Fourth Edition--Revised, Up-dated and Enlarged

The Men
Who Changed A Nation

The Tuskegee Airmen

By
Charles E. Francis
1st Lieutenant Army Air Force and
US Air Force (Reserve)

Edited, revised, up-dated and enlarged by
Adolph Caso
Colonel USAR

BRANDEN PUBLISHING CO.
Boston

*Fourth Edition—revised,
up-dated and enlarged.*

Library of Congress Cataloging-in-Publication Data

Francis, Charles E.
The Tuskegee airmen: the men who changed a nation / by Charles E. Francis : edited, revised, up-dated, and enlarged by Adolph Caso. --4th ed., rev., up-dated and enl.
p. cm.
Includes bibliographical references and index.
ISBN 0-8283-2077-2 (paperback : alk. paper)
ISBN 0-8283-2029-2 (hard cover : alk. paper)
1. World War, 1939-1945--Aerial operations, American.
2. World War, 1939-1945--Participation, Afro-American.
3. Afro-American air pilots--History.
I. Caso, Adolph. II Title.
D790.F637 1997
940.54'4973--dc21 97-5027
CIP

BRANDEN BOOKS
(A division of Branden Publishing Company)
PO Box 812094
Wellesley MA 02482

Charles E. Francis, in his honor.

Colonel Benjamin O. Davis, Jr.

To my friends of the 99th Fighter Squadron, the 332nd Fighter Group, the 477th Bombardment Group and the 477th Composite Group, who made this story and the late Georgiana Simpson, one of my instructors at Howard University, who inspired me to write this book.

Contents

Abbreviations:

Officers:

GEN = General
LTG = Lieutenant General
MG = Major General
BG = Brigadier General
COL = Colonel
LTC = Lieutenant General
MAJ = Major
CPT = Captain
1LT = First Lieutenant (LT)
2LT = Second Lieutenant (LT)

States:

AL = Alabama
TX = Texas, etc.

Hall of Black Achievement Reception Honoring Tuskegee Airmen. Left to right: Ronald Lucas, National President Tuskegee Airmen, William E. Broadwater, Jack Bryant, Luther McIlwain, John Roach, Thomas Ross, Edward Hartgrove, Willis Saunders, Daniel Keel, Enoch O-Dwoodhouse, Howard Carter, Milton Hopkins, Francis Hector. (Photo, courtesy of D. Confar/Images Photography)

ILLUSTRATIONS

1. Charles E. Francis
2. Colonel Benjamin O. Davis, Jr.

2a **Hall of Black Achievement Reception Honoring Tuskegee Airmen.** Left to right: Ronald Lucas, National President Tuskegee Airmen, William E. Broadwater, Jack Bryant, Luther McIlwain, John Roach, Thomas Ross, Edward Hartgrove, Willis Saunders, Daniel Keel, Enoch O-Dwoodhouse, Howard Carter, Milton Hopkins, Francis Hector. (Photo, courtesy of Office Public Affairs, Bridgewater State College)

3. Eugene Bullard
4. Bessie Coleman
5. Chief Anderson and Colonel Caso
6. Roscoe Draper, Fred Witherspoon, Philip Lee, Edward Gibbs, Ernest Henderson Sr., Joseph Ramos, James Hill
7. Civilian Primary Instructors: Bob Terry, John Young, Stevens, Charles Fox, Roscoe Draper, Sherman Rose, James A. Hill, Adolph Moret, Ernest Henderson, Matthew Plummen, Linwood Williams, Daniel C. James, Lewis Jackson, Milton Crenshaw, Perry Young, Charlie Flowers, Claude Platt, "Chip" Anderson, C.R. Harris, Wendell Lipscomb, J. E. Wright
8. LTC Hazard with MAJ Boyd
9. COL Frederick V. Kimble, second Commanding Officer
10. Cadet Color Guards
11. Post Headquarters, Tuskegee Army Air Field
12. Cadets in training at Tuskegee
13. Mechanics check a P-40
14. First class graduates TAAF: L-R: George Roberts, B. O. Davis Jr., Charles Debow, COL Robert Long (instructor), Mac Ross, Lemuel R. Custis
15. COL Noel Parrish and LTC George S. Roberts
16. LTC Noel F. Parrish flanked by BG Benjamin O. Davis, Sr. LTC Benjamin O. Davis, Jr. visiting at Tuskegee
17. Members of the original 99th Fighter Squadron
18. Secretary of War Stimson inspects the 99th

19. Irene Turner admiring expert aerial gunnery medal of her son LT Leon L. Turner

20. LT Wilmeth W. Sidat, star football player Syracuse U., with mother and fiancee

21. LT Lloyd R. Radcliffe surrounded by his proud family

22. LT Surl Smith and his proud family

23. Ground crew of the 99th

24. Captain Charles B. Hall

25. CLASS 45E, BASIC SINGLE ENGINE, ADVANCED MULTI-ENGINE PILOTS: *Rear Row Standing*: John S. Harris, John B. Roach, Mexion O. Pruitt, Joseph C. Bryant, Mitchel N. Toney, Walter N. O'Neal. *Middle Row Kneeling*: Jerrold D. Griffin, Harold B. Maples, Clifford E. Mosley, Harry E. Ford, Jr. *Front Row Sitting*: Albert Whiteside, John C. Curry, William H. Taylor, Jr., George A. Brown, William E. Broadwater

26. CLASS 45e, ADVANCED SINGLE ENGINE PILOTS: *Rear Row Standing*: Wesley D. Hurt, Roger B. Duncan, Henry T. Tolland, Clinton E. McIntyre, William A. Fuller, Jr., Martin G. Saunders, Joseph P. Scott, Eugene W. Williams. *Middle Row Kneeling*: Leonard W. Wiggins, Logan Roberts, Aaron C. Gaskins, Russell L. Collins, William H. Bailey, George G. Turner. *Front Row Sitting*: Marvin C. White, Herman A. Barnett, Isaac R. Woods, Clarence E. Reynolds, Jr., Reginald V. Smith

27. Elsberry discussing flying with LT M. Rodgers, COL Davis, MAJ Gleed and CPT McDaniels

28. Men of the 332nd Fighter Group prepare for deployment at Selfridge Field in late 1943, courtesy of Luther McIlwain.

28a BG Benjamin Oliver Davis, Sr., First Day of Issue, Washington, DC, 28 January 1997, 20066

29. Brigadier General Benjamin O. Davis, Sr.

30. BG Benjamin stamp First Day of Issue, Jan 28, 1997.

31. Posing with his wife, LT Thomas Malone, who was awarded the Purple Heart for combat in Sicily

32. Greeting nurses, a Colonel shakes hands with Chief Nurse Della M. Raney

33. Captain Eldridge and the Tuskegee boxing team

34. *Miss Gridiron*, Edna B. Bouldin, greeting SGT Jerry Williams and LT Ira J. O'Neal of Tuskegee's *Warhawks*

35. Medical Staff of the 99th and 332nd: MAJ Marchbanks and CPT Allen, Moloney and Waugh
36. Four pictures: Black nurses "keep them flying"
37. Major Campbell and Airman before takeoff
38. Major William T. Mattison and Crew Chief
39. Pilots of the 332nd Fighter Group: LT Morgan, Woods, Nelson, CPT Turner, and LT. Lester
40. LT Andrew Marshall hit by flak in a strafing mission, Greeee
41. Veterans of the 332nd: Haywood, Mosely, Robinson, Faulkner and Weathers
42. Spencer, Punch, Houston, Custis, Perry, Ed Thomas, Payne, Blackwell, M. Rodgors, Gene Brown, Hardy, Gaines
43. Captain Edward Toppins
44. Major Andrew D. *Jug* Turner
45. BG B.O. Davis, Sr. decorates B.O. Davis, Jr., Joseph Elsberry, Jack Hokar, and Clarence Lester
46. BG Davis, Sr. decorating pilots of the 332nd
47. Captain Luke Weathers scored two victories in one day
48. Captain Woodrow Crockett posing on his plane (notice the names of Parks and Fernandez)
49. Pilot of the 477th Bomber Group warming up plane at Godman Field
50. Marcus Ray, Aide to the Secretary of War, at Tuskegee with CPT Driver, McDaniel and CPT Friend
51. The 332nd returning to the States
52. Colonel Benjamin O. Davis, Jr., receiving Legion of Merit
53. Major Fred Minnis, greatly responsible to the success of the Tuskegee experiment
54. Leaders of the 332nd *Red Tails*: LTC Roberts, MAJ Brooks, CPT Lucas, and MAJ Letcher
55. Members of the first AAF class, Hondo Army Air Field, Texas
56. LT Cyril Burke and F/O Daniel Keel receive their wings at Midland Army Air Field
57. Formation of Black Cadets at Hondo Army Air Field
58. Cadets May, Trotter, and Evans at Midland Army Air Field
59. Mayor Fiorello LaGuardia greeting Hondo Air Field flyers
60. F/O Levert V. Middleton, Bombardier Navigator; 2LT Eugene Henderson, Co-Pilot; 1LT Henry P. Hervey, Pilot, SGT Charles

Jones, Tail Gunner, PVT Frank Hector, Radio Operator, Gunner; FFC John E. Starks, Engineer, Gunner

61. Atlanta, GA August 12, 1995, Roger C. Terry, President of the Tuskegee Airmen, is surrounded by Colonel Caso, Frank *Fuzzy* Hector, and admirer, celebrating the vindication of over one hundred Tuskegeeans who had held fast against segregation and racism, photo courtesy of Sylvia Freeman

62. MAJ Mattison, CPT Temple, LT Stewart, LT Harvey and LT Alexander

63. LT Harvey and members of 332nd Gunnery Team, 1949

64. Major General Lucius Theus

65. General Daniel C. James

66. Four Astronauts: COL Guion S. Bluford, Dr. Ronald E. McNair, COL Frederick D. Gregory, and LTC Charles F. Bolden.

67. COL McPhearson, A. Cisco, L. Jackson, H. Baugh, *Ace* Lawson, Dempsey Morgan, and L. Turner

68. Veteran Tuskegee Pilots attend reunion in Tuskegee, in 1977. Left to right: Alva Temple, Lowell Steward, Four Star General Daniel *Chappie* James (names of other two gentlemen unknown)

69. The author, Charles E. Francis, with his son, daughter-in-law and grandchildren (1987)

70. Former pilot with 99th, Dr. Curtis C. Robinson and Mrs. Florie Robinson

71. Former test pilot for the 99th, Wylie Selden and wife June at a celebration party at Howard University

72. COL William Campbell, 1987 San Francisco TAAF Convention

73. Airplane Armorer, SGT Conway Waddy at an air base in Italy

74. The author, Charles E. Francis, in 1944

75. Italy 1944--Tuskegee Airmen Ground Support

76. Italy 1944--SGT George Watson, Sr. with an Italian boy

77. James A. Hurd, Pilot 477th, and Crew

78. Luther A. Goodwin, John Rector, Robert C. Brown, Augustus Brown, James A. Hurd, Warren E. Henry, Russell C. Nagle, Frederick Samuels, Paul C. Bonseigneur, (unknown)

79. CPT Herbert Carter and LT William W. Green, veteran combat pilots of the 99th and 332nd

80. Dual-rated Pilot-Navigator Officer LT Turner, LT McIntyre, LT Choise, LT William Williams, LT C.C. Moseley, LT Maples, and LT H.J. Holland

81. James A. Calhoun, "To My Darling" Wife

82. LT Calhoun and his fellow classmates

83. The Cross

84. The Purple Heart

85. 2LT LeRoy A. Battle on leave in Brooklyn, NY with his mother and his aunt

86. Midland Army Air Field, 8 September 1944--Advanced Bombardier/Navigation Cadets drawing parachutes for a night mission: Robert S. Lawrence, Benjamin J. Williams, Ivan G. Bynoe, LeRoy A. Battle, and Robert A. Lee

87. Italy 1944--Tuskegee Airmen Ground Support

88. Italy 1944--SGT George Watson, Sr. with an Italian boy

89. LT James L. Warthall

90. MAJ Gabe Hawkins

91. COL Donald McPhearson

92. LT Luther Davenport

93. LT Richard Kraft

94. LT Owen Peterson

95. LT Philip H. Heard

96. LT Wayne E. Cook

Acknowledgements

First and foremost, I would like to express my sincere apology to Mrs. Helen Holmes Robinson, Miss Kate Broadus, Mr. William Scott, Mrs. Jane E. Hughes, and to the family of the late Catherine Holmes. They gave me invaluable assistance in the preparation of my original manuscript, but because of an error on my part they were not given the acknowledgment they deserved.

I am deeply indebted to Mr. Leo Kerford, former Public Relations Officer of Tuskegee Army Air Field, whose cooperation and assistance enabled me to gather much of the materials for this book. I am grateful to my late friend, Major Ulysses G. Lee, US Army Historical Division, and Dr. Vincent J. Brown, former Professor of Political Science and Administrative Assistant to the President of Howard University. I am also grateful to my wife, Frances Holmes, who gave me great assistance in the preparation of my original manuscript.

I wish to thank those who labored so hard deciphering my poor handwriting and typing my manuscript: Miss Kate Broadus, Mrs. Jane E. Reeder Hughes, Mrs. Ruth Johns, Mrs. Jennifer Odum, Mr. Joseph W. Francis, Sr., Mrs. Marilyn Atkins Francis, and especially Mrs. Thelma Francis Adams, who stuck with me through my many revisions and corrections. Of course, I am indeed indebted to Dr. Stephanie Francis Locke and Mrs. Helen Holmes Robinson for their skilled assistance in editing my manuscripts.

I believe all Americans are indebted to LTG Benjamin O. Davis, Jr. (retired), who commanded all of the black combat units of the Army Air Forces during World War II, and BG Noel F. Parrish, who commanded Tuskegee Army Air Field and was responsible for the training of all black pilots during the war. It was through their abilities and outstanding leadership a new source of manpower was added to the US Air Force.

Finally, I wish to thank my friends: COL Spann Watson, COL Harry A. Sheppard, COL Ernest J. Davis, Jr., COL Elwood Driver,

LT Alfred McKenzie, and Mr. Samuel O'Dennis for their encouragements and assistance in the preparation of this revision of the book.

(And special thanks to Eunice Mosher, COL John Roach, LT LeRoy Battle, SGT George Watson Sr., Luther E. McIlwain, and *Fuzzy* Hector for their assistance in preparing this enlarged and comprehensive Fourth Edition--the Editor).

A Word from the Editor

This book, *The Tuskegee Airmen*, has come to me by inheritance. After Bruce Humphrey Company sold out to Branden Press, I acquired a majority in Branden Publishing Company, thus becoming its editor and publisher. Out of the hundreds of titles in the warehouse, one stood out, not because it looked better than the others or because the graphics were exciting; it stood out because it purported to tell the history of the integration of the U.S. Armed Forces. The subject intrigued me.

Though I was a Colonel in the USAR, during my active duty tours as well as those in Reserve Training, I had not seen integration as a problem in the military. However in 1963, I saw the two sets of water faucets in a Georgia airport.

After reading the book, I decided to promote it because I believed the story needed to be known by all Americans. With a review in hand (you may have read it on the flaps of the jacket of this book), I sent it to various military magazines for publication. As a result, and with a newly-found collaboration with Charles Francis, we began to see both enthusiasm and demand for the book. The first edition sold, we prepared a second one, and a third edition still. Except for a few copies remaining of the uncorrected special edition dedicated to Charles Francis, the 1993 edition sold out. Therefore, I decided to edit and to enlarge on Mr. Francis' third edition by bringing out the present fourth. I hope that the Tuskegeeans in particular and Americans at large will enjoy this volume for its comprehensive breath and for its historical accuracy, having made every effort to include as many Tuskegeeans as possible in names (see the extensive Index) and in stories so as to create as complete a record as possible of what those individuals achieved for themselves, for their families and for all of us. The nation is indebted to them.

Unbeknown to me, I became indirectly aware of the Tuskegee Airmen when I was a child growing up in Italy in a village not too far from the airstrip at Ramitelli. I saw just about every aspect of the war, from the movement of numberless troops and huge armaments by the Germans, to the Salerno invasion whose ships lit the night sky some sixty miles away, to the artillery barrages whistling over my head, to the dive-bombing and machine fire of Allied planes on the retreating Germans, to the first American foot-soldiers battling the remnant German infantry. These things happened around me to the same extent that I was as much a recipient of that fire as were the Germans.

I also remembered the almost daily flights of bombers in tight formations going northward, always escorted by single engine fighter planes doing battle with similar attacking monoplanes. What impressed me about those many aerial dogfights was that neither one single engine plane nor one bomber ever went down, except for the attacking planes.

Now, some forty years later, an officer in the U.S. Army, fate would have that I should inherit Charles Francis' *The Tuskegee Airmen*, and discover, to my amazement, that those pilots, who fought above my head, who sent so many planes down in smoke and flames--the same pilots whose rounds struck my house, are also the ones who have enriched my imagination with their deeds and their goodwill.

Older, and because of this unexpected association with so many Tuskegeeans, I feel my time also coming. When it comes, I will not hesitate to continue my relationship, for I shall promptly seek out the Lonely Eagles of the sky.

ADOLPH CASO
COL USAR

Preface

Dramatic and exciting as any adventure story ever written are the memories of every combat pilot. He may never express it in words, but every combat pilot has some particular incident indelibly fixed in his mind: lifting a wing at the last split second over a silenced flak tower, peeling off in a whistling dive to attack a roundhouse or marshalling yard, seeing the bright lines of tracers streak past as an enemy fighter comes out of the sun, hitting the deck and roaring across enemy territory at tree top level, dodging flak and small arms fire after attacking an enemy airfield, watching a locomotive speed hopelessly down the rails trying to outrun attacking planes, watching an enemy pilot throw back his canopy and bounce high out of his smoking plane, plowing through a formation of enemy fighters, getting back in friendly territory with plane torn practically apart with hardly enough gas to land, or not getting back and bailing out in unknown territory. Yes, these are but a few memories that perhaps every fighter pilot recalls when he thinks of this combat days.

This story of the part played by the Air Force cannot be told by the generals, the military analysts, the war correspondents, even the historians, however gifted they may be. It can only be told by the pilots, crewmen, and ground complements of the US Air Force--the men who actually made the history and survived. For years to come, they will tell it in corner drug stores and barber shops, at home and on the streets throughout the country, wherever people talk about the war.

This narrative has a manifold purpose which has interwoven threads of deeds, actions, thoughts, and ideals into one composite story. It is not only the story of Negro airmen who went to war as members of the 99th Fighter Squadron and the 332nd Fighter Group as integral parts of the 12th and 15th Air Forces, but the story of the 477th Bombardment and Composite Groups that fought the battle on the home front by challenging the discrimination and segregation practices of the War Department and the nation.

This narrative does not pretend to be a complete record or an exact appraisal of what black airmen accomplished. It does not pretend to prove that black airmen who fought over Europe won the war for the Allies, nor does it attempt to give black airmen sole credit for changing the nation. The significance must not be lost, however, that it was as American citizens these men served, fought and died with the hope that by their efforts and sacrifices, they would achieve for black Americans, the same rights, privileges, treatments and opportunities enjoyed by white Americans.

Unfortunately, the war and the victory brought little change in the minds and attitudes of most military leaders and white Americans as a whole, towards Blacks. They, to a large extent, wanted to maintain a government of white supremacy that hypocritically expounded the ideals and principles of Democracy, but sanctioned racial discrimination and segregation.

Since World War II, many journalists and historians have attempted to tell the story of the Tuskegee airmen. They have used as a source of their information the voluminous records, opinions and reports prepared by prejudiced military leaders to forestall the integration of the services. With such bias information many writers have drawn erroneous conclusions about the performances of the Tuskegee Airmen. This author believes the story of these airmen has been so fragmentally told that the true story is still unknown. This book has been revised and enlarged in an attempt to tell as completely, accurately, and objectively as possible that story.

It will be noted that in this revision, the words *Negroes* and *Blacks* are used interchangeably. This is done to placate those affected by the change of time. Today, the terms Blacks, Black Americans and African Americans are used interchangeably. It should also be noted that Army Air Corps and the Army Air Forces are likewise used. Prior to the outbreak of World War II, the Army Air Corps was the air arm of the Army. However, on June 20, 1941, the Army Air Forces was organized and on March 9, 1942, it was officially established. General Henry *Hap* Arnold, who was the Chief of the Army Air Corps and a member of the Army Staff, was appointed Chief of the Army Air Forces. His primary duty was to coordinate the various air components of the Army. He was replaced by General George Brett as Acting Chief of the Army Air Corps.

Prologue
The Roads to the War and the American Conflict

The roots of World War II were planted with the surrender of Germany in World War I and the signing of an Armistice on November 1, 1918. Although the fighting ended, its roots of racial hatred and jealousy between the peoples of the world remained alive.

Following its defeat, Germany was forced to sign a harsh treaty that required the government to pay reparations far beyond its ability to pay. The heavy indemnities left the people so humiliated, demoralized and destitute that they were willing to follow anyone who offered hope to alleviate the deplorable condition. Such a man was Adolf Hitler, a native of Austria, who had volunteered for service with the German Army at the outbreak of the war.

In October 1918, Hitler, who had advanced to the rank of Corporal, was temporarily blinded by mustard gas in a British attack near Comines. While he lay helplessly in the hospital, he brooded over Germany's defeat. As a young man growing up in Vienna, he had associated with German Nationalists who instilled in his mind that wealthy speculators and Jews were responsible for undermining the government and exploiting the people. In the hospital with nothing to do, his thoughts led to anger and to an overpowering hatred of Jews and wealthy speculators, whom, he reasoned, were responsible for the defeat of Germany.

When Hitler was finally released from the hospital, he was disheartened and angered to find that the defeat had left the people destitute, that law and order had collapsed and that the government was in a state of turmoil.

In September 1919, Hitler attended a rally in Munich, sponsored by the German Weimar Party. There he met others who voiced opinions similar to his. He joined the Party and in February 1920, at a mass meeting of the Party, held in Munich, he emerged as a dominant figure. Thereafter, he channeled all of his energy towards the expansion of the Party.

By November 1923, Hitler had gathered a hard core of determined nationalists among whom Hermann Goering and Rudolph Hess were most prominent. They decided to seize the government of the State of Bavaria, but were unsuccessful. Twenty demonstrators were killed, but Hitler managed to escape. However, in April of 1924, he was arrested and sentenced to serve four years, but later his sentence was reduced to thirteen months. During his imprisonment, he completed his book, *Mein Kampf*, a treatise that outlined his political philosophy.

After being released from prison, Hitler was determined to reorganize his movement and to lead Germany to her rightful position of leader of the world of governments. This was not easy and years passed before the National Socialist Party, termed the Nazi Party, was able to gain a stronghold on the German people. This was accomplished by taking advantage of the deplorable poverty of the German people and the lust for revenge. With colorful banners waving, passionate, patriotic mass meetings were frequently held at which hate propaganda was voiced against Jews, a German minority.

Jews were used as scapegoats, depicted as the profiteers, who were responsible for Germany's defeat. Then through a secretly organized para-military force known as the Brownshirts and a smaller disciplined core of Storm Trooper, Hitler terrorized those who voiced opposition or even failed to publicly display enthusiasm for his movement.

By 1930, Hitler and his para-military forces had grown so strong and feared that the German General Staff, the military that had controlled Germany for generations, began to fear that Hitler and his forces would seize control of the government. In a move to maintain its control, the German Staff, known as the *Reichswehr*, decided to seek an agreement with Hitler. The Staff proposed to Hitler that if he curtailed the activities of the Brownshirts, and made them subordinate to the General Staff, it would consider Hitler for a position of Chancellor of Germany. If the Brownshirts refused to submit to the agreement, they would be liquidated.

Hitler welcomed the proposal by the General Staff. He recognized that it was the official, legally accepted controlling body of the government. To be accepted by that group meant he was officially accepted to run the government. This he saw as the opportunity to solidify the German movement without opposition.

Hitler agreed to the proposal and shortly afterwards, the General Staff pressured Marshall Hindenburg to reluctantly appoint Hitler as Chancellor of Germany. On January 30, 1933, Hitler took office.

Immediately after taking office, Hitler set about to gain complete control of the government. On February 2, 1933, he forbid all meetings of the German Communist Party and began to round up all weapons secretly held by the Communists. On February 27, 1933, the Reichstag building was mysteriously set afire. Brownshirts and Storm Troopers were called out and over four thousand arrests were made including the Central Committee of the Communist Party. Then on March 24, the Nazi Party, that had gained the majority of the Reichstag, voted Hitler complete emergency power for four years.

Hitler was now ready to move towards other modern nations of the world. In March 1935, he denounced the provision of the Versailles Treaty regarding disarmament of Germany and he re-instituted conscription. With British sanction by a separate agreement, he began to rebuild a Navy, with U-boats of the British scale. Meantime, Germany had secretly developed an Air Force which she openly claimed to be the equal of the British Air Force.

On March 1, 1936, Hitler made his first move of revenge. Two hours after proposing a twenty-five year peace pact with Britain, France, Belgium and Italy, German troops moved into the Rhine lands. This accomplished, Hitler assured the world that Germany's territorial objectives had been satisfied. However, approximately two years later, on February 4, 1938, he assumed command of the Armed forces of Germany and on March 13, German troops, with the aid of Austrian Nazis, captured Vienna. Hitler declared the dissolution of the Austrian Republic and the annexation of Austria to the German Reich.

The easy victories with relative no bloodshed encouraged Hitler. On September 26, 1938, he announced the Czechoslovakians "must clear out of the Sudetenland". He based his claims on the large numbers of people of German descent that lived in the area. At the same time, he announced that "this is the last territorial claim I have to make in Europe."

Shortly after stating his position on the Sudetenland, Hitler invited British Prime Minister Neville Chamberlain, France Prime Minister M. Daladier and Mussolini to Munich. On September 30, the four leaders agreed to what was termed the *Munich Pact*. It provided that the Sudetenland was to be evacuated by the Czechs in five stages beginning October 1, 1938. In March 1939, German troops moved into Prague and took control of the country.

Czechoslovakia had hardly been brought under Germany's domination when Hitler began his propaganda against Poland. He insisted that Germans, who were members of the *master race*, were being maltreated by the Poles--an inferior people. He argued that the existence of the *Polish Corridor* which divided East and West Prussia was agonizing to Germany and insisted that Danzig, a port city made up largely of Germans be returned to Germany.

Following a threat against Poland in May 1939, Britain and France warned Hitler that they would support Poland if Germany attempted to settle the Danzig question by aggression. However, the warning came too late. Hitler's chain of successes had made him a hero to the German people. He was the conqueror who was only revenging the harsh treatment that had been forced on Germany--that he was only retaking areas that rightfully belonged to Germany.

At dawn on September 1, 1939, the German war machine charged into Poland. Fifty-six divisions, including nine armored and motorized divisions with over fifteen hundred aircraft, struck (in what was termed the *Blitzkrieg)* at Polish cities and at a much smaller Polish Army. The Polish Air Force, caught by surprise saw its planes destroyed on the ground. By the end of the second day of battle, the remaining force was virtually destroyed.

On September 17, the Russians, in accordance with the secret provisions of the Hitler-Stalin Pact, rushed into Poland and drove westward. On September 18, German and Russian forces met at Brest-Litovsk. The Germans captured Warsaw on September 27 and the following day Germany and Russia signed a treaty that partitioned Poland between the two nations. Many Polish citizens were forced into slave labor, but the Polish Jewish citizens were rounded up and exterminated.

Meanwhile on September 3, Great Britain had declared war on Germany and dispatched an expeditionary force to France. By mid-October, four divisions were stationed along the France-Belgium frontier and by March 1940, six additional divisions joined the force.

On December 14, 1939, a former Norwegian Minister of War and a member of the Norwegian National Party, Vidkun Quisling, visited Hitler. Shortly after the visit, Hitler ordered his Supreme Command to prepare plans for an operation against Norway. The objective was to secure air bases for attacks against Britain.

In April 1940, German troops aided by Norwegian traitors, seized all the important points on the Norwegian coast. British and French troops were rushed into the battle, but they were no match for the German forces.

The failure of British forces in Norway brought a storm of protest from the British people and the British Parliament against Prime Minister Chamberlain and his cabinet. On May 10, 1940, he resigned and Winston Churchill was named Prime Minister. The same day Churchill took office, Hitler opened an assault on the Netherlands, Belgium and France.

The Belgian forces that bore the brunt of the German attack was no match for the Germans. On May 28, 1940, Belgium was forced to surrender, exposing the entire northern flank of the remaining allied forces in Belgium, to the relentless attacks from German forces. They were forced to retreat towards the sea. Unable to halt the attacks, the British forces of 136,000 men, together with approximately 20,000 Polish troops that fought with the British, were finally evacuated on June 4, 1940.

The Germans, unable to stop the evacuations, went all out to conquer France. On June 8, German forces crossed the Aisne and Somme rivers and, two days later, on June 10, Italy declared war on France and invaded southern France.

The Germans moved so quickly into France that on June 10, Paris was declared an open city. The Germans entered Paris on June 14, and Verdun the next day. The great French fortress that controlled the French Maginot Line was captured. The French Government collapsed. On June 16, Premier Paul Reynault resigned and eighty-four year old Marshal Petain assumed the position of Premier. He immediately begged Germany for an Armistice.

Hitler agreed to an armistice; but, to humiliate the French and to satisfy German lust for revenge, he arranged for the Armistice talks to be held in the forest of Compiegne, where, in a railroad car twenty-two years earlier, French Marshall Ferdinand-Foch had dictated to the Germans the Armistice terms of World War I. On June 22, in the same car, the French accepted the harsh terms imposed by the Germans.

Meantime in the United States, the people had been aroused by the war in Europe. No one wanted war and as a whole, Americans were reluctant to join Britain and France in the war. President Roosevelt, however, had realized that the United States entrance into the war was inevitable and had begun to prepare the American people for war.

On January 4, 1939, Roosevelt declared that "it had become increasingly clear that peace is not assured and urged Congress to make provisions for adequate defenses and proclaimed that "this generation of Americans has a rendezvous with destiny." Aware that the United States had only a small Air Force made up of a small group of Army Air Corps officers and a relative small number of obsolete aircraft, Roosevelt urged Congress to give priority to the Air Force in its appropriations. Congress responded to the President's appeal by not only appropriating money for the massive production of aircraft, but also for all the training of pilots and other air crewmen.

America, however, had its own minority problems that had existed much longer than the problem Hitler had managed to stir up against the Jews in Germany. For 250 years, Negroes had been subjected to slavery. After being freed in 1865, they were subjected to brutality, humiliation, discrimination and segregation by the white majority.

The treatment of Negroes, however, was not uniform. In the South, Negroes were forced to observe strict codes of social etiquette that made them submissive and subservient to whites. They were employed only for the menial jobs, and were expected to respect all whites at all times. Any Negro, who dared to show disrespect or dared to challenge the subservience whites expected, was arrested, severely beaten and even lynched.

Negroes born in the North had little first-hand knowledge of the treatment of Negroes in the South and their daily reminders of supposed inferiority. Many northern Blacks lived in segregated neighborhoods, and on the whole received little harsh treatment from whites. Whites in the North were more subtle in their discrimination practices, which for the most part were in the areas of job opportunities, employment and advancement.

When the massive war mobilization program began, Negro leaders--especially the editors of the *Negro* press, who had for generations voiced the cause of Negroes against discrimination, segregation, and had decried the abusive, humiliating and terroristic tactics used against Negroes in the South--saw the war crisis as the opportune time to demand the Federal Government to take positive steps to uphold the Constitution that proclaimed equal treatment for all Americans. They anticipated that no provisions would be made to permit Negroes to participate in the war effort either as members of the Armed Services or in war production industries, except in the most menial and subservient capacities.

As anticipated, the Federal Government poured millions of dollars into training personnel in an effort to gear the nation to war production, but Negroes, none the less, were overlooked. The largest training program, the Vocational Educational Defense (VED) was operated by the Department of Education. Its leaders on the national and local levels were on the whole against altering the existing policy involving racial discrimination. They worked closely with business and labor unions, and both were more or less against the training of Negroes as skilled workers. The few Negroes accepted for training lived in the north and of that few only a small percentage were trained in welding, machine shop and aircraft production where skilled workers were mostly needed. Negroes as a whole were accepted only for nonessential training. Likewise, Negro youths were wanted by the Armed Services only in menial and subservient roles.

The attitudes and apathy of the Federal Government and military officials aroused Negro leaders, the press and their white supporters to put pressure on President Roosevelt in an effort to have him take positive actions in the utilization of Negroes. On September 27, 1940, Roosevelt, the Assistant Secretary of War, Robert P. Patterson, and Secretary of the Navy, Frank Knox met with three Negro leaders: A. Phillip Randolph, Walter White, and T. Arnold Hill to consider the utilization of Negroes in the Armed Services.

Following the conference, Secretary Patterson issued a memorandum to the press that stated the War Department policy towards the use of Negroes would be on a fair and equitable basis; that Negroes would be used in proportion to the total population. The memorandum further stated that the policy of the War Department was not to intermingle colored and white enlisted personnel in the same regimental organizations. It implied that the Negro leaders supported the War Department's stance.

The black leaders were angered at the implication that they supported the War Department policy. They immediately issued a statement which denied they approved segregated units and stated that "official approval by the Commanding Chief of the Army and Navy of such discrimination and segregation is a stab in the back of democracy."

President Roosevelt repudiated the statement by the War Department which, however, refused to change its policy. But under pressure from black leaders and the black press, plans were being made for the activation of a segregated air field and a black flying unit. On March 21, 1941, it activated the 99th Pursuit Squadron and, four months later, work began on the construction of the Tuskegee Army Air Field in Tuskegee, AL. The activation of the 99th Fighter Squadron and Tuskegee Army Air Field began what the War Department called the Experiment, making possible, therefore, the emergence of our black pioneers.

PIONEERS OF BLACK AVIATION

Although black youths were turned down by the Army Air Force because there were no established black units, and with the excuse that Blacks did not appear to be as interested in flying as much as whites, nevertheless, there were already over 100 licensed black pilots at the time. The flight of the Wright Brothers in 1903 sparked enthusiasm for aviation by black youths, but racial hatred and discrimination was so deeply embedded in American life that Blacks were excluded from flight instruction. It was a wide-held belief that Blacks had neither the mentality, aptitude nor reflexes to fly. However, black youths were fascinated with flying and were determined to learn to fly. Two youths, Eugene Bullard and Bessie Coleman started the break through for Blacks to fly. Bullard learned to fly and earned his wings as a pilot in the French Air Force during World War I. Likewise, Bessie Coleman learned to fly in France and returned to the United States where, in 1922, she became the first licensed black pilot in America. However, she died in a plane crash in 1926.

Eugene Bullard flew combat missions with the French against the Germans, and is credited for having ambushed a Pfalz D.III. Forgotten in America, Bullard was remembered in France. In 1954, he was one of three men to light the Flame of the Unknown Soldier, and in 1959, he was made Knight of the Legion of Honor.

The historic flight of Charles Lindbergh across the Atlantic inspired more youths to seek instructions to fly. In 1929, a small group of aviation enthusiasts, led by William Powell--one of the first black pilots, organized the Bessie Coleman Aero Club in Los Angeles to promote aviation in the black community. On Labor Day, 1931 it sponsored the first all black air show in the United States.

Los Angeles became the important center for black aviation, but Chicago quickly became its rival. Inspired by the legacy of Bessie Coleman, a group of young Blacks organized the Challenger Air Pilot Association and at the Harlem Airport, the Coffey School of Aeronautics offered flight instruction. The school was run by Cornelius R. Coffey, a certified airplane and engine mechanic, who had been trained at the Curtiss-Wright Aeronautical School.

Along with Cornelius Coffey, his wife Willa Brown, and other struggling black pilots, there was also another very important aviation enthusiast by the name of Janet W. Bragg; she purchased the first aircraft for the Challenger Air Pilots Association.

Ms. Bragg was a graduate nurse, who had attended Spellman College and did post graduate at Cook County Hospital and at Loyola University in Chicago. In 1933, she attended the Aeronautical University of Chicago where she studied Theory of Flight and other ground courses. After completing flying instruction, she joined the Coffeys in flying from a small field in Robbins, IL. However, the complaints of the noise made by the planes caused them to move to Harlem Airport on the outskirts of Chicago. Ms. Bragg was instrumental in developing the first college preparatory Training Flying Program. This was a pre-aviation cadet Evaluation Program to initiate prospective Army pilot trainees into the world of flight. These programs were funded by the United States Government to prepare candidates for military flying after graduating from college.

In 1942, Ms. Bragg attended Tuskegee Institute's Civilian Training School. Under Chief Anderson, she prepared for a Commercial Pilot License, which she received in 1943 at the Palwaukee Airport in Chicago.

In that age of discrimination and segregation there was very little social contact between the races; as a result, whites knew very little about Blacks and Blacks knew very little about whites. Blacks, like Hubert Julian, pursued careers as showmen by conducting Air Shows and performing at various circus-type events. Then there was John C. Robinson, the president of Chicago's Challenger Air Pilot Association, who, in 1935, was advising Haile Selassie on building an Ethiopian Air Force when Italy invaded Ethiopia. Robinson was fortunate to escape the Italians and return to the United States.

In May 1939, two young black pilots, Dale L. White and Chauncey E. Spencer--sponsored by the National Airmen Association and the "Chicago Defender"--flew from Chicago to Washington, DC to dramatize the goal of Blacks to participate in aviation careers. On landing in Washington, they were met by Edgar G. Brown, a popular Civil Rights leader and by Senator Harry S. Truman to promote their cause. It was these black pilots who opened the door for other pioneers of military aviation.

Willa C. Brown Chappell

Willa Brown Chappell was truly one of the pioneers of Black Aviation. She was born in Glasgow, KY in 1906. She received a bachelor degree from Indiana State Teachers College and taught at Roosevelt High School in Gary, IN before moving to Chicago in 1932.

While studying for a master's degree at Northwestern University, she became interested in flying. She was graduated from the old Aeronautical University in the South Loop in 1939 and was awarded a pilot's certificate.

After receiving her pilot's certificate, Ms. Brown organized the National Airmen's Association of America, the first black aviation association. The same year she married Cornelius R. Coffey, also a black pioneer; together, they opened the first flight school owned and operated by Blacks. Mrs. Brown was director and coordinator of civilian pilot training at the Coffey School of Aeronautics, which was located at the Harlem Airport in Oak Lawn.

In 1940, the US War Department contracted with the school to conduct an experimental program to prove that black youths could be taught to fly and become flight instructors. The success of the program led to the organization of the 99th Pursuit Squadron and the establishment of Tuskegee Army Air Field. Ms. Brown headed a program for the recruiting and training of black combat pilots from 1940 to 1945. In 1942, she became the first black woman to serve in the US Army Air Corps Civil Air Patrol. The flight school closed after the war. She remarried, changed her name to Willa Chappell, and resumed teaching in the public school system. She retired from Westinghouse High School in the 1970s and died in Chicago on July 18, 1992 at the age of 86.

James Herman Banning 1900-1933

Born and reared in Oklahoma, as a youth, he was fascinated with flying and dreamed of becoming a pilot. In the 1920s, he moved to Chicago where he tried to enter an aviation school, but was turned down because of his color.

Banning was determined not to be discouraged. He moved to Des Moines, IA, where an Army Officer, LT Raymond Fischer taught him to fly. He moved to the West Coast in the late 1920s; in 1932, he made his first and only transcontinental flight. He was killed in a plane crash in 1933.

Charles Alfred Anderson

Affectionately addressed as Chief Anderson by all who trained as pilots at Tuskegee, he is one of the pioneers of black aviation and Blacks in military aviation. He was born in Bridgeport, PA in 1907, attended Drexel Institute in Philadelphia, the Chicago School of Aeronautics, and the Boston School of Aeronautics.

The Civil Aeronautics Administration awarded him a private pilot license in 1929 and a Transport Pilot License in 1932. In 1933, Mr. Anderson completed a transcontinental round-trip with Dr. Albert E. Forsythe. This was the first such accomplishment by Blacks. In the same year, he began flight training for Blacks, which resulted in many

Blacks learning how to fly. In 1937, he introduced ground school aviation training in the black high schools of Washington, DC

In 1938, Anderson conducted a civilian pilot training program at Howard University. He conducted the flight training at the Hybla Valley Airport in Washington, DC, the only airport Blacks were permitted to use. At Howard, he was instrumental in inspiring many Howard students to press for their right to be accepted for Army Air Corps pilot training.

In 1940, Dr. Frederick D. Patterson, President of Tuskegee Institute, persuaded Chief Anderson to head up the Civilian Pilot Training Program at the Institute--a lucky move for basically two reasons: Chief Anderson's influence on black pilots has not abated to this day, and he may have served as a stimulus toward the eventual integration of the black pilots and soldiers into Armed Forces of this country.

At a time when few people had faith in the ability of Blacks to fly, Eleanor Roosevelt visited the Institute to see for herself whether Blacks could or could not fly. To gain this knowledge, she chose to fly with Chief Anderson. Thanks to his skill and obvious abilities, the First Lady returned to the White House convinced about the Blacks' capabilities not only to fight in the Air Corps, but to fight as well in the Army and in the Navy.

The flight proved to be of great historic importance. Her positive experience served as ammunition in reporting to President Roosevelt, who in turn convinced enough of the critics that Blacks could fly and that America needed to establish and to support a viable and operational black pilot training program at Tuskegee.

It is a shame that in the HBO movie version of *The Tuskegee Airmen*, another cadet is given the credit for having flown Mrs. Roosevelt on that historic and significant flight. These un-necessary revisions wherein fiction replaces fact is harmful to the real individual and to history itself, thus cheating everyone.

Among Chief Anderson's significant colleagues was James O. Plinton Jr., one of the first flight instructors of the 99th (who was appointed Vice President of Eastern Airlines in 1971), and Joseph T. Camilleri, who, because of his Naval Air Reserve training, was to become the first instructor for the Tuskegee Airmen.

The success of the Civilian Pilot Training Program was instrumental in influencing the Army Air Corps to establish its Primary Training Program at the Institute with Chief Anderson as Director. Roughly 1000 pilots who successfully completed the Army Air Corps Training Program were under his tutelage in the primary phase of flight training. He now serves as Director of the Negro Airmen International (NAI) Summer Flying Camp at Tuskegee University.

The beloved Chief Alfred Anderson passed on in 1996 to join his many Lonely Eagle comrades.

Dr. Albert Forsythe

Dr. Forsythe was born in Nassau in 1897 and reared in Jamaica. As a child, he dreamed of flying, but it was not until he had earned his Medical degree from McGill University in Montreal, Canada and established a medical practice in Atlantic City that he set about to make his dream a reality. He approached a flight instructor at a small field in Pennsylvania and asked "will yo teach me to fly." To his surprise, Ernie Buehl, the instructor, said, "Yes." In the 1930s, most instructors refused to teach Blacks.

Once Dr. Forsythe had gained his license, he made plans to prove that black pilots were as capable as white pilots. With his friend Charles Anderson as co-pilot, he made three long distance flights: one from Atlantic City to Los Angeles and back, a second form Atlantic City to Miami and back, and a third from Miami to the West Indies and South America. The only instruments they had were a compass and altimeter. They had no lights, no radio, no parachutes.

After completing his missions, Dr. Forsythe continued his medical practice in Atlantic City until 1951. He then moved his practice to Newark, N.J., where he retired in 1978. In 1986, he was inducted into the Aviation Hall of Fame of New Jersey and February 7, 1986 was proclaimed "Albert Forsythe Day" by the Mayor of Newark.

John W. Greene

One of the pioneers of black aviation, John Green lived in the Washington, DC area for many years. He was born on December 25, 1900 in Atlanta, GA, the son of John W. Green, Sr. and Rosa Reasley Green. He attended public school in Atlanta, GA and was graduated in 1922 from Hampton Normal School, in Virginia as a machinist. In 1933, he received a Commercial Pilot's License, the second black to do so. He was also one of the earliest Blacks to secure a Transport Pilot License and the first black to receive an Aircraft and Engine Mechanic License.

Mr. Greene moved to Washington, DC in 1940, organized and taught Aviation mechanics at Phelps Vocational High School, and later taught at Armstrong High. In 1941, he joined the Cloud Club, an organization of black youths interested in flying. He was appointed flight instructor and manager of the Columbia Air Center located in Croome, MD. The Center was the first black owned and operated licensed airport in the United States.

During World War II, Greene was employed as an aircraft mechanic at Camp Springs Army Air Field, now renamed Andrews Air Force Base. Later he was employed as an instructor at the University of Colorado National Aviation Education workshop. He died in Washington, DC at the age of 88, on March 23, 1989.

Early Pioneers: Eugene Bullard and Bessie Coleman.

Chief Anderson with Colonel Caso, Editor
(courtesy of Michael Ciccarelli).

Chapter 1
The Fight For The Right To Fight

Far down in the deep south in Tuskegee, AL, approximately twelve miles from the famous Tuskegee Institute, stands an abandoned Army Air Field. Today, this field is only a memory for thousands of Negroes throughout the United States, military and civilian, men and women, who in answer to the call of their country, came here to develop this site as a training center for Negro pilots. Today, this ghost field in a beautiful rolling valley is a desolate place. How different from the days when it was teaming with activity--with planes zooming overhead at all hours, and happy, singing cadets marching to and from classes. How different from the day when the first Negro cadets were commissioned as pilots of the United States Army Air Force.

It was March 7, 1942, that five young men stood stiffly at attention on Tuskegee Army Air Field's lone runway. The occasion was the first graduation exercise of Negro pilots into the Army Air Force. A brisk March breeze tugged at these happy cadets' officers' blouses as they stood smartly at attention before General George E. Stratemeyer, the guest speaker. A hush fell over the throng of friends and relatives as the Chief of the Army air Staff arose to speak.

"I am sure," remarked General Stratemeyer, "that everyone present, as well as the vast unseen audience of your well wishers, senses that this graduation is an historic movement, filled with portent of great good. Our country is engaged in a hard fight for its security and freedom. Here today is opened up a new source to wage that fight. It is my hope and my confident expectation that by your skill, courage, and devotion to duty you will fully justify that confidence and trust reposed in you, and that your service records will constitute bright pages in the annals of our country." Looking directly at the graduates, the General continued: "You will furnish the nuclei of the 99th and the 100th Pursuit Squadrons. Future graduates of this school will look up to you as *Old Pilots*. They will be influenced profoundly by the examples which you set. Therefore, it will be of the highest importance that your service be of a character worthy of emulation by younger officers."(1)

After the address, the five new Army Air Corps pilots stepped forward snappily and received their wings and commissions. CPT Benjamin O. Davis, Jr., of Washington, DC, the son of the Army's only Negro General Benjamin O. Davis Sr., was the first to receive his wings. The others were Charles Debow Jr., of Indianapolis, IN; Lemuel R. Custis, of Hartford, CT; George S. Roberts, of Fairmont, WV; and Mac Ross, of Dayton, OH.

The five proud young men had come a long, hard way to become members of the United States Army Air Corps and at this graduation exercise they began to realize the great responsibility that rested upon them--for upon their shoulders not only rested perhaps the future of their country, but the future of Negro youths who might aspire to become pilots. These young pilots were also aware of the hardships encountered before they were admitted into the Cadet Corps. However, their experiences were only a small part of the long struggle by Negro youths to be accepted for the Army Air Corps pilot training. Actually, the battle by Negroes to be accepted for military pilot training began during World War I.

In 1917, Negro youths tried to enlist in the Air Service of the Signal Corps as Air Observers. However, the applicants were informed that "No colored aero squadrons were being formed at the present time...but, if later on, it was decided to form colored squadrons, recruiting officers would be notified to that effect."(2)

Four years later in 1922, Negro leaders urged the War Department to establish Negro Army Air Force Reserve units. To this request the Department replied that it was "impossible to establish such units because no Negro officers had previously held commissions in the Air Service and that since no Negro Air Units existed, there was no justification for the appointment of Negroes as flying cadets."(3)

In 1931, Walter White, Secretary for the NAACP and Robert R. Moton, President of Tuskegee Institute requested that the War Department accept Negroes in the Army Air Corps for pilot training. To this request the War Department stated that from the beginning the Air Corps had selected men with technical and mechanical experience and ability, that the colored man had not been attracted to flying in the same way or to the extent of the white man and that it had received so many applications from college trained white men that many white applicants had to be turned down.(4)

In reply to this letter, White wrote: "It is obvious that colored men cannot be attracted to the field of aviation in the same way or to the extent as the white man, when the door to that field is slammed in the colored man's face... There are thousands of excellent colored mechanics in the country and if the War Department did not prejudice the case by definitely excluding them, we feel sure that there would be no difficulty in finding and developing men with all the qualifications required of pilots, mechanics, and all the other functions included in the air service."(5)

The reluctance of the War Department to accept Negroes for flying training led many to feel that, only through legislation by Congress, would Negro youths be assured acceptance into the Air Corps. Senator Harry H. Schwartz of Wyoming was one of those who felt that legislation was the only guarantee. When Public Law 18, an appropriation bill, was being considered, he introduced an amendment. Enacted as a part of the Appropriation Bill passed on April 3, 1939, it read, "The secretary of War is authorized, in his discretion and under the rules, regulations, and limitations to be prescribed by him, to lend to accredited civilian aviation schools one or more of which shall be designated by the Civil Aeronautics Authority for the training of any Negro Air Pilot, at which personnel of the Military Establishment are pursuing a course of education and training pursuant to detail thereto under competent orders of the War Department, out of aircraft, aircraft parts, aeronautical equipment and accessories for the Air Corps, on hand and belonging to the Government, such articles as may appear to be required for instruction, training, and maintenance purposes."

The passage of Public Law 18 caused considerable concern to high air force officials. BG Barton K. Yount, Chief of the Training Group of the Air Corps, directed the Air Plans Section to prepare a plan for the training of Negro pilots and a Negro unit, on the assumption that it would be necessary for the Air Corps to begin such training. However, a study by members of the General Staff and by Civil Aeronautics Authority came to the conclusion that such a plan would not be necessary. "...the bill merely authorized the Secretary of War to lend equipment to accredited civil aviation schools at which personnel of the Military Establishment were pursuing a course under competent War Department orders."

The Judge Advocate General was informed of the Air Corps interpretation and was requested to give his interpretation. He agreed with the Air Corps. He further construed the Law to contain a directive to the C.A.A. with absolutely "no duty imposed by such language on the War Department."

The War Department, however, decided that in spite of the interpretation, it would cooperate with the Civil Aeronautics Authority in carrying out what appeared to be the intent of Congress. It directed the Air Corps to confer with the C.A.A., to obtain its designation of an accredited civilian flying school and to agree upon the aircraft and equipment required.

It was believed by Negro leaders and supporters of the amendment Public Law 18, that its enactment had settled the discussions of whether or not the Air Corps would train Negro pilots. However, the Air Corps' slow pace in implementing the training program brought many inquiries. The Air Corps prepared a letter which explained its interpretation of the law. The letter was to be sent to Senator Morris Sheppard, Chairman of the Senate Military Affairs Committee; but before it could be sent, the Office of the Chief of Staff informed the Air Corps that "for the time being" the War Department would take no action in connection with the training of Negro pilots and that "no more publicity will be given this matter than is absolutely essential."(6)

The continuous delay in training Negro pilots caused Senator Schwartz to make a personal visit to the office of General Arnold and General Yount and demand that Negro pilots be trained. Representatives of Negro organizations also called on the generals and expressed the opinion that they would continue to agitate in Congress for the passage of additional legislation if something definite was not done for training Negroes as pilots in the very near future.

On June 5, 1939, during a hearing of the House of Representatives on a Supplemental Military Appropriation Bill, Congressman D. Lane Powers of New Jersey asked Secretary of War Harry H. Woodring if under Public Law 18, one or more schools would be designated for Negro pilot training. Secretary Woodring replied that they were trying to work out a program of fairness "to those Colored people who are rightfully entitled to the training" that would honestly meet the interest of every citizen of the United States. Congressman Powers was not satisfied with his answer and asked if he definitely was going to train Negro pilots. To this, Secretary Woodring replied: "We are planning to do so."(7) However, when Negro youths applied for such training, the War Department had a prepared answer: "It has been a policy of the War Department not to mix Colored and white enlisted men in the same tactical organization and since no provision has been made for any Colored Air Corps unit in the Army colored persons are not eligible for enlistment in the Air Corps."(8)

When the Appropriation Bill was being considered, Congressman Louis Ludlow of Indiana offered an amendment that one million dollars of the eight million dollars proposed for expanding the training of military pilots and for materials, be set aside exclusively for the training of Negro pilots. He argued, "There is nothing in the record of Negroes in war that serve as a reason for refusing to give Negroes their proportionate share of air pilot training... How can we justify such discrimination before the court of public opinion and before the higher court which we may humbly agree knows no color line when it comes to judging acts of loyalty and devotion.(9)

Secretary Woodring says, on page 281 of the hearing on this bill, that "We are trying to work out a plan whereby we shall have a program under which Negroes can be trained!

"The Secretary of War's words are an eloquent acknowledgment of the justice of giving this training to Negro pilots. Yet not one cent is provided for such training. I appreciate the good intentions, but why should there be such delay in providing this training? ...Available land and facilities for these Negro training units are being offered free of charge at Tallahassee, FL, and at Tuskegee."

Congressman Dirksen continued the argument for black pilot training. "Mr. Chairman, the amendment offered by the gentleman from Indiana is similar to an amendment I have pending on the clerk's desk... There is certainly justification for the amendment, and it should be adopted... It is proposed that this training camp be established at Tuskegee Institute, Alabama. At Tuskegee, they have a Reserve Officers Training Corps at the present time, which is officered by a Negro First Lieutenant, who is a graduate of West

Point, and whose father, I am informed, is the Colonel of the Fifteenth Infantry in New York, COL B.J. (B.O) Davis, Sr. In the second place, they have a mechanical school at Tuskegee. So this appropriation can be very conveniently adapted for the purpose of training civilian Negro pilots at Tuskegee Institute in order to carry out and effectuate the purpose of section 4 of the act approved in April of 1939."

Although the Air Corps refused to accept Negro youths for pilot training, in the fall of 1939, the Civil Aeronautics Authority organized civil pilot training units at some Negro colleges and permitted some Negro youths to enroll in pilot training courses at white colleges. The C.A.A. also announced that the North Suburban Flying School at Glenview, IL had been designated as the school required by Public Law 18. However, no Negroes were sent to the school, although white flying cadets were being sent there for training.

One of the Negro colleges selected by the C.A.A. for Negro pilot training was Tuskegee Institute. On October 15, 1939, President Frederick D. Patterson of Tuskegee Institute was notified by Robert H. Hinckley, Chairman of the Civil Aeronautic Authority, that Tuskegee Institute had been approved for participation in the civil pilot training program. It was stipulated that Tuskegee Institute and the Alabama Air Service, a commercial flying service, would use the Municipal Airport in Montgomery, AL, jointly to conduct flying classes. Tuskegee Institute, however, was to conduct ground training on its campus.

In January 1940, flight training for civilian pilot trainees of Tuskegee was begun at the Municipal Airport in Montgomery with Mr. George L. Washington, Chief Aeronautics, Tuskegee Institute as its Director.

The daily 80 miles trip soon proved expensive and tiresome. Cognizant of this handicap, Washington set about to establish an air field in the vicinity of the Institute. As a result, in March 1940, Tuskegee Institute's Airport # 1 was opened. Meantime, while these plans were in the making, the training had progressed. In May 1940, 19 trainees completed flight training in the primary course and were granted private pilot certificates.

Director Washington was informed in June, 1940, by the civil Aeronautics Authority that Tuskegee Institute had been approved for a second unit of the primary course which was to begin on June 15. A short time afterwards, Dr. Patterson was notified that pilots trained at Tuskegee were eligible for two of the one thousand training scholarships being made available by the Civil Aeronautics Authority for the summer of 1940. This meant that civilian pilots trained at other colleges such as Hampton Institute, West Virginia State College, Howard University, Lincoln University, A & T College and Delaware State College were also eligible for two of the scholarships.

Upon receiving the information that Negro civilian pilots were to be given advanced flying, President Patterson and Director Washington held a conference with high officials of the Civil Aeronautics Authority. Shortly after the conference, it was announced that advanced civil pilot training would be held at Tuskegee Institute beginning July 22, 1940. Letters were addressed to the coordinators of civil pilot training of the various Negro colleges by Director Washington urging them to canvass their rosters of civil pilots to secure members for the advance course. These letters were promptly complied with and the course began as scheduled. Howard University sent three trainees: John Perry, Yancey Williams, and Elmer Jones; Hampton Institute sent two: Roscoe Draper and Philip Lee; West Virginia State University sent one: Hector Strong; North Carolina A & T College sent one: Reginald Smith; and Tuskegee Institute supplied three: Erwin Lawrence, Milton Crenshaw and Sherman Rose.

Although Negro youths were permitted to participate in the civilian pilot training program, they were denied the right to enter military flying. Public Law 18 did not grant Negroes acceptance into the Air Corps as military pilots, but it did give Negro youths pilot training and a chance to prove Negroes could be taught to fly. However, it was little known, but there were at the time over 100 black pilots.

The legislation that primarily affected the employment of Blacks by the Army was the Selective Training and Service Act of 1940. When the act was being discussed Negro leaders and supporters remembered that Public Law 18 did not gain acceptance of Negroes as military pilots. To assure that Negro youths would not be discriminated against and that the Act would not be interpreted as Public Law 18 had been interpreted, Congressmen and Negro leaders proposed amendments which they believed would specifically state the intent of congress.

On January 25, 1940, during a hearing on a Supplemental Military, Naval Appropriation Bill, Senator Bridges of New Hampshire brought to the attention of the Senate that provisions of the last military appropriation bill had not been carried out. The bill referred to was approved on April 3, 1939 and provided for the training of Negro pilots. As evidence of the War Department's refusal to comply with the mandate of Congress, he read into record a reply by the War Department, dated September 23, 1939 to an applicant, Mr. Frank S. Reed of Chicago.

Dear Sir:

With reference to your application for appointment as a flying cadet, you are informed that the War Department has taken final action on your application and that your transcript of college credits and other supporting papers have been returned to this headquarters with the statement that in as much as there are no units composed of colored men in the Air Corps at the present time, no provision has been made for their flying training, and therefore, the War Department can take no further action with a view to giving you flying training at this time.

Your transcript of college credits and other papers which accompanied your application are returned herewith.

It is regretted that the nonexistence of a colored Air Corps unit to which you could be assigned in the event of completion of flying training, precludes your training to become a military pilot at this time. (10)

Very truly yours,
J. G. Brackinridge,
MAJ, A.G.D.

Senator Thomas of Oklahoma tried to defend the actions of the War Department in ignoring the Act of Congress relating to the training of Negro pilots. "Mr. President, the Army is becoming a highly efficient organization. It is a highly scientific organization. If anyone had the time to spend and inspect the exhibit at Bolling Field the past ten days, no doubt he was edified and gratified to see there the component parts which goes into the making of an airplane. I had no idea that there were so many parts to an airplane... I am advised that to make one of the larger airplanes it takes about 4500 parts. These parts of course are of various kinds and characters. From the outside the parts are not discernible, but when we go and look at the inside of an airplane, look at the engine, look into the control room, and at the various parts of the plane, we find that it is a mass of intricate parts. I presume they are necessary. If they were not necessary, they would be eliminated."(11)

Senator Bridges, in response to remarks by Senator Thomas, remarked:

"I agree with everything the Senator has said about the efficiency of the War Department. I think it is one of the best departments of the government, and I think it is well administered, and I am in general sympathy with the pending bill and in general sympathy with the defense program. But I do desire to point out, and I do want it very definitely understood, that for some reason or other the act of Congress relating to the training of colored aviators has been ignored, and I think the War Department should have its attention called to that matter and that Congress should have some word as to why the administration here in Washington, headed by President Roosevelt, who claims to be so interested in these matters, has ignored the colored people of the country in that particular matter."(12)

Dr. Rayford W. Logan of Howard University, Chairman of the Civilian Committee on Participation of Negroes in the National Defense Program, testified before the House Committee on Military Affairs. He asked that a section be added to the bill to state that "No provision of the act shall be construed or administered so as to discriminate against any person on account of race, creed, or color," or as an alternative, "In the selection and training of men as well as in the interpretation and execution of the provisions of this act there shall be no discrimination against any person on account of race, creed or color."(13)

Charles H. Houston, the civil rights lawyer for the NAACP and Congressman Hamilton Fisk of New York urged the adoption of similar amendments, while Senator Robert R. Wagner of New York sought to include specific mention of aviation units as well as to make it mandatory that men be selected "without regard to race, creed or color."(14)

In reply to remarks by Senator Tom Connally of Texas, who opposed the amendment as unnecessary, Senator Wagner stated: "...I have received a number of communications from organizations such as the Association for the Advancement of Colored People, which have called attention to a rule adopted by the Army, particularly in the aviation units, that no matter how well fitted they may be physically, mentally, or in any other way, they will not take certain American citizens because of their color. I think we ought not in any way to approve such an un-American practice. This is the reason I have offered the amendment, with the sentiments of which I think the Senator will agree."(15)

Senator Connally stated that he agreed thoroughly with the sentiments expressed by Senator Wagner, but "...I think I know as much about the Colored race as does the Senator from New York. I was raised with colored people, and played with colored boys when I was a boy, and I worked with them side by side in the cotton fields and other places. I am ready to fight for the right of the colored man under the laws and the Constitution, not simply during election time, as the Senator from New York.

"But I realize better perhaps than the Senator from New York that constitutional and legal rights are one thing, and the right to select one's associates socially is another thing. There is something in the Anglo-Saxon written in the Constitution of the race, there is something written in the statues of our blood, *Do not compel me to accept any man, whether he is white or black or yellow or red, as my social companion and equal, if I do not want to accept him*."(16)

The Selective Service Act when passed contained a provision which was suggested by Dr. Rayford Logan of Howard University. "That in the selection and training of men under this act, and in the interpretation and execution of the provisions of this, there shall be no discrimination against any person on account of race or color."(17)

On the surface, it appeared that Congress had taken a positive step against discrimination in the selection and training of men by the Army. However, there was an additional provision in the act that caused great concern to Negro leaders and later was used by the Army, as they had suspected, to continue its discriminatory practices. The provision (Section 3) provided "That no man shall be inducted for training and service under this act unless and until he is acceptable to the land or naval forces for such training and service and his physical and mental fitness for such training and service has been satisfactorily determined." It further provided "That no man shall be inducted for such training and service until adequate provision shall have been made for such shelter, sanitary facilities, water supplies, heating and lighting arrangements, medical care, and hospital accommodations, for such men, as may be determined by the Secretary of War or the Secretary of the Navy, as the case may be, to be essential to public and personal health."(18)

Concerned with the possibility of the Armed Services using this section to limit the service of Negro youths, several Negro leaders met and formulated a memorandum, which they considered outlined the minimum request for the employment of Negroes. The memorandum was submitted to President Roosevelt, Secretary of the Navy, Frank Knox, and Assistant Secretary of War, Robert P. Patterson at a White House conference on September 27, 1940. The following proposals were made:

1. The use of presently available Negro reserve officers in training recruits and other forms of active service. At the same time, a policy of training additional Negro officers in all branches of the services should be announced. Present facilities and those to be provided in the future should be made available for such training.

2. Immediate designation of centers where Negroes may be trained for work in all branches of the aviation corps. It is not enough to train pilots alone, but in addition navigators, bombers, gunners, radiomen, and mechanics must be trained in order to facilitate full Negro participation in the air service.

3. Existing units of the army and units to be established should be required to accept and select officers and enlisted personnel without regard to race.

4. Specialized personnel such as Negro physicians, dentists, pharmacists and officers of chemical warfare, camouflage service and the like should be integrated into the services.

5. The appointment of Negroes as responsible members in the various national and local agencies engaged in the administration of the Selective Service Training Act of 1940.

6. The development of effective techniques for insuring the extension of the policy of integration in the Navy other than the menial services to which Negroes are restricted.

7. The adoption of policies and the development of techniques to assure the participation of trained Negro women as Army and Navy nurses as well as in the Red Cross.(19)

On September 5, 1940, however, President Roosevelt had directed the War Department to prepare and hold a statement to the effect that "colored men will have equal opportunity with white men in all departments of the Army." At a cabinet meeting on September 13, President Roosevelt stated that "he had been troubled by representations of the Negroes that their race under the draft, was limited to labor battalions." The Army informed the President that it planned to give Negroes "proportionate shares in all branches of the Army, in the proper ration to their population--approximately 10 percent." The President then suggested that the War Department, "in conjunction with the Navy" publicize this fact.(20)

As a result of the conference to September 27, Assistant Secretary of War Patterson submitted to the President a full statement of policy informally approved by the Secretary of War Stimson and the Chief of Staff, Marshall. President Roosevelt approved the policy report and on October 9, the report was released to the press by the White House. The policy statement read:

It is the policy of the War Department that the services of Negroes will be utilized on a fair and equitable basis. In line with this policy, revision will be made as follows:

1. The strength of the Negro personnel of the Army of the United States will be maintained on the general basis of the proportion of the country.

2. Negro organizations will be established in each major branch of the service, combatant as well as noncombatant.

3. Negro reserve officers eligible for active duty will be assigned to Negro units officered by colored personnel.

4. When officer candidate schools are established, opportunity will be given to Negroes to qualify for reserve commissions.

5. Negroes are being given aviation training as pilots, mechanics and technical specialists. This training will be accelerated.

6. At arsenals and army posts Negro civilians are accorded equal opportunity for employment at work for which they are qualified by ability, education, and experience.

7. The policy of the War Department is not to intermingle colored and white enlisted personnel in the same regimental organizations. This policy has been proved satisfactory over a long period of years, and to make changes now would produce situations destructive to morale and detrimental to the preparation for national defense. For similar reasons the department does not contemplate assigning colored reserve officers other than those of the Medical Corps and chaplains to existing Negro combat units of the Regular Army. These regular units are going concerns, accustomed through many years to the present system. Their morale is splendid, their rate of reenlistment is exceptionally high, and their field training is well advanced. It is the opinion of the War Department that no experiments should be tried with the organizational set-up of these units at this critical time.(21)

Negro leaders and the Negro press, while praising the signs of change within the army and pointing out that under the new policy Negroes would have broader opportunities than in the past, nevertheless continued to attack the Army's segregation policy.

In response to the mounting criticisms, the War Department made plans for the activation of several new Negro units and on October 25, 1940, nominated COL Davis, Sr. for promotion to BG. The same day, Secretary of War Stimson, who had succeeded Woodring, appointed Judge William Hastie, Dean of Howard University Law School, as Civilian Aide on Negro Affairs.

In October 1940, the War Department announced that Negroes were in training as pilots, mechanics, and technical specialists, and that Negro Aviation units would be organized as soon as the necessary personnel were trained. Judge Hastie later repudiated this announcement. He related that when the announcement was made the only aviation training Negroes were receiving, was training in civil flying at a few Negro Colleges and one private field under the supervision of the civil Aeronautics Administration.(22)

Judge Hastie took office on November 1, 1940 and his duties as described by Secretary Stimson were "to assist in the formulation, development and administration of policies looking to the fair and effective utilization of Negroes in all branches of the military services."(23)

When Judge Hastie began service, most of the policy proposals affecting Negroes were referred to his office for comment and approval. This did not last. He soon complained that too frequently, policies had been formulated and presented for final approval before they were submitted to him. Following the complaint, the chiefs of arms and services and the General Staff divisions were instructed that "Matters of policy which pertain to Negroes, or important questions arising thereunder, will be referred to Judge William Hastie, Civilian Aide to the Secretary of War, for comment or concurrence before final action."(24)

Judge Hastie was assured at the beginning of his service that Negroes would not be excluded from any of the armed services. He was assured also that Negro flying units would be activated when the National Youth Administration and the Civil Aeronautics Authority program had trained sufficient civilian pilots, mechanics and ground personnel.

In December 1940, the Air Corps submitted a plan for the establishment of a Negro pursuit squadron, a base group detachment, a weather and communication detachment and a service unit. The plan provided for white noncommissioned officers to be used as inspectors, supervisors, and instructors for an indefinite period of time. The initial training of technical and administrative officers and enlisted men was to be given at Chanute Field. Negro officers, when qualified, would replace white officers in the squadrons and in administrative positions. Negro graduates of the C.A.A. civilian pilot training courses were to be selected for military flying training and the initial primary flying training course was to be omitted.

When it was agreed that Negroes would be accepted for military flying, three principal military centers were considered as possible locations for the training of cadets. They were the West Coast, Texas, and the Southeast center of Maxwell Field in AL. But Tuskegee Institute, wrote Judge Hastie, "with a small civilian pilot training program already inaugurated, was willing and anxious to cooperate with the Air Command at Maxwell Field in the development of a military aviation training program at Tuskegee to be coordinated with the Tuskegee Institute program. In the very first step, the selection of a site for a Negro training base near Tuskegee Institute, the Administration of the school was active in the location and negotiation for the necessary land."(25)

Judge Hastie wrote in regard to the maneuver of the administration of the Institute: "In view of notorious racial attitudes prevalent in the Alabama and Texas areas, the integration of Negroes into the West Coast training center was the obvious course which would immediately suggest itself to anyone concerned primarily with working out a sound program."(26)

In the spring of 1941, Secretary Patterson presented to Judge Hastie a plan for the establishment of a flying training school at Tuskegee. Judge Hastie objected to the plan that proposed to establish a segregated field in the south and commented that "there would unquestionably be very great public protest if the proposed plans should be adopted."

The Air Corps related that Randolph, Maxwell, and Moffett Fields were already congested and that a field at Tuskegee would provide a minimum of delay in getting the training program for Negroes started. It related also that the school would be under the direct supervision of the Commanding General of Maxwell Field. On January 8, 1941, Judge Hastie withdrew his formal opposition to the plan, although he was not satisfied with the plan.

The newly proposed Tuskegee Army Air Field was to be used in the second phase of Army Aviation training. The instructors were to be military personnel. They were trained to instruct cadets who had received primary training under civilian instructors at privately operated schools contracted by the army.

In organizing its primary training program, the Air Force again solicited the cooperation of Tuskegee Institute. It requested the use of the facilities of the Institute for the training of cadets in the primary phase of Army flying. A contract was signed which stipulated that the Institute would furnish flying instructors, ground personnel, and the necessary physical facilities. It also provided for the stationing of a detachment of officers and enlisted men to supervise the cadet training program at the Institute's field. The responsibility for the operation and training in the flying school was left to the Aeronautical division of the Institute. This contract brought into being the 66th Air Force Contract Flying School at Tuskegee Institute.

The establishment of a segregated primary school also brought protest from Judge Hastie. He wrote: "Although my own objections to a segregated Army training base were overruled in the War Department, I had persisted in contending that Negro cadets should be sent for primary training to the various contract schools, many of them outside the south where white cadets were being trained. But the plan of the Southeast Center and Tuskegee Institute prevailed. Tuskegee Institute was given a contract for the primary training of all Negro cadets. The Air Command had accomplished its design for a completely segregated Negro training program.(27)

The Tuskegee Institute still maintained a private civil pilot training program which had no connection with the Army training program. Many Negro youths enrolled in the civilian course with the belief that it would entitle them to further training under the Army program. Recognizing this misconception, the Institute made a request to the War Department that graduates of its civil course be given priority in admission to the Army training course. This request was readily granted by the War Department.

In spite of the commitment of the War Department to give Negroes military pilot training, the Air Force continued to refuse applications from Negro youths. In January 1941, a Howard University student, Yancey Williams, filed suit under the sponsorship of the National Association for the Advancement of Colored People to compel the Air Corps to admit him to one of the Army Air Force training centers. In early March 1941, the Air Corps began accepting applications from Negro youths. This was followed by an announcement made by the Selective Service Headquarters on March 25, 1941. It stated: "The War Department has announced that pilots will be selected from those who have completed the secondary course offered by the Civil Aeronautics Authority. The Negro pilots, it was said, will be trained at Tuskegee, in connection with Tuskegee Institute. Thirty-three pilots and twenty-seven planes make up the normal complement of the squadron, which was begun in February."(28)

Meantime, numerous Negro youths who had been denied applications for pilot training sought aid through the National Association for the Advancement of Colored People. In a letter to Louis R. Purnell, a hopeful pilot candidate, the Association wrote on May 16, 1941:

As one of those who have written to the NAACP requesting information regarding application to join the Air Corps of the United States Army, we are sending you herewith an application form. We secured these from the War Department because of the numbers of persons who had written to us, as you did.

In making application we suggest that you request that you be given training at the training school nearest your home. Our reason for making this suggestion is because the present plan is to send such Negroes as are accepted for training to a segregated training school at Tuskegee Institute.

Signed:
Walter White
Secretary.

Shortly after the Air Corps began accepting applications from Negroes, the War Department announced that it was planning to establish an Air training center to train a Negro Squadron for pursuit flying. Following this statement by the War Department, Dr. Patterson announced that he had received a letter from the Assistant Secretary of War stating that the War Department was proceeding immediately with plans to establish a Negro Pursuit Squadron. this Squadron was to consist of 400 enlisted men, 33 pilots, and 27 planes. In addition, $1,091,000 had been appropriated for the establishment of an air field at Tuskegee.

Rear L-R: Roscoe Draper, Fred Witherspoon, Philip Lee, Edward Gibbs. Front: Ernest Henderson Sr., Joseph Ramos, James Hill

Civilian Primary Instructors: Top: Bob Terry, John Young, Stevens, Charles Fox, Roscoe Draper, Sherman Rose, James A. Hill, Adolph Moret, Ernest Henderson, Matthew Plummen, Linwood Williams, Daniel C. James, Lewis Jackson, Milton Crenshaw. Bottom: Perry Young, Charlie Flowers, Claude Platt, "Chip" Anderson, C.R. Harris, Wendell Lipscomb, J. E. Wright.

Top left to right: Executive Officer LTC Hazard with Operations Officer MAJ Boyd; COL Frederick V. Kimble, second Commanding Officer. Bottom: Cadet Color Guards and Post Headquarters, Tuskegee Army Air Field.

Chapter 2
A Dream Comes True

By the Spring of 1941, it was becoming apparent that definite plans were in the making for the acceptance of Negroes in military aviation. A new primary training school was being organized and 24 civilian pilots were being trained by the Army Air Force to qualify them as instructors of cadets. In the meantime, on March 21, 1941, the 99th was officially activated.

On July 10, 1941, the War Department announced that the quota of pilots for the 99th was to be about 33, but a total of approximately 100 men would be trained annually. At the same time, it also stated that 271 enlisted men were already in training at Chanute Field, IL, as ground crews for the 99th Squadron. These men were to be sent to Tuskegee at the completion of their training and with seven more to be entered, making a total of 278, the full ground complement would be getting technical training. The types of training, these men were depicted as undergoing, included airplane mechanics, aircraft armorer, aircraft supply and technical clerk, instrument and weather forecasting.

The big day for air-minded youths came on July 19, 1941 when an inaugural exercise, marking the beginning of military pilot training for Negro youths, was held at the Booker T. Washington monument, located on the campus of Tuskegee Institute. The most memorable day for the people of the little town of Tuskegee came a month later on August 25, when the first class of cadets was given the initial flying instructions.

While the first class was receiving primary training, construction of the Army Air Force Advanced Flying Field was being rushed. Early in 1941, the Army awarded a contract to McKissack and McKissack, an organization headed by a Negro architect and contractor, the contract calling for the conversion of a wooded graveyard site to an airfield. On July 23, 1941, the engineers began leveling hills and uprooting trees in preparation for laying runways.

Almost at the same time that the engineers began to work, the Army sent MAJ James A. Ellison to Tuskegee to command the new field. On arriving at Tuskegee, he immediately began plans for the activation of the field. However, it was not until a month later that the real organization began.

In the latter part of October, 1941, the initial ground crew of the 99th arrived at Tuskegee Army Air Field. A few weeks later, on November 8, 1941, the first class of cadets was transferred from Primary Field to the Army Air Field and operation began.

Although MAJ Ellison made great progress in organizing Tuskegee Army Air Field, he was transferred on January 12, 1942 to the Air Corps Ferrying Command, Wayne County Airport in Romulus, MI. It was alleged that his removal was due to his courage in opposing local civil authorities who had disarmed a Negro sentry for challenging a white civilian. MAJ Ellison was succeeded by COL Frederick V. H. Kimble, a West Point graduate with 24 years of flying experience. It was during the period that COL Kimble was commanding officer that the field developed from a mere plan on paper to an actual functioning unit in the Army Air Corps. The organization of this field was not an easy one, for in addition to public sentiment, which definitely affected the program, there were also flying difficulties.

When the first class completed primary training and arrived at the Advanced Flying Field, it found the field incomplete. Only one runway was sufficiently ready for flying. The ground school was located in a temporary wooden structure which housed the offices and classrooms. One of the unusual things about the building interior was that there were no partitions separating the classes from the offices. The babble of voices was accompanied by the clicking of typewriters. Concentration was most difficult for the cadets. The six cadets were divided into three classes. One could almost take lecture notes from the different classes at the same time.

Although many handicaps were present, the training went on without interruptions. In the following months, more cadets were graduated as pilots and nearly every day new ground officers arrived at the field to add to the ground complement. The field was also developing rapidly. A new ground school building was constructed together with barracks, office buildings, warehouses, and a large commissary.

The organization of Tuskegee as an Air Force installation progressed so rapidly that by September 1942, COL Kimble, in addressing Class 42-H, was able to remark that, though the field was still incomplete in many details, its form, utility and purpose were well established. The following month, in addressing another class, he said that in the establishment of Tuskegee Army Air Base, there appeared, in the minds of those who went through its early days, a far-off goal to be realized only by a long struggle of construction difficulties. As the weeks and months wore on, the goal to train pilots, to develop mechanics and to equip and organize a fighter squadron began to take tangible form and then become a concrete reality. "Today," remarked COL Kimble, "it is no longer difficult to see the initial goal for which you and your predecessors have stood. The Fighter Squadron exists in full fact and beyond this there are other squadrons already taking shape. The material aspects of this school are no longer difficult of realization."

Even though steady progress was made at the field, the War Department was reluctant about increasing the quota of cadets admitted for training as pilots. The order to allow only ten cadets to enter training every five weeks worked great hardship on Negro youths. Many who made applications for cadet training were delayed so long that they were called into other branches of services. Some even waited so long that they became ineligible because of the Air Corps age limit. Mr. Langston H. Caldwell, chairman of the Tuskegee Airmen Association, in a telegram to Secretary Stimson, called attention to the fact that a large number of qualified men were kept from serving their country by the ten percent restriction. "More than 100 private pilots trained at Tuskegee have filed applications to become cadets in the Air Corps, but to date only two have been called."

The NAACP requested that the War Department accept and train Negro cadets on the basis of fitness without regard to racial quota. The Association stated that it had received numerous letters from bewildered and disappointed young colored men who stated they had passed their physical examination but, because their actual enlistment had been delayed so long by the restricted quota system, they were being called by their local draft boards for general military service.

On December 26, 1942, COL Kimble was transferred to Cockron Field, Macon, GA to command the 27th Training wing. He was succeeded by COL Noel F. Parrish, a native of Lexington, KY, born on November 11, 1909, who obtained his elementary education in the schools in Kentucky, Georgia, and Alabama. In 1928, he was graduated from Rice Institute, with a Bachelor of Arts Degree. After one year of graduate study, his aspirations as a teacher gave way to a desire for travel and activity in the regular Army.

Entering the Army in July 30, 1930 as a private, COL Parrish spent one year with the 11th Cavalry before being appointed as a flying cadet. On the completion of his primary training at March Field, CA, he was transferred with the first basic class to be trained at the newly constructed Randolph Field. COL Parrish completed his advanced pilot training at Kelly Field in July 1932, and was assigned to the 13th Attack Squadron then stationed at Fort Crockett, Galveston, TX. In February 1934, he was assigned to the First Provisional Transport Squadron, commissioned as second lieutenant in the regular army in July 1935, and reassigned to the 13th Attack Squadron at Barksdale Field, LA. Later he was sent to Randolph Field, as a primary flight instructor.

When the civil pilot training program was inaugurated, COL Parrish was ordered to Chicago School of Aeronautics as an Air Corps supervisor. In May 1941, he was sent to Tuskegee Institute to command the newly activated 66th Army Air Force Training Detachment. He and the first class of cadets to complete primary training were transferred to the Advanced Flying School at the new Tuskegee Army Air Base in November 1941. It was at this time that he was made Director of Training.

COL Kimble's policy of catering to local prejudices and his determination to maintain a segregated policy on the field aroused considerable resentment. It was hoped that COL Parrish would change the practices at Tuskegee, but he made no substantial changes. In spite of this, COL Parrish's administration was more favorable than that of COL Kimble. COL Parrish was a soldier and a gentleman, with understanding and patience. He read extensively, met Negro leaders, and talked freely with everyone. As a result, he developed a keen awareness of the psychological effect of the traditional southern practices upon Negroes. This enabled him to carry out his and the policy of the War Department, in regard to Negroes, without arousing too much resentment.

Following COL Parrish's elevation to the position of Commanding Officer of Tuskegee, the War Department broke its long silence concerning plans for Negro pilots in combat service. It announced that it expected the first Negro Squadron would be on active duty overseas very soon. It also expressed satisfaction over the results obtained in the experimental training of Negro Flyers. In reference to the success of the cadets at Tuskegee, MG James R. Ulio, Adjutant General of the Army, stated: "From results so far obtained, it is believed that the Squadron will give an excellent account of itself in combat and that it will be a credit to its race and to Americans everywhere."

COL Davis, Jr., who took over the command of the 99th on August 24, 1942, also expressed confidence in the ability of the Squadron. Speaking to an assembled group of 99th pilots and guests on the occasion of a Field Day program in December 1942, he remarked: "The success of the combat unit will prove to be the opening wedge for the air minded youths who aspire to the field of Aviation. The records, so far, by the cadets at Tuskegee Army Flying School do not compare unfavorably with those records made by cadets at other fields. My greatest desire is to lead this squadron to victory against the enemy."

By February 1943, it had become apparent to all at Tuskegee that definite plans were being made for the 99th to enter combat. The pilots and ground crew were given intensive training in combat tactics. Daily they were told that they must grasp as quickly as possible the various phases of training because the possibility of going into combat was great. The results of this intensive training program were evident by the remark made by Secretary Stimson on his visit to Tuskegee in February 1943, when he stated that the outfit looked as good as any he had seen.

It was shortly after Secretary Stimson's visit that the possibility of active overseas duty seemed to become a probability. COL Parrish, addressing the 99th on February 12, hinted as much when he said: "All of you know that at any time you may be sent into an active combat zone. Since none of us can foretell the day of your departure from the station and the command, I shall take this occasion to speak a few words of farewell.

"You are fighting men now. You have made the team. Your future is now being handed into your own hands. No one knows what you will do with your future as fighting men, you yourself do not know. Your future, good or bad, will depend largely on how determined you are not to give satisfaction to those who would like to see you fail."

The War Department had planned to send the 99th to Liberia. The success of Rommel and his Afrika Korps against the British in Libya had posed a threat to the Middle East and Africa. In early 1942, the Liberian government granted to the United States the right to construct such airfields as it deemed necessary. Black troops were rushed to Liberia to provide for the defense of the country and to build air bases. They built Roberts Field, but after Rommel was driven out of Africa in the Tunisian Campaign, the German threat to Liberia became remote.

During the Tunisian Campaign, the Allies began making plans for a swift move into Sicily. The Allies had rushed into the Tunisian Campaign with very limited forces. They suffered such devastating losses to win the victory that they decided that in the Sicilian Campaign they would employ sufficient troops to battle the Germans, who, they expected, would be even more determined.

Both General Eisenhower and General Arnold urged the War Department to send more troops. The 99th Fighter Squadron was one of the fighter units sent overseas in answer to these calls. Spann Watson, one of the original 99th pilots sent into combat, related that after months of intensive training, they were told that they were now to begin studying radio communication and radar. It was emphasized to the pilots to pay particular attention to the instructors and learn radio communication and radar, because, where they were going, they would be alone. Spann remarked: "They had the complete set-up at Tuskegee. You know Luther Pugh, a member of our East Coast Chapter, was one of the instructors. They taught us how to follow planes on the scope, control them, direct them on missions and bring them back home. That course was a real drag, but it was something we had to know.

"Then the word got out that white pilots were being rushed overseas to England and Africa soon after graduation. White boys didn't get five weeks of training. After they were graduated, they were gone. Black newspapers got on the story. They said, like the 24th Infantry and anything else, they wanted to make a service unit out of the 99th or put it on patrol somewhere, reported to be Liberia. They said, we want our boys to get over there like everybody else.

"They agitated and agitated. Mind you, my class graduated on July 2. It supplied almost enough pilots, not enough, but almost enough pilots to fill out the squadron.

"The black newspapers stated that it was Christmas and we still hadn't gone anywhere--and now they were talking about sending the squadron on patrol in Liberia with a black company. The papers stated, let them get over there and fight like everybody else. We are all Americans, like everybody else and we got to pay the price.

"They kept that up and even General Parrish made a comment about it. We were somewhere, I can't recall where, and he said, 'Yes, they are saying that you are not going anywhere, just by sitting around Tuskegee, but remember the white boys are over there fighting and dying and making a name for themselves.'"

Throughout the month of March 1943, the 99th went through intensive and rigorous training. The pilots were not only drilled in the fundamentals of aerial combat, formation flying, and night flying but, with the ground complement, were subjected to long forced marches and drilled in bivouac and air base maintenance procedures. Spann Watson, commenting on the training experience, said: "They made us fly all Christmas Day and New Years Day. You know, even in combat they wind down for Christmas. It is an unwritten agreement by the enemy and the Allies that they would respect the Lord's birthday. We knew it, and we were angry. We said the sneaky bastards just wanted to give us a hard way to go."

Finally, on the morning of April 1, 1943, the 99th began making preparations for its departure from Tuskegee. Although the movement of the Squadron was suppose to be kept as confidential as possible, the news of its leaving for combat spread throughout the little town of Tuskegee. The next day, April 2, hundreds of well wishers and friends gathered at the depot to bid the men farewell and good luck as they boarded the evacuation train.

Top Picture: Cadets in training at Tuskegee. Middle Picture: Mechanics check a P-40. Bottom Picture: First class graduates TAAF: L-R: George Roberts, B. O. Davis Jr., Charles Debow, COL Robert Long (instructor), Mac Ross, Lemuel R. Custis.

Chapter 3
The Road to War

Although the members of the 99th had suspicion that they were headed for overseas duty, they were not convinced until they arrived at Camp Shanks, NY, a port of embarkation. Upon arrival, they were given quarters, fed, and, for the remainder of the day, they were allowed to lounge around and rest. The next morning the long tedious job of being processed began. This lasted for ten days. Finally, on the morning of April 14, COL Davis, who was to be senior officer aboard the transport ship, was directed to select a staff consisting of an Adjutant, Mess Officer, Provost Marshal, and Police Officer to aid him as Executive Officer in carrying out the orders and policies of the Transport Commander. It was now obvious that their stay in the country was to be only a matter of days.

The order to board ship came sooner than many expected. Early next morning, April 15, the Squadron was ordered to board ship. This was it! Although everyone saw it coming, the news was still a surprise. For a moment there was almost a complete silence; then confusion reigned. All of the men began talking simultaneously-talking of seeing their kids once more, of their wives and loved ones, of being back on *Main Street*, of their chances for survival, of the war in general.

A few hours later, the transport, filled to capacity with approximately 4,000 troops, white and colored, officers and enlisted men, hoisted anchor and stole out of the harbor. It was still dark and seemingly more quiet than usual as the ship moved lazily down the Hudson towards the sea. Its deck was crowded to capacity with men trying to get their last look at their native land.

The ship was far out at sea when the sun rose. The men could still see the majestic skyscrapers towering in the sky. Sadness filled their hearts as they watched the last vestige of their country slowly disappear in the hazy distance.

The first day at sea many of the men suffered from sea sickness. But as the days passed they became more accustomed to the water.

They moved about more at ease, played games, and met members of other squadrons. Still they could not completely relax for they lived in anticipation of attacks by enemy U-boats.

For eight days the ship moved steadily ahead. On the morning of April 24, land was sighted. There was a mad rush for the deck, every porthole and window. "Land! Land!" was the cry on every lip. As the minutes and the hours passed by slowly, the men became restless. Everyone now was excited and curious. It seemed as if they would never reach shore.

Finally, in the late afternoon, the ship entered the harbor and shortly afterwards dropped anchor. The wharves were crowded with Arabs who begged for candies and cigarettes, fighting among themselves over the prizes tossed from the ships by the soldiers.

The job of disembarkation was long and tedious. After casting anchor, the ship stood at dock for hours before the first troop disembarked. When the movement finally began, only one outfit at a time was permitted to leave the ship. It was hot and the waiting seemed endless to the men who were now almost exhausted from the heat and the long voyage.

When the 99th's turn came, the men hurried down the gang-plank. On reaching the ground, they were besieged by a host of Arabs swarming around them, begging for cigarettes and food.

The squadron was met by COL Alison of the Northwest Training Command. After greeting COL Davis, he directed the movement of the squadron to its bivouac area.

En route to the new station, the convoy passed through the city of Casablanca. The men observed the white buildings and green squares. They saw Moroccans in their bright red uniforms; they viewed French Colonials sitting at the tables of sidewalk cafes and noticed Arabs in turbans, sandals, and dirty white robes milling about the streets.

It was late afternoon when the convoy reached the bivouac area. Although tired and hungry, the men went about in good spirit to set up camp. COL Davis, meanwhile, was busy seeking information relative to his new station.

When the sun went down the temperature dropped considerably. By now, the men were almost exhausted; so, after a hearty meal, they turned in for a good night's rest.

The following day, COL Davis and his operations officer, CPT George S. Roberts, were taken by COL Alison to see General Cannon, who commanded the Northwest Training Command. The General persuaded COL Davis to remain in the area until the squadron was satisfactorily equipped for combat. He also sent COL Davis on a preliminary reconnaissance of his new station, which was located about 150 miles inland in French Morocco near the town of Fez in North Africa.

After the 99th was equipped to the satisfaction of COL Davis, arrangements were made to move by rail to the new station. It was a slow, tiresome ride, and to these men, who had come across the ocean with expectations of finding everyone rushing with excitement, this was a great disappointment.

It took the train 17 hours to cover the 150 miles. During the trip, COL Davis complained about the slowness of the train. He was informed that he was lucky to move at such a fast rate of speed.

Upon arrival at the new station, which was located at OuedN'ja, a little town near Fez, the 99th immediately began setting up camp. Knowing that they would be stationed here for a while, the men set about to make their quarters as comfortable as possible.

A service command was stationed near the 99th's new location. It was commanded by a COL Phillips. A fighter-bomber group was also located nearby. It was commanded by COL Stevenson, a West Point graduate whom COL Davis had met at the Academy. COL Davis, relating the experiences at OuedN'ja, said: "Our stay there was probably our most pleasant stay overseas. Most cordial relations existed between the members of the Squadron and the members of the fighter-bomber group nearby. The pilots of the two organizations engaged in impromptu dog fights to determine the relative superiority of the P-40 and the A-36. Enlisted men of the two groups got along together very well in all types of athletic contests and other means of recreation.

"The town of Fez was found to be one of the most delightful spots that any of us had ever visited. One unusual feature of our stay there was that members of my organization and members of these organizations visited the town of Fez every single night for over a period of a month, and not one unpleasant incident arose.

"The officers of the squadron were made socially secure in the town by the visit of Josephine Baker. Miss Baker insisted on presenting several different groups of our officers to the prominent French and Arab families in the town. All in all, Miss Baker was very largely responsible for our most pleasant social relations in the town of Fez.

"It was during our stay here that four P-39 pilots, whom we had met on the boat on the way over, came to visit us. They were ferrying some P-39's from Oran to Casablanca and, en route, they, of their own volition, simply stopped over to pay us a visit. I mention this simply to indicate that a considerable bond existed among those who fly regardless of color or race.

"Our equipment was of the best. We ferried in 27 brand new P-40 and all of us experienced for the first time the thrill of flying a brand new airplane. LTC Cochran--the Flip Corkin of *Terry and the Pirates*--was our most capable instructor. He imbued all of us with some of his own very remarkable fighting spirit, and in addition to that he taught us what to do and what not to do in aerial combat.

"We had two other instructors who were with us until we left for Tunisia, MAJ Keyes and a CPT Fechler. Both of these officers had extensive combat training, one in England and one in the African campaign, and both had just been returned to the training command for instructional purposes. These officers worked unceasingly to make us ready for the real test and all of us felt very grateful for their efforts."(1)

COL Noel Parrish and LTC George S. Roberts.

Top: LTC Noel F. Parrish flanked by BG Benjamin O. Davis, Sr. LTC Benjamin O. Davis, Jr. visiting at Tuskegee. Middle: Members of the orininal 99th Fighter Squadron. Bottom: Secretary of War Stimson inspects the 99th.

Chapter 4
A Taste of Combat

The members of the 99th soon learned that the unit was not as static as it appeared. After spending a month of intensive combat training at OuedN'ja, the Squadron was ordered to move to a new base on the Cape Bon Peninsula, near Fez in North Africa.

On May 31, 1943, after one month at the town of QuedN'ja, the 99th was moved to a new base at Fardjouna, Cape Bon Peninsula. The 99th was attached to the 33rd Fighter Group, commanded by COL William Momyer.

It was now evident to the pilots of the 99th that they were gradually being integrated into the great fighting machine that was taking the battle to the enemy. At this station, they received first hand information from pilots who were meeting the enemy daily. They saw planes return to the base riddled with holes from enemy machine gun fire. They saw planes hobble home almost torn apart. They waited for friends who never returned. They saw pilots die. These things brought the war home to the members of the 99th. Now they realized that they had no time to waste--that their futures were left up to themselves.

The first combat assignment of the 99th came on June 2, 1943. The mission was a strafing mission against the heavily fortified island of Pantelleria. In reference to the Squadron's entrance into combat, COL Davis said: "I personally believe that no unit in this war had gone into combat better trained or better equipped than the 99th Fighter Squadron. We were weak in one respect only and that was simply that the Squadron Commander, myself, and the flight commanders had had no actual combat experience. That is a very desirable feature because it gives a bit of confidence to those who are led that the man who is in charge of the formation knows what he is doing, and frankly, I didn't know initially, nor did my flight commanders. On the other hand, this deficiency was balanced by the fact that my pilots averaged about 250 hours in a P-40, and a young pilot, in these days, who has 250 hours in a P-40 before he goes into combat, is a hard man to find."

COL Davis assigned four men to his pioneering role. The pilots assigned to make the first combat missions were LT Charles B. Hall, William A. Campbell, Clarence C. Jamison and James T. Wiley. Another pilot, Lemuel R. Custis, was also chosen to be one of the pioneers, but at the time had not arrived at the base because his plane had developed engine trouble en route from OuedN'ja. All of these men were to fly as wingmen for pilots of the 33rd Fighter Group.

The morning of June 2 was one of the most important days for the squadron, for it was on this morning that LT Hall and Campbell received the necessary briefing for their first combat mission. After the briefing, Hall and Campbell were taken to the dispersal area in a jeep. On arrival at the area, they jumped out of the jeep and walked swiftly toward their planes. When they reached their planes they climbed in and, with the aid of their crew chiefs, adjusted their equipment. This completed, the crew chiefs stepped down off the wings of the planes. The two pilots then started their engines and taxied up the runway for the take off. Hall led and Campbell followed closely behind. As they reached the edge of the runway, they stopped their planes and raced their engines. The roar of the two planes sounded unusually loud, but, to the jubilant members of the squadron, who had assembled to watch the take off, there was indescribable beauty in this roar.

When the planes were sufficiently warmed up, and the pretakeoff checks had been completed, Hall and Campbell taxied onto the runway, applied takeoff power to the engines and rose swiftly into the air. The crowd kept its eyes on the two planes until they disappeared into the distance.

At eight o'clock, LT Jamison and Wiley left on the squadron's second mission; later in the afternoon, the same pilots made another flight to Pantelleria, but no enemy aircraft was sighted that day, and on the whole the initial mission was un-exciting.

The 99th flew missions to Pantelleria for seven days without sighting the first enemy aircraft. Finally, on the morning of June 9, a flight led by LT Charles Dryden of New York City was attacked by a group of enemy aircraft.

Just before reaching his rendezvous point, Dryden heard a call over his radio, "Unidentified aircraft approaching the island." Immediately, Dryden reefed his plane around with his flight following him. Behind him were LT Lee Rayford of Ardwick, MD; Willie Ashley of Sumter, S. Carolina; Spann Watson of Hackensak, NJ; Sidney P. Brooks of Cleveland, Ohio; and Leon Roberts of Pritchard, AL.

Training a pilot is a long process. Flying an airplane is only a part of that process. The rest has to be gained through experience. The fighter pilot gains the greater portion of his knowledge from his fellow pilots and from the enemy.

There are two things a fighter pilot must have to be successful in combat: confidence in his ability to kill, and confidence in his ability to get away when in trouble. These can only be acquired through active participation in combat. If the pilot feels he can kill and feels that the enemy can't kill him, then he has the offensive spirit. Without that offensive spirit--the ability to attack instantaneously and automatically like a tiger the moment he spots an enemy plane, he is lost. If he hangs back and is afraid to take the offensive, he eventually gets shot down. Realizing that they would probably be attacked, the pilots settled tight against their seats and tensed a little against the pull of their planes' engines. They were nervous, of course, because this was to be their first encounter with the enemy who had been credited as having shrewd and capable pilots. But though they lacked the confidence in their ability to shoot down the enemy and figured they didn't know enough about the business of fighting with planes to match the enemy skill, they realized that they also had to fight to survive.

As they climbed to gain altitude for an attack, the enemy planes dodged in over the sea. Suddenly, LT Roberts spied the enemy flight as it dived out of the sun. Roberts broke to the right to evade the enemy aircraft that were now coming down on his formation at great speed. As he broke, the rest of the flight broke with him. But, though previously warned by the air observer, they had been caught by surprise. It was impossible for them to maintain company front against the Germans who were diving in close formation of two's at approximately 450 miles an hour.

LT Dryden, after turning, found himself far out beyond the enemy aircraft, with the bombers passing about 5000 feet above. He pointed the nose of his plane upward and began climbing towards the bombers. After climbing far above the enemy formation, he circled and fell into a dive. He dived at full speed across the tail end of the enemy formation and sprayed the enemy ships with volleys of 50 caliber fire as he went along. On pulling up, he noticed a dog fight. Without hesitation, he went to the aid of his comrades who were battling desperately to match the skilled and experienced German pilots.

In the meantime, Rayford was having trouble with two Focke-Wulf which had caught him alone. They kept charging at his plane and each time he attacked one, the other would attack. Although this was Rayford's first engagement, he kept his composure and fought back with great determination. A 20 millimeter cannon shell shattered his right wing, but he fought back. He had been taught that the best defensive against the enemy was a determined offensive, and in battle the lesson stuck with him. The Germans pressed the battle with equal determination. They attacked from all angles and maneuvered to line him up for the kill. Just when it seemed that they would be successful, LT Watson came to the rescue of Rayford. Watson opened up at long range on one of the attacking planes and to his surprise hit the target. The Germans, seeing that opposition was gathering against them, retreated.

At the initial turn, LT Ashley's plane had gone into a spin, causing him to lose considerable altitude. When he came out of the spin, he saw another plane out alone. Thinking it was a friendly plane, he decided to join the aircraft; but, as he closed in on the plane, he found it to be a Focke-Wulf. He moved in closer and began to fire. He sprayed the enemy aircraft with several volleys before it began to smoke and headed downward. Ashley dived after the smoking plane, but as he approached the ground the enemy ground force sent up a heavy barrage of flak and machine gun fire. Ashley was forced to turn back, and as a result probably lost the opportunity of being the first Negro to destroy an enemy aircraft in aerial combat.

This air assault on Pantelleria, which began on May 30, 1943, caused the Italian island of 11,500 population to surrender on June 11. Thus, for the first time in history, air power alone had completely destroyed all enemy resistance.

On June 12, Lampedusa, another island off of Sicily, succumbed to the Allied air attack, and the following day, Limosa, a third island off of Sicily, also surrendered. The capture of these islands gave allied sea power complete control of the sea lanes to the island of Sicily and to mainland Italy.

Top: Irene Turner admiring expert aerial gunnery medal of her son LT Leon L. Turner. Bottom: LT Wilmeth W. Sidat, star football player Syrcuse U., with mother and fiancee.

Top: LT Lloyd R. Radcliffe surrounded by his proud family. Bottom: LT Surl Smith and his proud family.

Chapter 5
The Sicilian Campaign

After the fall of Pantelleria, the Allies turned their attention to the island of Sicily. By capturing Sicily, they believed that allied troops would be in a position to successfully invade Italy. However, the immediate objective of the Allies was to capture Messina, an enemy port in northeastern Sicily. Through this port almost all enemy supplies flowed, and once it was secured, the position of the enemy in Sicily would be hopeless.

On June 29, the 99th Fighter Squadron moved to El Haouria on the tip of Cape Bon. Here it began operating with the 324th Fighter Group which was engaged in the battle of Sicily.

The 99th's first mission to the island was on July 1, 1943, when it was assigned to escort medium bombers to the western sector of Sicily. Although the mission was successful, it was un-exciting, for the pilots encountered very little enemy opposition.

The next day, July 2, the 99th was assigned to escort medium bombers to the coast of Sicily in the Castelvetrano area. The pilots who were to make the flight reported at the briefing room after an early breakfast. The Intelligence Officer began the briefing immediately. He revealed the target, the amount and position of enemy anti-aircraft batteries, and the number of enemy fighters expected to be encountered in the target area. When the Intelligence Officer finished, the Weather Officer gave his weather report. The pilots were then told to synchronize their watches. The briefing was over.

After leaving the briefing room, the pilots rode to the dispersal area where the planes had already been warmed up and were ready for the take off. A few minutes later, the first plane broke ground. Others followed at short intervals. As they climbed, they circled the base until the flight was assembled. Then the flight headed towards the coast and picked up the bombers.

The sky was clear although there was a slight ground haze. Only a few minutes had elapsed before they were over the Mediterranean, which was calm, clear, and remarkably blue.

Once clear of the land, the pilots tested their guns. As they engaged their triggers, the sharp rat-a-tat-tat of the practice shells sang out above the noise of the engines. Satisfied that their guns were in firing condition, the pilots fell into position to cover the bombers.

On arriving in the target area, the bombers began to unload their bombs. Clouds of smoke arose from the explosions. This was answered by volleys of inaccurate, large, black flak bursts. Almost immediately, a group of enemy fighters came up to attack the bombers.

When the enemy planes were sighted, the 99th attacked. In the ensuing battle, the 99th received its first aerial victory when LT Charles B. Hall of Brazil, IN, shot down a Focke-Wulf 190. Relating his victory, Hall said: "It was my eighth mission and the first time I had seen the enemy close enough to shoot at him. I saw two Focke-Wulfs following the bombers just after the bombs were dropped. I headed for the space between the fighters and bombers and managed to turn inside the Jerries. I fired a long burst and saw my tracers penetrate the second aircraft. He was turning to the left, but suddenly fell off and headed straight into the ground. I followed him down and saw him crash. He raised a big cloud of dust."

At the time Hall was gaining the Squadron's first victory, LT Charles Dryden and his wingman LT James B. Knighten were fighting a grim battle against four German aircraft. When the formation broke to attack the enemy planes, Dryden noticed two Messerschmidt 109s making passes at the outside bomber element. After the enemy attacked the bombers, they pulled up and began to split "S". Dryden, who was above the attacking enemy aircraft, made a dive for the enemy as his wingman followed. He was about to fire on one of the enemy ships when two Focke-Wulfs opened up on him. He was forced to break off his attack and go into a series of tight turns to avoid being shot down.

The Germans were determined to make the kill. They pressed the attack and maneuvered to line up the fleeing planes. But, after following the attack for a long while and seeing that they were being led too far from their base, the Germans broke off the attack. When Dryden landed at the base, he found his ship had been severely damaged.

The success of LT Hall was received with praise by the Allied Commanders. General Dwight D. Eisenhower made a special visit to the base and upon arrival exclaimed, "I would like to meet the pilot who shot down the Jerry." Among General Eisenhower's party were General Spaatz, Major General Doolittle, and Air Marshal Cunningham of the Royal Air Force.

Amid the joy and celebration of LT Hall's victory, there was also sadness. A few hours earlier, LT Sherman White Jr., of Montgomery, AL, and James L. McCullin of St. Louis, MO, collided while taking off on an early morning mission. Both pilots were killed.

Throughout the first week of July 1943, the 99th continued its attacks on Sicily. It escorted medium bombers to bomb the coastal batteries and enemy installations. It strafed enemy air fields and dive bombed supply centers and communication lines.

These relentless attacks played a potent part in a softening up of the island for the invasion of the ground forces. On July 7, the invasion fleet slipped out of the harbor of North Africa and headed for Sicily. Ernie Pyle, one of the most outstanding War Correspondents, vividly described the invasion of Sicily:

"Our first day at sea was like a peacetime Mediterranean cruise. The weather was something you read about in travel folders, gently warm and sunny and the sea as smooth as velvet.(1) On the second day, the dawn came up gray and misty with a 40 mile an hour gale. The sea was rough, and all day long the invasion troops were harassed by the continuous rocking, bouncing, and swaying of the ship. At ten o'clock, I lay down with my clothes on. There wasn't anything I could do and the rolling sea was beginning to take nibbles at my stomach, too. As I finally fell asleep, the wind was still howling and the ship was pounding and falling through space.

"The next thing I knew a booming voice over the ship's loudspeaker was saying, 'Stand by for gunfire. We may have to shoot out some searchlights.'

"I jumped up, startled. The engines were stopped. There seemed to be no wind. The entire ship was motionless and quiet as a grave. I grabbed my helmet, ran out on the deck, and stared over the rail. We were anchored, and we could see the dark shapes of the Sicilian hills not far away. The water lapped with gentle caressing sound against the sides of the ship. We had arrived. The storm was gone. I looked down and the surface of the Mediterranean was slick and smooth as a table top. Already assault boats were skimming past us towards the shore. Not a breath of air stirred. The miracle had happened."(2)

It was approximately 2:45 A.M., July 10, when the first wave of troops stormed the beaches. As they waded in, the guns from the naval vessels kept up a continuous barrage of fire. They were answered by the enemy batteries which were located on the hills back of the beaches. Throughout the early morning, the battle raged. Finally, the enemy fire began to dwindle, and the superiority of the Allied force became evident.

Daybreak found the shores of Sicily clustered with assault boats and the American Flag flying majestically above an enemy fort. The allies had landed safely and established the beachhead as planned.

COL Fred M. Dean, writing of this experience in the Sicilian invasion related: "There was scarcely any contest in the sky over Sicily. The few fighters we met seemed more interested in turning tail and evading combat than attempting to press interference with our invasion operations. The transport and bomber encounters likewise were easy pickings. Enemy Air activity was relatively negligible and we were surprised with the lack of opposition."

In the meantime, the 99th was doing its part in making the invasion a success. While the invasion fleet was at sea, the 99th guarded the fleet against being attacked by enemy planes. It made numerous divebombing and strafing missions and escorted medium bombers to the island.

On the afternoon of July 10, LT Richard Bolling of Hampton, VA, was shot down while patrolling the invasion area. His plane was severely damaged by flak and started to burn. Bolling bailed out of his burning ship and landed in the Mediterranean Sea. LT Samuel Bruce of Seattle, WA, circled Bolling and pin-pointed his position before returning to the base.

After spending 24 hours drifting helplessly, Bolling was picked up by an American destroyer and set ashore in Sicily. Several days later, he boarded a ship for North Africa and returned to the base. Meantime, on July 10, the 99th completed its operations with the 324th and prepared to move to a new base in Sicily. In the 11 days of operations with the 324th, it flew 175 sorties, divebombing and strafing enemy positions.

By this time, the American Seventh Army had swung west and north from Licata and Gela to mop up the western half of the island, while the British Eighth Army under General Montgomery advanced up the east coast from Noto and Syracuse towards Messina. The strategy was to trap the enemy in the Northeastern corner of Sicily to prevent the enemy from escaping across the Strait of Messina to Italy.

On July 14, the Americans captured the Biscari Airfield which assured them a good base for aerial operation against the enemy. On July 19, the 99th moved to Licata, Sicily, a city of 35,000 inhabitants, located on the coast of the Mediterranean Sea.

On July 23, the 99th received its first group of replacement pilots. They were: LT Howard Baugh of Petersburg, Virginia; Edward L. Toppins of San Francisco, CA; John Morgan of Carterville, GA; John Gibson of Chicago, IL; and Herman A. Lawson of Maryville, CA.

Meantime, on July 22, the coastal city of Agrigento was captured, and a week later Palermo fell to the swiftly advancing Americans. The Allied troops advanced so rapidly that the Axis Forces began preparing to withdraw across the Strait of Messina. A race began for the Strait, with the British pushing up from the South and the Americans driving in from the North.

The 99th was still in operation against the enemy. It dive bombed strongholds, strafed enemy troops, patrolled the areas, and performed armed reconnaissance. On August 11, LT Paul Mitchell of Washington, DC, was killed when his plane collided with a plane piloted by Lt Bruce. Fortunately, Bruce escaped death by parachuting to safety.

In spite of the all-out drive by the Allied Ground Forces, the 12th Air Force, and a series of amphibious landings, the Germans were able to retreat across the Strait of Messina. On August 17, 1943, the US 3rd Division pushed into the town of Messina. A little later, a detachment from the Eighth Army arrived in Messina. The remaining element of the enemy forces was soon eliminated. It had taken just 38 days to capture the Island and approximately 100,000 prisoners.

Top: Ground crew of the 99th. Bottom: Captain Charles B. Hall.

Chapter 6
The Dark Days

While the Sicilian Campaign was in progress, preparations were being made for the invasion of Italy. The Allied Strategy called for the landing of troops at Reggio Calabria on the toe of Italy and further up the coast of Italy at Salerno.

The invasion of Italy actually was designed as a new strategy. The Mediterranean theatre was no longer to be given top priority for new equipment and supplies. It was now to play a secondary role to the European theatre. It was believed that if Italy could be forced out of the war and if a sufficient portion of the country could be occupied by Allied forces, then air bases in the occupied territory could be used for strategic operations against Germany and her satellites.

The landing at Reggio Calabria by a British invasion force termed Bayton was scheduled for September 3. It was to be made by the British Eighth Army's 13th Corps with air support from the British Desert Air Force. The plan provided for two divisions to cross the narrow strait of Messina, land at Reggio Calabria and Gallico/Catona, capture the nearby airfield, then drive northward to make contact with the right wing of the American invasion force termed Avalanche, that was to land near Salerno. These forces were then to fan out towards the east and link up with another British force which was scheduled to land near Taranto. The Avalanche Force plan provided for the Fifth US Army to capture Salerno and the airfield at Montecorvino, then capture Naples and near-by airfields.

In planning the invasion, the most perplexing problem faced by Allied air planners was how to furnish air cover for the assault and the initial ground operations. This task had been assigned to the 12th Air Support Command, which consisted of the 27th, 86th, 31st, 324th, 33rd, the 99th Fighter Squadron "separate" and the 11th Observation Squadron. The P-40's and P-39's with auxiliary tanks could fly a radius of only 150 miles, the A-36, 300 miles; Beaufighter, 300 miles; Spitfire, 180 miles; and the P-38, 350 miles. For this reason, it was planned that the primary objective of the Salerno landing was to capture Montecorvino Airfield, ten miles from Salerno. This accomplished, aviation engineers were to be sent in to construct landing strips in the Paestum area. The fighter units would be transferred to Italy from Sicily immediately after the strips were laid and begin operations from these strips and continue until other permanent bases could be seized from the enemy, especially bases in the Naples and Foggia areas.(1)

The Avalanche invasion plan provided that on D-Day, September 9, the Coastal Air Force, consisting mostly of British forces, would protect shipping to within 40 miles of the beaches, then the Tactical Air Force would furnish cover for the convoy with two squadrons of P-38s, one squadron of A-36s and one Spitfire squadron.

The first invasion movement began on September 3, 1943, when General Montgomery slipped two divisions of the British Eighth Army across the Strait of Messina to Reggio Calabria and advanced up the Italian coast against slight resistance. This followed by a landing in the Salerno area by American forces on September 9, and an invasion by the British First Airborne Division that captured the Taranto Naval Base. LT William Murphy, a P-38 pilot whose group covered the assault troops over Salerno, related, "We left at dawn and picked up warships, transports, and landing craft just off Salerno. I could see the activity beneath us and it appeared that there was not much in the way of opposition. We assumed our position over the beachhead in groups of four in stepped down strings. Throughout the first day, we didn't have any aerial opposition. We just went up and back, up and back, without any trouble. There were control boats in the water to warn us of approaching planes, but during the first day there just wasn't anything to warn us about."(2)

The same was true for the top cover Spitfires--no German aerial activity--according to CPT Dale E. Shafer: "I was over the invasion area with the first element, and it was just like a practice mission. All we did was fly around for a while and then go back to our base while another took over."(3)

The short range P-40 units unable to give assistance to the initial invasion forces remained more or less idle from September 1 through September 11. On the morning of September 11, a detachment of the 817th Engineer Battalion that had been sent ahead on D-Day to construct a landing strip completed the strip at Paestum. On the same day, one officer and 78 enlisted men of the 99th were flown to Italy and landed near Battipaglia. This was to be the advanced echelon for the 99th scheduled to be moved to Italy.

On September 13, two aircraft of the 59th Squadron of the 33rd took off at 0945 from Milazzo, Sicily on a permanent change of station at Paestum. The following day the remainder of the 33rd flew from Termini, Sicily to the new base at Paestum. The Germans, who had only mildly contested the invasion forces, began to counter attack on September 13. The enemy counter attacked with such fury and fierce fighting that the Allied forces were forced to retreat towards the beach. The enemy drove to within two or three miles of the beach and for a while it appeared as though General Clark and his Fifth Army would be captured or destroyed. To halt the German drive, every available soldier, which included the advanced detachment of enlisted men of the 99th that arrived at Battipaglia on September 11, were pressed into battle. Although these men had practically no training in the handling of guns and fighting equipment, they were issued guns and rifles, and placed on defensive lines. Spann Watson, one of the pilots of the 99th, later recalling the incident, remarked: "You know, we never did see some of these men again."

The threat of the German offensive caused British Air Chief Marshal Tedder, who was supreme allied air commander of the Mediterranean Air Force, to order air commanders to concentrate their full strength on attacks against the Germans. The 33rd, which had arrived in Paestum on September 13 and 14, was thrown immediately into the battle. At 0730 hours on the morning of September 15, 1943, 8 P-40s of the 59th Squadron of the 33rd Fighter Group, patrolling the beaches in the vicinity of Paestum observed six or more FW 109s attacking the shipping in the harbor. The flight dived on the attacking aircraft and destroyed one, probably destroyed another, and damaged one aircraft. However, in the battle the flight lost one pilot, MAJ Crest, who was shot down. On another mission at 11:15, a flight of eight P-40s of the 59th intercepted eight FW 190 about one mile from Paestum's landing strip and destroyed four more enemy aircraft and possibly another. The same day, a flight from the 60th Squadron patrolling at Battipaglia and the Airdrome, intercepted ten FW 190 as they made runs on ships at Agropoli. The flight destroyed one FW 190, probably destroyed another and damaged two FW 190's. On September 16, the 58th, patrolling Peach Beach, shot down one FW 190 and probably destroyed a second FW 190. Then at 1345 hours, a flight from the 58th intercepted six plus FW 190s while bombing. The flight destroyed one FW 190 and probably another. On September 17, the 33rd gained its last victories of the year, and had no more victories before the Anzio-Nettuno battle in late January 1944. On the 17th, four P-40s of the 59th Squadron covering a C-47 landing at Paestum Airfield were attacked by eight enemy aircraft. In the ensuing battle, the flight shot down three of the enemy planes, one pilot claiming two of the victories. After shooting down one aircraft, he pulled up and observed another enemy ME 109 within range. He fired a short burst, hit the target and sent the ME 109 crashing to earth.(4)

While the 33rd had moved with the battle to Italy and was gaining victories, the 99th was still in Sicily. It had moved from Licata on the south shore of Sicily to Barcellona on the northern coast of Sicily, in the vicinity of Messina. At Barcellona, the 99th was based far from the actual war zone and was unable to participate directly in the battles. It covered shipping in the Sicily area, and made a few escort missions to Italy, but on these missions encountered no enemy aircraft. For example, on September 16, MAJ George *Spanky* Roberts with a flight consisting of LT Mills, Deiz, Dryden, Wiley, Lewis C. Smith, Clark, Toppins, Lawson and Lane rendezvoused at 1630 with twenty four Martin A-30 Baltimores and twelve B-25s over Milazzo, Sicily and escorted the bombers to Nola, Italy. On the same day, at 1700, ten P-40s led by CPT Charles Hall, accompanied by LT Baugh, Carter, McCrumby, Jamison, Rogers, Roberts, L.C. Brooks, Campbell and Rayford rendezvoused with 24 Baltimores in the vicinity of Milazzo and escorted them to the vicinity of Salerno.

On September 17, CPT Hall led a flight of seven that consisted of LT Toppins, Roberts L.C., Clark, Baugh, Lawson and Smith that met 24 B-25s over Milazzo at 1500 hours and escorted the bombers to the vicinity of Salerno where the bombers dropped bombs from 10,000 feet. On September 18, 1943, the Squadron lost one of its pilots, LT Sidney Brooks of Cleveland, OH, who was killed while taking off on a bomber escort mission.(5)

When MAJ George Spencer Roberts returned to the States in the early part of 1944, he spoke as guest speaker at a ceremony held at Abraham Lincoln Garden located at East Boulevard and Wade Park Avenue, Cleveland, OH. The occasion was the planting of an evergreen tree as a memorial for LT Brooks. During the course of the speech MAJ Roberts remarked:

"Sidney Brooks fought and stood for the things that are America. America is its people--you. We are finding that the color of a man's skin, the blood in his veins, or his religion makes no difference in finding whether he is or is not a man. The privileges of America belong to those brave and strong enough to fight for them."

Mayor Frank. J. Lausche spoke of the death of a young man who gave everything in defense of a democracy, he did not enjoy, in the hope that his death might make it possible for the living to continue to fight for an America that would be free, just and fair for all people.

The 99th had been sent overseas at a time when preparations were being made for the Sicilian Campaign. In the North Africa Campaign, the Allied Forces had encountered superior German forces. In the battle for Sicily, it was believed that the Allied would encounter even larger enemy forces. It was decided to bolster the strength of Air Force groups by adding a fourth squadron. For example, the 79th and the 324th were temporarily broken up and their squadrons were added to other Groups.

The 99th Fighter Squadron was sent overseas to bolster the strength of the 33rd Fighter Group. However, COL William Momyer, the Commander of the 33rd did not want the 99th attached to his Group.

Spann Watson, relating his experience with COL Momyer, said: "During the Sicilian Campaign, the pilots of the 33rd and 99th used the radio code *needless* to indicate they had encountered enemy aircraft. We went for months without seeing enemy aircraft. COL Momyer knew it. He waited until all of his squadrons had gained victories in the invasion of Italy, then criticized us. We didn't get a chance to gain victories because we didn't go with the invasion force to Italy. We remained in Sicily, hundreds of miles from the battle zone.

"I will never forget COL Momyer. One morning, COL Davis dispatched us to fly to COL Momyer's Headquarters for a combat briefing. You know, COL Davis was strict. If he sent you any place, you better be there on time or have a damn good excuse.

"Anyway, we arrived at the appointed time, only to learn that the briefing was ending. We were surprised because we knew we were on time. COL Momyer informed us that the briefing was over and said, 'You fellows follow my men'. Spann said, 'Now I ask you, what way was that to brief pilots going on a combat mission where their lives were at stake?' COL Momyer was just plain prejudiced towards us.

"During the Sicilian Campaign, the 33rd and the 99th were assigned to tactical duty, such as dive bombing, bombing and strafing. The failure of the 99th to gain victories, however, caused some high army officials to suspect its pilots courage to fight. They charged the 99th with being a failure and clamored for more action. However, while the 99th was being criticized, LTC Philip C. Cochran, one of the United States Army's greatest dive bombing expert, was praising the 99th as 'a collection of born dive bombers.'"

Although the 99th was criticized for failing to register aerial victories on dive bombing and strafing missions, seemingly, the records of other dive bombing units were not taken into considerations. For instance, Ernie Pyle, who covered the Mediterranean Theatre of War, during the Sicilian and Italian Campaign wrote: "For several reasons our dive bombers didn't have much trouble with German fighters. First of all, the Luftwaffe was weak over there at the time. Then too, the dive bombers' job was to work on the infantry front lines, so they seldom got back to where the Germans fighters were. Also, the invaders were such a good fighter that the Jerries weren't too anxious to tangle with them.

"There were pilots in the squadron who had finished their allotted missions and gone back to America without even firing a shot at an enemy plane in the air and that's the way it should be, for their job was dive bomb, not to get caught in a fight."(6)

On August 15, 1942, CPT Harry C. Butcher, US Naval aid to General Eisenhower, wrote in his diary: "Had Chief of Radio and Press Bureau, principal staff officers of PRO and editor of Stars and Stripes for a buffet luncheon today. A correspondent expressed concern that at least one irresponsible and biased reporter was about to start trouble by sending articles back home on the color question. Someone raised the point that existent censorship rules bar Negro stories of these types. Ike said, 'Take it off.' Later, he was importuned by a small group of first rate correspondents to reconsider his decision, but he stuck to it, said in the long run it would be better for the news, good or bad to flow freely, might just as well let the American public know what the problems are, our success or failure in meeting them."(7)

It appears the 99th was the victim of such irresponsible and biased reporters. On September 20, 1943, the *Time* Magazine carried an article entitled "Experiment Proved". The article stated that unofficial reports from the Mediterranean Theatre had suggested that high air force officials were not altogether satisfied with the performance of the 99th. It revealed that plans were being discussed to disband the organization as a fighter unit and attach the squadron to the Coastal Air Command, where it would be assigned routine convoy cover.

The basis of the article was a critical and prejudicial report by COL Momyer, Commanding Officer of the 33rd Fighter Group to which the 99th was attached for operations. The report submitted to MG Edwin J. House's Headquarters, 12th Air Support Command, read in part: "The general discipline and ability to accomplish and execute orders promptly are excellent. Air discipline has not been completely satisfactory. The ability to work and fight as a team has not yet been acquired. Their formation flying has been very satisfactory until jumped by enemy aircraft, when the squadron seemed to disintegrate. This has repeatedly been brought to the attention of the Squadron, but attempts to correct this deficiency so far have been unfruitful. On one particular occasion, a flight of twelve JU 88s with an escort of six ME 109s, was observed to be bombing Pantelleria. The 99th, instead of pressing home the attack against the bombers, allowed themselves to become engaged with the 109s. The Unit has shown a lack of aggressive spirit that is necessary for a well organized fighter squadron. On numerous instances, when assigned to dive bomb a specific target in which the anti-aircraft fire was light and inaccurate, they chose the secondary target which was undefended. On one occasion, they were assigned a mission with one squadron of this group to bomb a target on the toe of Italy; the 99th turned back before reaching the target and pressed back home. As later substantiated, the weather was considered operational. Based on the performance of the 99th to date: "It is my opinion that they are not of the fighting caliber of any squadron in the group. They have failed to display the aggressiveness and desire for combat that are necessary to a first class fighting organization. It may be expected that we will get less work and less operational time out of the 99th than any squadron in the group."(8)

Shortly, after the article appeared in the *Time*, COL Davis, who had been recalled to the States on September 2, held a press conference at the War Department. In relating the attitude of his Squadron, COL Davis said that the members of the 99th realized that the Unit was a test to determine whether the Negro pilot was physically, mentally, and emotionally suited to the rigors of combat flying. They understood that the future of the Negro in the Air Corps probably would be largely dependent upon the manner in which they carried out their mission. Hence, the importance of the work done by the squadron meant that very little pleasure was to be had by anyone, until the experiment was deemed an unqualified success. He added that the outfit was hurt by adverse publicity it received during the training period at Tuskegee. The men, however, had the sense to realize that the best means they had to defeat the ends of supporters and philosophers who relegated them to a subsidiary role in the life of the United States was to do their job in such a way that they would know that they were capable of performing a highly specialized and technical piece of work in a creditable manner.

MAJ George S. Roberts, who also commanded the 99th Fighter Squadron, said: "People assume the 99th was not producing because they were Negroes. It was remarkable that the men kept their morale, being under such a strain because of the civilian attitude. We went for months without seeing an enemy aircraft, not to mention shooting one."

The War Department repudiated the story that it was contemplating the deactivation of the 99th. It stated that it felt keenly about the report *Time*. An Air Force officer stated that the Office of the Assistant Chief of Air Staff, Operations, Commitments and Requirements had no knowledge of such a proposal, and that so little operational data on the 99th had reached Washington that it was impossible to form a conclusive opinion about the pilots. He added that the 99th had apparently seen little action compared with many other units, but seemed to have done fairly well.

However, unofficial reports from the Mediterranean Theatre had suggested that the top air command was not altogether satisfied with the 99th performance. Although the War Department denied it had considered disbanding the 99th, it was no secret to COL Davis and his staff that General Arnold, the Wartime Chief of the Army Air Force, had listened to the unofficial and prejudiced reports and had considered the disbandment of the Squadron. MAJ Roberts, in relating a visit of General Arnold to the base, said: "I never felt so bad in all my life. While he stood there discrediting the men who were doing their best under the circumstances, I felt like crying. I could see that COL Davis was deeply hurt."

On September 20, 1943, the same day the article on the 99th appeared in *Time*, Montecorvino was freed of enemy artillery fire. Montecorvino Airport immediately became the principal airdrome in the Salerno area. Air units stationed at the airdrome began attacking other enemy air bases and giving support to the allied ground forces.

On September 23, ten aircraft of the 99th was sent from Barcellona to Paestum, and immediately went into action. At 0840, a flight of three aircraft piloted by LT Morgan H. Lawson and Jamison left on a patrol mission that patrolled an area between Agropoli and Salerno. A flight of four, consisting of CPT Custis, LT Fuller, Campbell and Gibson patrolled an area east of Salerno from 1050 to 1310. At 1248, a third flight consisting of MAJ Roberts, LT H. Lawson, Carter and Clark left on a mission that patrolled the area south of Albanella to north of Battipaglia.

Then at 1450, a flight of four consisting of LT Fuller, Morgan, Jamison, and Gibson, left to patrol the area south of Albanella to north of Battipaglia. On the return flight, LT Jamison's plane's Prestone temperature dropped causing the engine to become excessively hot. He successfully forced landed his plane north of the base.

The landing of General Clark and his Fifth Army in Salerno area forced the Germans to shift some of its forces from the east, enabling General Montgomery to accelerate his advance. On September 16, the left flank of his Eighth Army made contact with the right flank of the 5th Army, just south of the Salerno Bay. Meanwhile, the right flank of the Eighth Army moved forward and joined up with the British First Airborne Division that had invaded Italy at Taranto and was pushing northward towards Foggia.

The Germans, under heavy pressure, began to withdraw to the north followed by the Fifth and Eighth Armies. On September 23, 1943, Oliveto was captured by the Eighth Army. The Germans then fell back to defend Naples.

The Allied Air Force met little opposition from the German Air Force. It was no longer the superior force it had been earlier in the war. Another reason for the lack of opposition was that Allied long range bombers had forced the Germans to move most of their aircraft further away from the battle area, from southern Italy to central and northern Italy.

In the last ten days of September, the Allies dispatched special missions against enemy forces in Corsica, the Leghorn sea area, and against enemy evacuation routes from Corsica. The Germans had only recently been forced out of the island of Sardinia and now were being forced out of Corsica by French troops and Corsican patriots aided by Allied bombing attacks. Yet, in spite of the heavy pressure, the Germans were successful in evacuating 25,000 of its personnel and approximately 600 tons of supplies. To accomplish this feat, the Germans were forced to shift many of the fighter aircraft that were giving support to ground troops in Salerno and eastern Italian battle areas. The absence of air support made it difficult for the ground forces to sustain their positions against the Allied offensive, especially in the eastern sector. There, General Montgomery's Eighth Army advanced at a steady pace. On September 27, it captured the Foggia Airdrome complex which was to later play an important role in the conquest of the Italian peninsula.

General Mark Clark's Fifth Army had a more difficult task and moved at a slow pace in its drive towards Naples. Although Marshal Kesserling lacked sufficient air support, his artillery and small rear guard units--placed at strategic positions together with incessant rains, heavy winds and glutinous mud--made it very difficult for the Fifth Army to advance. From September 24 to the end of the month, bad weather forced the curtailment of a large percentage of air and ground operations, and the few air units that were able to take off ran into heavy clouds that obscured the targets. This, however, did not stop the Fifth Army's drive. By September 28, it had reached the outskirts of Naples. Meantime, other than the detachment of ten pilots and planes that arrived at Paestum on September 23, the main body of the 99th was still operating from Barcellona, Sicily, far from the battle area.

CLASS 45E, BASIC SINGLE ENGINE, ADVANCED MULTI-ENGINE PILOTS: *Rear Row Standing*: John S. Harris, John B. Roach, Mexion O. Pruitt, Joseph C. Bryant, Mitchel N. Toney, Walter N. O'Neal. *Middle Row Kneeling*: Jerrold D. Griffin, Harold B. Maples, Clifford E. Mosley, Harry E. Ford, Jr. *Front Row Sitting*: Albert Whiteside, John C. Curry, William H. Taylor, Jr., George A. Brown, William E. Broadwater.

CLASS 45e, ADVANCED SINGLE ENGINE PILOTS: *Rear Row Standing*: Wesley D. Hurt, Roger B. Duncan, Henry T. Holland, Clinton E. McIntyre, William A. Fuller, Jr., Martin G. Saunders, Joseph P. Scott, Eugene W. Williams. *Middle Row Kneeling*: Leonard W. Wiggins, Logan Roberts, Aaron C. Gaskins, Russell L. Collins, William H. Baily, George G. Turner. *Front Row Sitting*: Marvin C. White, Herman A. Barnett, Isaac R. Woods, Clarence E. Reynolds, Jr., Reginald V. Smith.

Chapter 7
From Failure To Success

The capture of Salerno was a strategic gain for the Allies. They were now in a position to take the offensive against the enemy forces stationed in Italy. The Germans began to withdraw to the North followed by the Fifth and Eighth Armies. On September 23, 1943, Oliveto was captured by the British Eighth Army. The Germans then fell back to defend Naples. On October 7, the Fifth Army, with the aid of uprising civilians, forced the Germans to surrender the city of Naples and fall back to the steep northern bank of the Volturno River.

There was no rest for the Germans. On October 9, 1943, the 79th Fighter Squadron moved to Foggia and, on October 17, was joined by the 99th. The 99th was received on a more friendly and equal basis with the 79th than it had been with the 33rd. COL Earl Bates, the Commander of the 79th, was a fair minded and impartial leader, who accepted the 99th as one of his squadrons. He not only integrated the Group by assigning the pilots of the 79th to lead or fly with pilots of the 99th on combat missions, but flew missions with the 99th. He also permitted pilots of the 99th to fly with squadrons of 79th.

On October 16, the enemy was forced to retreat from its position on the Volturno. However, in retreat, the Germans destroyed bridges and left land mines and small groups of snipers that forced the Allies to move with caution.

The 99th went into action with the 79th Group by attacking targets in the Isernia-Campione area and later shifted to the network of roads northwest of Sangro. On the first mission with the 79th, LT Martin of the 79th with Knighten, Jamison, Watson, Carter, Lawrence, Campbell, Wiley, Clark, and CPT Roberts, Custis and Hall of the 99th dropped 250 pound bombs on a wooded area suspected of being a communication and fuel dump in the Chieti area. The next day, LTC Grogan of the 79th led a formation of 12 P-40s of the 99th on a mission to bomb and strafe hidden guns and troop concentrations in the area of Chieti. On the 25th, the 99th bombed bridges at

Tarino. On October 26, the 99th dropped fragmentation bombs on store dumps at Campione. On the 27th, MAJ Leon Roberts--accompanied by LT Mills, Baugh, Driver, Morgan, Rice, Toppins, Fuller, Watson, Roberts, Hall, Roberts and Bruce--dropped fragmentation bombs on a road junction in the Naples area.

Progress was slow on all fronts, but the Allies continued their relentless attack. On October 29, General Marshall called General Eisenhower and suggested that an increase in operations of medium, light and fighter bombers would be adequate help for the Fifth and Eighth Armies. This, he stated, would free the heavy bombers to attack the nine rail lines entering the Po Valley. Marshall's call was a result of a memorandum prepared by General Kuter. The memorandum stated that the destruction of eleven bridges, nine major rail lines, and five bridges on a line extending from Pisa to Ancona might force the Germans to withdraw into the Po Valley.

The 99th was assigned the task of carrying out all types of missions. It performed as dive bombers and fighter bombers; it escorted medium bombers, heavy bombers and C-47s and carried out strafing and fighter sweep missions.

On November 19, the 99th moved with the 79th to Salsale, an airdrome near Modena, a coastal strip near Termoli. But the bad weather limited flying. In the last two weeks of November, the weather deteriorated to such an extent that only a few missions could be dispatched. The muddy season had also set in, making the task of following the retreating enemy all the more difficult. Herbert L. Matthews, a noted War Correspondent, wrote of the mud of Italy: "No mud could be deeper or stickier or more persistent. On flat ground you plow disgustingly through it, often getting into it well over your ankles. But on a climb you do worse. You slide, slip, fall all over yourself and get covered with it from head to feet. The more tired you get the more you slip and fall, the dirtier you get, the harder it is to stand up again and plug on."(1)

Clear weather on November 30 permitted the 79th Group to set a record by flying 26 missions. The Group also had good weather on December 1, 1943. In the two days of flying, it dropped 65 tons of bombs on heavily defended area around Orsogna. In one day, the 99th flew nine missions and the 87th flew eight. This included loading bombs, cleaning guns, refueling and repairing. Damaged aircraft were repaired, props were changed, and instruments adjusted practically on the spot. Not only were the crew chiefs kept continuously busy, but the armorers, fitters, and mechanics worked right up to the last minute. These missions enabled the 8th Army to establish a beachhead across the Sangro and won for the 79th Fighter Group many congratulatory messages.

The 79th, with the 99th fighting as a component, averaged 36 to 46 sorties a day, striking close support targets on the lateral roads and roads branching out of Chieti. After dropping their bombs, the pilots strafed troop concentrations, gun positions, and convoys. Intense small arms fire, supplemented by heavy and light anti-aircraft fire and extremely bad weather, made the mission very hazardous, but the pilots refused to quit.

A series of close support targets was communicated to the 79th Group by the Air Support Control of the 8th Army. These targets extended from Ortona to Orsogna and as far west as Chieti. They were important because it meant defended positions, mortars, big guns, or troop concentrations standing in the way of General Montgomery's advance up the east coast. On the missions many pilots suffered ack-ack hits before their dive bombing attacks, but chose to complete their assignments.

The bravery of the pilots in carrying out their missions brought numerous commendations to the 79th, both from the British and Dominion Commanders of the 8th Army. It was related that the air attacks caused countless German casualties, destroyed vast amounts of enemy equipment and buildings and forced the Germans to make hasty withdrawals. This enabled Allied troops to enter the areas without too much resistance from the disorganized enemy forces.

On December 18, 1943, an all out air assault in support of New Zealand and Indian Divisions thrusting towards Orsogna and Tollo was called. Thirty missions were flown by the 57th and 79th Groups, the RAF 239 Wing and SAAF Spitbombers of Squadron No. 4 against enemy gun positions and installations. However, bad weather hid many of the targets. In spite of the indifferent weather, by noon of the 18th, 14 missions had successfully bombed their targets. Nine missions bought back their bombs, while four bombed alternate targets they discovered through the gaps in the clouds.

Meantime, early in December, General Clark's Fifth Army cleared the Germans out of the Camino hills. It then consolidated its position for a drive on the winter line in mid January. To break the winter stalemate, the Allies planned an end around the assault at Anzio.

On January 17, 1944, the 99th moved with the 79th from Salsale Airdrome near Modena to the Capodichino Airdrome near Naples. Here it began operations on January 20, with an Orientation Fighter Sweep termed *A Party*. This mission was designed in preparation for the assault on Anzio and comprised the 85th, 86th, the 87th of the 79th and 16 aircraft of the 99th. The formation took off from the Capodichino Airdrome, proceeded to the Gulf of Gaeta, flew up the coast to the vicinity of Rome and returned to base.

At 0500 hours on January 21, the first ships of the Allied invasion forces left Naples and headed towards Anzio. It received air protection to the Ponziane Island by the Coastal Air Force. From Ponziane Island to the Anzio beaches fighters of the 12th Air Support Command covered the convoy.

On January 22, 1944, three divisions of Allied troops landed at Nettuno and Anzio while the Allied Air Forces struck at targets around the beachhead and in Southern France.

The Germans preoccupied at Cassino, were taken by surprise and the quick Allied drive moved within Aprilia before gathering German resistance stopped its advance. Here three Axis Divisions, including the Italian Fascista, still held the heights commanding the beachhead. Ernie Pyle wrote of the battle that followed at Anzio:

"On the beachhead every inch of our territory was under German Artillery fire. There were no rear areas that were immune, as in most battle zones. They could reach us with their 88s and they used everything from that on up... The land of the Anzio beachhead is flat and our soldiers felt strange and naked with no rocks to take cover behind, no mountains to provide slopes for protection. It was a new kind of warfare for us. Distances were short and space was confined. The whole beachhead was the front line, so small that we could stand on high ground in the middle of it and see clear around the thing. That's the truth, and it was no picnic feeling either."(2)

In the ensuing battle that followed the Allied landing at Anzio, the 12th Air Force was made responsible for isolating the battle area and preventing the enemy from bringing up the reinforcements and supplies necessary for a successful counterattack. In carrying out this assignment, the squadrons of the 79th Group, including the 99th Fighter Squadron were assigned to support the ground troops by dive bombing and strafing rail yards, troop concentrations, highways, bridges, ports and supply centers. However, hard luck continued to follow the 99th Squadron. The Squadron on January 3, 1944, lost LT John H. Morgan of Centerville, GA, who died from injuries sustained in a crash while slow timing his plane. Twelve days later on January 15, LT William C. Griffin of Birmingham, AL, crashed landed his plane in enemy territory after being hit while dive bombing. Upon landing, Griffin was captured by the Germans and held as a prisoner of war until the end of the war.

Since being attached to the 79th Fighter Group on October 1943, the pilots of the 79th and the 99th had flown integrated missions almost on a daily basis. On January 16, the pilots of the 79th flew for the last time with pilots of the 99th. On that day, LT Wiley of the 99th led a formation of 12 planes, one of which was flown by LT Bech of the 87th. The formation bombed a fork where roads crossed at the river Ariolle. In the afternoon of the same day, MAJ Roberts led another 12 planes on a mission that bombed in the Chieti area.

On January 22, the three squadrons of the 79th Fighter Group, the 85th, 86th and 87th were assigned to patrol the assault beaches at Anzio, while the 99th was assigned to convoy patrol between Ponzione Island and the assault beach. On January 23rd, 24th, and 25th, the 99th was assigned to patrol X-Ray and Peter Beaches. Then on January 26, the 99th was assigned three convoy patrols missions. The first missions led by CPT Hall accompanied by LT Robinson, Bruce, Smith, Lane, Dunlap and Lawrence covered 50 plus ships in the patrol area that ran from Ponzione Island to Anzio. After months of flying without sighting enemy aircraft, two FW 190s were sighted approaching the formation at 8,000 to 11,000 feet. Immediately, the pilots jettisoned their belly tanks and tried to intercept the enemy aircraft, but the enemy turned quickly and fled. The second and third missions were led by CPT Custis and Jamison, but no enemy aircraft were encountered.

The squadron could show only one victory at the completion of six months of combat duty. This was disheartening and the morale of the 99th was far from high. The ground crewman had just about lost faith in their pilots' courage to engage the enemy. To make matters worse, in five days of battle, the pilots of the 79th had engaged the enemy, destroyed 11 aircraft, one probable, and damaged seven.

The opportunity to prove that they were capable pilots presented itself on the morning of January 27, 1944. A flight of twelve planes, led by CPT Clarence Jamison, of Cleveland, OH, spotted a group of enemy planes. They met the enemy at all angles and refused to give ground although they were outnumbered almost two to one. This was a desperate group of men determined to gain victories or die trying. This was the opportunity they had prayed for; therefore, they had to make the best of it. The battle didn't last long, but in less than five minutes they had knocked down five of the enemy aircraft. The remaining enemy pilots, seeing that they were fighting a losing battle turned tail and headed for home.

As the victories and happy pilots returned to the field, their morale was high. They buzzed the field several times and each made a victory roll before landing. This was the biggest day in the Squadron's history. The morale of the whole squadron, pilots and ground crewman, reached a new heighth and the victorious pilots were heartily received. The pilots credited with victories were as follows: LT Willie Ashley Jr. of Sumpter, SC; Leon Roberts of Pritchard, AL; Robert W. Deiz of Portland, OR; Edward L. Toppins of San Francisco, CA; and one victory between Howard L. Baugh of Petersburg, VA; and Clarence Allen of Mobile, AL.

All 12 of the planes returned safely. MAJ Roberts' plane had a huge hole torn in its left wing. LT Henry Perry of Thomasville, GA, was hit by an 88 shell that ripped a hole in his left wing. The plane of LT Pearlee Saunders of Bessemer, AL, developed engine trouble on the mission and was forced to return to the base. LT Walter Lawson of Newton, VA, and Albert Manning of Spartanburg, SC, also participated in the mission.

Another patrol flight over the Anzio beachhead was led by LT James T. Wiley on the afternoon of the same day. A flight of FW 190s escorted by ME 109s enemy fighters were sighted by the patrol as soon as it arrived in the Anzio area. With the morning's victories still fresh in mind the pilots vigorously attacked the enemy formation. In the battle that followed, CPT Lemuel R. Custis of Hartford, CT; LT Charles Bailey of Punta Gorda, FL; and Wilson Eagleson of

Bloomington, IN, shot down three more enemy aircraft, which brought the total of victories to eight for the day.

LT Bruce was the only casualty listed for the entire day. He was last seen chasing two Focke-Wulf 190s and therefore had to be considered missing in action. Lt Allen G. Lane of Demopolis, AL, was forced to bail out of his plane, which was set afire by a flak burst. He landed safely near an airfield at Nettuno and returned to the base two hours later in a Cub plane piloted by S\SGT William R. Lynn of Milbury, MA. A third pilot, LT John A. Gibson of Chicago, IL, was forced to crash land his plane when he returned to the base because his hydraulic system had been damaged by flak.

At the end of the day, the victorious pilots were anxious to relate their experiences. They had a large audience. CPT Lemuel Custis, commenting on their success, said: "It was the roughest day of the campaign, but the hunting was good all day." MAJ *Spanky* Roberts remarked: "We've been looking forward to such a happening, but this is the first time in five months that we have encountered enemy opposition. The whole show lasted less than 5 minutes. It was a chasing battle, as the Germans were always on the move. We poured hell into them." LT Willie Ashley remarked: "I saw a Focke-Wulf 190 and jumped directly on his tail. I started firing at close range, so close that I could see the pilot. After blasting away with all my ammunition, I saw the enemy plane smoking and fire flaming from its left side." At this time, LT Baugh entered the conversation. "I saw 12 or more Focke-Wulf 190s cut away from our ships and hit the deck. I was flying about 5,000 feet and went down firing. I gave three or four bursts of fire, then saw one plane skid along the tree tops, throwing clouds of dust as it hit the ground."

The Allied Air Force had one of its best combat days in the Italian Campaign on January 28. Fighter planes protecting the Anzio beachhead knocked 21 enemy aircraft out of the sky, while Flying Fortresses raiding Southern France destroyed 14 enemy planes. In two days of fighting, Allied fighter planes destroyed 85 and Allied bombers destroyed 50 enemy planes. During the battle of January 28, CPT Charles B. Hall destroyed two enemy aircraft, LT Deiz of Portland, OR, and Lewis C. Smith of Los Angeles, CA, shot down one each. On returning to the base, the victorious pilots were congratulated by MG John K. Cannon, Commanding General of Northwest African Training Command.

LT Curtis C. Robinson, whose friends addressed him as C.C., recalling CPT Hall's victories, said: "That mission gave me the scare of my life. I recall I was frightened on my first mission. I arrived overseas at the time the 99th was flying dive bombing and strafing missions. On my first mission, we were sent to dive bomb an enemy stronghold. When we reached the target area, our leader rocked his wings, turned over and started down and others followed. When my turn came, I rolled over and followed, but I worried that I would be hit by gun fire or wouldn't be able to pull out of my dive.

"On Charlie's mission, I got the scare of my life. On January 28, CPT Hall led a flight consisting of myself, Toppins, Smith, Knighten, Dunlap, Deiz and Eagleson to patrol the beach. We followed a course along the coast to the vicinity of Ponzione Island and then flew inland to the beach area at 5,000 feet.

"I had been flying dive bombing and strafing missions. I had never seen any enemy aircraft. At the time we were flying in a straight formation, a formation the Americans had learned from the British. I was supposed to be Charlie's wing man. Anyway, when we reached the beach, I heard a loud blast in the back of my ship. I pulled up and looked back, but saw nothing. I looked around and all of the planes in my formation had disappeared. When I looked down, I could see all of the planes way down below engaged in a battle. I started to dive for the scene of the battle, but shortly after beginning my dive an enemy aircraft shot across my plane. I immediately opened fire, but just as I began to fire, Charlie Hall crossed in front of me. He was firing away at the enemy ship. I just knew I had hit Charlie's ship. I turned and followed Charlie and saw his shots hitting the enemy aircraft. The enemy aircraft finally spun into the ground.

"When I returned to the base, I was anxious to see Hall's plane because I was sure I had damaged it in the battle. I was happy to find that I had missed and I was most happy to verify his victory."

Despite the aerial losses over the beachhead, the Germans continued to send over large forces of aircraft in an effort to halt the Allied all out drive. Seventeen planes were engaged over Anzio on February 5, by a flight of seven led by CPT Clarence Jamison. Although outnumbered over two to one, the flight destroyed one of the enemy planes. LT Elwood T. Driver was credited with the only victory.

While LT Driver was gaining his victory, CPT Jamison and his wingman, LT McCrumby were having trouble. McCrumby's plane was hit by an ack-ack burst and went into a dive at 4,000 feet. LT McCrumby related: I tried to pull out, but had no control of my elevators. Seeing that I had lost control of my plane, I tried to climb out of the left side of the cockpit, but the slip stream knocked me back into the plane. Then I tried the right side and got half way out when the slip stream caught me and threw me away from the plane, where I dangled until the wind turned the ship at about 1,000 feet from the earth, shaking me loose. I reached for the ripcord six times before finding it. My parachute opened immediately and I floated to a safe landing in a cow pasture."

The broadcast of the celebration of the third anniversary of Tuskegee Army air Field, August 9, 1944, was the occasion for CPT Jamison to relate his story: "It was over Anzio beachhead. I was leading a flight of seven planes that day. We'd been up a short time when we got word over the radio that a flight of 17 Focke-Wulf aircraft were coming at us. When we saw them, they were too high for us to catch them until they'd dropped their bombs, and then we closed in. I took off after four of them, when all of a sudden my guns jammed. A Focke-Wulf got on my tail, and I couldn't shake him off. I dropped on deck and hedge hopped along, but he chased me ten to 15 miles before he lost me. By that time, he had hit my engine and I knew I had to get out of there. I tried to climb high enough to jump, but I couldn't make it. So I made a crash landing. I didn't know just where I was, of course, but when I found I was all in one piece, I began to look around. I saw three American paratroopers motioning to me. I was only 200 yards from the German line and 300 yards from our forward position."

The success of the 99th brought an official commendation from General Arnold. It read: "The results of the 99th during the past two weeks, particularly since the Nettuno landing, are very commendable. My best wishes for their continued success."

The 99th was credited with three more victories on February 7, when LT Wilson V. Eagleson, Leonard M. Jackson, and Clinton B. Mills were each credited with an enemy aircraft. LT Jackson, a slender Texas lad, related: "On February 7, 1944, during the hot Anzio battle, I scored my first victory. I was patrolling over the beachhead in a formation of eight P-40s. The mission had been uneventful for 45 minutes, then it happened. Sixteen FW-190s came over to dive bomb Anzio Harbor. The enemy was sighted and called in by our ground control. We saw the enemy planes as our flight passed heading south. As the Focke-Wulf pulled out of their dive, they turned into our tails. Three members of our four ship element, which included LT Eagleson, Knighten, C. B. Mills, and myself, pulled around into a tight 180 degree turn. As the turn was initiated, the Jerries broke away and started climbing. I was on the right side and turned away from my element leader into the enemy. On recovery from the turn, I observed a Jerry plane pulling away from my plane. I gave him one burst at 150 yards and another at about 200 yards. I was about to break off my attack when I saw the Jerry plane turn over and tumble to the ground. I expected him to pull out and come back after me, but the ship continued to plunge earthward. The pilot bailed out of the damaged plane at 1,500 feet."

Late in January, 1944, the United States 34th Division managed to break through the northern end of the Gustav Line. The French Corps simultaneously captured key hills east of Mount Cairo, which dominated the Cassino area. An attack was launched on the heavily defended town of Cassino by the Allies on February 1, 1944. Support for the ground troops was again supplied by the 99th. The elaborate fortifications and an estimated 100,000 men of Marshal Kesserling, Commander of the German forces, could not stem the Allied tide. The hills to the north and northwest of the famous Hill 516 on which stood the ancient Benedictine Monastery were captured by the Allies after twelve days of fighting. All attempts by the Allied ground forces, however, to take the town were repulsed by the Germans, even though the 12th Air Force had plastered the town with bombs. On February 13, the 79th Group flew 131 sorties against German strongholds, supply dumps and troop concentration. The 99th flew 33 of the sorties.

Early in February, the New Zealand Corps of the Eighth Army, together with the Fourth Indian Division, relieved the Second Corps of the Fifth Army. They were assigned the mission of capturing the town of Cassino. The New Zealand Corps managed to take roughly one third of Cassino, but, due to bad weather, it was forced to postpone its assaults. Although the ground battle ended, the 79th Fighter Group, the 99th Fighter Squadron and other Air Force units kept continuous pressure on the enemy. The objective was to deny the enemy not only additional manpower, equipment and supplies, but to deprive the enemy of the ability to hold its present position or to withdraw troops from Italy to use against *Operation Overload* invasion forces. On February 14, the 99th bombed enemy forces in the Cisterna area; the next day, it bombed supply dumps at Valmontone and on the 16th attacked a supply dump near Rome. It attacked a supply dump and bridge in the Rome area on the 17th and, from February 19th to the 29th, bombed troop concentrations and patroled the assault beach area in the vicinity of Rome.

Meantime, misfortune struck the 99th again on February 21, 1944. LT Alwayne W. Dunlap of Washington, DC, was killed as his plane crashed when he overshot a landing strip on the Anzio beachhead. Nine days later on February 29, LT George McCrumby pulled out of his formation near Gaeta Point. He radioed that he was returning to the base because his plane had developed engine trouble. He was never seen or heard from again.

Records of the 79th's victories from January 9, 1943 to February 10, 1944, and of the 99th from its entrance in combat June 1943 to February 10, 1944, are as follows:(3)

SQUADRON	PROBABLE DESTROYED	DESTROYED	DAMAGED
85	29	8	11
86	17	2	9
87	41	7	24
99	17	4	6

Record of the 79th Fighter Group and the 99th Fighter Squadron from October 22, 1943 to April 1, 1944. The 99th was attached to the 79th and the results are as follow:(4)

SQUADRON	PROBABLE DESTROYED	DESTROYED	DAMAGED
85	15	2	8
86	2	2	2
87	15	13	3
99	16	2	2

Chapter 8
The 99th Fighter Squadron and Operation Strangle

During the lull in the fighting at Cassino, plans were made for an all out spring offensive against the enemy. It was believed that the enemy's ability to supply, reinforce, and shift his forces could be so weakened that he could neither withstand determined ground attacks nor withdraw in an orderly way. Using these views as a central theme, Allied Air Force commanders developed and put into effect a plan known as *Operation Strangle*. Needless to say, the aim of this operation was to reduce the flow of enemy supplies far below requirement.(1)

While the ground troops rested and prepared for the spring campaign, the Mediterranean Air Force, commanded by LTG Ira C. Eaker, was active. It plagued communication and supply lines far up the peninsula and harassed enemy troops in the Cassino area.

The Allied ground forces together with the Air Force opened their spring campaign in March 1944, with an assault on Cassino. A terrific aerial bombardment by more than 500 planes, including planes from the 99th, practically levelled Monte Cassino. When the New Zealand Corps tried to advance, it found roads so cratered and choked with debris that tanks could not be used. The stubborn Germans fought off all attempts to take Monte Cassino, and as a result, General Alexander, the Allied Commander, was forced on March 23 to call off the battle.

From March 24 until the fall of Rome on June 4, 1944, the Allied Air Force kept up a continuous attack on the enemy forces. Two interdiction lines were maintained across Italy which prevented through trains from running from the Po Valley to the front lines. This forced the Germans to move practically all their supplies south of Florence by truck.

The enemy attempted to use ships to bring in supplies, but heavy bombers attacked the key ports and coastal aircraft attacked the vessels. The enemy resorted to motor trucks to haul supplies around the broken bridges and eventually all the way from Florence to Rimini. This operation, however, could only be carried out at night because Allied strafing attacks made any daylight attempt impossible.(2)

Meantime, the pilots of the 99th were kept active. On March 23, the 99th struck gun positions east of Anzio and Nettuno. Gun positions north of Ardea were the next to be attacked on the following day by the Squadron under the leadership of LT Walter Lawson. On March 25, a flight from the 99th dive-bombed targets in the Palestrina area. During the mission, LT Clarence Dart's ship was set afire by a flak burst. He rode his plane down from 12,000 feet and landed in friendly territory.

The Squadron suffered a casualty on March 28 when LT Edgar L. Jones, of New York City, was killed. While taking off on an early morning mission, his plane collided with several parked planes on the side of the runaway. Two days later, LT John Stewart Sloan, of Louisville, KY, was shot down by enemy ack-ack guns as he pulled up from dive-bombing a target in the Cassino area. Shrapnel pierced the bottom of his plane and fractured his upper thigh bone. Immediately after the hit, Sloan called his element leader, LT Robert W. Deiz and reported that he was badly hurt. A little later, Sloan lost control of his aircraft. He bailed out of his crippled plane and landed safely. The following day, he returned to his base.

Throughout the month of March, the 99th, fighting with the 79th Fighter Group, supported Allied ground troops in the Cassino and beachhead areas. During the month, the group flew 172 missions. However, at the end of March, the 99th was released from operations with the 79th Group as a result of the Group's reassignment to bomber escort duty.

The 99th moved to Cercola on April 1 and was attached to the 324th Fighter Group. Upon arrival at its new base, the Squadron was reorganized and CPT Erwin B. Lawrence succeeded MAJ Spencer Roberts, who returned to the States.

Shortly after receiving his appointment as commanding officer of the 99th, CPT Lawrence addressed the Squadron. He said: "I am happy to have a bunch like you to work with me. You are all good men. We will try to live up to the record made by the Squadron under our two former leaders, COL Davis and MAJ Roberts, and if possible, to continue to improve. It will be tough for me to follow in the footsteps of these men, but I will do my best."

Throughout April 1944, the 99th dive-bombed and strafed enemy positions in the Anzio and Cassino areas. The success of the squadron was expressed by General Ira C. Eaker, Mediterranean Allied Air Force Commander, when he inspected the Squadron on April 20. He said: "By the magnificent showing your fliers have made since coming to this theatre and especially in the Anzio beachhead operation, you have not only won the plaudits of the Air Force, but have earned the opportunity to apply your talent to much more advanced work than was at one time planned for you."

The sustained offensive by the Air Force practically eliminated the use of rail transportation by the Germans. They resorted to the use of motor trucks for long supply hauls, but they were unable to build up significant reserves.

Around the first of May 1944, preparations were made for the spring offensive against the enemy. Air and Ground Forces were given two complementary objectives. The Mediterranean Allied Air Force was assigned to the mission "to make it impossible for the enemy to maintain his forces on its present line in Italy in the face of combined Allied offensive." The Ground Forces were "to destroy the right wing of the German 10th Army; to drive what remains of it and the German 14th Army north of Rome, and to pursue the enemy to the Pisa-Rimini line, inflicting the maximum losses on him in the process."(3)

On May 11, the big drive against the enemy began. The Fifth and Eighth Armies charged forward. The 99th also went into action as support for the ground troops. On D-Day, May 11, it flew 31 sorties and dropped 30,000 pounds of bombs on enemy positions. However, the Squadron suffered a casualty when LT Neil V. Nelson of Amarillo, TX and also from Chicago, IL, failed to return from a mission. He was last observed pulling into formation after making his bomb run. According to pilots who made the mission, visibility was so poor in the target area that they were forced to pick their way through clouds. This factor and the high concentration of flak was attributed to the probable cause of Nelson's failure to return from the mission.

The following day, the 99th flew 28 sorties against a bridge spanning a valley between the Germans north of Cassino and German supply dumps. During one of the missions, LT Elwood Driver's plane was severely damaged by flak, but he was able to nurse the ship back to the base. LT Theodore Wilson of Roanoke, VA, was forced to bail out of his ship when it was damaged by a flak burst. Fortunately, LT Wilson landed in a friendly hospital area and was able to secure another plane to fly back to his base.

The coordinated operations of the Air Force and Ground Forces worked as planned. The enemy's night convoys were unable to meet the added requirements for rapid movement of troops and materials to the front. Desperate for supplies, the enemy attempted to use his motor transports in daylight convoys. These convoys were extremely vulnerable to Allied Air attacks, and as a result, the enemy suffered heavy losses, both in troops and supplies. The enemy's line broke under the impact of the air and ground offensive. The Germans were unable to withdraw in an orderly way because of their disrupted transportation system. Within a week, General Clark's Fifth Army surrounded Cassino, and on May 17, the town was captured.

General Clark complemented the 99th on May 16 for the support it gave his ground troops. The citation read: "They contributed materially in forcing the German units to surrender to advance Allied infantry in the current all out offensive." MAG Cannon, Commanding Officer of the Twelfth Air Force, also praised the 99th as "battle hardened and one of the most experienced in giving close air support to ground troops in the entire theatre of operation."

The pilots of the 99th were told on May 22 that the second phase of their campaign against the enemy would start at 6:30 A.M. on the morning of May 23. The Anzio beachhead was to be expanded and the battle line would be continued from the Fifth Army bomb line until the beachhead forces and the Fifth Army met. The 99th's immediate mission was to strike targets northwest of the beachhead and south of Rome.

As planned, the Anzio garrison burst from its confines on the morning of May 23, 1944. In a wild battle at Cisterna, the Allied Forces repelled seven German counter-attacks and took the town. Later, the Anzio troops were joined by the Fifth Army which came up the West Coast. Together, they pursued the retreating German

14th Army which fell back to protect the Alban Hills and the city of Velletri.

The 99th flew an armed reconnaissance mission northeast of Lake Albano on May 26. During the mission, LT Woodrow Morgan developed engine trouble. He landed by mistake on an enemy airfield located west of Frosinone and was seized as a prisoner of war. LT Robert Deiz, who covered the disabled pilot, was hit several times by enemy gun fire but was able to return to his base. A third pilot, LT Alva Temple, had his rudder shot out, elevators practically shot off, and large holes ripped in his fuselage. In spite of these damages, Temple landed his plane safely at the base.

General Mark Clark sent the following message to the Twelfth Air Force headquarters on May 27: "Greatly pleased with splendid effort of Air Force. We have put the enemy on the run. Good hunting to all." The next day, the 99th continued its attacks on the enemy by dive-bombing in the vicinity of Frosinone. Though the squadron effectively carried out its assignment, one of its members, LT James B. Brown failed to return from the mission. LT William H. Thomas, relating what happened to Brown, said: "Brown went down in the lower layer of clouds which was bout 1,500 feet. A pilot flying in a rear element saw a plane dive through the clouds and later heard Brown cry out that he had been hit. LT Dart went down below the clouds and saw Brown's plane hit in a forest area and skid about 50 feet. He didn't see J. B. get out. He saw some peasants around the plane. Later, however, it was picked up in a prison camp that J.B. was captured by the Germans and marched away. But while marching down the street, J.B. was hit by American artillery shell fire. Some Allied Intelligence officers found J.B.'s dog tags and underwear."

On June 1, the Germans were forced to retreat from their stronghold in the city of Velletri. With their Alban Hill defense broken, the Germans retreated to Rome. Two days later, Allied troops entered the Eternal City and forced the Germans to retreat further north. Following the capture of Rome, General Clark, on June 5, stated that the 12th Air Force support "had enabled us to show the enemy how irresistible the Air-Ground combination can become."

The capture of Rome was the occasion of celebration throughout the world. To the soldiers, however, it marked only a milestone back to the States. The Germans were on the retreat and there was no time to give them rest.

The 99th flew armed reconnaissance north of Lake Bracciano on June 5. The next day it strafed vehicles on a highway between Lake Bolsena and Lake Vico. During the assault, LT Leonard Jackson's plane was severely damaged by flak. Seeing that he could not keep his plane in the air, Jackson glided it across Lake Bracciano and landed in a wheat field. As he climbed out of his ship, he was greeted by a small band of American soldiers. The soldiers had recognized the American plane and had come up hurriedly to offer assistance. Jackson learned that the soldiers were volunteers sent out to search a house for snipers.

While Jackson talked with the search party, he noticed two German soldiers waving a white flag from a ravine. He motioned them to approach and took their arms. Jackson turned the Germans over to the search party and then proceeded to Rome. Here he was interrogated and returned to the Squadron.

LT Clarence Allen was also shot down by flak during his mission. He landed in enemy territory but managed to hide himself before the Germans reached him. The entire area was sprayed by machine gun fire when Allen refused to surrender. Several attempts were made by the Germans to force Allen from his hiding place, but all failed. Seeing that their efforts were not successful, the Germans gave up and departed.

The next morning, Allen crawled out of the cave and found he was less than 100 feet from a German machine gun nest. That afternoon, an American tank squad entered the area and forced the Germans to move. Circumstances being very favorable, indeed, Allen decided to make a break. His efforts to reach friendly territory were met with success. He was able to reach a camp of French soldiers after sliding down a whole mountain side. Exhausted from his hazardous trip, Allen collapsed before he could identify himself. He was revived and carried to the French headquarters. Here he was questioned and given a physical examination before being returned to his Squadron.

Fate seemed to have been against Allen. A week later on June 14, he was again shot down. This time, it was a strafing mission over Southern France. Again, he was lucky. He escaped being taken by the Germans. Upon arrival at the base, he was returned to the States.

Meantime, on June 8, 1944, the 99th lost CPT Lewis C. Smith, who was shot down by small arms fire while dive-bombing and strafing. After bailing out of his disabled plane, Smith was set upon by a mob of angry civilians. He was rescued by a squad of German soldiers who carried him to Florence. Ten days later, he was shipped to Frankfurt on the Main. Not long after this, he was moved again to Sagan, Silesia, where he remained until January 22, 1945. At this time, he was transferred to Stalag Luft 7-A in Moosburg, Germany. Smith was held prisoner here until liberated by the Allies on April 29, 1945.

The capture of Rome placed the Germans in a strategically vulnerable position. They fell back in good order to defenses 150 miles north on the Arno River. The weary enemy troops were given no respite as the Allied ground and Air Forces continued to press them The 99th joined the 86th Fighter Group at Ciampino, Italy, on June 11, and immediately went into action dive-bombing and strafing the enemy troop concentrations and strongholds in the Rome area. On June 12, the Squadron strafed in the Rome area where it encountered heavy flak and machine gun fire. It dive-bombed a bridge at Macchie on the 15th and on the following day dive-bombed and strafed in the San Quirico area.

The 99th moved to Albinia on June 20, 1944, with the 86th Fighter Group. Here it went into action dive-bombing and strafing in the Florence-Pisa areas. On the 21st, the Squadron dive-bombed a railroad east of Pisa. The next day, it continued its attacks. From June 23-27, it dive-bombed railroads northeast of Florence.

On June 29, the 99th was sent to the Po Valley to knock out some 500 railroad cars. Heavy concentrated flak greeted the squadron as soon as it reached the Po area. LT Floyd Thompson was hit by flak bursts which severely damaged his plane. He was forced to bail out of his plane in the vicinity of Florence. He was taken prisoner by the Germans and held until the end of the war.

LT Charles Bailey, of Punta Gorda, FL, became excited when heavy flak bursts rocked his ship. Thinking his plane was damaged, he requested escort back to the base. LT Heber Houston of Detroit, MI, was assigned to escort Bailey on the return trip. Checking his ship after landing at the base, Bailey found it was not damaged as badly as he thought. Only a few small flak holes were found in the wing and tail assembly.

July 2, 1944 was the last day on which the 99th flew as a separate unit. It was on this day that the Squadron, which had ended operations with the 86th Fighter Group on June 29 and moved to Orbetelli, left to join the 332nd Fighter Group. The next day, the 99th joined the 332nd at Ramitelli, and was immediately integrated into the group.

The Allies took Siena on July 3, and on the 19th, Polish troops captured Ancona on the Adriatic. Meanwhile, British troops, advancing through central Italy over difficult terrain, passed around both sides of Lake Trasimeno, took Arezzo, and opened up the road to Florence. The Germans retreated to the Pisa-Florence-Rimini line where they prepared for an all out offensive.

Elsberry discussing flying with LT M. Rodgers, COL Davis, MAJ Gleed and CPT McDaniels.

Men of the 332nd Fighter Group prepare for overseas deployment at Selfridge Field in late 1943 (courtesy of Luther McIlwain).

Chapter 9
The 332nd Fighter Group
The Red Tails

Originally, the 332nd consisted of three Squadrons: the 100th, 301st and 302nd. Shortly after entering combat, the group was enlarged by the integration of the 99th.

The 100th Fighter Squadron was the first of these to become active. Under the leadership of LT Mac Ross of Dayton, OH,the 100th was activated at Tuskegee on May 26, 1942. LT George L. Knox and Charles Debow, both from Indianapolis, IN, were assigned as adjutants of the newly formed squadron. The Squadron remained at Tuskegee until March 27, 1943, and was then transferred to Selfridge Field, Mt. Clements, MI as a component of the 332nd Fighter Group.

Changes in officer personnel were made in July of the same year. LT Mac Ross now became the Group Operation Officer. The promotion of Ross left the squadron without a Commander, the vacancy quickly filled by the appointment of LT Knox as Squadron Commander. LT Elwood Driver took over the command in December, 1943, but his assignment lasted only a week. He was succeeded by LT Robert B. Tresville, a graduate of the United States Military Academy. In June 1944, LT Tresville failed to return from a mission. LT Andrew D. Turner of Washington, DC, then became the squadron leader. He commanded the squadron until hostilities ceased in the European Theatre. When Turner returned to the States, CPT Roscoe Brown of New York City was appointed, commanding the squadron until it returned to the States in October 1945.

The 301st Fighter Squadron was activated at Tuskegee in the early part of 1943. It, too, like the 100th, had a series of squadron commanders, CPT Charles Debow being the first. During his command, the squadron was ordered overseas. CPT Debow was relieved of his command in April 1944, with MAJ Lee Rayford of Ardwick, MD, replacing him.

MAJ Rayford was returned to the States after completing his tour of duty and MAJ Armour C. McDaniel of Satunton, VA, took over the command. A change in command was again necessitated when MAJ McDaniel was shot down over Berlin in March 1945. CPT Walter Downs then became the new leader and held this position until the outfit returned to the States at the close of the war.

The 302nd was the last of the group to be activated, in March 1943, under the leadership of LT William T. Mattison of Conway, AR. This particular unit of the group, however, encountered adverse conditions. In the beginning, the unit was considered only a pool for the other two squadrons. Most of its personnel, both officers and enlisted men, were considered the least desirable members of the group.

The seeming disregard for the ability of the members of the 302nd, however, played a very potent part in welding it into a capable and effective outfit. The men realized that whatever they did wrong would reflect on the Squadron and at the same time substantiate opinions about their characters and abilities. They were determined to do everything a little better than the other squadrons. The 302nd began demonstrating its possibility as a fighter unit on maneuvers in the North Woods of Michigan. Here it developed the team spirit that it carried into combat.

Late in the summer of 1943, LT Mattison was replaced by LT Tresville, who commanded the Squadron only a short time before being transferred to the 100th Fighter Squadron. LT Edward G. Gleed of Lawrence, KS, succeeded Tresville and carried the Squadron overseas. On April 10, 1944, it received a new commanding officer, CPT Melvin T. Jackson of Warrenton, VA, commanding the Squadron until he returned to the States in the spring of 1945. CPT Vernon C. Haywood, the next commander, carried out his duties until the Squadron was deactivated in March of 1945.

Although the first squadron of the 332nd was formed in May, 1942, the group was not officially activated until October 13, 1942. On that date, LTC Samuel Westerbrook was appointed to command the 332nd, and plans for actual organization began. A month later on November 13, 1942, the first cadre of enlisted men were transferred from the 318th Base Headquarters and Air Base Squadron at Tuskegee to the group.

Under the command of LTC Westbrook , the 332nd was transferred to Selfridge Field on March 27, 1943. But the stay at Selfridge was brief for the majority of the Group's personnel. On April 13, the 100th moved from Selfridge Field to Oscoda, MI, for a temporary change of station. The 301st followed on May 5, and by May 21, most of the Group had moved to Oscoda with the exception of radio mechanics and other technicians of the 302nd who remained at Selfridge Field. The 302nd, the last of the fighter squadrons to be activated, did not have sufficient line personnel to function as a unit at Oscoda; consequently, only the pilots of the 302nd underwent the initial training phases.

COL Robert R. Selway Jr. took over the command of the 332nd in June 1943. Under his direction, the group was reorganized and an effective training plan put into action. Intensive training in combat tactics was given by LT Richard Suer, veteran of the Aleutian Campaign.

The instruction given by Suer did not fall on barren soil. Within a comparatively short period of time, the 332nd developed into a combat unit whose motto was summed up in the slogan, "Get to your damn guns" which was adopted by COL Selway.

The training program at Selfridge Field, however, was not without casualties. Shortly after it went into training, the 332nd lost one of its most popular pilots in the death of LT Wilmeth Sidat Singh. A native of New York, he had already gained national recognition for his participation in football and basketball at Syracuse University long before entering the army.

After completing his studies at Syracuse, Singh moved to Washington, DC, where he became a member of the Metropolitan Police Force. It was during this time he played professional basketball with the famous *Washington Bears*. By his superior playing, he was instrumental in leading the *Bears* to the National Professional Basketball Championship.

Singh enlisted in the Air Corps on August 7, 1942, and was sent to Tuskegee as an aviation cadet. On March 25, 1943, Singh was commissioned as a 2LT in the Air Corps and sent to Selfridge Field where he became a member of the 332nd Fighter Group. While flying over Lake Huron on a routine training mission on May 9, 1943, his engine burst into flame. No alternative being possible, he bailed out of his ship into the water. Forty-nine days later, his body was recovered by a coast guardsman and turned over to the Group.

After nine months of intensive training, the 332nd was considered ready for combat. On October 5, 1943, COL Davis assumed command of the group and immediately made preparation for combat. He was assured of experienced leaders when CPT Louis Purnell, CPT Lee Rayford, LT Elwood Driver, and LT Graham Smith reported to the group on December 2, 1943. These men had served their tour of duty with the 99th Fighter Squadron and had volunteered to return to combat with the 332nd Fighter Group.

On December 23, 1943, the 332nd was transferred to the Port of Embarkation at Camp Patrick Henry, Virginia. Here the members of the 332nd received their final processing before embarking for overseas duty on January 3, 1944.

BG Benjamin Oliver Davis, Sr., First Day of Issue, Washington, DC, 28 January 1997, 20066

Left: Brigadier General Benjamin O. Davis, Sr. Center: BG Benjamin O. Davis Sr. stamp First Day of Issue, Washington, DC 20066, Jan 28, 1997. Bottom: Posing with his wife, LT Thomas Malone, who was awarded the Purple Heart for combat in Sicily.

Chapter 10
The 332nd Fighter Croup Enters Combat

The destination of the 332nd was no longer a secret. After three weeks of sailing, the first ship carrying personnel of the 301st and 302nd arrived at Taranto, Italy. Other ships of the convoy arrived intermittently until February 3, 1944, when the final ship landed. Meantime, the 100th Squadron under CPT Robert Tresville landed at Naples, where it set up camp at the Capodichino Airport. Here it went into action on February 5, flying a coastal patrol mission to Naples Harbor under the leadership of CPT Andrew Turner of Washington, DC.

A few days after the final convoy ship disembarked at Taranto, the 301st and 302nd moved by truck to Montecorvino. Here the 332nd replaced the 81st which had performed coastal patrol and was being transferred to Burma.

After spending a short time at Montecorvino, the 302nd and Group headquarters moved to the Capodichino Airport in Naples. The 301st under MAJ Lee Rayford remained at Montecorvino supporting ground troops fighting in the Anzio area.

The entrance into combat on the part of 332nd was quite unlike that of the 99th. Almost immediately, the group encountered enemy aircraft. On February 18, LT Lawrence D. Wilkins of Los Angeles and his wingman, LT Weldon K. Groves of Edwardsville, KS, sighted a TU 88 near Ponsa Island off Gaeta Point. They chased the enemy aircraft as far as the Anzio Beachhead and were successful in getting several bursts into the enemy plane before they were forced to turn back because of a shortage of gasoline and a faltering gun.

LT Roy N. Spencer of Tallahassee, FL, and his wingman, LT William R. Melton of Los Angeles, encountered an enemy reconnaissance plane near Ponsa Point two days later. They sprayed the enemy ship with volleys, but failed to make the kill. LT Spencer's guns jammed just after he had lined up the enemy aircraft and prepared to fire. Melton took up the attack, but he was unable to make a direct hit on the enemy plane that maneuvered to keep from being shot down.

No battle has been fought without some casualties and the battle waged by the 332nd was no exception. On February 24, a flight of four, engaged in a routine training mission, ran into a bad storm while flying over the Adriatic Sea. LT Harry J. Daniels of Indianapolis, IN, was reported missing in action when he failed to return to the base. He was last seen trying to fight his way through heavy walls of clouds closing on his plane. LT Ulysses Taylor of Kaufman, Texas, was forced to bail out of his ship after losing control. He was rescued by an Allied vessel and carried ashore where he was hospitalized and treated for severe shock received from hitting the water.

The group lost LT Clemenceau Givings, a member of the 100th Squadron, on March 18, 1944. Returning from a mission, his plane spun into the Adriatic Sea. His body was recovered by an Italian fisherman, and on March 19, he was laid to rest in an American Cemetery near the Capodichino Airport.

LT John B. Quick, the Intelligence Officer of the 100th, said the last words over the body. As the burial party stood around the grave with heads bowed in silent prayer, LT Quick said:

"There are some men in an outfit that you always expect to find around. *Wild Bill* Walker was one, Clem Givings was another. Givings, the latest of our group to meet his death, was perhaps the most unique personality among us. He was strictly Air Corps, incorporating in his decorum all the zest, cock-suredness, pride, and braggadocio that is the essence of a fighter pilot's makeup. He was always talking about flying, about women, about everything a dare-devil talks about, and while he talked, we all listened. We had to; his voice was loud and never faltered for lack of words, and his speech was as colorful as a night full of ack-ack. To him, being a pilot was a great achievement and, to rate with him, one had to have wings. Well, he's gone now. The Squadron has lost its first pilot in combat. While he lived, he lived a symbol of the Air Corps, and dead he is no less."

During a training mission of May 28, 1944, the engine in the plane of LT Roger B. Brown of Glencoe, IL, conked out while he was flying 2,000 feet above water. After unsuccessfully attempting to start his engine, Brown found himself only 800 feet above the water and falling too fast to jump with his parachute. He jettisoned the doors of his P-39 Airacobra, unfastened everything he could, cut off his switches, placed his hands over his gunsight, and held his plane off the water until his air speed was less than 120 miles an hour. When his ship hit the water, he abandoned it in less than three seconds. Yet, despite his swiftness in getting out, the tail of his fast sinking plane struck him.

LT Brown was rescued by a British vessel shortly thereafter. For his accomplishment, he was officially commended for being the first pilot to the United States Air Force known to have successfully crash landed a P-39 Airacobra at sea.

In spite of the casualties suffered by the 332nd, it effectively carried out its assignments of coastal patrol dive-bombing and strafing in support of ground troops fighting in the Rome area. When the 12th Air Force and Bombers denied the enemy the use of rail transportation and enemy motor convoys could not bring in ample supplies, the Germans resorted to the use of ships to bring in the much needed supplies. The 332nd, together with other coastal Air Force units, made these attempts unsuccessful. The Germans' supply problems were rendered so acute that when the Allies finally started the push on Rome, Marshal Kesserling was unable to halt the drive. On Sunday, June 4, 1944, the Allies entered Rome and forced the Germans to retreat northward.

Even before the fall of Rome, it had become apparent to Allied commanders that the network of roads, over which the Germans transported supplies and the supply centers further north and in Southern France, had to be destroyed. Strategic bombing of these roads, bridges, enemy coastal ships, harbor installations, and supply centers was decided upon as the most effective means of crippling the German war machine. As a result, many Tactical Fighter Groups were relieved of tactical operations and assigned to strategic bomber escort duty. The 332nd was one of the groups affected by this operational change. On May 31, 1944, it was transferred from the 12th Tactical Air force to the 15th Strategic Air Force and assigned new P-47 Thunderbolt planes for escort duty.

The War Department had planned to continue the 332nd in tactical operations. It had planned to re-equip it with P-63s, the King Cobra, and improved models of the P-39. It was the idea of General

Eaker that the 332nd be equipped with P-47s and P-51s, and reassigned to strategic escort duty.

General Eaker had had a long and frustrating career in trying to develop the 8th Air Force Daylight Strategic Bomber Command, because of changing war plans, and the lack of a good long distant fighter plane. In February 1942, he and six US Army Air Force Officers arrived in England and announced that they intended to organize an American Daylight Bomber Command. British Air Force officers, however, were apprehensive as to the effectiveness of the plan. They insisted that it was almost impossible to precision bomb Germany in the daylight from high altitudes and especially while being attacked by anti-aircraft guns and enemy fighters.

General Eaker was determined to organize an American Bomber Force. But he soon found the British prediction to be accurate. On August 17, 1942, the 8th flew its first mission, escorted by British fighters to France. It bombed marshalling yards at Roven-Sotteville without a loss. However, on a mission to Vegesack, Germany on January 29, 1943, the Germans waited until the fighter escort turned back because of the shortage of fuel, then appeared in full force. They shot down two B-24 and one B-17.

General Eaker learned from the mission that the Germans were reluctant to attack bombers when escort planes were present. He ordered 6,000 200 gallon wing tanks for the P-47, but they had to be designed, built and tested before being sent to England.(1) Meantime, the General continued his attempt to penetrate into Germany.

On February 4, 1943, he sent out a force of 86 planes to bomb the industrial city of Emden. The Germans jumped the straggling formation and shot down five B-17. On March 4, a large force was sent to destroy the railroad yards at Hamm. En route from the target area, one unit of the formation was attacked by about 50 German fighters, destroying four B-17. On April 17, 1943, 115 bombers were dispatched to bomb the Focke-Wulf plant at Bremen. About 150 enemy fighters intercepted the bombers and shot down 16 of them and damaged 46 others.(2)

In April 1943, General Eaker received a shipment of auxiliary drop tanks, designed to extend the range of the P-47 to 400 miles, still far short of the necessary range to cover the bombers all the way on missions into Germany. However, he felt it would help tremendously in giving the bombers close support further into Germany.

However, the drop tanks brought Eaker more frustrations. His fighter commander, General Hunter looked with disfavor on the idea of close support and the use of drop tanks. He believed that a more effective tactic was to have fighters sweep an area of enemy fighters for the bombers could pass through unmolested. He argued that the tanks lowered the speed and maneuverability of the planes and were "powder kegs waiting to be set off by enemy guns." Furthermore, he could not see any purpose for the fighters, because the bomber crews would get all the credit for the victories. However, he reluctantly agreed to use the tanks, but permitted his pilots to drop the tanks as soon as they reached ceiling. This caused more arguments.

After listening to one of the arguments, COL Emmet *Rosey* O'Donnel, one of General Arnold aides, sent a memo to General Arnold, stating that the fighters were not doing the bombers much good: "...if their participation in the bomber offenses comprises escort across the Channel only... they simply insure the bombers safe delivery into the hands of the wolves."(3)

Shortly after receiving the memo, General Arnold, a personal friend of General Eaker, informed Eaker that he still had confidence in his ability, but believed he was too loyal and easy on incompetent aides, that he wanted him to come out of this a real commander. "You have performed an excellent job but there are times when you will have to be tough. So be tough... In any event, a definite change seems in order..."(4)

General Eaker got the message that his career was on the line. At his request, General Hunter was relieved of his command and reassigned as commander of the First Air Force. In this position, he became one of the most determined adversaries of integration. However, in preparation for the Cross Channel invasion of France, General Eaker was reassigned to command the newly activated 15th Air Force stationed in the Mediterranean.

In December 1943, General Eaker took over the command of the 15th. He soon found the same reluctancy of white commanders and pilots of the 15th Air Force to give bombers close support. In March 1944, he summoned COL Davis to his headquarters and related the trouble he was having with the white fighter commanders and pilots in carrying out his ideas of close support for bomber crews. He revealed that on some missions, he had lost 25 or more bombers with crews of 11 men each, because white pilots wanted to score victories for their personal glories rather than protect the bombers. He remarked that this resulted in a "tremendous loss of lives and bombers." He stated he wanted fighter commanders and pilots who would protect the bomber crews. COL Davis assured him that he would carry out his orders.(5)

On March 14, 1944, General Eaker informed General Barney M. Giles that "In the Anzio bridgehead battle, the Colored combat pilots have demonstrated that they fight better against Germans in the air than they do on the ground support missions. The only point raised against this is the fact that bombardment accompanying missions are high altitudes and colored troops do not normally stand cold weather very well. The P-47 is a warm airplane, however, and we believe it will work. COL Davis and his colored pilots are most enthusiastic to undertake the program and I am confident that they will do a good job."(6)

On May 31, 1944, the 332nd was transferred from the Tactical Air Force to the 15th Strategic Air Force and assigned new P-47, Thunderbolt planes for escort duty. On June 1, 1944, General Eaker informed General Arnold: "Yesterday, we transferred the 332nd, completely equipped with P-47s to the Strategic Air Force. These colored pilots have very high morale and are eager to get started on their new Strategic task accompanying long-range bombers. I talked with General Strothers, their Wing Commander, today. He has watched them closely, in their indoctrination phase and he feels, as I do, that they will give a good account of themselves."(7)

Fighter pilots are fighter pilots regardless of race, color or nationality. COL Davis soon learned that the idea of "Close Support" was as unpopular with his pilots as with the white pilots. They also wanted to gain credit for personal victories. He called an assembly and informed the pilots that their primary duty was to protect the bomber crews by giving close support, that if it were ever reported to him that anyone left the bombers to chase after an enemy aircraft, he would not only ground that pilot but subject him to court martial. Of course, the pilots disliked nothing more than to be grounded.

Greeting nurses, a Colonel shakes hands with Chief Nurse Della M. Raney.

Top: Captain Eldridge and the Tuskegee boxing team. Bottom left: *Miss Gridiron*, Edna B. Bouldin, greeting SGT Jerry Williams and LT Ira J. O'Neal of Tuskegee's *Warhawks*. Bottom right: Medical Staff of the 99th and 332nd: MAJ Marchbanks and CPT Allen, Moloney and Waugh.

Four pictures: Black nurses "keep them flying."

Chapter 11
The 332nd and the Fifteenth Air Force

The capture of Rome gave the Allies added incentive to attempt an invasion of western Europe. On June 6, just two days after the conquest of Rome, the long awaited assault on the coast of France was launched. While the invasion of western Europe was taking place, the battle of Italy was being accelerated. The Allied strategy in Italy was to keep the enemy forces fully occupied so that it would be impossible to withdraw any troops from Italy to help defend the coast of France.

The capture of Rome also held special significance for the Mediterranean Allied Air Force and, more specifically, for the Twelfth and Fifteenth Army Air Forces. It marked the culmination of the largest scale Tactical Air Force campaign to date and the emergence of strategic bombing as an important Air Force strategy in the Mediterranean theatre.

One of the main objectives of the Italian campaign was to capture the Foggia plains. Army Air Force planners had long recognized the fact that Southern Italy could be used as bases for bombers to strike at the Balkans and at the industrial plants moved by the Germans beyond range of the British base bombers.

In September 1943, Foggia was captured by the British Eighth Army. Almost immediately afterwards, engineers began developing and repairing the numerous fighter plane bases that the Germans had constructed in the area. However, the bases had been built for lighter aircraft and the damages suffered by continuous bombings made it impossible for the Allies to make immediate use of the bases for bomber operations.

The Fifteenth Air Force was activated on November 1, 1943, and immediately went into operation on a small scale against enemy production centers. Meantime, throughout the winter of 1943, new groups were crossing the Atlantic to join the new Air Force. By April 1944, the 15th had grown to such an extent that it was ready for large scale operations. Its bombers and fighters were sent to attack strategic targets beyond working range of the British based bombers. It was obvious, however, from the beginning that the success of strategic operations depended on a degree of air superiority, providing freedom for the heavy bombers to fly over enemy territory. The Germans had converted the aircraft industry to fighter production and moved it as far from the British based threat as possible--Bavaria, Austria, and Hungary. The Fifteenth met opposition from these enemy fighters in its attacks on the production centers and suffered a large number of casualties.

The assignment of the 332nd to bomber escort brought the pilots in contact with more enemy aircraft and gave them a chance to register more aerial victories. A fighter sweep to the Po Valley on June 7, led by COL Davis, was the first assignment of the 332nd with the 15th. The next day, the group escorted bombers to Pola Harbor in northeastern Italy. Both missions, however, were uneventful in that no enemy aircraft was encountered.

The first big day of the 332nd with the 15th Air Force came on June 9, 1944. The group was assigned to fly top cover for heavy and medium bombers to the Munich area. On approaching the Udine area, four ME-109s were observed making attacks from 5 o'clock high on a formation of B-24s. As each enemy aircraft made a pass at the bombers, it fell into a diving turn to the left. LT Wendell Pruitt described the situation as follows:

"As the Jerries passed under me, I rolled over, shoved everything forward, dove and closed in on one ME-109 at 475 miles per hour. I gave him a short burst of machine gun fire, found I was giving him too much lead so I waited as he shallowed out of a turn. Then I gave two long two-second bursts. I saw his left wing burst into flame. The plane exploded and went straight into the ground, but the pilot bailed out safely."

LT Frederick Fundenburg of Monticello, GA, sighted two ME-109s 400 feet below at 9 o'clock. He peeled down on one of the enemy ships and fired a burst. He noticed pieces flying off the enemy ship as he continued in his dive. Then he made a steep climbing turn and found two ME-109s coming head on at him. He flew straight towards the Germans and fired until one of the enemy ships exploded.

Meantime, LT Robert H. Wiggins saw a ME-109 coming at his level. He turned into the enemy plane and fired a burst. His fire finding its mark, the enemy plane began to smoke and fell into a shallow dive. However, a few minutes later, it gained speed and pulled away from LT Wiggins, who was attempting to follow up his attack.

LT Melvin *Red* Jackson, relating how he got his victory, said, "We were flying P-47 Thunderbolts. COL Davis was leading. Over the Udine valley, COL Davis observed a group of ME-109s coming in on our bombers. Skipper called in that enemy fighters were attacking. 'Go get them.' Immediately, I peeled off, out of formation and with my wingman following, went back to the scene of engagement. I noticed about seven ME-109s coming in at 5 o'clock, so I radioed my flight to drop belly tanks and prepare for attack. then I fell in behind the second enemy aircraft which was coming down in string formation. Having a faster plane than the enemy, I overshot him. However, my wingman, LT *Chubby* Green, and LT Charles Bussey, who were behind me, shot the enemy ship down.

"When I pulled out of my dive, I started to climb. I noticed a ME-109 headed straight down at me, blazing away with all his guns. At the same time, my plane seemed to be dragging on the climb, so instantly I realized that I hadn't dropped my tanks. I tried to drop them but they were stuck. Then I applied my water booster. This gave me additional speed and enabled me to pull away from my attacker.

"Below were the Alps with their high peaks, and just above a mountain top hung a layer of clouds. So finding myself hindered by the wing tanks, I decided to drop out of the battle and seek refuge among the clouds. I dived into the clouds, but as I broke out into the clear on the south side of the Alps, I found my pursuer waiting to shoot me down. He made a pass at me, but somehow he missed me. I fell in behind him. Realizing I was on his tail he began weaving from side to side. Every time he turned I gave him a short burst of fire. On the fourth burst, his plane began to smoke. I saw the canopy come off the ME-109 in two pieces. A little later, I saw the pilot jump and his parachute open. I circled the helpless pilot for a while. But looking down I saw that I was directly over an enemy airfield. I dove down on deck and headed for the Adriatic Sea. About ten miles out, I gained altitude, settled down and cruised home happy over my victory."

The 332nd was credited with five victories during the mission. The victories were credited as follows: LT Frederick D. Funderburg, two ME-109s; Melvin T. Jackson, and Wendell O. Pruitt, one ME-109 each; Charles M. Bussey and William W. Green shared credit for destroying one ME-109.

LT Cornelius G. Rogers failed to return from the mission. Lee Rayford was wounded when his ship was badly damaged by a flak burst. The plane of *Drink* Hunter was literally shot from under him by flak. When he arrived at the field he called his crew chief and remarked, "Horse, how about putting a few patches on our gal?"

Throughout the month of June, 1944, the 332nd escorted bombers to targets in Italy, Southern France, and the Balkans. On June 22, the 332nd was assigned to make a low-flying mission over water to strafe the Aircasea-Pinerolo landing ground located a mile and a quarter west of Aircasea, Italy. This was considered to be one of the most important enemy supply lines. On the morning of the mission the group was briefed to fly very low over the Tyrrhenian Sea to Corsica. This was designed to avoid being picked up by enemy coastal radar equipment.

The mission was carried out as planned until the group reached a point about 30 miles from the coast of Corsica. At this point, LT Charles B. Johnson, a member of the 100th Squadron, who was flying No. 4 position in the third flight of planes, developed engine trouble. When the engine cut out, the plane, flying just above the water, almost immediately hit the water. He pulled his ship up a little, but it failed to catch up. This time, Johnson made a beautiful belly landing, but he forgot to open his canopy before hitting the water. The ship sank so rapidly, Johnson could not get out.

Shortly after Johnson went down, CPT Tresville made a slight turn. Because Tresville was flying so low, the rear flights were forced to pull up to avoid collision when he made the turn. The 100th led by CPT Tresville was flying beautiful formation and as yet no one in the lead squadron knew that Johnson had gone down.

As the fight skirted low over the water, it met with another accident. LT Earl Sherrod of Columbus, OH, permitted the belly tank of his plane to hit the water. He tried to pull up but the heavy tank pulled the plane down and caused the wing to hit the water.

Seeing that he could not get his ship up again, Sherrod quickly got out of the ship, walked out on the wing, pulled off his *chute* and inflated his dinghy. A few seconds later, the plane sank below the surface of the water.

On seeing Sherrod's plane hit the water, Samuel Jefferson, who was flying to the right of Sherrod, made a tight 180-degree turn and attempted to circle the helpless pilot. But in making the turn, a downward slip stream caught his ship and threw it into a flat spin. It crashed, exploded, and, in burning, left a huge cloud of black smoke.

Not long after LT Jefferson went in, the flight reached the coast of Europe, between Southern France and Italy, approximately 60 or 80 miles above the spot where the flight was to dive-bomb. Somehow, on the initial turn, CPT Tresville had turned east when he should have turned due north. Upon becoming aware he was flying off course Tresville made a 90 degree turn and flew up the coast of Italy, about ten miles off shore.

The 100th was still flying very low. This fact made those who flew the mission conclude that Tresville was still unaware that he had lost several men. They reasoned that if he had been aware of the accidents, he would have pulled up higher above the water. LT Spurgeon Ellington, who flew opposite Tresville on the mission, related that Tresville was glancing at his map when his plane slid off course and plunged into the water. On hitting the water, the plane was completely engulfed by a huge wave. After traveling under the water about 50 feet, it emerged above the water, pulled up above the water, slipped over a plane piloted by his wingman, LT Dempsey Morgan, and fell back into the water.

Immediately after Tresville went down, LT Woodrow Crockett, the deputy flight commander, took over. He continued the mission but, unable to find a break in the weather suitable to approach the target, he decided to return to the base.

When the Group returned to the base, it found four members, CPT Tresville, LT Samuel Jefferson, Charles B. Johnson, and Earl Sherrod were missing. However, LT Sherrod was rescued by a British coastal ship and returned to the base the same day.

The casualties suffered on the mission affected the morale of the members of the 322nd greatly. LT Carl E. Johnson of Charlottesville, VA, wrote to the wife of LT Charles B. Johnson:

"My dear Isabelle, I cannot express to you how hard it is for me to write you at this time. You know that there is much in life that we do not understand, the ways of man, the movement of the elements and strange ways of God. Yet he is my one and only hope now. "This week will live in my heart and memory in infamy. Your great and heavy loss has been mine. I cannot tell you how deeply hurt I am. He meant more to me than a brother. I would like to express my deepest and most sincere sympathy to you and your family at this hour and time in our lives.

"It will perhaps help some if I should say that he is not known to be lost. There is still a faint hope that he is still alive. But in the annals of war, time makes a record. However, you must believe that the War Department will continue to make every effort to ascertain his whereabouts. The entire squadron maintains a hope and prayer that all is well. Yet if such is to be his case to give life, remember that he gave it in the line of duty, faithful and obedient to his mission against odds of battle and elements. This is all I can say... Today a storm rages. It touches every little brook, every river, every nook. Yes, even the far distant edges of the sea. But tomorrow--the sun, isn't it bright."

In spite of the tragic mission and the great losses suffered by the 332nd there was no hesitancy on the part of its members to carry the battle to the enemy. On June 25, the Group was assigned to strafe some roads in northern Italy, which were known to be the enemy's main supply routes for troops fighting in sections further south. At the briefing, CPT Joseph Elsberry, who was to lead the flight of 12 planes on the mission, was told that there were a large number of enemy troops coming out of Yugoslavia to reinforce lines in northern Italy. The flight was briefed to fly to Ancona, a port city on the Adriatic Sea, and fly over the water up the coast of Yugoslavia until it reached its target zone in the Pola area.

After the briefing the flight took off and headed for Ancona. On reaching Ancona it skirted low over the Adriatic and turned north towards the Pola area. However, the wind was stronger than the pilots had contemplated, and without realizing it, they were blown off course into Trieste Harbor.

As the planes roared over the harbor the pilots spotted a vessel. At the briefing, the pilots were told that they would find no Allied vessels in the area so they were at liberty to shoot at any vessel sighted. At first sight, the vessel looked like a small American destroyer, but as the flight approached the ship, they saw that it was an enemy ship. By now, the ship's crew, realizing that they had been spotted, began to open up with all the ship's guns and hid the vessel beneath a thick layer of black smoke. LT Henry B. Scott, relating the battle that followed, said: "The flak was so thick when the destroyer opened up it looked like a blanket. It was throwing everything it had at us and, at 9 o'clock in the morning, it was so dark you'd think it was midnight."

CPT Elsberry led the attack with LT Henry B. Scott, Joe Lewis, and Charles Dunne following at close intervals. After they attacked and pulled up, Wendell Pruitt and Gwynne Pierson went in. CPT Pruitt made a direct hit that set the ship afire. LT Pierson followed and made another direct hit that caused the destroyer to blow up, scattering debris so high into the air that his plane was almost knocked out of the sky.

After the victory, the flight continued to its target area but on arrival sighted no troop movement. It circled the area for a while thinking maybe the enemy had camouflaged its movement. Unable to observe any activity, CPT Elsberry decided to return to the base.

On the way back to the base, LT Joe Lewis and Charles Dunne flew up and down the coast of Italy shooting at everything they saw. Suddenly they sighted 12 enemy planes in the distance, but before they could radio the rest of the flight, Lewis' plane was hit by a flak burst that damaged his instrument panel. He tried to fly back to the base, but was forced to land before reaching the field. LT Dunne circled the disabled ship until it landed, then after pin pointing its location returned to the base. Later a command car was sent out to pick up Lewis.

The news of the victory was received with great joy by the members of the 332nd. After the pictures of the battle with the destroyer were developed, CPT Pruitt was credited with making a direct hit on the ship, but LT Pierson was officially accredited as being responsible for the sinking of the ship. As a result of this victory, both pilots were awarded the Distinguished Flying Cross in a ceremony which took place later.

The following day, on June 26, the 332nd was assigned to provide penetration escort for bombers which were to strike in the Lake Balaton area. Although the mission was successfully carried out, the group lost two pilots. LT Andrew Maples Jr. was forced to bail out of his ship when it began to act up in the vicinity of Termoli. A second pilot, LT Maurice V. Esters, was forced to bail out in the vicinity of Vetachandrija. Neither of the pilots was ever seen or heard from again.

LT William Faulkner, a close friend of LT Maples, wrote to Mrs. Maples:

"My dear Mrs. Maples,

By now you must have received word that Andy is missing, and I feel you undoubtedly would like to know whether it is true, how it happened, and the possibilities of his coming out safely.

"On the morning of the mission, he was scheduled to lead a flight of four ships, one of which was mine. Because of engine trouble, I was unable to take off with him, but the rest went on.

"After about 15 minutes, he called that he had developed mechanical trouble and was returning to the base. Since he was close to base, his wingman did not return with him, but continued on with the formation.

"A few seconds later, he called in that he was bailing out and a fix (by radio) was taken on his position. Some of the men in the squadron following his formation saw his plane strike the water about five miles from shore in the midst of about a 100 small Italian fishing boats. None saw a parachute.

"All of this, of course, was on this side of the front line. When I learned that he had bailed out, I got two fellows to go with me over the water to look for him. For three hours, the limit of our plane's endurance, we searched a 50-mile radius about the point down on the water, but saw no rubber boat, no parachute, no oil slick. Since then, we've heard nothing.

"At first we thought he might have parachuted down near a fishing boat and he'd return in a couple of days. After four days passed, we considered maybe he was being cared for by a fisherman's family, which may still be the case. There is also the possibility that the fisherman was a Fascist and took him up to the German side or he may have become entangled with the plane and gone down with it."

The victories and tragedies of 332nd Fighter Group seemed to follow the pattern of a river tide. When the tide was in, the Group registered a series of victories. When the tide was out, the Group registered a series of tragedies. On June 28, the 332nd lost two pilots, LT Edward Laird of Brighton, Al, and Othel Dickson of San Francisco, CA. LT Laird died when his plane spun into the runway at Ramitelli while taking off on a routine mission. LT Dickson was killed when he attempted to slow roll his plane over the Ramitelli Airport. The death of Dickson was typical of many casualties suffered by young, eager pilots during the war. He had just arrived overseas and was taking transition training when he met death.

While a cadet at Tuskegee, he had won recognition as a promising combat pilot. He was acclaimed top aerial gunner of the Eastern Flying Command and third best cadet gunner of all Army Air Force cadets at a meet held at Eglin Field. These honors made him the envy of all cadets of his class and to maintain this recognition as a "hot pilot" he took unnecessary chances which finally led to his death.

Meantime, the ground battle had progressed. The defeat on the outskirts of Rome placed the Germans in a strategically vulnerable position. Unable to halt the Allied drive, the enemy retreated northward to the Pisa-Florence-Rimini line, along the Arno River. Here it dug in and prepared for an all out defensive campaign.

Top: Major Campbell and Airman before takeoff. Bottom left: Major William T. Mattison and Crew Chief. Bottom right: Pilots of the 332nd Fighter Group: LT Morgan, Woods, Nelson, CPT Turner, and LT. Lester.

Chapter 12
The 99th Joins the 332nd Fighter Group

The retreat of the German army to the Pisa-Rimini line set up a new problem for the Allied Mediterranean Air Force. *Operation Strangle* had cut the rail lines in central Italy on a route by route basis, but the complexity of the rail system in the Po Valley precluded any operations of similar scope in the north.

To cope with the new problem, a division in the assignments of the Strategic and Tactical Air Forces was instigated. The Tactical Air Force was assigned to cut and keep cut all lines supplying the German front. The Strategic Air Force was assigned to hit the marshaling yards in northern Italy, southern France, and Germany beyond the reach of the Tactical Air Force. The new plans also called for a large scale determined ground attack to force the enemy to use up, at a very fast rate, whatever supplies he had left. This was an operation designed to make the enemy "burn both ends against the middle."(1)

Meantime, new developments were taking place that affected the 332nd Fighter Group. The 332nd was transferred to a new base in Ramitelli, Italy. On July 3, 1944, the 99th, which had previously been attached to the 86th, joined the 332nd at Ramitelli.

The transfer of the 99th to the 332nd brought new problems. The members of the 99th were satisfied being attached to the 86th, though it was an all white outfit. When the 99th received orders to join the 332nd, many of the 99th's members felt that the War Department was reverting to segregation policies practiced in the States. The pilots of the 99th who had fought with tactical outfits ever since entering combat felt that color and race should not be used as a basis for transferring the unit to a strategic outfit. On June 1, 1944, the late CPT Edward Thomas of Chicago, wrote in his diary: "We received orders to join the 332nd Fighter Group today and everyone is unhappy."

COL Davis also met operational difficulties by the transfer of the 99th to the 332nd. A fighter group as a rule consists of three squadrons. When the 99th joined the 332nd plans had to be made for the extra personnel. This required a great deal of extra planning and reorganizing. Many of these changes brought dissatisfaction and unfavorable comments. MAJ George S. Roberts, relating the situation, said: "COL Davis and I saw the condition and immediately endeavored to eradicate it. When the actual combining of the units took place I was in the States. When I got back and actually saw the jealousy among the men, I felt ashamed of my race. The members of the 99th hated to lose their identity by being integrated into a larger unit. They imagined themselves with 50 or more missions flying as wingmen for men who had no combat experiences. On the other hand, the members of the 332nd feared the experience pilots of the 99th would be assigned to all the responsible positions. Anyway, we set about to integrate the units and it took us about three months to do it. We who tried to straighten out the matter, stuck our necks out and were scorned by members of the 99th. However, we finally got the men together as a team."

Not long after the 99th was integrated into the 332nd, CPT Mac Ross, of Dayton, OH, was killed. The death of Ross aggravated the strife between the members of the two organizations. Mac Ross, a rather reticent lad, was one of the most conscientious workers of the Group. Shortly after winning his wings at Tuskegee Army Air Field he was appointed as commanding officer of the newly activated 100th. He was relieved of his assignment before the Group embarked for combat and appointed as Group operation officer. When the 332nd entered combat, Mac Ross served as principal pilot of a C-78 which was used as the Group's business transport plane. This assignment kept him busy and as a result he received very little combat experience.

The job of Operation Officer required an experienced man. COL Davis realized that the success of the Group depended largely on effective operations. Therefore, he relieved Mac Ross of his assignment and appointed LT Alfonso W. Davis of Omaha, NE, a pilot with two years combat experience as operations officer. On July 11, shortly after being relieved of his assignment, Mac Ross was killed while taking transition training in one of the Group's newly acquired P-51 Mustangs. It was alleged that he was very despondent over being relieved as operation officer and his mind was not on flying when he flew his fatal mission.

The Group suffered another loss in the death of CPT Leon Roberts. At the time of his death, Roberts was operation officer of the 99th. He was the youngest member of the original 99th and had completed 116 missions. CPT Edward Thomas noted in his diary: "CPT Roberts crashed and was killed. He was operation officer for the 99th. A damn good pilot, too. Think altitude got him. He was about 30,000 feet, peeled away from formation, and wasn't seen again until his wrecked plane and remains were found."

In war, a combat unit cannot take time out to mourn the death of its members. Death is accepted as routine. This was true in the 332nd as in all other combat units. Though the 332nd lost two of its members on July 11, the next day it was in the air again. On July 12, the Group escorted B-17s of the 5th Bombardment Wing to southern France to bomb a marshalling yard. During the mission, pilots of the 332nd were attacked by a formation of enemy fighters. In the ensuing battle, CPT Joseph D. Elsberry of Langston, Oklahoma, shot down three of the enemy aircraft and Harold E. Sawyer of Columbus, Ohio, shot down one enemy plane.

LT Sawyer, a tall, handsome lad, was a proud pilot when he returned to the base. Relating how he scored his victory, he said: "The weather was so bad our group was the only group able to get through. Near the target we were jumped by 25 enemy aircraft. After three of the enemy aircraft had attempted to attack the bombers, LT *Bernie* Jefferson and I followed them down. I pulled up behind one of the enemy planes and got a burst into its tail section. Immediately the enemy plane began making split S's while diving towards the ground. I followed the enemy until I saw him crash."

In every combat outfit during the war there were certain men that stood out as having unusual amount of "guts". CPT Joseph D. Elsberry, without a doubt, was one of these men. This was the man that three unfortunate German pilots tried to do battle with on the morning of July 12, 1944.

When the flight took off, the weather in the immediate vicinity of the base was bad and the ceiling was less than 12,000 feet. On the take-off, CPT Elsberry, who was assigned to lead the Group, instructed the flight leaders of the 302nd and the 100th to take their squadrons up separately in small units over the overcast. Elsberry figured that it would be too risky to have so many planes flying on the same level in such bad weather. This, however, required a relatively long time and resulted in the squadrons being approximately 40 miles apart.

During the take-off, several members of the 100th got lost in the overcast and not being able to locate their flights returned to the base. One member of the 100th, LT George Rhodes, developed engine trouble and was forced to bail out of his plane in the vicinity of Rome. He was picked up by friendly natives and taken by motorcycle to an English mission where he stayed until he received transportation back to his base at Ramitelli. LT Woodrow Crockett, another member of the 100th, was unable to find his squadron. He joined up with a flight from the 301st and continued on the mission.

The 332nd reached the rendezvous point two minutes late, but fortunately, the bombers were five minutes late. This put the 332nd three minutes early. Finding that it was ahead of the bombers, the Group made a fast 360 degree turn and fell in over the formation and began to weave over the bombers. About three minutes later the formation crossed the coast of Southern France. Approximately ten minutes later, it sighted a group of aircraft at a distance at 10 o'clock high.

As the fast approaching planes closed in, they turned in the direction of the bombers and came in on the bombers in a trail formation. On recognizing the planes as enemy aircraft, Elsberry instructed his men to drop their auxiliary tanks and prepare for attack. When the Jerries saw the tanks fall from the planes, they turned away from the bombers. In turning, they left themselves exposed to attacks from the rear. Seizing this break, the pilots of the 332nd pulled in behind the enemy planes and started firing.

CPT Elsberry opened fire on one plane at long distance. Although his shots hit the target, he realized no results. Not long afterwards, an enemy aircraft turned in front of Elsberry's plane. Elsberry gave his plane the gun (throttle), overtook the FW-190, pulled up behind it in a good shooting range, lined up his sight and fired away. A mild explosion occurred midway the fuselage of the enemy plane as a few short bursts hit the mark. A few more bursts sent the enemy plane into a roll and finally it wandered off to the right and headed downward to earth.

Just after Elsberry finished destroying his first plane, a second enemy plane crossed in front of him, reefing at a 70-degree bank. Immediately, Elsberry rolled in on the enemy and fired 80 to 90 degrees around the turn. The enemy plane began to smoke and fell into a dive towards the ground.

A third enemy plane shot down across Elsberry's plane at about 45 degrees. Elsberry rolled his ship to the left, followed him and started firing. When he began firing, the enemy plane broke into split S's to evade Elsberry's guns. Elsberry followed him down to about 11,00 feet, then, looking back, noticed four planes of the 332nd following closely behind. Elsberry broke off his attack and joined his comrades. The enemy pilot, thinking he was still being followed, continued his dive. Just before reaching the ground, he attempted to pull his plane up, but the plane crashed into the ground.

The 332nd flew its first four squadron escort missions as protective cover for the 15th Air Force heavy bombers on July 15. On July 17, the 322nd provided penetration target cover and withdrawal for the 304th, which had been assigned to bomb the Avignon marshaling yard and railroad bridge. Approximately 19 enemy aircraft were seen in the target area. Three of the enemy planes attempted to intercept the bombers and were shot down. Credit for the victories was given to LT Robert H. Smith of Baltimore, MD; Luther Smith of Des Moines, IA; and Lawrence D. Wilkensof Los Angeles, CA. However, the most interesting story of the mission was told by LT Maceo Harris of Boston, MA. He related:

"My flight leader and I went down on two bogies and after they split S'd from me at about 18,000 feet, I pulled up all alone in a tight chandelle to the left. I tried to join another ship, but lost him when I peeled off on two more bogies which were after some bombers. The bogies, seeing me coming in on them, turned steeply to the left. Seeing some P-51s in the vicinity, I decided to stay with the bombers because they were now hitting the target. Flak was intense over the target. I kept an eye for the enemy planes that might come in when the bombers left the target area.

"Upon leaving the target, I joined another P-51 and tried to contact him by radio. My attempt was unsuccessful, so I peeled off alone on three bogies who were approaching a bomber from the rear. At first, they looked like P-51s so I rocked my wings, but as they swung left away from the bombers I could see they were enemy aircraft.

"I circled the bomber because the top turret gunner was firing on me. Finally he recognized me and stopped firing. I came in very close to survey the flak damage. The number two engine was feathered and the number one was smoking moderately. I received the bomber on Channel A, but he could not receive me because my signal strength was low.

"We used the sign language and I conveyed to the pilot the info that he should not crash land on the French coast since his number one engine looked as though it would hold out for a while. I used five fingers to show the fellows that we'd be in Corsica in 40 minutes and they understood perfectly. Their compass was out, so I put them on course and brought them into Black Top at Corsica. My radio was out so I buzzed the field several times to clear the runway. They landed O.K.--partly on their belly. Only the tail gunner was injured. They took him out on stretchers. The B-24 pilot was from San Francisco. He is in the 459th Bomber Group and his ship number is 129585. He and the co-pilot appreciated my friendly aid and kissed me several times after the manner of the French."

Early in the morning of July 18, the 332nd took off to escort bombers of the 5th to Memmingen airdrome. As the formation approached the Udine and Treviso areas, it was attacked by 30 or 35 ME-109s and FW-190s. In the encounter, the Group shot down 11 enemy planes and damaged another. The most successful pilot of the mission was LT Clarence D. Lester of Chicago, who was credited with three of the victories. The other members of the Group who gained victories were: LT Jack Holsclaw of Portland, OR, two; Lee Archer of New York, one; Roger Romine, one; Walter J. Palmer of New York City, one; Edward L. Toppins of San Francisco, one; Charles P. Bailey of Punta Gorda, FL, one; Hugh S. Warner of New York City, one; Andrew D. Turner of Washington, DC, severely damaged an enemy aircraft, but was unable to confirm his victory.

The 332nd victories, however, were not gained without losses. Three of its members, LT Oscar Hutton, Wellington G. Irving, and Gene C. Browne, failed to return to the base with the rest of the flight. LT Hutton was last seen flying northeast of Venice headed towards the base. LT Irving and Browne were lost in the Kempton area. However, LT Browne landed safely in enemy territory and was held as a prisoner of war until he was freed by the American ground forces at the end of the war.

LT Browne, a short, small built lad who looked more like a high school kid than a combat pilot, related: "I was chasing a ME-109 and had him lined up in my sights when another ME-109 stole up behind me and began to fire on me. LT Joseph Gomer tried to warn me that the ME was on my tail, but I was so eager to make the kill his warning didn't register in my excited brain. My plane was so badly damaged I was forced to crash land.

"I was sent to Ausburg where I stayed two days. Then I was sent to Frankfort. I stayed there three days. From Wetzlar, I was sent to Stala Luft 7-A near Munich. I was held there ten months. Here I also met several members of the Group, namely: LT Alfred Carroll, Sterling Penn, Griffin, Gould and many others."

The 332nd escorted B-24s of the 47th Heavy Bombardment Group to Friedrichshafen in the Munich area on July 20. On the morning of the mission, the sky was filled with heavy clouds and a heavy mist covered the air base. In spite of the weather, the flight took off with success. On arriving at the rendezvous point over the Udine area, northeast of Venice, it sighted the bombers being attacked by a squadron of ME-109s. Immediately the 332nd dropped its wing tanks and started after the Jerries. The enemy planes were split S-ing from about 33,000 feet down on the bombers. At the time, the 332nd was at 29,000 feet and the bombers were 27,000 feet.

Unable to intercept the enemy planes because of the enemy's advantage of altitude, orders were given to concentrate on the enemy planes as they started away from the bombers. One by one, the pilots of the 332nd fell in behind the Jerries as they left the bombers. Finally CPT Govan, the Group's leader, seeing the bombers were being left without protection, ordered the pilots to return and cover the bombers.

Just as the flight led by CPT Joseph Elsberry reached the bombers, a Jerry plane which had just completed its attack on the bombers, swept across Elsberry's plane. Elsberry immediately turned in behind the Jerry and at the same time called CPT Govan and reported he was following a "bogie" that he had lined up. After chasing the enemy a short distance, he opened up with a few short bursts that hit the enemy ship. The enemy plane burst into flames, rolled over and started straight down.

At this point, Elsberry looked back and saw another enemy aircraft between his plane and his wingman, Flight Officer Gould. Elsberry decided not to follow up the disabled plane because he was sure it was through. So, yanking back on his flaps to about 35 degrees and making a turn and a quarter, he fell in behind the Jerry. However, in the maneuver, he had lost considerable altitude and, forgetting to turn on his defroster, ice formed on his windshield. Although his vision was impaired, he was determined to make the kill. He chased the fleeing German for a distance, but before he could open fire, he found himself running into a mountain. Relating his mission, Elsberry said: "This was the last time I engaged an enemy aircraft at close range and my failure to register this victory meant the difference of being cited as an ace."

In the meantime, while Elsberry was having his engagement, LT Lee Archer attacked one enemy plane while LT Charles Bussey attacked another plane. The plane LT Bussey was following made a steep diving turn in front of Archer. Archer fell in behind it with Bussey following on his wing. They chased the enemy until he crashed into the side of a mountain after being hit by a volley from Archer's guns. However, Archer's victory could not be confirmed, and, as a result he lost the chance of being cited as an *ACE*.

When the victories pilots returned to the base after the mission, they were as happy as a group of kids on Christmas morning. LT Toppins was as much elated over his third victory as was LT Langdon Johnson over his first victory. Perhaps the happiest pilot of the Group was CPT Armour McDaniel, who had gained his first victory. McDaniel, a stocky built Virginian, who appeared older than he actually was, related how he scored his victory. "After Elsberry attacked the leader, I attacked the leader's wingman. I couldn't catch him somehow, but glancing downward, I saw another enemy pilot trying to make his getaway. I dived on him, dropping from 27,000 feet to 10,000 feet. When I fired on him, he dove through some clouds and crashed against a mountain. I pulled up just in time to miss crashing into the mountains."

LT Andrew D. Marshall hit by flak in a strafing mission over Greece.

Chapter 13
Striking Oil

While the 332nd was engaged in the Italian campaign, it was also taking part in the Allied Air Force offensive against German oil supply centers. As far back as 1940, the Royal Air Force struck specific oil targets in the Ruhr and elsewhere. However, it was not until the Allies had driven the Nazis out of Africa and gained limited air superiority that the smashing of Nazi refineries and synthetic plants could assume its rightful priority.

The principal German oil centers in Germany were the synthetic plants in the three main coal regions of Silesia, the Ruhr, and around Leipzig. Various coke ovens, gas works, and L. T. carbonization units added a little to the German supply, but by far the greater percentage of Germany's natural sources were scattered throughout the German occupied countries.

It was realized at the beginning of the oil offensive that an effective reduction of Nazi output called for neutralization of the Luftwaffe to permit a concentrated assault. There had been successful missions against the Nazi oil centers before 1944, notably the attacks on Ploesti oil fields in August, 1943, but the Nazi fighter strength was so strong that such missions could not be carried out without great losses. The Allied Air Force, therefore, concentrated on the demolition of aircraft plants, ballbearing factories, and related industrial installations. By May 1944, this objective had been so effectively carried out that the Luftwaffe could not seriously interfere with Allied operations. Nazi single engine fighter production had been cut by more than eighty percent. The Germans also had lost thousands of their combat planes and many of their best pilots.

The field was now clear for an all out offensive against the Nazi oil centers. The Royal Air Force was assigned to attack petroleum plants in the Ruhr. Central, northern, and eastern Germany, western Czechoslovakia, and western Poland was the area designated for the operation of the Eighth Air Force. The Fifteenth Air Force was to strike at Southern Poland, Austria, Hungary, Italy, Southern France, and the important Balkan countries including Rumania.

The Germans made frantic efforts to reduce the vulnerability of their oil centers. For example, at Ploesti the oil region covered an area of 19 square miles which was densely crowded with refineries and pumping stations interconnected with a railway network. In May 1944, when the oil offensive began, heavy bombers went into action against the refineries. The Germans counteracted with active and passive defenses. Their fighters were sent up in force, with Rumanian and Nazi pilots flying fast ME-109s. Anti-aircraft guns, including four-barreled 20MM, 88MM, 105MM, and 128MM, threw up protective curtains of intense and accurate flak.

Fighter interception and ack-ack were not the sole extent of Hitler's defense preparations. Beginning with the last allied raid in May 1944, the whole Ploesti area was screened by a thick swirling artificial fog. Approximately 2,000 smoke generators were employed and functioned every time Allied airmen came over.

Another defensive feature at Ploesti was the concentration of high blast walls. These walls were built around every installation at each refinery. Nothing quite like them had been seen. Some were six feet thick at the bottom and tapered upward to a height of 20 feet, where they were two feet wide. Even a series of three pumps had a complete square of blast walls around it, and from the air the whole arrangement had the weird, dazzled, painted appearance of a gigantic, one-story, multi-room roofless house.

In July 1944, the 15th air Force struck at oil targets and related installations 17 days of the month. The 332nd shared in many of these missions. On July 4, it struck at Pitesti, Romania. On July 8, it was over Vienna. It escorted bombers to the Ploesti oil field on July 13, and took part in a fighter sweep to Vienna on July 16. The Group was credited with two victories on July 16, as a result of the guns of LT Alfonso W. Davis and LT William W. Green.

LT Eugene D. Smith, a member of the flight, related: "We were returning from the target at 28,000 feet when our flight leader, CPT *Preflight* Davis, spotted a lone B-24 bomber in trouble headed for home about 10,000 feet below us. He called the flight and said he would take the bomber home. Almost immediately after his call he rolled over into a vertical dive followed by LT Green and myself. I didn't see immediately what he was after, but in a short order I saw two Macchi 202s starting a dive behind the bomber.

"CPT Davis gave chase and lined up the rear fighter, but he was traveling so fast he overshot it. He continued on to line up the first enemy plane. LT Green took the last one and I followed CPT Davis, who opened fire and the Macchi started smoking. However, CPT Davis was traveling so fast he was overtaking the enemy so he broke rather than overshoot. The enemy plane, however, had been badly damaged and went into the ground in a diving turn. Meantime, Green got his plane and we returned home with two aircraft to our credit."

On July 21, the 332nd furnished withdrawal escort for bombers in the 15th's first mission to the Brux oil refineries in Bohemia. The next day the Group escorted bombers to the famous Ploesti oil fields. The mission was carried out as planned, but, returning from Ploesti, CPT Walker, the flight leader, was shot down over central Yugoslavia. Like many pilots on similar missions, he made the mistake of flying over a small town which looked harmless. Walker's plane was so severely damaged that he was forced to bail out. He landed in friendly territory and was taken to an underground hideout by some friendly peasants. A few days later, he was joined by a crew of nine white airmen who also had been shot down.

After remaining in the hideout a short while, CPT Walker and the other airmen started out together for their respective bases. They covered 300 miles, over rough and mountainous country, wading through snow and water, before they received transportation to their bases.

CPT William Faulkner of Nashville, TN, led an escort mission to Linz, Austria, on July 25, 1944. On the way to the target, the bomber formation was intercepted by a group of 30 enemy aircraft. In the battle that followed, two members of the 332nd, LT Alfred Carroll of Washington, DC, and Sterling Penn of New York were shot down. A third member of the Group, LT John Leahr was not so unfortunate, but he was a very disappointed pilot when he returned to the base. During the battle he was able to get two enemy planes lined up in his sights, only to be disappointed by the failure of his guns to fire. When he arrived at the base he found his gun heater had been improperly connected, causing his guns to freeze.

CPT Joseph Elsberry related, "the flight was about 15 minutes from the rendezvous point when an estimated 12 enemy aircraft were sighted making vapor tracks about 11 o'clock high from the leading squadron. CPT Jackson called in that a group of bogies had been sighted. At the time we were weaving above our bombers, Faulkner, who was leading an element of the 301st, immediately began spreading out and as a result was drifting away from the bombers. I called *Bubble Blue leader*, the code name for the 301st, to come back over the bombers, that we were getting too far away from them. By this time the Jerries were close enough to be seen clearly and instead of 12 there were approximately 40 of those S.O.Bs. LT Faulkner's element, however, was caught out by itself and the enemy diving from about 5,000 feet above knocked Carroll's plane's tail off with a 20MM shell and continued on in to attack the bombers. My flight was still weaving about the bombers. The enemy then began lobbing 20MM shells into Faulkner's flight of eight planes. This forced Faulkner to turn back towards the Jerries in order to protect himself.

"In the meantime, Faulkner began calling for me to join in the battle. There was so much confusion over the radio at the time that I couldn't hear Faulkner; and, instead of helping the distressed pilots, I began to order them back into formation over the bombers. In the meantime, LT Sterling Penn was shot down.

"I consider this my luckiest mission. Several times when I saw Jerry dodging back and forward above me, I felt like leaving my position with the bombers and going after them. But on the way back home I found out how lucky I was in not following my temptations. When I tried to drop my wing tanks I found them to be stuck. I tried to fire my guns with the hope of shaking them off, but to my surprise my guns wouldn't fire. CPT Cisco also told me later that there were two enemy planes following an aircraft that had dodged across me. If I had followed him I probably would have run into a lot of trouble, especially with no guns and two heavy wing tanks to hold me down."

LT Harold Sawyer also vividly described the mission: "We were covering B-17s. After we intercepted the bombers each flight was assigned to cover certain portions of the bombers. Faulkner was leading the Group. He also led a flight of four. We saw a group of MEs and decided that as long as they didn't attack us we wouldn't leave the bombers. They came in at 4 o'clock to 6 o'clock putting them behind us with altitude. As we climbed up they came down. About 30 jumped our flight of eight. I saw smoke rings over my canopy. We got into a tight luffberry. A little later I noticed one enemy aircraft coming in at 3 o'clock. Meantime, LT Leahr called in that his guns were frozen. The enemy broke into us and immediately I started firing. I fed him a lot of rounds that damaged his ship severely and sent it into a spin. I couldn't follow him down as other enemy planes were still up there. A few minutes later, CPT Faulkner called that the other bandits had gone. We then caught up with the bombers and continued on our mission."

The 332nd escorted heavy bombers to Vienna on July 26. Just before reaching the target the Group encountered a group of enemy aircraft which was sent up to intercept the bombers. The encounter that followed brought the 332nd more victories. LT Weldon Groves of Edwardsville, KS, and William W. Green of Staunton, VA, shared one victory; Freddie F. Hutchins of Donaldsonville, GA, Leonard M. Jackson of Forth Worth, TX, and Roger Romine of Oakland, CA, each received a victory.

CPT Jackson, in relating the mission, said: "We were escorting B-24s to Vienna when I got my second Jerry plane. CPT Edward Toppins was leading my flight when we sighted three FW-90s ten minutes before reaching the target. CPT Toppins turned into them and fired, but they were out of range for effective shooting. Toppins damaged one on the tail of the formation, then we reassembled in battle formation. Just then we sighted three ME-109s above us making vapor trails. We were at 28,000 feet. We climbed as the ME-109s started a gradual climbing turn. I knew CPT Toppins was not going to let them get away, so I prepared for a good fight.

"Their ships decreased in rate of climb and we gained altitude on them while climbing to 36,000 feet. We closed in on them, and I had an enjoyable feeling for it was the first time I had seen Jerry when he couldn't run away or out climb me. When our ships closed in at 500 yards the Germans decided to quit the trail. The MEs pointed their noses toward the earth and began to dive. We reeled around and began to follow them. I gave a short burst at 150 yards, then we broke through a layer of stratus clouds at 20,000 feet. When we broke out of the clouds I saw a Jerry spinning and burning. As I pulled away I saw a second ME going down in flames, the victim of CPT Toppins' guns."

On the way back to the base after the mission the plane of LT Charles S. Jackson Jr. of Chicago, developed engine trouble while he was flying over Yugoslavia. Before bailing out of his ship, Jackson radioed his element leader, CPT Lowell C. Steward of Los Angeles, and reported that he could not keep his ship in the air. Cpt Stewart circled Jackson until he landed safely, then returned to the base and reported the incident.

The next day, the 332nd led by MAJ Lee Rayford escorted bombers to Budapest to bomb the Mannifred Wiess Armonenof works. Over Lake Balaton the Group encountered a group of ME-109s. It was successful in destroying eight of the enemy aircraft. CPT Edward C. Gleed and LT Alfred M. Gorham each were credited with two enemy aircraft. CPT Claude B. Govan, LT Felix J. Kirkpatrick, Richard W. Hall and Leonard M. Jackson were each credited with one victory.

The all out offensive against Nazi oil producing centers reached its climax during the month of July 1944. By the end of the month almost all of the important refineries and synthetic oil plants had been attacked by the Allied Air Force. Conservative estimates showed that the loss of output of the plants attacked between May and July was in excess of 400,000,000 gallons. By August, German gasoline production had been reduced to 20% of its minimum requirement.

The persistent bombing of Germany's oil industries had a costly effect on her war machine. The Luftwaffe was left without sufficient gasoline for training pilots. Panzer divisions were left stranded for lack of fuel, and civilian use of gas and oil was virtually prohibited.

In spite of the success of the Oil Campaign, Allied leaders were aware of the ingenuity of the Germans and were determined to keep the fuel centers from recovering. Allied intelligence was also aware of Albert Speer, Hitler's Minister of Production determination to restore the oil production centers. With an army of 35,000 laborers, mostly foreigners, he had restored bombed plants at a faster rate than thought possible. In addition, the Germans were dispersing and camouflaging plants to make them difficult to be located.

During the month of September, the 15th dispatched formations of 100 to 150 bombers that dropped 287 tons of bombs on Blechhammer North, 235 tons on Oswieicin, 272 tons on Odertal, and 253 tons on oil centers in Budapest. On all of these missions, the 332nd was sent as escort.

During the month of October, the three Strategic Air Forces dropped 12,592 tons of bombs on oil centers. Although bad weather hampered the 15th operations, it had a good month. It attacked the synthetic plants at Brux which had been out of operation for four months; bombed Blechammer South on October 7 and 12; Blechhammer North and Odertal on October 14; and on October 7, 11, and 16 attacked the three major oil centers in Austria.(1) The 332nd was called upon to provide escort for bombers on all of these missions.

Wherever the 15th bombers flew, the 332nd was there to protect the bombers. On October 16, COL Davis led a formation of 64 planes that escorted the 5th Bomb Wing to the Brux oil refineries. On the 17th, the 332nd flew two missions. The first, led by CPT Arnold Cisco, escorted B-17s to Bucharest. The second, led by CPT Melvin Jackson, escorted the 5th Bomb Wing to Blechhammer South. On October 21, MAJ Roberts led a formation of 64 planes that escorted bombers of the 5th to Brux, while LT Eagleson led a flight that escorted a Catalina on a rescue mission.

Despite all the concentration and continuous bombings of enemy oil centers, Allied oil experts estimated that Germany's oil production had increased in October seven points or to 30% of the pre-campaign level. They concluded that the Germans were drawing their petroleum supply mainly from benzoil plants and from what remained of her crude oil plants.

The benzol plants were very difficult to locate because they were small and hidden in complex urban centers. It was recommended that more reconnaissance planes be sent out to locate the plants. The 332nd was frequently called upon for escort duty, not only as escort for reconnaissance aircraft, but for special missions and air-sea rescue missions.

The 15th carried out its greatest attacks on German oil production centers on November 5 and 6, 1944. Approximately 500 bombers dropped 1,000 tons of bombs on the crude oil refinery at Floridsdorf on November 5, and 400 tons on Moosbierbaum the following day. On the same day, MAJ Lee Rayford led a formation of 55 aircraft that escorted the 5th Bomb Wing to Floridsdorf. The next day, CPT Melvin Jackson, with a formation of 70 aircraft, escorted the 5th Bomb Wing to the Moosbierbaum Oil Refinery in Vienna.

There was no let-up in the hunt and attacks on German oil centers until the war ended. The 332nd was kept busy. For example, on December 20, MAJ William Campbell with 50 planes escorted the 5th to Brux, and LT Charles Dunne with six planes escorted a P-38 on a photo reconnaissance mission to Prague. On the 22nd., LT G. Gray with six aircraft escorted a P-38 photo reconnaissance mission to Ingolstadt, and the following day, MAJ Andrew *Jug* Turner with five planes escorted a P-38 on a reconnaissance mission to the Praha, Czechoslovakia area. Then LT Jack Holsclaw led the Group's last mission of the year with a formation of 60 aircraft that escorted the 304th to attack targets at Muldorf and Landshut.(2)

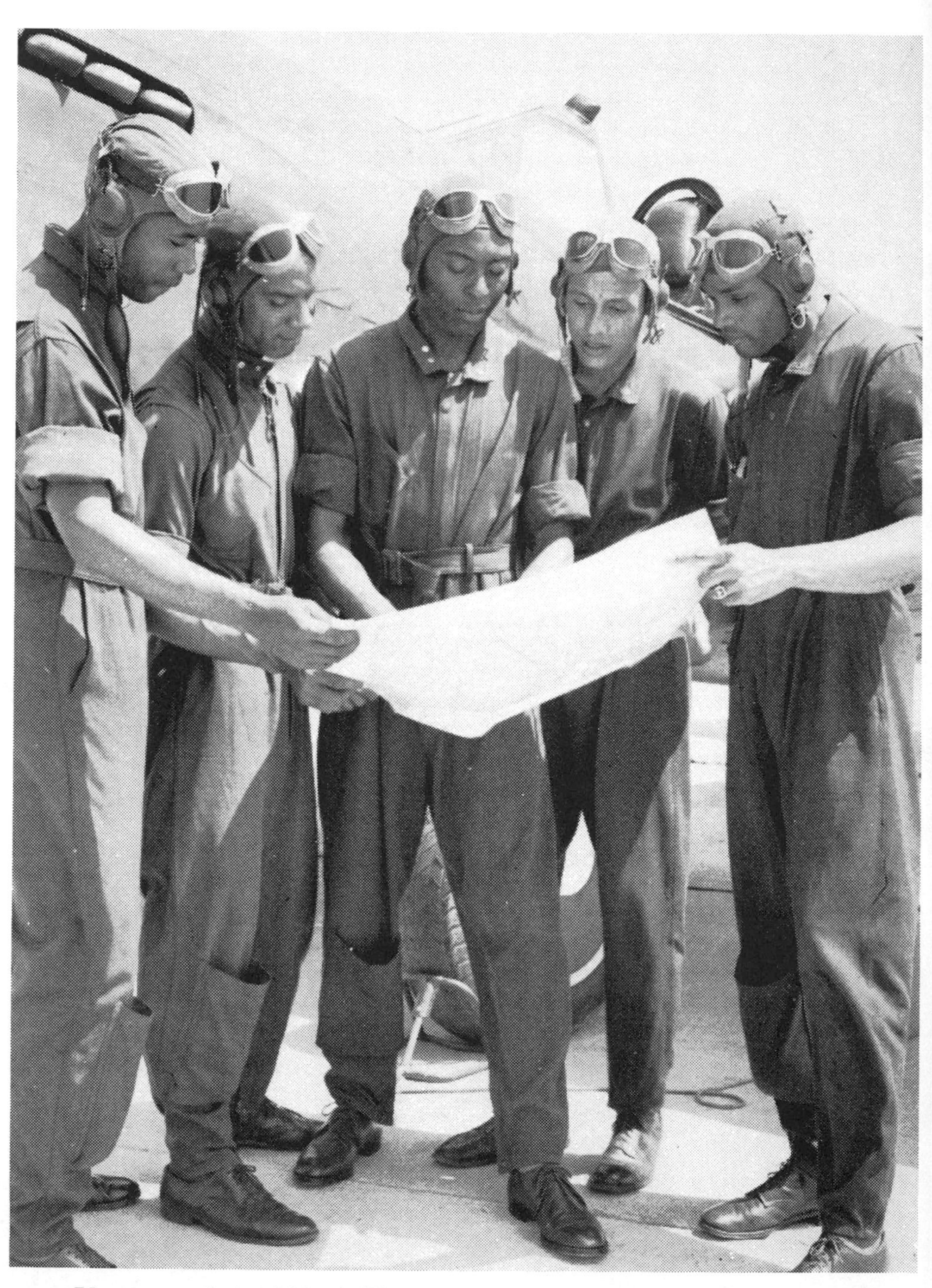

Veterans of the 332nd: Haywood, Mosely, Robinson, Faulkner and Weathers.

Standing L-R: Spencer, Punch, Houston, Custis, Perry, Ed Thomas, Payne. Squatting L-R: Blackwell, M. Rodgors, Gene Brown, Hardy, Gaines.

Chapter 14
The Invasion of Southern France

Early on the morning of June 6, 1944, more than 4,000 Allied vessels steamed across the English Channel. A few hours later, Allied troops successfully landed on the coast of France and quickly pushed inland. Within five days, the Allies had landed 16 divisions on Normandy. By June 12, they controlled 80 miles of the Normandy coast. So rapid was its advance that by June 18 the Americans had swept across the Contentin Peninsula, established a corridor seven miles wide, and continued their advance to the outskirts of Cherbourg.

At Cherbourg, the Allies met with stiff resistance. For five days, the Germans fought off the American assaults. Finally, on July 25, the enemy was forced to retreat.

"When Cherbourg and the Contentin Peninsula had been won, the Americans turned south, broke through the German left flank at Avranches, drove into Brittany, swung around and outflanked Paris from the south. Two weeks of savage fighting had won Saint Lo on July 18, opening the way to a breach of German lines."(1) Meanwhile, the British Second Army fighting at Caen had also met success in its campaign against the Germans. The town of Caen was the pivot of the German Seventh Army in Normandy and the German Fifteenth Army along the channel coast to the east. The Germans, therefore, put up great resistance to hold Caen.

Even as the Germans were fighting desperately to withdraw their battered armies from Normandy and trying to pull out of Paris, they were threatened with a new invasion from the south. As early as April 1943, Allied leaders began to make plans for an invasion landing in southern France. This invasion termed Anvil was to be a diversionary attack to be coordinated with the main invasion in northern France. It was believed that an invasion in southern France would open up ports outside of Normandy which could be used for the shipment of troops, supplies and equipment for the re-enforcement of divisions already fighting in France.

D-Day for the invasion of southern France was initially set for May 1944. This decision was based on the assumption that by May the Allied forces in Italy would be driving on the Pisa-Rimini line. It was reasoned that from this point troops could be withdrawn to make up the invasion forces. However, the Germans put up such a stiff resistance that a stalemate developed in the Italian campaign.

The Allies, unable to break the stalemate despite all-out efforts, decided to put off the invasion until conditions in the Italian campaign improved. However, General Eisenhower informed MAG Thomas T. Handy, Chief of the War Department Operational Division that he had to have either Bordeaux or Marseille before he could hope to deploy all available forces in the minimum of time.(2)

On July 2, 1944, the Combined Chiefs of Staffs directed General Sir Henry Wilson, the Commanding General of the Mediterranean Expedition Forces to launch the invasion of Southern France as early as possible and to make every effort to meet a target date of August 15, 1944. Meantime, the planning for the invasion continued.(3)

The final invasion plan provided that assault troops would go ashore east of Toulon and over the beaches between Cavalaire Bay and Cape Roux. The main assault would be three divisions of the US Seventh Army, seven divisions of French troops would go ashore on and after D-Day plus 3, and drive on Toulon and Marseille. When these cities were captured, the American and French troops both under the command of LTG Alexander Patch would move toward Lyon and Vichy with the objective of linking with the Eisenhower forces.

Soon after General Wilson received the directive, the Allied Air Forces went into action in preparation for the invasion. The 15th bombers and fighters kept the coast of France under continuous bombardment. In the weeks before D-Day, medium bombers knocked out all the enemy airdromes in the Po Valley; and with the help of fighters, they carried out concentrated assaults on gun positions, radar stations and the Italian Riviera.

The 15th carried out six important missions in preparation for the Anvil invasion, all of its units participating in these invasions; but the 52nd and the 332nd carried the brunt of the work.(4) On July 5, 1944, 319 B-24s and 228 B-17s were dispatched and successfully bombed Montpelier and Beziers yards and sub pens and installations at Toulon. On the 5th, COL Davis with flight leaders CPT Rayford, LT Foreman, Williams, D. (Dudley) Watson, Sheppard, Haywood, Kirkpatrick, Pullam, Ellington, Holsclaw, and Palmer led a formation of 52 planes that covered the 304th Bomb Wing. On the 11th, B-24s saturated Toulon Harbor with 200 tons of bombs. CPT Melvin Jackson led the 332nd formation that provided cover for the 47th Bomb Wing that bombed submarine docks at Toulon. On July 12, 315 B-24 dropped 760 tons of bombs on yards at Miramas and Nimes while 106 bombers attacked bridges at Theoule sur Mer and across the Var River. The 332nd covered the 49th Bomb Wing on this mission. Then on July 17, 162 B-24 were sent to attack rail bridges at Arles and Tarascon and bridges and yards at Avignon. The 332nd, led again by CPT Melvin Jackson, covered the 304th Bomb Wing that hit targets in the Avignon area. A week later, 145 B-24 dropped 30,700 x 20 frag bombs on airfields at Chanoines and Valence. However, on this day, the 332nd led by Rayford was dispatched to provide penetration, target cover and withdrawal for the 47th Bomb Wing that bombed the Mannfred-Weiss Armament Works in Budapest, Hungary. The final special mission of the 15th in the pre-invasion campaign came on August 2 which resulted in rail cuts being made between Lyon and the mouth of the Rhone River. The 332nd, for the third time led by CPT Jackson, covered the 5th that attacked the Ponsin Oil Storage and the Portes Les Valence marshalling yard.(5)

On August 6, 1944, CPT Howard Baugh led a formation of 72 P51 that covered the 55th on the mission to knock out railroad bridges at Avignon. The pilots observed a heavy smoke screen and flak over the target. During the attack, one B-24 was seen hit and destroyed by a flak burst. However, five chutes were observed to open soon after the hit. On the second mission, a flight of eight aircraft led by CPT Jackson provided escort, landing and withdrawal for a B-25 to Yugoslavia.

The most important pre-invasion assaults on Southern France for the 332nd came on August 12 and 14, 1944. On August 12, a flight led by CPT Alton F. Ballard of Pasadena, CA, escorted bombers to Marseilles Harbor to knock out coastal radar stations. Over the target the flight encountered dense and concentrated flak and machine gun fire. The radar stations were destroyed but in fulfilling its mission the

332nd lost several pilots: LT Alexander Jefferson, Langdon E. Johnson, Robert H. Daniels, Richard Macon, and Joseph Gordon.

CPT Woodrow Crockett, a tall, slender quiet youth, was one of the pilots who flew on the mission. He related, "We went into the target at about 15,000 feet. Then we began our dive on the target which was in Marseilles harbor. As we dived for the target, the Germans began firing on us. Just as I approached the target, my wingman, LT Langdon Johnson, crossed in front of my plane and shot out to sea on deck. Instead of pulling his plane up, he allowed his plane to hit the water. It hit, skipped two or three times, tearing off the plane's right wing, and sank below the water. I didn't see Johnson get out of the plane."

CPT Marion Rodger, a rather modest Detroit youngster, vividly described the August 12 mission: "It was my first strafing mission. We went into the target area at 15,000 feet. I was number four-man in the lead flight. Our leader brought us over the target, which were radar stations near the coast. Then he rolled his plane over on its back and went down on the target in almost a vertical dive. I had been nervous up to this time but when I started my dive it all left me. Now my attention was centered on bringing my ship out of the dive because it had gathered tremendous speed and the ground was rushing towards me. I still hadn't located the target. I was slightly to the right of the ship ahead of me and I saw him veer off to the right rather sharply, but I followed the other ships ahead of me while still pushing my own ship through a near split S.

"As my ship leveled out about 50 feet above the ground, I had glimpse of something that looked very much like the picture we had seen of radar stations. I had a chance to hold my trigger down for two seconds, then zigzagged out to sea on the deck.

"When I returned to the base, I found out that our flight of eight had lost two ships, one of them being the ship that had veered to my right. I had no vision of the flak. I had thought there was none over the target area."

There are some pilots who survived combat by sheer luck or miracles. Such a pilot was LT Richard D. Macon from Birmingham, AL. A tall, slender, soft-spoken lad, he stated that an act of God saved his life. While participating in the mission of August 12, he ran into a cloud of flak that sliced his aileron controls and flipped his plane over on its back. The plane burst into flames and as he fought to straighten it out, he lost consciousness. While unconscious, his body evidently slumped against the control stick and pushed it forward. This threw the plane into an outside loop and tossed him out of the plane. In some inexplicable manner, the parachute opened in time to partly break his fall and he landed in a ploughed field.

When he regained consciousness, 45 minutes later, he found himself looking at three Germans. He was taken into a field hospital where he was found to have a broken shoulder and a broken neck. The doctors set his shoulder but the invasion of the area by Allied troops forced the Germans to move before they could set Macon's neck.

Two weeks later, Macon arrived in Sagan, Silesia, where he was placed in a hospital staffed by French personnel. Here his neck was x-rayed and set. Before he could recuperate from his injuries, the Russians forced the Germans to move out of Sagan. Macon, with his neck in a cast, was taken to Nurnberg. The advance of the American troops on Nurnberg forced the Germans again to move, this time to Moosburg. Here Macon was held until he was liberated by the American Army.

In spite of the losses suffered by the 332nd on August 12, the mission was considered successful. All of the enemy's radar stations were knocked out as planned. The next day, August 13, MAJ Mattison, with flight leaders Curtis, Palmer, Briggs of the 100th Squadron; Thomas, Lawson, Campbell of the 99th; Elsberry, Downs, Sawyer, Cisco of the 301st; and Pruitt, Spencer, Kirkpatrick, and Smith led a formation of 67 aircraft on a mission as escort, cover and withdrawal for B-24s of the 304th Bomb wing that bombed railroad bridges at Avignon. This mission was uneventful, but the mission the next day, August 14 was more exciting.

On the 14th, a formation of 64 planes led by CPT Pullam was dispatched to strafe targets at Cape Blac, Camerat, Dapet, and La Ciotat. Two squadrons of the formation were assigned to conduct a fighter sweep of targets in the Toulon area.

When the fighters reached the target area, the 99th and 100th conducted the fighter sweep while pilots of the 301st and 302nd strafed radar stations. LT Weathers, Williams, and Smith hit the base of a station and saw it crumble. Another flight attacked an antenna and saw it topple over, and a third flight silenced a gun position and strafed a building from which enemy gunners were firing.

Over the Toulon area, a large force of enemy aircraft were sighted. Four of the enemy aircraft, 2MM 109's and 2FW 190's attacked the last flight of the formation, coming in from five o'clock high. The story as to what happened was told by LT George Rhodes, who was credited with a victory.

George Rhodes, a Brooklyn youth, was a quiet, unassuming fellow. He loved to fly and throughout his tour of duty, he exhibited courage that won the respect of those who flew with him. On one mission over Rome, he was forced to bail out of his ship. Returning from another mission he was forced to crash land. A few seconds after he stepped out of his ship, it burst into flames and exploded, scattering its wreckage over the runway.

Relating how he scored his victory on August 14, Rhodes said, "About 40 enemy fighters came up after us. Two made passes at us as we were flying formation. I spotted them coming down and I turned to intercept one of them. I fell on his tail and followed him down from 15,000 feet to 4,000 feet. I closed in on him and shot his right wing off and he went into a downward spin. At this time, I heard a lot of bombs dropping and suddenly realized I was all alone, so I pulled up to 25,000 feet and headed back for the base. During the battle, I lost my wingman, LT Robert O'Neill. He landed in the hills of France, joined a group of partisans, and fought with them. Later, he returned to the base and was immediately sent back to the States."

On August 15, the large invasion force landed on the coast of southern France and swept swiftly inland. The 332nd was kept busy during the invasion. CPT Alfonso Davis with flight leaders LT Manning, Thomas, Campbell, and Dart of the 99th; LT Crockett, Morgan, Pullam, Steward of the 100th; Dunne, Downs, and Cisco of the 301st; D. Watson, Suggs, Wilkins and Spencer, led a formation of 71 P-51s that provided escort, cover, and withdrawal for the 55th that attacked target at Point St. Esprit, Donzere, Le Teil, Bourg and St. Andeal.

The invasion forces moved so swiftly that by the end of the first week, the two most important Nazi-held cities, Toulon and Marseilles, were isolated. On August 28, both cities were occupied. Meantime, the advance up the Rhone Valley was being pushed at full speed. On September 3, the 36th Division reached Lyon. Eight days later, on September 11, the French First Armored Division took Dijon and in the vicinity of Somberon, linked up with the right flank of General Patton's Third Army. Four days later, the southern France invasion campaign was completed when General Wilson transferred the operation to General Eisenhower.

Meantime, while the Allied ground troops were advancing in southern France, the 332nd, together with other fighter and bomber groups, were kept busy. They struck targets to the north of the retreating Germans. They harassed the enemy ground troops, destroyed bridges, marshalling yards, supply dumps and communication centers. The 332nd main efforts, however, were directed towards enemy oil production centers, airdromes and marshalling yards in Germany and her satellite countries. For example, on August 16, LT Pruitt led a formation that escorted the 55th Bomb Wing on a mission to destroy the Ober Raderach Chemical Works in Germany. On August 17, 18 and 19, the 332nd escorted bombers to bomb the Ploesti Oil Refineries and on the 20th, CPT Gleed led a formation that escorted the 5th Bomb wing to attack the Oswiecim Oil Refinery.

The assignments of the 332nd varied; it provided escort landing and withdrawal for six C-47s from Brindisi to Yugoslavia on August 22. It escorted the 47th Bomb Wing to attack the Miskoic marshalling yard in Hungary on August 28 and escorted the 5th the following day to bomb the Bohumin and Privoser Oil Refineries and the Morvaska Main marshalling yard. During this mission, LT Emile C. Clifton, a member of the 99th, was forced to bail out of this plane over Yugoslavia when it developed engine trouble. Fortunately, he landed safely and was able to return to the base.

Chapter 15
Striking Around The Clock

At the same time the 15th Air Force was participating in the Southern France campaign, it was performing other important assignments. It was aiding the partisans in Yugoslavia, flying shuttle missions to Prussia, hammering axis ports in Greece, pounding the Brenner Pass, through which materials were flowing to the stubborn German armies in Italy, participating in the oil blitz, and aiding the Russians by striking Balkan communications and strong points.

The multiple assignments of the 15th Air Force kept the 332nd active continuously. On August 6, while some flights of the 332nd escorted bombers to southern France, other flights of the Group escorted bombers to Budapest. During one of these missions to Budapest, enemy fighters attempted to intercept the bombers before they could drop their bombs. However, the Germans were driven off by fighters of the 332nd, and LT Carl E. Johnson, of Charlottesville, VA, was credited with shooting down one ME-109.

The 332nd furnished escort for the 15th bombers on August 19, in an attack on the Ploesti oil refineries. On August 23, it escorted bombers to Austria to knock out an enemy airfield which stood in the way of the Russian advance towards Berlin. Just before the formation reached the target area it was intercepted by a flight of seven ME-109s. In the ensuing battle two members of the 332nd, LT Luke Weathers and William Hill, shot down one of the enemy aircraft.

The next day, the 332nd returned to Austria. Again it encountered enemy fighters and added three more enemy planes to its list of victories. The victorious pilots were: John F. Briggs of St. Louis, MO; William H. Thomas of Los Angeles, CA; and Charles E. McGee of Champaign, IL.

On August 25, the 332nd escorted bombers of the 5th over Germany. The mission, however, was carried out without resistance by enemy fighters. The next day, the 332nd escorted B-17s and B-24s to the heavily fortified Ploesti oil fields. Although the mission was successfully carried out, LT Henry A. Wise of Cheriton, Virginia, was forced to bail out of his ship which developed engine trouble on his return to the base.

The fact that LT Wise volunteered to fight the Nazi is sufficient evidence of his fighting blood. In July, 1942, when the Allied's chance of winning the war looked very dim, Wise volunteered for the Army. In spite of the numerous stories of Allied losses in the air, he applied for cadet training. He was sent to Tuskegee Army Air Field where he earned his wings. In July 1944, he joined the 99th and flew 13 missions over France, Romania, Germany, and Italy before he was forced to parachute from his plane.

When the men returned to Tuskegee after the war, most of the evenings were spent "shooting the breeze" about combat experiences. Wise had his story to tell, and this is how he related what happened to him after bailing out of his ship: "Returning from the mission to Ploesti on August 26, I was forced to bail out of my plane at 9,000 feet. Immediately after hitting the ground, I was captured by a group of Bulgarian soldiers and taken to prison. I was placed in a local guard house at the nearest enemy camp. I stayed there only two days, but in those two days, I almost starved because I couldn't eat the type of food they gave me.

"On the third day, I was placed under a guard and carried across country to a prisoner of war camp. The camp was a lone stone building constructed to hold about 100 men. But already there were about 300 men at the camp, all Allied fliers, British, North Africans, Yugoslavians, Australians, Poles, and Americans. Officers and enlisted men were all encamped together, dirty, hungry, and definitely in need of clothing because all of it had been taken when they were captured.

"I was the only Negro in the camp. However, I got along as well as the others and no difference was shown by the Bulgarians or my fellow prisoners. We shared the same beds, same foods, and same difficulties. We suffered no physical punishment such as torture and beatings. Three weeks after I arrived at the prison camp, the Russians moved into the country and forced the Bulgarians to sign peace terms. We were freed and immediately sent across the border."

Blechhammer, Germany, was the target for the 15th bombers on August 27. After escorting the bombers over the target, the 332nd attacked an enemy airfield while en route to the base. The enemy was caught by complete surprise and 22 planes were destroyed on the ground. On the mission, LT Emile C. Clifton, a member of the 99th, was forced to bail out of his plane over Yugoslavia when it developed engine trouble. However, he later returned to the base.

CPT Alfonso Davis led the 332nd in an attack on an enemy airfield at Grozwarden, Romania, on August 30. The 332nd was credited with 83 enemy aircraft destroyed on the ground. These planes had been evacuated previously from other enemy fields because of the rapid advance of the Russians. CPT Davis, happy because of his success, said, "They were parked like sitting ducks and all we had to do was line up our sights and shoot." LT Roger Romine remarked, "When we went over the airport, we looked like a cloud of grasshoppers swarming over a field of ripened wheat."

On August 31, the 332nd escorted B-17s of the 5th to Bucharest, Romania. The mission was to evacuate American pilots and crewmen who had been shot down. This mission was particularly risky because the enemy still held the heavily defended territory. However, the mission was carried out with great success.

The flight leaders of a combat unit play a very important part in making a mission successful. The amount of confidence the men have in their leaders often determines the outcome of a battle or mission. On this mission to Bucharest on August 31, the 332nd was led by such a man as LT Lawrence B. Jefferson of Grand Rapids, MI. "Bernie," as he was known by his comrades, had gained national fame before volunteering for pilot training. While attending Northwestern University he won recognition as a football star. When the war started, this broad shouldered, unassuming lad volunteered for cadet training and was sent to Tuskegee. After gaining his wings he joined the 332nd and was sent overseas with the Group in January, 1944. Though never a colorful nor eager pilot, Bernie's stability under pressure made him a valuable man to the Group.

Wherever German armies fought, Allied airmen carried the battle to them. On September 1, the 332nd was over Pitesti, Romania. The next day, it flew missions to Belgrade and Neskrs. Four days later one flight of the Group attacked a bridge south of Budapest, while another flight escorted bombers to Romania. On September 8, the

332nd had another big day. It was credited with 36 of a total of 76 aircraft destroyed on airdromes in Yugoslavia by the 15th Air Force.

The 332nd took time out from combat on September 10 to reward four of its outstanding pilots. The four heroes were led to the runway by a parade of Group members. Here the four heroes were called to the front by the Group's adjutant to receive decorations for bravery in combat. The first to be decorated was COL Davis, Jr. It was an extra special occasion for him because the decorating officer was his father, BG Davis Sr. As the proud father stood before his son one sensed the personal delight that the occasion meant for him. He paused a while as if he was to shake hands with the hero and then as a General and a proud father remarked, "I am very proud of you." Shortly afterwards, the citation was read:

Benjamin O. Davis Jr., COL, Air Corps.,

For: Extraordinary achievement--in an aerial flight as pilot of a P-47 type aircraft, led his Group on a penetration escort attack on industrial targets in the Munich area June 9, 1944. The bomber formation was attacked by more than 100 enemy fighters near Udine, Italy. Faced with the problem of protecting the large bomber formation with the comparatively few fighters under his control, COL Davis so skillfully disposed his Squadron that in spite of the large number of enemy fighters, the bomber formation suffered only a few losses.

CPT Elsberry was the next pilot to be decorated. His citation read:

For extraordinary achievement in aerial flight against the enemy in the North African and Mediterranean Theatres of operations, CPT Elsberry consistently aided in the success of combat operations. Against heavy opposition from both aggressive and persistent fighter aircraft and intense, heavy, and accurate enemy anti-aircraft fire, he has battled his way to his targets, defeating the enemy in the air, and destroying his vital installations on the ground. Through severe and adverse weather condition over treacherous mountain territory, he continuously surmounted overwhelming obstacles for successful completion of his assigned mission to attack and destroy the enemy.

The third hero to be decorated was LT Clarence D. Lester. His citation read:

On July 18, 1944, as a pilot of a P-51 type aircraft, Lt. Lester participated in an escort mission for heavy bombers attack on enemy installations in Germany. En route to the target, the bomber formation was attacked by approximately 300 enemy aircraft, but despite the superiority in numbers of hostile ships, Lt. Lester immediately engaged the hostile force in the ensuing engagement, displaying outstanding aggressiveness and combat proficiency. With complete disregard for his personal safety, he destroyed three enemy fighters, thus materially aiding in preventing the enemy from making concentrated attacks on the bombers.

The last to be decorated was LT Holsclaw:

On July 15, 1944, in an aerial flight as pilot of a P-51 type aircraft, Lt. Holsclaw led his flight as escort to heavy bombers attacking enemy installations in Germany. Despite severe and adverse weather conditions, he brought his flight through to engage an enemy force of approximately 300 enemy fighters. With complete disregard for his personal safety, Lt. Holsclaw with an outstanding display of aggressiveness and combat proficiency, destroyed two enemy fighters and forced the remainder to break off their organized attacks.

After the ceremony, the decorated pilots were congratulated by several high officials of the Air Force. Among those present to congratulate the heroes were LTG Ira C. Eaker, Commanding General of the Mediterranean Allied air Force; MAG Nathan P. Twining, Commanding General of the 15th; and BG Dean C. Strother, Commanding General of the 306 Fighter Wing, of the 15th Air Force.

The Legion of Merit was presented COL Davis by General Eaker a week later. This citation created by Congress on July 20, 1942, is "Awarded to personnel of the Army of the United States and of the Armed Forces of friendly foreign nations, who have distinguished themselves by exceptional meritorious conduct in the performance of outstanding service."

In September 1944, news reached the 332nd that the Germans were perfecting a jet plane that was capable of flying much faster than the conventional planes. On September 12, 1944, CPT Edward Thomas noted in his diary: "All bomber Wings bombed airdromes and aircraft factories in the Munich area. We escorted the B-17 Wing and hit targets at Lechfeld, Germany. Reports say that the new German jet propelled plane can climb vertically and has a level flight speed in excess of 500 M.P.H."

Heavy bombers escorted by the 332nd struck Blechhammer, 150 miles east of Berlin, on September 13. Over the target, LT Wilbur F. Long's plane was hit by flak. His canopy was destroyed and his cooling system was severely damaged. Long was forced to crash land in Hungary. Upon landing he was captured by a group of civilians and turned over to the Germans.

The 332nd suffered another loss on September 22, when F/O Willette was shot down while on a mission to Blechhammer. The following day it was on escort to Regensburg. The Germans fought desperately to stave off defeat, but the continuous, around-the-clock attacks by the Allied Air Force had telling effect on the German war machine.

Top left: Captain Edward Toppins. Top right: Major Andrew D. *Jug* Turner. Bottom left: BG B.O. Davis, Sr. decorates B.O. Davis, Jr., Joseph Elsberry, Jack Hokar, and Clarence Lester. Bottom right: BG Davis, Sr. decorating pilots of the 332nd.

Chapter 16
The Battle of Greece

In the latter part of September 1944, the weather in Italy was very bad. In fact, the weather was so bad that the whole 15th Air Force was grounded. For eight days a steady downpour kept the Allied air Forces in Italy on the ground. But in some respect it gave the battle-tired pilots the much needed rest they had so valiantly earned.

In the meantime the German control in the Balkans was collapsing under the pressure of the Russian drive. The rapid sweep of the Russians through southeastern Romania threatened the Nazi control of the Balkans. Alarmed over their failure to halt the Russian drive, the Germans began evacuating several garrisons.

Near the end of September, British forces invaded Greece which also was in the process of being evacuated by the Germans. A week later, on October 4, the weather broke in Italy and the 15th was sent into action against German Forces in Greece. The 332nd as a component of the 15th was assigned to strike enemy airfields in and around Athens which were threatening the British campaign.

CPT Erwin Lawrence led the Group on a mission to Greece on October 4, to knock out an enemy airfield. Just before reaching the target area each of the four squadrons that comprised the Group was assigned different targets. These targets were enemy airfields at Eleusis, Totoi, Kolamoi, and Megara.

After the Group had split up to attack the different targets, CPT Lawrence instructed CPT Edward Thomas, the leader of the second element of the 99th, that upon arrival over a target he was to furnish cover for the attacking flight.

Immediately upon reaching the enemy field, CPT Lawrence fell into a dive with his flight following in string formation at close intervals. But the Germans were prepared for the attack and opened up with all their guns. Just as CPT Lawrence was about to pull out of his dive his ship was hit by a barrage of machine gun fire. Shortly afterwards the ship spun into the ground. CPT Thomas then took command of the squadron and continued the attack until the field was a mass of wreckage. Meantime CPT Freddie Hutchins of Donaldsonville, GA, a member of one of the other flights, had been knocked out of the sky at Megara. Freddie, a small, round-faced, jovial lad, related: "We were just approaching the target and I was flying with LT Wilson on his first mission. As we approached the target run I told Wilson to start his run. However, it being Wilson's first mission, he became excited and was slow in opening up his plane. This retarded my run and cut down my speed. As I pulled up off the target I was hit by a volley of flak. I looked to my right and saw that my right wing tip was torn off completely. Looking back I noticed my tail assembly was practically shot apart. At this time flak was hitting my ship pretty consistently. I scooted down into my seat to get protection of the armored plates, but just at this time a volley of flak burst through the floor of my plane and struck my leg.

"I called CPT Dudley Watson, our flight leader, and told him that my plane had been damaged badly and that I couldn't stay up long. At the same time by some miracle I continued to gain altitude. I headed for friendly territory or rather a clear spot.

"I managed to clear a mountain peak by a few inches and then my plane began to lose altitude. I was now headed for some trees in a valley. I had very little control, but managed to miss the trees and crash landed into a small opening.

"I was knocked unconscious by the shock of the crash. When I came to, I found myself sitting at my controls with the engine of my plane lying several hundred feet away. My goggles were smashed on my forehead. My head was aching and my legs felt like they were broken. However, after examining my legs I found that they were all right except a deep flak wound on my left leg."I was pulled out of my ship by some Greeks who arrived at my plane shortly after it crashed. I walked a few steps, then passed out. Some men raised me up and began to walk me around. Then they put me on a donkey and walked the donkey around in a circle. They did this to restore my respiration. However, my back hurt me so badly I begged them to stop. I was then carried to a doctor who rubbed my back with some home made olive oil, strapped me up and put me to bed. The fleas had a wonderful time off me that night. The next day I decided I couldn't live through another such night so I made plans to leave though I was still in pain. I was taken into the city. There I gained transportation back to the base."

Meanwhile, LT Kenneth Williams had also run into trouble on the mission. While strafing an enemy airfield his plane was hit. He managed to gain sufficient altitude to bail out of his ship safely, but only to find his canopy was damaged and wouldn't open. He made a forced landing but was captured and taken to prison at an airfield. Later he was taken to the Luftwaffe headquarters in Athens and interrogated. Here he was joined by two more of his friends, LT Joseph Lewis and Carroll S. Woods, who were shot down two days after he went down.

"Six days after I was shot down the three of us, a British pilot, and a British navigator, were placed aboard an evacuation train with a company of German soldiers. We traveled two weeks before arriving in Skopia, Yugoslavia. On the train I noticed the German soldiers were arrogant. They believed that a new weapon they had would change the tide of the war.

"At Skopia we learned that the Russians had cut the rails to the north. We were placed on a JU-52 and flown to northern Yugoslavia. We were held at a local prison to await a train to Budapest. "The next morning we boarded a fast express to Budapest. At Budapest we were placed in solitary confinement for five days. During the time we were in solitary confinement the Russians attacked Budapest. Several bombs struck near the jail damaging it considerably, breaking windows and shaking the building.

"On the fifth day we were sent to Frankfurt on the Main. We stayed here five days then were carried to Wetzlar, a city about 70 miles from Frankfurt. This was the first prison camp where we were allowed a little freedom and received Red Cross parcels. We stayed here three days; then on November 28, 1944, were sent to a permanent prison camp at Baleric, Germany. We hiked about 100 miles to Spremberg before boarding a train. We ended up in Moosburg. This camp was overcrowded because the Germans were attempting to crowd prisoners from all the surrounding camps into this one camp. We were finally liberated on April 29, 1945 by the 3rd Army."

The mission to Athens on October 4 was not altogether unsuccessful. LT George R. Rhodes, George Gray, Shelby E. Westbrook and CPT Edward Thomas scored victories. CPT Henry B. Perry of

Thomasville, GA, and LT Milton Hayes of Los Angeles, were jointly credited with a victory. CPT Samuel Curtis' plane was damaged by flak, but he was able to nurse it back to the base and land safely.

On October 6, the 332nd returned to the Athens area to complete its assignment. The success of the mission can best be told by the citation of the late CPT Thomas, who was awarded the Distinguished Flying Cross by the War Department. The citation reads:

Edward M. Thomas:

For extraordinary achievement in aerial flight P-51 type aircraft in the Mediterranean theatre of operation. Lt. Thomas' outstanding courage, aggressiveness and leadership enabled the formation to inflict damage upon a heavily defended airdrome in Athens, Greece. On October 6, 1944, Lt. Thomas flew as a flight leader in a formation of 14 aircraft assigned to strafe the heavily defended Totoi Airdrome. Upon arrival in the target area, Lt. Thomas observed the position of the airdrome and the surrounding terrain. Upon approach of the formation towards the airfield, Lt. Thomas' aircraft was hit by flak. Disregarding all thought of personal safety, Lt. Thomas courageously pressed his attack to deck level and destroyed two enemy aircraft and damaged another. Due to his exact judgment, skill and aggressiveness, a total of 11 enemy aircraft was destroyed or damaged without loss to any aircraft of his section. Flying over treacherous, mountainous terrain, under adverse weather condition and against severe enemy opposition, Lt. Thomas flew 81 hazardous combat missions for a total of 205 combat hours. His outstanding courage, judgement, unquestionable devotion to duty and professional skill have reflected great credit upon himself and the Armed Forces of the United States of America.

Although the mission was successfully carried out, the Group lost two members, LT Carroll Woods and LT Joe Lewis. Both were shot down by flak bursts and were taken as prisoner by the Germans. They were held as prisoners at Moosburg, until General Patton's 3rd Army released all prisoners at the camp on April 29, 1945.

The Athens area was attacked by the 332nd for the third time on October 7. On this mission, LT Andrew D. Marshall, of Bristol, VA, was forced to crash land his plane when it developed engine trouble while flying over the target area. Fortunately, however, he landed among some partisan Greeks who hid him from the Germans.

A week later, on October 14, after the British forces had consolidated the territory they had taken from the Germans, Marshall, astride a white horse at the head of a procession of several hundred peasants, rode from the hills of Megara into town. Here he received transportation back to the 332nd base. But fate was against Marshall. In December 1944, he failed to return from a mission to Germany.

Chapter 17
The Balkan Campaign

While the British were driving the Germans out of Greece, other Allied forces were charging hard against Germans in the Balkans. In Yugoslavia, an army of partisans under Marshal Tito was driving toward the Danube to meet the swift moving Russians. In Albania and Czechoslovakia, small specialized forces were harassing the Germans.

Meantime, the Russians had met with great success. Russia's northern armies had repulsed German counter attacks in the Baltic, along the border of east Prussia, around Warsaw and Krakow. On August 20, an offensive launched from Jassay and Bessaralin had forced the Rumanian government to turn against the Germans and their ally, Hungary, on August 23.

The Germans were angered by the action of the Rumanian government. It retaliated by attacking Bucharest with her Air Force elements stationed at the Bucharest/Otopeni airfield and German troops stationed at the near-by Baneasa barracks were alerted to crush the Rumanians.

In response to an appeal from the Rumanian General Staff, the Mediterranean Strategic Air Force dispatched 114 bombers that dropped 205 tons of bombs on the barracks, military stores and gun positions at Baneasa, while 115 B-24s dropped 258 tons of bombs on the airfield. On August 26, CPT Lawrence, with flight leaders, Campbell, Dart, Crockett, Morgan, Briggs, Curtis, Govan, Foreman, Ballard, Haywood, McGee, and Smith, led a formation of 66 planes that escorted the 304th that bombed the Baneasa barracks.

The success of the Russian troops in the Balkans deprived Germany of all her allies except Hungary and opened the southern flank of Germany to the threat of an invasion through Hungary and Czechoslovakia. The continued drive by the Russian armies through Romania pushed west to the Iron Gate leading into Yugoslavia, where for more than a year partisan guerrillas under Marshal Tito had kept 125,000 enemy troops occupied. With the British advancing in Greece, the Germans could only hope to retain control of escape routes through Yugoslavia.

The 332nd played varied roles in the Balkan campaign. It escorted bombers of the 15th to strike targets throughout the Balkans. It aided partisan forces in Yugoslavia and Czechoslovakia and dive bombed and strafed Nazi strong points that hindered the advance of the Russian Army.

LT Hubron Blackwell, a small youngster from Baltimore, liked to relate two of his most memorable missions. One was to attack a heavily defended installation in the Balkans. When the Group started its attack, the Germans began throwing up such heavy flak and gun fire that he was sure that he would not survive. When he started his run of attack, with guns blazing away, "I visioned my mother crying in grief when notified of my death."

Blackwell's other most memorable mission was more amusing. It involved CPT Melvin Jackson, a quiet, modest youngster from Warrenton, VA, who appeared to have had no fear of death. From all outward appearances, including skin color, Cpt Jackson could be mistakenly considered a 'white' American. Those who did not know him would suspect that he was a member of any of the fighter groups, except the 332nd. No doubt, he was second to none as a combat fighter pilot, and would have been chosen as a leader by any group. He, perhaps, led as many missions as anyone and was respected by all of his comrades as being one of the best leaders in the group.

One day, COL Davis was directed to dispatch a mission to Yugoslavia to escort a plane loaded with American pilots and crewmen, who had been shot down. The mission was particularly risky because the enemy still held the country. There were hundreds of hidden air strips constructed in the forest and valleys by the partisans and they were so camouflaged that they were difficult to locate. To reach a particular air strip, it was necessary to navigate accurately. A slight error in navigation meant a mission was lost.

The Colonel briefed the pilots before the mission was launched. When the briefing was completed, he turned to Jackson, and said sternly, "CPT Jackson, you will complete this mission successfully."(1)

Blackwell related that en route, he was amazed to see CPT Jackson navigate so accurately. He was hitting every check point on time. When the formation reached Lake Balaton, one of the last check points, a voice came over the radio. "Do any of you fellows see the lake." Immediately, CPT Hutchins replied: "Damn Jack, I was just admiring your navigation, now I find you don't know where the hell you are. I know it is a little hazy, but if you cock the wings of your plane, you'll see we are flying over the lake. Now this mission will be completed successfully or, tomorrow, little Freddie will be your squadron commander." Blackwell related that when they arrived at the designated air strip, nothing was moving, they could see no one, then it was a beautiful sight to see a plane burst from under its camouflage, speed down the runway and take off. They surrounded the aircraft and escorted it home safely.

On October 7, 1944, the 332nd strafed targets in Yugoslavia which were causing the partisan forces under Marshal Tito considerable trouble. While strafing, LT Robert H. Wiggins' plane was damaged by a flak burst. Wiggins attempted to fly his ship back to the base, but while en route was forced to land on the Isle of Vis.

After repairing his ship, Wiggins took off again for his base. En route, he picked up a crippled C-47 and escorted it to the Foggia area. Then, after seeing the bomber land safely, he struck out for home. Somehow, he wandered off course and crashed into the Adriatic Sea. Later his body was recovered and buried in the American Cemetery in Bari.

On October 11, the 332nd, led by LT George E. Gray escorted bombers to Hungary. En route to the base, the Group attacked an enemy airfield and destroyed a locomotive and several oil tankers. The next day, the 322nd lost LT Walter L. McCreary. While on an escort mission to Hungary, his plane was hit by a flak burst. He bailed out of his ship in the Lake Balaton area. Upon hitting the ground, he was pounced upon by a mob of angry civilians. Fortunately, he was rescued by a group of German soldiers who broke up the mob and led McCreary off to prison.

As the Germans retreated before the Russian Army, McCreary was moved from prison to prison. He finally ended up in Moosburg, where he was held a prisoner until the American 3rd Army captured the city and released all the prisoners.

Nine enemy aircraft were shot down and 26 were destroyed on the ground during an attack on Blechhammer, by the 332nd on October 12, 1944. LT Lee Archer was top scorer with three victories, CPT

Wendell Pruitt was credited with two victories, and CPT Milton R. Brooks was credited with one enemy aircraft. LT William W. Green, Luther H. Smith Jr., and Roger Romine also were credited with a victory each.

One Saturday afternoon, I ventured down to the Operation Office at Tuskegee to talk with CPT Baugh and Archer. Sometime during the course of our conversation we began to talk about Pruitt, who had been killed a short time before in a plane accident near the field. This led to the mission of October 12, on which Archer and Pruitt scored victories. This is how Archer related what happened on that day.

"The mission was bomber escort to Blechhammer. On this mission the 302nd was the low squadron and we flew to the extreme right of the other squadrons. We had just crossed Lake Balaton when I spied a group of enemy aircraft at two o'clock on the tree top. These planes were just beginning to take off from an enemy airfield.

"I called in the bandits and Pruitt was the first to pick up my message. He reeled off from the formation, rolled his plane over, and dived for the enemy aircraft. I followed close behind him as he made two passes at a HE-111.

"A short while later, I looked down and saw about 12 enemy ships taking off on the runway. They seemed to have been escort planes for the HE-111 that was just beginning to take off from the runway. I called in that 12 enemy aircraft were taking off below. somehow I didn't receive any answer from the rest of the Group. I later learned that LT Smith and Green had engaged the enemy ships and were successful in shooting two of them down.

"In the meantime, Pruitt made a third pass at the enemy plane and as he pulled up I notice the enemy plane smoking. I followed Pruitt's victim and gave him a long burst and the ship disintegrated in the air. However, I couldn't claim this victory because Pruitt had damaged the plane so badly that it was only a matter of seconds before it would have spun into the ground.

"Just after we had destroyed our first plane, Pruitt noticed the formation of enemy planes coming directly toward us. Instead of avoiding them, Pruitt flew directly into the formation with his guns blazing away.

"We made a tight turn and fell in behind three enemy aircraft. After getting within shooting distance I fired a couple of short bursts at one of the planes. My fire was accurate and I tore off the wing of the plane. It tumbled down to earth. Then I slid my plane down below Pruitt's plane which was now on the tail of a second plane. However, before I could fire, Pruitt's shots hit the target. The plane burst into flame.

"At this time a ME-109 came in from the left and slid in behind Pruitt, who was now on tail of a third enemy plane. I immediately pulled up behind him and gave a few short bursts, the plane exploded, throwing the pilot out of the cockpit and then fell to the ground.

"Pruitt was still chasing the plane he had lined up. However, on his third burst, his guns jammed. As I pulled up beside him I could see him fiddling with his controls trying to start his guns. Seeing that Pruitt wasn't getting any results, I told him to move over and let a man shoot who could shoot. He pulled over and I eased my plane into his position. I gave the enemy plane a long burst. Then the ME-109 went into a dive for a runway that I observed below. Seemingly, he had decided to land. I gave him another long burst and he crashed on the runway. The German ground crew opened up with all their guns. Lights were blinking at me from all directions. For a few seconds, I had to dodge flak and small arm fire that burst all around my ship. But I was lucky and managed to wiggle out."

On Sunday afternoon, a group of us held a little "bull session" in LT William Thomas' room down at Tuskegee. Thomas, a slender Californian, loved music. He had records of most of the outstanding orchestras and a selection of classical records that ranked among the best on the post. Naturally, this was an ideal place to lounge around and pass away Sundays which were usually dull and un-exciting. Anyway, the conversation got around to experiences in combat.

I asked Thomas if he had known Westmoreland. "Yes, Westmoreland was one of my best friends," said Thomas. "He was a very likable fellow, rather quiet and unassuming. You know, he was the nephew of White, Secretary of the NAACP.

"Anyway, a few weeks before I arrived in Naples, he had bailed out of a P-39 Airacobra and hurt his leg. When I arrived overseas he was using a crutch to get around. But he recovered and resumed flying.

"On October 12, 1944, the Group was assigned to escort heavy and medium bombers to Blechhammer, about 125 miles from Berlin. Before we took off we agreed we would strike anything we saw on the way back to the base.

"During the mission Dubois Ross had trouble with his plane so LT Lee Archer had to follow Ross until his plane straightened out. Near Lake Balaton we spotted an enemy airfield and we decided to strafe it. Before this, however, we made passes at a shipping port and hit a ship. Anyway, on the enemy airfield, there was a high building. As we made our run in to attack the field, we noticed small lights blinking at us, so we knew the enemy was firing on us from the building.

"When the time came for me to make my run I headed towards the building with all my guns blazing away. As I pulled up I noticed I was almost out of ammunition, so I decided to take pictures of the action. I decided to circle the field and make my run in from the entrance pattern. As I reached the entrance point I noticed one of our ships going into the field with all of its guns blazing away at the building. As the ship pulled up I noticed smoke coming from it. Then the plane rocked and headed into the field. I watched the plane as it hit the field, skipped a good distance, and turned over on its back tearing off its wings.

"After making my second pass, I pulled up and circled over the wrecked plane, but I didn't see Westmoreland get out of the plane. Then I rejoined my formation.

"Immediately after rejoining the formation CPT Melvin Jackson, our flight leader, decided to brave the enemy guns and go down to take pictures of the wreckage. He went down in spite of the heavy enemy machine gun fire and took pictures of the wreckage. Then he rejoined us and we returned to the base. The pictures were immediately developed, but they revealed nothing to give us hope that Westmoreland had come out of the accident all right."

While CPT Jackson's flight was attacking the enemy airfield, another flight led by CPT Pruitt was strafing a railroad junction. They shot up box cars, locomotives, and buildings. Two pilots of the flight, LT Luther "Preacher" Smith and William W. "Chubby" Green, hit a large barn filled with explosives. The barn blew up so suddenly that the debris damaged the planes in flight.

Not long after Smith went down, Green noticed the temperature of his gauge rising fast. He called his flight leader, but received no response. CPT Jackson later related that he heard Green say that he was forced to bail out of his ship. He was picked up by a group of partisans and taken to a divisional headquarters of Marshal Tito's army. The following day he volunteered to help a British supply mission drop supplies to Tito's men scattered in various sections of the country. (At the end of the war, LT Green received the order of the Partisan Star III class. This award by the government of Yugoslavia was presented to him by COL Davis Jr. in a colorful review ceremony at Godman Field.) Four days later, some Russian pilots landed at the base where Green was staying and they agreed to fly Green back to his base in Naples.

While Green and Smith were having their troubles, LT Archer was also having trouble. Archer's plane had been hit in the propeller when he followed his last victim down too close to the enemy airfield. CPT Pruitt decided to escort him to the base. While flying over a high mountain range on the return to the base, Archer's plane began to act up. He managed to keep his plane in the air and continued on to the Isle of Vis.

On landing, CPT Pruitt gassed up and shortly afterwards took off for his home base. LT Archer immediately set about to replace the propeller of his ship with another he took from a junked plane. He returned to his home base the following day.

The 332nd was again sent to Blechhammer on October 14. On this mission LT Ruall Bell was shot down ten miles northeast of Zagreb. During the battle he was wounded. He bailed out of his ship and on landing he was picked up by British solders and sent to an American hospital in Bari, Italy.

On the same day, CPT Alfonso Davis led an escort mission to Southeastern Germany to strike the Odestal Oil Works. During the attack, LT Robert J. Friend of Washington, DC, strafed an oil barge, pouring 50 calibre bullets into its hull. The bullets found their mark and all of a sudden the barge belched a huge mushroom shaped flame just as Friend's ship reached her. The flames completely engulfed the diving plane. Luckily, Friend managed to pull his plane through the flames without damage.

CPT Armour McDaniel sprayed another barge and was also fortunate in clearing the deck just as a tremendous blast ripped the barge to pieces. The force of the blast was so great that all of McDaniel's wing guns were ripped out of his ship. In spite of the severe damage he was able to nurse his plane back to the base in Naples.

COL Davis led the 332nd on a mission to Austria on October 15, and the following day CPT Melvin Jackson led a mission to Upper Silesia. On October 20 the Group escorted bombers to Brux. Three days later it was over Regensburg and Yugoslavia. Most of these missions were uneventful; but on the mission to Yugoslavia, the Group lost LT Robert C. Chandler of Allegan, MI, and Shelby F. Westbrook of Toledo, OH, both shot down by enemy ack-ack guns.

Throughout the last two months of 1944, the 15th Air Force, cooperating with the swiftly moving Russians, struck targets throughout the Balkans and Europe. On November 7, the 332nd escorted bombers to southeastern Austria. En route to the base after completing its mission the Group flew high over a slight overcast. In the vicinity of Reuhenfels, Austria, CPT William Faulkner peeled off from his formation and headed straight downward.

Upon receiving the news that Faulkner had broken formation, the flight leader made a quick turn and at the same time ordered his men to watch for the missing pilot. They combed the area and went down as close to the ground as safety permitted, but no trace of Faulkner's ship could be found. The flight then assembled and continued its journey back to the base. No information as to what happened to CPT Faulkner was ever obtained. It is the belief of those who flew with him on the fatal mission that his oxygen tank failed him. Evidently, high altitude and the lack of sufficient oxygen (hypoxia) caused him to pass out.

The 332nd added another victorious page to its record on November 16 as a result of the success of CPT Luke Weathers, a native of Memphis, TN. After escorting bombers to the Munich area, together with CPT Melvin Jackson and Louis Purnell, Weathers was detailed to escort a crippled bomber to its base. Over northern Italy, eight enemy planes were sighted at 2 o'clock high. However, when first sighted, they were too far off to be identified as enemy aircraft. As the planes approached, they were recognized as ME-109 and preparations were made for the attack. CPT Weathers, who was flying escort on the side of the approaching aircraft, peeled off and met the enemy planes in a head on attack. When they got within shooting distance, he opened fire. After a few burst from his guns one of the enemy planes fell into a dive and began to split S down to earth. At this time, Weathers began to notice little red balls sailing past his canopy. He glanced around in time to notice that a second enemy aircraft was on his tail and was blazing away, trying desperately to make the kill.

Meantime, CPT Jackson and Purnell had noticed the enemy aircraft following Weathers. They fell in behind the enemy plane, but before they could open fire, they were attacked from the rear by the remaining enemy planes. They were forced to go into a dive to avoid being shot down.

Instead of the enemy pilots pressing their attacks on Jackson and Purnell, they decided to concentrate on Weathers. They circled him and closed in from all directions as their comrade followed close on Weathers' tail. This was the German "Wolf Pack" and with the battle in its favor it was determined to make the kill.

Though he was greatly outnumbered, Weathers kept his composure. He refused to be shot down. Relating how he escaped being shot down, Weathers said: "It looked like they had me so I decided to follow the falling plane. I made a dive, came out of it and looked back. One plane was still on my tail. I was headed back towards Germany and I didn't want to go that way. I chopped by throttle and dropped my flaps to cut my speed quickly. The fellow overshot me and this left me on his tail. He was in range so I opened fire. A long burst and a few short bursts sent him tumbling to the ground."

In combat a man is respected if he has "guts" no matter where he is from, what his religious beliefs are, or the color of his skin. CPT Weathers experienced this in Naples. A pilot from another fighter group joined CPT Weather's party one night while at a little club in Naples. In the conversation that followed the new acquaintance mentioned that he was a cousin of a former governor of Mississippi. He then stated that he had the utmost respect for members of the 332nd because some pilots of the Group had probably saved his life when he was being attacked by a group of German fighters. After hearing the incidents of the mission CPT Weathers decided that he himself was one of the members of the escort mission that had fought off the Germans.

CPT Weathers was given the keys to the city by the mayor of Memphis on June 25, 1945, on the occasion of the Seventh War Loan Drive. The *Commercial Appeal* and the *Press Seminary*, two of the leading newspapers of Memphis, carried Weathers' picture and his speech. This was an honor never before bestowed on a Negro by that city.

The victories by the 332nd on November 16 were not gained without price. While taking off on the mission, planes flown by LT Roger Romine and William Hill collided. Romine was killed and Hill suffered severe facial and body burns as a result of a fire started by the collision. LT Hill was pulled out of his ship and sent to an American hospital at Bari where he recuperated.

Early in November 1944, heavy bomber crews reported attacks by enemy fighters based in northern Italy. On November 16, bombers returning from missions to southern Germany were jumped by 30 to 40 enemy aircraft stationed in the Udine area. The enemy fighters concentrated on the stragglers of the bomber formation and were successful in shooting down 14 bombers.

It was estimated that approximately 100 enemy fighters were stationed at four fields: Aviano, Vicenza, Villafranca, and Udine. On the night of November 17 and the day of November 18, the 15th sent out large forces of bombers escorted by 186 fighters to destroy the airfields. On November 18, MAJ George *Spanky* Roberts with flight leaders, CPT Daniels, Pullam, Down, Cisco, Govan, and Jackson, and LT Gaither, Rhodes, Nelson, Friend, Ballard, Pierson, and Thomas led a formation of 53 aircraft that provided escort, cover and withdrawal for bombers that bombed airdromes in the Vicenza-Villafranca areas.(2)

The pilots of the 15th encountered no enemy aircraft in the two days of bombing the airfields. But most disappointing to Allied leaders, the bad weather that set in immediately after the bombings prevented them from evaluating the extent of the damages inflicted in the attacks. However, when the weather finally cleared, enemy aircraft were noticeably absent. In fact, after the attacks the Luftwaffe was never again a force to fear in the Mediterranean.(3)

On 22 November 19, LT Quitman Walker of Indianola, MS, and Robert B. Gaither of New Jersey, were shot down while strafing in Hungary. Both pilots survived the experience of being shot down in enemy territory. Gaither evaded the Nazis four days before he was captured. Then he was taken to Gyor where he joined six other airmen who also had been shot down. A few days later the prisoners were marched to a railroad station for shipment to Germany. At the station they were pounced upon by a mob of angry civilians and severely clubbed before the guards decided to come to their rescue. Bruised and bleeding, the prisoners were then placed on a train and shipped to Vienna. From Vienna they were sent to Germany where they were held until released by the Allied army at the end of the war.

The day after Walker and Gaither were shot down, LT Maceo Harris of Boston, failed to return from a mission over Germany. This loss was followed by another seven days later when LT Elton N. Nightingale failed to return from a mission to southern Germany.

Nightingale was flying as wingman for CPT Stanley Harris when he disappeared. Relating the mission, he stated that they were flying above a heavy layer of clouds at approximately 30,000 feet. They broke into a small opening and saw the bombers they were assigned to protect, flying directly below. Upon spotting the bombers. CPT Harris made a tight turn in order to place his flight in a position to go down to protect the bombers. In making the turn, however, he lost Nightingale. Realizing that he had lost his wingman, he turned back to catch up with Nightingale. Meantime, Nightingale had turned back to join the flight. This placed Harris and Nightingale still traveling in opposite directions. By this time, the clouds had closed in. This made it impossible for Harris to locate the missing plane. However, he was able to contact Nightingale by radio. He gave Nightingale his course and told him to strike out for the base. For a while they kept contact with each other, but later lost contact. Nightingale failed to return to the base and was never heard from again.

On December 2, LT Cornelius Gould Jr. failed to return from a mission over Czechoslovakia. He became a prisoner of war and was held until the end of the war. LT Andrew D. Marshal of Bristol, Virginia, and Frederick Funderburg of Monticello, GA, failed to return from a mission on December 28. The next day, while returning from a mission over Vienna, LT Lewis W. Graig, a member of the 99th, was forced to bail out of his ship while flying over the Adriatic. In the fall, Craig dislocated his shoulder, but fortunately was rescued from drowning by some Italian civilians. He was placed on a British hospital ship and carried to an American hospital at Bari, where he was treated.

By the end of 1944, the Germans were practically without an ally. They had lost considerable ground in the east and had been pushed out of Russian territory. The Balkan countries were practically lost, Finland had turned upon Germany, half of Poland had been liberated, and the assault on Warsaw was about to begin. Though far from defeated, Germany was definitely on the defensive.

Top left: Captain Luke Weathers scored two victories in one day. Top right: Captain Woodrow Crockett posing on his plane (notice the names of Parks and Fernandez). Bottom left: Pilot of the 477th Bomber Group warming up plane at Godman Field. Bottom right: Marcus Ray, Aide to the Secretary of War, at Tuskegee with CPT Driver, McDaniel and CPT Friend.

Chapter 18
The Collapse of Germany

By January 1945, the effects of the Allied Air offensive against the Germans were becoming apparent. The Air Force had achieved remarkable success in depleting the enemy's oil reserves, disrupting his transportation and communication systems, and demoralizing his troops. The Nazis found it increasingly difficult to transport reserve troops and supplies from one front to another, and their armies, on all fronts, suffered from the lack of fuel for vehicles.

Although Germany's defeat seemed inevitable, the Allies were cautious of her inventive genius. During the fall and winter of 1944, the Allied Army Intelligence staff reported that the Germans were making considerable progress in the development of jet planes. Increasing numbers of these heavily armed jets were seen in the sky, but they were neither sufficiently numerous nor sufficiently aggressive to constitute a major threat. However, reports of the speed and maneuverability of these new jets caused Allied Commanders to make immediate plans for the destruction of their factories. They knew that technically the jet was far ahead of any aircraft the Allies had in action. They also realized that should Germany succeed in putting into the air a considerable number of these new planes they could exact heavy losses to the Allied bombers operating against her.

To delay the production of jet planes the Air Force decided upon an all out campaign against Nazi aerial production centers. Early in January, Allied bombers and fighters were again sent out to strike enemy areas which were believed to be jet construction centers.

Meantime, while the war against German aircraft factories was in progress, other developments that would eventually spell finish for the German domination of Europe were in progress. The American and British Forces in the West were preparing for a swift campaign across the Rhine and into Germany. In the east the Russians were forging ahead in the Balkans. The great armies of Russia along the center of their 1000 mile front were reorganizing for a final lunge. In the southern sectors of the Russian line, Russian armies were driving into Hungary and Austria, seeking to outflank Germany from the south in one of the greatest encircling operations in military history.

At the beginning of the new year, the Russian campaign in the east seemed distant and somewhat confused. But her new offensive which started on January 12, 1945, was one of phenomenal success. In three weeks the Russians drove 275 miles from Warsaw, Poland, to Frankfurt on the Oder.

The 15th was also doing its part in the offensive to crush Germany. It operated against German jet production centers, hit targets in central and southern Germany, and dive bombed and strafed enemy troops and supplies in all sectors. It struck targets in Czechoslovakia, Yugoslavia, Hungary, Austria, and Poland.

Pilots of the 332nd shared with their comrades of the 15th in bringing the war in Europe to an end. Wherever its bombers flew, the 332nd acted as escort. They were over Vienna one day, over Budapest the next day. They struck targets in Munich and battered German airmen over Berlin. They went on fighter sweeps into Poland and blasted Nazi supply lines and communication centers in Yugoslavia.

Throughout the months of January and February 1945, the 332nd was kept continuously busy. On February 1, it escorted bombers to Yugoslavia. This mission was led by CPT Armour McDaniel of Martinsville, VA. However, no enemy aircraft were encountered during the mission.

MAJ George Roberts led a strafing mission to the Munich area on the same day. On this mission, the 332nd scored its first aerial victory of the new year when LT William S. Price of Topeka, KS, shot down a German ME-109. The Group was also credited with destroying five enemy aircraft on the ground, seven locomotives, five box cars, and one flat car. The victorious pilots were LT Henry R. Peoples of St, Louis, with three locomotives; Jimmie D. Wheeler of Roseville, MI, with one locomotive; Roscoe C. Brown of New York City, with one locomotive; Harry T. Steward of Corona, IL, with one JU-52 transport plane destroyed on the ground; Lionel Bonan of Pascagoula, MS, with one FW-109 destroyed on the ground; John W. Davis of Kansas City, with five box cars and one flat car; F/O James

Fischer of Stoughton, MA, with one locomotive; and Wyrian T. Schell of Brooklyn with one locomotive.

The 332nd escorted heavy and medium bombers to Vienna and Moosbierbaum on February 8. The next day, it escorted bombers to Vienna to destroy a huge ordnance depot. On February 12, COL Davis led a mission to Vienna. The success of the mission is best told by CPT Louis Purnell, a youthful MD lad, who had entered combat with the original 99th: "It was a beautiful sight. Looking off the corner of my left wing I saw a terrific explosion and then clouds of smoke rose high. The explosion flames must have risen at least 200 feet. The sight made me think of the old days over Ploesti targets."

On February 13 and 14, the 332nd escorted bombers to Vienna to knock out a central repair depot. Nurnberg was attacked by the Group on February 17. The next day, it returned to Vienna. A marshalling yard in Brenner was the target on February 20. Two days later, the Group escorted bombers to the Munich area. It aided in knocking out a marshalling yard in Gmunden, Austria on the 23rd, and returned to the Munich area on the 25th.

During the mission of February 25, the 332nd lost two of its members: LT George Iles and Wendell W. Hochaday. While strafing in the Munich area. Iles' ship was knocked out of the sky by enemy ack-ack guns. He was taken to prison and held until released by the American Third Army. Hochaday allowed the wing of his ship to hit a locomotive while strafing. He managed to pull his ship up after it had been severely damaged. A little later, he was forced to bail out over the Alps when his ship began to falter. He was never seen or heard of again. It is the belief of many of his friends that he was killed when he hit the rocky mountains.

The day-to-day experiences of a fighter group are as varied as life itself. Unexpected things happen each day. The 332nd flew missions to San Marino, on March 1. On the 7th, the Group lost F/O Thomas Hawkins when his plane crashed on the runway while taking off on a mission. On March 14, LT Samuel Washington was shot down over Vienna while strafing a freight train. A flak burst damaged his fuel line and hydraulic system. A second burst severely damaged his instrument panel. Despite the damages, he stuck with his crippled plane and nursed it into friendly territory in Yugoslavia. He landed in a field and was later picked up by a British liaison pilot and carried to Zagreb where he stayed four days before returning to his base.

Another member of the 332nd, LT Harold Brown also went down the same day. A locomotive that he had just strafed blew up under his plane. He was forced to bail out. Twenty minutes later after hitting the ground, he was picked up by some civilian policemen and turned over to the Germans. He was held as a prisoner of war until released at the end of the war by Allied troops.

The 332nd escorted bombers to Linz, Austria on March 20. Over the target, LT Newman C. Golden's plane developed engine trouble which forced him to bail out 50 miles west of the target area. He was captured and held as a prisoner by the Germans. Three days later LT Lincoln Hudson's plane was hit by flak burst while on a mission to Ruhland, 75 miles south of Berlin. He attempted to fly to the Russian line but en route his engine failed. He landed in Czechoslovakia. His escort, Lt Rapier circled the helpless pilot until he landed safely, then returned to the base.

On March 24, COL Davis led the 332nd on one of the longest missions (1600 miles) ever attempted by the 15th. The pilots were briefed to bomb the Daimler Benz Tank Works in Berlin. However, the mission was actually designed as a diversionary effort to draw off German fighters based in central Germany which might otherwise have been committed against the airborne landings north of the Ruhr.

It was planned that the 332nd would relieve a P-38 Fighter Group at 11 o'clock over Brux and carry the bombers to the outskirts of Berlin. At this time, the 332nd was to be relieved by another P-51 group which would escort the bombers over the target. Upon the arrival at the point where it was to be relieved, the 332nd was instructed to continue over the target because the relief group was late.

Just before reaching the target, COL Davis' plane developed engine trouble which forced him to turn back. CPT Armour McDaniel then took over the command. Over the target, the 332nd encountered the new German jet planes for the first time. In the ensuing battle, pilots of the Group destroyed three of the jets. CPT Roscoe Brown of New York, LT Earle R. Lane of Wickliffe, OH, and F/O Charles V. Brantely of St. Louis, MO, were credited with the victories.

The mission, however, was not without losses. During the battle, LT Ronald Reeves and Robert C. Robinson were shot down. Both pilots failed to return to the base and later were listed as missing in action. CPT McDaniel was also shot down. Captured by the Germans, he was held as a prisoner of war. LT Spears was forced to land in Russian held territory when his plane was severely damaged. A fifth member, Lt Hannibal Cox, was forced to crouch to keep from being shot down by enemy aircraft.

LT Jimmie Lanham, relating the mission, said: "I was flying in the *thin man's* (COL Davis) flight on the mission. I was an element leader and Whitney (Yenwith) was my wingman. McDaniel had blue flight. COL Davis' plane developed engine trouble just before we reached Berlin so he returned to the base and McDaniel took over the Group. After we were attacked by the jets, I heard Schell (Wyrian) say, 'McDaniel just got shot down.' Someone said, 'There he goes.' I heard Walter Manning say, 'Here's a whole bunch of them.' A jet came in at 90 degrees to attack the bombers. We made a 180 degree turn, but the jets went over the horizon before we could get to the attack point. There were about 25 enemy planes in the air."

Although heavy losses were sustained, the mission was successfully carried out. For successfully escorting the bombers, the Group was awarded the Distinguished Unit Citation:

WAR DEPARTMENT
BUREAU OF PUBLIC RELATIONS
PRESS BRANCH

October 16, 1945
IMMEDIATE RELEASE

332ND FIGHTER GROUP WINS
DISTINGUISHED UNIT CITATION

In the name of the President of the United States, as "public evidence of deserved honor and distinction," a Distinguished Unit Citation has been conferred upon the all Negro 332nd Fighter Group for outstanding performance of duty in armed conflict with the enemy, the War Department announced today.

The citation reads as follows:

"On March 23, 1945, the group was assigned the mission of escorting heavy bombardment type aircraft attacking the vital Daimler-Benz tank assembly plant at Berlin, Germany. Realizing the strategic importance of the mission and fully cognizant of the amount of enemy resistance to be expected and the long range to be covered, the ground crews worked tirelessly and with enthusiasm to have their aircraft at the peak of mechanical condition to insure the success of the operation.

"On March 24, 1945, 59 P-51 type aircraft were airborne and set course for the rendezvous with the bomber formation. Through superior navigation and maintenance of strict flight discipline the group formation reached the bomber formation at the designated time and place. Nearing the target approximately 25 enemy aircraft launched relentless attacks in a desperate effort to break up and destroy the bomber formation.

"Displaying outstanding courage, aggressiveness, and combat technique, the group immediately engaged the enemy formation in aerial combat. In the ensuing engagement that continued over the target area, the gallant pilots of the 332nd Fighter Group battled against the enemy fighters to prevent the breaking up of the bomber formation and thus jeopardizing the successful completion of this vitally important mission. Through their superior skill and determination, the group destroyed three enemy aircraft, probably destroyed three others and damaged three more. Among their claims were eight of the highly rated enemy jet-propelled aircraft with no losses sustained by the 332nd Fighter Group.

"Leaving the target area and en route to base after completion of their primary task, aircraft of the group conducted strafing attacks against enemy ground installation and transportation with outstanding success. By the conspicuous gallantry, professional skill, and determination of the pilots, together with the outstanding technical skill and devotion to duty of the ground personnel, the 332nd has reflected great credit on itself and the armed forces of the United States."

The 332nd scored one of its most outstanding victories on Saturday, March 31. While on a strafing mission near Linz, it encountered a flight of enemy aircraft. In a wild dog fight, the Group was successful in shooting down thirteen of the enemy planes without losing a plane. The victorious pilots were:

MAJ William A. Campbell, Tuskegee, AL: 1 ME-109

LT Robert W. Williams, Ottumwa, IA: 2 FW-190
LT Bertram W. Wilson, Brooklyn, NY: 1 FW-190
LT Daniel L. Rich, Rutherford, NJ: 1 ME-109
LT Ruall W. Bell, Portland, OR: 1 FW-190
LT Thomas P. Braswell, Buford, GA: 1 FW-190
LT John W. Davis, Kansas City, KS: 1 ME-109
LT James L. Hall Jr., Washington, DC: 1 ME-109
LT Hugh J. White, St. Louis, MO: 1 ME-109
LT Roscoe C. Brown, New York City: 1 FW-190
LT Earle, R. Lane, Wickliffe, OH: 1 ME-109
FO John H. Lyle, Chicago, IL: 1 ME-109

LT Robert W. Williams, who was credited with two victories, related: "I dived into a group of enemy aircraft. After getting on the tail of one of the enemy planes, I gave him a few short bursts. My fire hit the mark and the enemy plane fell off and tumbled to the ground. On pulling away from my victim, I found another enemy plane on my tail. To evade his guns, I made a steep turn. Just as I had turned another enemy plane shot across the nose of my plane. Immediately, I began firing on him. The plane went into a steep dive and later crashed."

The next day, April 1, the 332nd led by CPT Walter H. Downs, of Oakland, CA, provided escort penetration, target cover, and withdrawal for B-24's of the 47th to St. Polten marshalling yard. It encountered a group of enemy aircraft near Vels, Austria, and destroyed 12 more planes. This brought the total victories for two days of fighting to 25 enemy planes destroyed in the air.

The top scorer of the day was LT Harry T. Stewart of Corona, Long Island, who was credited with three victories. The others were credited as follows: CPT Charles White of Oakland with two aircraft; LT Earl Carey of St. Louis with two; LT John E. Edwards of Steubenville, OH, with two; Harold Morris of Portland, OR, with one; Walter Manning with one; FO James Fischer with one.

Perhaps the luckiest pilot on the mission was F/O Fischer. In fact, he felt that he was one of the luckiest pilots in the world. The story he related seems to substantiate this fact. This is his story of the mission on April 1:

"COL Davis flew with our Squadron, the 301st, on this mission. On the way to the target he told us that on our return from the mission we were free to hunt trouble. After fulfilling our mission, the 301st broke away from the rest of the Group and flew straight down the Danube River. We found nothing of interest in the Danube area, but when we got to Linz we met a great deal of flak. Frankly, we were looking for enemy barges on the river, but instead sighted enemy planes.

"Our leader, LT Charles White, called in the enemy aircraft. However, just at this time, I began having trouble. When I tried to release my wing tanks, I found that they were stuck. By the time I was able to release them the fight was on. At this time, the Jerries were attacking us from the rear. I wheeled my plane around and ploughed through the enemy formation and in spite of the concentration of enemy fire I didn't get hit. But after I had passed through the formation I found myself somewhat alone. So I immediately turned and rejoined my formation.

"In the distance I saw an enemy aircraft smoking and, looking downward, I got a glance at one of our planes crashing to the ground. Above me I saw smoke streaming from another P-51 as it made a steep turn. A FW-190 was directly behind it, firing away with all of its guns.

"I pulled up behind the Focke-Wulf that was firing on the smoking plane. I gave him several bursts from my guns. After I made several hits on the enemy ship it made a dive for the ground. I followed him down, but as I approached the ground, I met a volley of fire from the enemy ground crew. I was hit several times. My rudder and canopy were damaged. By some miracle, my ship managed to stay in the air. A few seconds later I dropped down behind a hill and out of range of the enemy ground force. I checked my plane and found that rudder cable was badly damaged. I called my leader and told him that my plane was damaged so badly that I was heading for Russian held territory. I was at this time about ten to fifteen miles from Vienna.

"I flew to Vienna and turned south with the idea of landing in Yugoslavia. I started climbing about this time to get above the Alps. As I crossed a small factory town, the enemy opened up with their 88's. They tore a hole in my wing. My plane began to lose gas and a little later my engine quit. I switched tanks and the engine caught up.

I was left with about 55 gallons of gasoline on the north side of the Alps. My engine had only about one-third of its power, because I had run it at top speed too long.

"I called Big Friend, our distress code call, but received no answer. Finally, after several calls, a British Commando radio emergency station picked me up and steered me to Zagreb. Just as I got over the coast line, my ship ran out of gas. I was flying at 14,000 feet and the field was in sight. I glided my plane toward the field. Realizing that I had no rudder, I decided it was too risky to attempt a landing. I decided to jump. I was afraid to turn my plane over, so I crawled over the side of my ship and fell out. In my fall, I hit the damaged rudder and my plane fell into a spin. I pulled my chute cord as I fell out of my ship. When I opened my eyes I found myself upside down, floating down to earth with silk all over my head.

"When I landed, many Yugoslavian kids and grown-ups gathered around me. An L-5 observation plane came over a few minutes later and spotted me. A little later a jeep and ambulance arrived to take me to the emergency strip. I was put on a C-47 and sent back to Ramitelli in time for supper.

"When I arrived at the field, I learned that the two pilots I saw in trouble during the dog fight were LT Walter Manning and F/O William Armstrong. They failed to return from the mission."

By the first of April, 1945, the German army was completely demoralized. It had suffered an unbroken series of major defeats. Beginning with the Battle of the Bulge on December 17, 1944, the Allied war machine inflicted upon the Germans a series of losses and defeats. In both the east and the west, strong Allied forces were now operating in the homeland of Germany. The great industrial centers of Germany, the Ruhr, the Saar, and Silesia, were all lost to the enemy. Germany's remaining industries, dispersed over the central area of the country, could not possibly support her armies still attempting to fight. Communications were badly broken and no Nazi senior commander could be sure that his orders would reach the troops. Only on the northern and southern flanks of the great western front were there armies of sufficient size to do more than delay Allied advances.

On March 31, General Eisenhower issued a proclamation to the German troops and people urging the troops to surrender and the people to begin planting crops. He described the hopelessness of continuing the war and told them that further resistance would only add to the future miseries. In spite of the warning, the Germans, through the medium of the Gestapo and SS troops, continued to fight.

The 332nd strafed enemy motor transportation in the vicinity of Verona on April 4. While strafing, CPT Hugh White was shot down. He was captured by the Germans who at the time were retreating northward out of Italy because of the great Allied offensive. White noted that the Germans were so low on gasoline that they used horses and wagons instead of motor vehicles. Traffic moved at a snail's pace. The British Sixth South African Division caught up with the Germans at Padova and released White. He returned to the Group and was sent back to the States three days later.

On April 12, the 332nd lost LT Samuel Leftenant. His ship collided in mid air with a ship flown by LT James Hall of Washington, DC, while flying over Russian occupied territory. Both pilots bailed out of their planes but Leftenant was never seen or heard of again.

LT Hall landed safely, was picked up by the Russians, and sent to Russia. There he requested a plane to fly back to the base, but his request was refused. The Russians, for reasons unknown, had specific routes for evacuating Americans from their territories. Although transports left Russia daily for American ports, Hall was sent out of Russia by way of Bucharest.

The first great German capitulation came in Italy. Throughout the winter months, the lines in northern Italy had remained static. Neither side had launched any major offensive. In January and February, there were rumors that the Germans were withdrawing. These rumors, however, could not be substantiated by Allied Intelligence.

In April, General Clark announced an Allied spring offensive. At this time, the Allied line ran south of Bologna. In mid April, the Allied Army launched an attack which resulted in the capture of Bologna on April 21. The Fifth and Eighth Armies pursued the Germans who fled across the Po valley.

The 332nd also played its part in the final battles of the Italian campaign. On April 23, the 332nd flew two missions. The first mission was escort and target cover for B-24's of the Red force of the 55th and 304th Bomb Wings attacking Padova and Cavarzere. Upon completion of the target cover assignment, 16 aircraft of the Group conducted an armed reconnaissance of the Verona, Marostica, Padova, Cavarzere, Staghella, and Legnana areas. The second mission furnished general escort, penetration, and target cover for the Blue force of B-24 of the 55th and 304th attacking targets in the Padova and Cavarzere areas.

Meanwhile, the Allied Army in the west had contacted the Red Army on the Elbe. The Russians, who had launched a powerful drive on a 200 mile front from their Oder River position, had made speedy progress. General Eisenhower, describing the war in his book *Crusade in Europe*, wrote:

"Almost coincidentally with our arrival on the Elve the Red Army launched a powerful westward drive from its positions on the Oder. The attack was on a front of more than 200 miles. The Red drive made speedy progress everywhere. Its northern flank pushed in the direction of the Danish peninsula, the center towards Berlin, and the southern flank towards the Dresden area. On April 25th patrols of the 69th Division of the V Corps met elements of the Russian Army's 58th Guards Division on the Elbe. This meeting took place at Torgau some 75 miles south of Berlin."(1)

While Allied troops were swarming over Germany and swiftly pursuing the retreating Germans in Italy, there were few remaining targets against which the Air Force could be directed without danger of dropping their bombs on Allied troops. As a result, on April 26, the 15th flew its last mission. This was a Photo Reconnaissance mission to Prague. During the mission, three members of the 332nd were credited with destroying four enemy aircraft and one probable. The pilots receiving credit for victories were: LT Jimmie Lanhan, who was credited with one enemy plane and one probable; LT Thomas Jefferson, who received two victories, and LT Richard A. Simons with one victory.

On April 29, the German forces in Italy surrendered to the Allies. This made it impossible for the German First and Nineteenth Armies, just to the north of Italy, to continue fighting and as a result they surrendered to the Allies on May 6. Meanwhile, on May 1, the 332nd moved further north in Italy to Cattolica, where it prepared for a final offensive. However, plans for the unconditional surrender of Germany were already in the making. On May 7, Admiral Doenitz, the new commander in chief of German Forces, instructed two of his emissaries, Admiral Friedeburg and General Jodl, who had proceeded to General Eisenhower's advanced headquarters at Reims, to sign the unconditional surrender terms, thus bringing an end to the war in Europe.

With the war in Europe over, the members of the 332nd looked forward to taking the battle to the Japs. COL Davis addressed his men soon after Germany surrendered. He remarked: "Our growing pains are now over. We know our job and how to do it. In the Pacific, we should be more successful as a result of our experiences in this campaign. I am personally quite happy that this end of the war is over, but we won't be able to really celebrate until we know that the entire war, including the Pacific, has been finished."

On June 8, 1945, COL Davis was awarded the Silver Star for gallantry in combat. This award was presented to him at a farewell ceremony held prior to his departure to the United States for a new assignment as commanding officer of the newly created 477th Composite Group. In his departing speech, he remarked, "Our mission here has been completed. We have fought the war and I think the group has done very well."

General Dean C. Strother, Commanding General of the 15th Fighter Command, praised COL Davis in a conversation with an Afro-American War Correspondent, when he said, "He is a fine soldier and has done wonders with the 332nd. I am positive that no other man in our Air Corps could have handled this job in the manner he has."

LTC Roberts, Deputy Commander of the Group, succeeded COL Davis. At the same time, other changes were made. CPT Wendell Lucas of Fairmont Heights, MD, succeeded MAJ William A. Campbell as Commanding Officer of the 99th; CPT Bertram Wilson of Brooklyn, NY, was appointed Operation Officer, and CPT Bernard Proctor of Philadelphia, PA, the Group's Mess Officer, was relieved of duty to return to the States.

While the 332rd waited return to the States, it lost two of its members: LT Charles Squires and James Coleman. Squires was killed when he flew to the Pisa area shortly after V-E Day to buzz the black

92nd Infantry Division. On arrival over the 92nd area, he attempted a victory roll while on deck. Just after he started his roll, his plane skidded off course and crashed. LT Coleman was killed when his plane exploded in flight while practicing divebombing.

The 332nd had one more mission to fly before returning to the States. The 99th Squadron of the 332nd was selected to demonstrate fighter tactic for Allied Air force leaders in appraising the war efforts in Europe. This was held in preparation for the campaign in the Pacific against the Japanese.

On August 7, 1945, the 99th intercepted B-25 of the 5th over Catania, and made simulated attacks on the bombers for ten minutes. The 99th started its attack from 22,000 feet and extended its attack down to 15,000 feet, demonstrating all of the fighter tactics it had experienced in combat during the war.

The 332nd returning to the States.

Top: Colonel Benjamin O. Davis, Jr., receiving Legion of Merit. Bottom left: Major Fred Minnis, greatly responsible to the success of the Tuskegee experiment. Bottom right: Leaders of the 332nd *Red Tails*: LTC Roberts, MAJ Brooks, CPT Lucas, and MAJ Letcher.

Chapter 19
The Organization of the 477th Bombardment Group

Perhaps no combat unit activated during World War II had a more difficult time organizing than the 477th Bombardment Group which was later redesignated as the 477th Composite Group. However, the problem of organizing was not entirely due to the men, but mostly to the racial problems that existed in the United States at that time and the problems encountered by the War Department in trying to organize an Air Force. LTC Willie Ashley (ret), a veteran of the 99th, commenting on the prejudice they encountered upon return from combat, said: "When we returned to the States with chests full of ribbons, we were very proud of what we had done for our country and we hoped others would be equally proud of us. But when we went into an officers club, we were marched through the kitchen, out the back door and told not to return. We were deeply hurt. We learned that we had helped to free everybody but ourselves."

Fortunately or unfortunately, the members of the 477th did not get the opportunity to engage in combat and gain recognition as combat pilots. The war ended just at the time they were preparing to venture to the Pacific area to enter combat against the Japanese. Nevertheless, the members of the 477th played a significant role in World War II. They fought the important battle on the home front against the long-standing discrimination and segregation practices against the Blacks of the United States. They, with the same courage and determination, brought freedom to the Blacks of America, just as the 99th and the 332nd in combat helped restore freedom for the people of Europe. They played a most significant part as the vanguards of a civil rights movement that changed the nation--a change that brought more opportunities, better treatment and more respect for the Blacks of the nation.

The story of the organization of the 477th is interwoven in that of the black pilot training program. To be accurately told, consideration must be given to the racial prejudices and division that existed in the United States at that time and the problems the War Department and Air Force faced in organizing to fight World War II.

When World War II broke out, black leaders saw it as a chance to gain for Blacks the same opportunity and treatment afforded whites. One such leader was Judge William Hastie, who was appointed Civilian Aide to the Secretary of War.

Judge Hastie took office on November 1, 1940 and his duties were to assist in the formulation and administration of policies affecting Negroes in the military.

When Judge Hastie began service, most of the policy proposals affecting Negroes were referred to his office. This did not last. His insistence that Negroes be integrated in the Services and be granted equal rights to other Americans provoked many high War Department and Air Force officials. As a result, he was left out of many important meetings relative to Negroes and his recommendations were virtually ignored.

Upon learning from a newspaper that plans had been made to turn Jefferson Barracks into a black base and establish a black Officer Training School at the Barracks, he was infuriated. Although he had been in continuous contact with the Air Force officials, he was neither consulted nor advised. On January 16, 1943, he submitted his resignation and asked his two assistants to stay on. On January 29, 1943, Secretary of War Stimson accepted his resignation.

Following the resignation, General Giles, one of General Arnold's aides, sent a memo to General Marshall, the Chief of Staff of the US Armed Forces, indicating that the problem of using Blacks was "political dynamite", and that he was of the opinion the War Department would be forced by public opinion to make a decision which it had been hesitant to make.

Judge Hastie was replaced by one of his aides, Truman Gibson. Although Judge Hastie and Gibson shared many points of view and pursued the same goal, their tactics were different. Judge Hastie was imaginative, outspoken, and somewhat arrogant. He made detailed critical reports and recommendations and doggedly prodded the War Department to act on his recommendations.

Gibson, on the other hand, was more diplomatic in his operations. He seldom criticized War Department and Air Force officials. He more often praised them for their efforts, but candidly suggested how improvements could be made. This approach gained for Gibson a much better working relationship with the War Department and Air Force officials than Judge Hastie had enjoyed. Truman Gibson, however, lost the respect of many black leaders. It appeared to them that Mr. Gibson was cooperating and siding with the War Department officials. On one occasion, Mr. Gibson expressed the opinion that some black leaders and organizations, including the NAACP did more harm than good, by insisting that the shortcomings of black servicemen, whatever the cause "should be rationalized and not publicly discussed."

Roy Wilkins, the Director of the NAACP, angrily assailed Mr. Gibson's defense of the War Department's actions as "indefensible by any standard." He rebuked Mr. Gibson for blaming black organizations and the black press and shifting responsibility for frictions and clashes to people and institutions "in your own racial group whom you know deep in your heart are morally correct 100 percent of the time and inaccurate and emotional only a small part of the time."

Grant Reynolds, the President of the Committee against Jim Crow, in the military service, labelled Mr. Gibson as "the War Department's mouth piece." The strongest criticism came from Representative Adam Clayton Powell, who stated that he would remember Mr. Gibson "as the rubber stamp Uncle Tom, who was used by the War Department."(1)

Despite the criticism, Gibson continued to work as he thought best. He worked with the War Department Advisory Committee on Negro Troops, headed by Assistant Secretary of War, John J. McCloy, and the Special Service Division, commanded by General Frederick H. Osborn.

On March 11, 1943, in a memo to General Osborn, Gibson outlined the problem of the Air Corps in utilizing Blacks. The memo was prepared to aid the general at a conference which was scheduled to be held with a Mr. Wilbur Laroe and a delegation from the Washington Federation of Churches. The conference was to discuss charges made by Judge Hastie and to discuss the War Department's policy relative to the utilization of Blacks in the war effort.

During the conference, several of the participants expressed dissatisfaction with the small number of black youths being trained as pilots by the Air Corps. Immediately following the conference, Secretary of the Air Force, Robert Lovett and General Stratemeyer agreed to expand the black pilot program and directed the Operation Division to develop a plan.(2)

The Operation Division recommended that a medium bombardment group and associated support units be activated. Such a group would satisfy the demands of political pressure, because black Americans would be receiving training in more than one type of military aircraft.

Shortly after receiving the report, General Stratemeyer directed the Air Force to make plans for the activation of a bombardment group. The Air Force responded by presenting a plan that designated Tuskegee Army Air Field as the training center for twin-engine pilots; Mather Field, as the transitional training base for instruction in flying the B-25 medium bomber; Eglin Field, for the training of gunners; Rosewell Field, NM, Hondo and Midland Fields, TS, for the training of bombardiers and navigators, and Selfridge Field, MI, as the home for the proposed 477th.

While plans were being made to expand the black pilot training program, the Air Force began to face a serious shortage of white pilot cadets. This shortage would greatly affect the black pilot program. The shortage of white cadets was primarily due to the over-zealous manner in which the Air Force had used a priority privilege to select pilot and aircrew trainees it had been given at the beginning of the preparation for war in 1939.

Before 1939, the Army Air Corps was a small elite organization made up college trained volunteers, mostly the sons of high military officials, Congressmen and wealthy civic and business leaders. Most of the graduates of the pilot training program received commissions in the Army Air Corps Reserve. They served terms ranging from six months to two years with tactical units, then returned to civilian life. Many found employment with private aviation companies.

The success of the German Blitz through Europe, propelled by the German Air Force however, caused President Roosevelt great concern. On January 4, 1939, he declared that, "it has become increasingly clear that peace is not assured." He urged Congress to give priority to the Air Force in its appropriation. Congress responded to the President's appeal by not only appropriating money for the massive production of aircraft, but also for the training of pilots, crewmen, and technicians.(3)

Because of the massive Air Force expansion program, it was decided that because of the large number of pilots and crewmen needed, changes had to be made in the recruitment standards. It was argued that the two years of college prerequisite was too restrictive to recruit large numbers of men with the desired mental and physical qualifications. General Spaatz, then the Chief of Air Staff, expressed the opinion that the existing educational requirement was "archaic" because it placed too much emphasis on formal education, "which may mean nothing and no emphasis on native intelligence which may mean everything."(4)

The recruiting of cadets was the duty of the Adjutant General. Because of the educational requirements, the source of cadet supply was the colleges. In early 1937, General Arnold had recommended that five traveling examination boards be organized to canvas the nine Corps areas of the army for aircrew trainees. The recommendation was adopted and in January 1938, the boards began visiting colleges throughout the United States. They were so successful that in 1940, the traveling boards were increasing from five to eighteen. However, Blacks at the time were neither considered, nor wanted, or accepted.

First on the priority list for appointment to flying cadet training with the Army Air Corps were graduates of the United States Military Academy, the US Naval Academy, and the Coast Guard Academy, "who apply for appointment as flying cadets within one year from the dates of graduation, who fail to receive commissions because of lack of vacancies and are recommended for appointment as flying cadets by the respective superintendents of those academies."(5)

GEN Davis, Jr., now retired, relating how he received approval for flying training, said, "when I was a student at the Academy, flying training was the 'hot subject'. Flying training was most appealing to the students. Flying was considered the most daring and glamorous profession. I was also captivated with the idea of a career as an Army Air Corps pilot. I applied for training and the Commandant of the academy approved my application. The application was sent to Washington for approval; however, the Adjutant General disapproved my application. He stated that since there were no black flying officers or units, my request could not be granted, but if and when such a unit was activated my application would be reconsidered.

"When the Air Force decided to activate the 99th Fighter Squadron, I was serving as the assistant to my father at Fort Riley, KS. One day, I received a letter from the Pentagon suggesting that I apply for Army Air Corps pilot training. I applied and shortly afterward was given a physical examination at Fort Riley, but was turned down because of a number of physical disabilities.

"The Pentagon was notified as to the result of my physical. A few days later, a plane arrived at Fort Riley with orders from the Adjutant General, directing me to report immediately to Maxwell Field, AL for another physical. In a matter of a few days, all of my disabilities had disappeared and I was found to be qualified for flying training."

Herman *Ace* Lawson, who served in combat as a member of the 99th, got pleasure out of telling his experience with a member of an examining board. He had just completed a Civil Aeronautical pilot training course, as the only black in his civil pilot training class at Fresno State College. On learning that an examination board was interviewing students for Army Air Corps pilot training, Lawson went with some of his classmates to apply for the training.

Lawson waited in a long line for an hour before he reached the interviewer, a Major who inquired as to what he wanted. When Lawson replied that he wanted to apply for pilot training, the Major grew angry and his face turned as red as a beet. Lawson related that he will never forget the Major's eyes and the expression on his face as he shouted, "Get the hell out of here boy, the Army ain't training night fighters." Of course, this is funny to Lawson now; but at the time, he was deeply hurt.

After the Japanese attacked Pearl Harbor and full mobilization began, the Air Corps was given more preferential treatment in its recruitment drive. One reason was the Air Force was assigned the responsibility for the early defensive and offensive actions in case of attacks by the Japanese. A second reason, it was realized that the number of men of military age with the physical and educational qualifications for pilot training was relative small. It was deemed vitally necessary for the Air force to recruit as many of these men as possible. Past experience had taught the Air Force officials that only one out of five applicants accepted for flying training would meet the qualification and of those accepted by the training schools, no more than 40 to 50 percent would complete the training.

On December 10, 1941, just three days after the attack on Pearl Harbor, General Arnold and General Stratemeyer proposed the following changes in recruiting and selecting aviation cadets: 1) increase the number of aviation examining boards, 2) give wide publicity to the recruitment program, 3) decentralize power to accept or reject aviation cadets applications by relegating it to the examining boards and authorizing them to enlist qualified applicants immediately upon acceptance, 4) authorize as a substitute for the college requirements, use by the examining boards an examination designed to test intelligence and ability to absorb training centers instructions, 5) remove the ban on married applicants for aviation cadet appointment, 6) enlist all successful applicants as aviation cadets and assign them to aircrew training, and 7) decide the type of training to be given to each individual after his arrival at an Air Corps replacement training center.(6)

On January 15, 1942, General Arnold's recommendations were approved by a special board appointed by him. The proposal that gave examining boards final decision to accept or reject applicants, however, did not apply to black youths or to those youths who had been citizens for less than ten years and those youths whose applications might need review by higher authority. Such youths were accepted only after the Office of the Chief of the Air Corps reviewed the application papers and made favorable recommendations to the Adjutant General's office.(7)

The examination adopted proved to be a good initial screening device, but more candidates passed the examination and were accepted than could be absorbed in the training program. Despite the restrictions placed on the acceptance of black youths, more black youths also passed the examination and were accepted than could be absorbed into the limited training program at Tuskegee. The Training Command was forced to place thousands of potential cadets on furlough because of the lack of training facilities.

In an attempt to limit the number of candidates accepted for training, the Training command decided to apply a second and more selected screening test. The test, known as the classification battery was designed to select only those with better than even chance of success in training as air crewmen and to assure that those accepted were placed in the specific type of aircrew training best qualified.

The test consisted of a series of psychological and psychosomatic tests which was designed to measure the extent to which each candidate possessed a certain aptitude. Each candidate that took the battery was given three scores, each of which was used to predict success in one of the three training positions, bombardier, navigator or pilot. The three scores varied and were given different weight as applied to the three positions.

The scores were converted into *stanines*, a term derived from the words standard nine. This term referred to the aptitude rating given each man on a scale that ranged from one to nine. A stanine of nine placed an individual in the highest category and a score of one placed him in the lowest category.

It was directed that after July 2, 1942, trainees assigned to navigator training had to have a stanine score of five or above; on November 28, a minimum stanine score of three was made the requisite for pilot or bombardier training.(8) In addition, to stem the flow of trainees into training centers, the Adjutant General, on March 5, directed the Corps Areas to place a quota on aviation recruitment. These measures brought some relief to the Air Corps training program, but did not satisfy the officials of Air Corps which needed thousands of young men to meet its increasing training demand. Air Corps officials considered any restrictions which discouraged men from applying or hampered the flow of men into the training program jeopardizing the Air Corps meeting its training goals.

Since the passage of the Selective Service Act in 1940, the primary objective of the Air Force had been the creation of a backlog of qualified applicants for flying training. The Air Force officials believed that the most practical way to insure against the loss of potential aviation trainees from the draft or from other services was to enlist qualified candidates in a reserve aviation cadet grade and place them on inactive status until such time as they could be called to active duty to fill training school quotas. They contended that such an arrangement was necessary to insure sufficient cadets for its training program which was being progressively expanded.

On April 1, 1942, the Air Corps won the approval for the establishment of an Air Corps Enlisted Reserve. It immediately launched a vigorous campaign to recruit not only cadets for its pilot training program, but to build up a pool of potential candidates. The number of traveling examination boards was increased from 18 to 32. They visited not only colleges and Army and Air Force bases, but traveled to areas where they believed candidates could be recruited. Anyone between the ages of 18 and 26 who could pass the physical and mental examination for pilot training was accepted. Each applicant who qualified could elect: 1) to enlist for active duty as a private unassigned in the Army Air Corps to await until assigned to a cadet training class, 2) enlist in the Air Corps Enlisted Reserve and remain in civilian life until called to active duty as an aviation cadet, 3) if enrolled as a full-time student in an accredited college, enlist as a private in the A.C.E.R. and continue in college until graduation or withdrawal with the understanding that the deferment could be terminated at anytime by the Secretary of War.(9)

One of such applicants was George Haley, a combat veteran of the 302nd Fighter Squadron. He was enrolled at Syracuse University when accepted. He withdrew from school with the idea that he would be immediately called. He had to wait nine frustrating months before he was called to active duty as an aviation cadet.

The recruitment practices of the Air Corps brought criticism from the draft board. It charged the Air Corps deferment practice helped young men dodge the draft. The Air Corps defended its practice stating that it was necessary to maintain at least six months supply of trainees to meet its expected expansion program.

Meantime, the nation was beginning to face serious manpower shortage which would affect not only the white pilot training program, but the black pilot expansion program as well. To insure that all branches of the Service would get a fair share of the available supply of eligible men, Congress and the President acted. On November 13, 1942, Congress lowered the draft age to include 18 and 19 year old youths. Those were ages the Air Corps had spent its efforts to recruit, because they were not eligible for the draft. They were now eligible for the draft.

On December 5, President Roosevelt went further and by an executive order terminated all military enlistments effective December

15. After that date, an applicant could apply for flying training only through the selective service, unless he was already in service. Quotas were also established for the various branches of service. It now became necessary for the Air Corps to get aviation cadets from the over-all manpower quota allotted it each month. This slowed not only the Air Corps recruitment program, but the black pilot expansion program.(10)

By April 1943, it had become apparent that the Air Corps monthly recruitment quota was not being met, and two months later the Air Corps faced an accumulated deficit of 40,317 cadets despite the fact it had a backlog of 93,000 men

Faced with the prospect of depleting its backlog and being unable to recruit a sufficient number of men to meet its training schedule, the Air Force again embarked on a recruitment drive. It began accepting 17 year old youths with the stipulation that they would be called within six months after they reached their 18th birthday. The Air Corps turned to voluntary induction of civilians and reduced the physical requirements. It also began an all out campaign to recruit service men. In addition, it made provisions for army reception centers to administer qualifying cadet examinations to all enlisted men who qualified and volunteered for flying training, made a score of 100 or better on the Army General Classification Test and passed the physical examination.

In its recruitment drive, the Air Corps again received criticism not only from the draft board, but from the other services. The services charged the Air Corps of not only grabbing the best civilian prospects, which they also needed, but luring many of their key personnel to apply for aircrew training.

General Arnold, disturbed by the mounting criticism and fearing the Air Corps would lose many of its recruited men by being drafted, made a recommendation that was approved by the Secretary of War in January 1943. The recommendation was that the Air Corps be permitted to call its recruits to active duty and give them a period of college training to help them make up their educational deficiencies. Tuskegee Institute was one of the colleges contracted for the training. Actually, the college training program was designed not so much to meet the educational needs of the recruits, but to keep them from being drafted.

In spite of the manpower crisis, the Air Corps was under pressure from black leaders and from some white leaders to activate the 477th. In addition, the Air Force had been directed to activate the Group. On May 13, 1943, it constituted the 616th Bombardment Squadron and two months later, on July 1, the squadron was activated, only to be deactivated on short notice on August 15. The apparent change of plans to activate the 477th brought a flood of inquiries from black leaders. They expressed concern about the seriousness of the Air Corps' intention to organize the Group.

In response to the inquiries, Assistant Secretary of War, John J. McCloy called a press conference on September 2, stating that black youths would soon begin bombardier navigation training and all the training will be with white students. The Air Corps, however, had made plans to establish the training program at Tuskegee. In fact, it had already begun sending enlisted men and non-rated officers to Tuskegee for the 477th.

COL Parrish and his staff disfavored the idea of stationing more troops at Tuskegee. In a communication to officials of the Air Corps, he stated: "For the last six months, enlisted men have been sent to this station, especially from the technical school of both the Air Corps and the Signal Corps, classified trained in jobs for which in the main, there are no positions at this station. At the present time the number is approximately 120 and this station is operating under a Manning Table and has no personnel available to care for these men. No further training can be given them as they are all specialists and in most cases due to their ranks are not suitable for reclassification nor for assignment to any other jobs on the station. Not only are these men presently at this station, but daily, men are being transferred into the station... This is certainly a waste of manpower and malassignment of personnel and a serious imposition on this station as these men are not needed, can serve no useful purpose at this station, and constitute a serious drain upon our personnel, which has to be assigned to care for them. This office has made repeated reports of this matter and to date no relief has been forthcoming."(11)

The news to activate an all black 477th was received with great enthusiasm at Tuskegee. The great thrill, however, came on September 24, 1943, when the first AT-10 twin-engine training plane arrived at Tuskegee and was assigned to the base.

The organization of the twin-engine training program began shortly after the arrival of the plane. CPT Clay Albright was appointed director of the twin-engine training school, LT Milton B. Hall of Owensboro, KY, a black man, was appointed as his administrative assistant, and LT Leonard C. Crozier and Robert B. Meagher were appointed as cadet instructors. To insure that the planes received the proper maintenance, a detachment of mechanics was sent to Tuskegee from Turner Field, GA, to instruct the mechanics at Tuskegee in twin-engine maintenance.

There was no end, however, to the problems that deterred the organization of the 477th. On September 20, 1943, *Time* Magazine carried the aforementioned article titled "Experiment Proved". The basis of the article was a prejudicial report by COL William W. Momyer, the highly respected commander of the 33rd to which the 99th was attached for operations in combat.

Although COL Momyer made accusations about the performance of the 99th in combat, actually the 99th performance compared favorably to the initial entrance of the 33rd into combat. The 33rd had arrived overseas in November 1943 with the North African Invasion Force aboard the Carrier *Chenango* which carried 75 aircraft of the 33rd. Five days later, 35 additional P-40's arrived off the coast of Morocco on the British carrier *Archer*. Of the 75 planes catapulted from the *Chenango*, two were lost and 17 crashed when landing at the Port Lyautey Airfield. Four of the aircraft catapulted from the *Archer* also crashed. The loss of the planes was attributed mainly to the inexperience of the pilots. This resulted in the organization of the Northwest African Training Command, headed by General John K. Cannon. It was established to give pilots sent overseas from the US additional training before being sent into combat.

The 33rd was sent into combat on January 1, 1943. On January 10, MAJ Philip Cochran dropped a 500 pound bomb that destroyed Hotel Spendida, a German Headquarters at Kairoun. A few days later, the 33rd shot down eight enemy aircraft that attacked its base.

The victories won for the 33rd the recognition as a "hot outfit". COL Momyer threw caution to the winds, despite warning by General Doolittle, Commander of the Northwest African Strategic Command

and General Howard Craig, Commander of the 12th to group commanders to conserve their strength for other campaigns to come. COL Momyer recklessly and aggressively sent small forces to areas far from the base, where the Germans were known to have overwhelming air superiority. In one month of battle, the 33rd was forced out of the war, and the few remaining survivors were sent to Morocco for a rest and to pass on their experiences to the pilots of the 325th that had just arrived overseas. Despite COL Momyer's heavy losses of men and planes, more men and planes were supplied and the 33rd returned to combat.(12)

Momyer's report spurred the War Department to act. On October 12, 1943, the McCloy Committee met to consider that report. During the hearing, Gibson charged that the Air Force initially believed that Negroes could not learn to fly, "Now it believes that they lack the ability to fight... that white squadrons had done worse upon commitment to combat." General Benjamin O. Davis, Sr. stated that veterans could not be made in one campaign and that he did not believe that the report justified scrapping the program.(13)

The War Department denied the report that it was considering disbanding the 99th, but it delayed the activation of the 477th. However, while the Department was vacillating as to what to do with the black pilot training program, Tuskegee was developing into one of the most unique air bases in the country. While other bases specialized in only one phase of pilot training, Tuskegee specialized in all phases of pilot training. It trained pre-flight, basic, advance, and transitional pilots training to fly the P-40. It trained liaison pilots for the Army Field Artillery, pilots for the government of Haiti, and French Colonial pilots. In addition, it trained pre-flight navigator and bombardier cadets and acted as a pool for unassigned enlisted men and non-rated officers.

On October 20, BG Marvin E. Gross wrote General Howard Craig, that a definite decision was needed soon because the training schedule being followed at Tuskegee would turn out more pilots than the fighter units would need. Otherwise, he wrote, "the Air Force would find it difficult to explain why it had trained so many men for which it had no need." On October 27, 1943, General Arnold ordered the 477th to be activated, trained and sent to the North African Theatre of war.(14)

Just as it appeared the 477th would be developed, reactionary forces began working to disband all black combat units. The 846th and 819th anti-aircraft battalions were disbanded and their personnel were assigned to the Quartermaster Corps. Other black combat units were likewise disbanded. Even the 9th and 10th Cavalries, two of the oldest established black combat outfits were not spared.

While the reactionary movement was in progress, the 99th began to prove that it was a fighting unit capable of competing with the enemy in combat. On January 27 and 28, 1944, it destroyed 12 enemy aircraft over the Anzio beachhead. Nevertheless, the 99th was also considered for disbandment.

The news of the plight of black combat units brought a storm of protest. In early February, 1944, John W. Martyn, the administrative assistant to the Secretary of War announced that Secretary Stimson would make a full and comprehensive report on the status of Negro soldiers. This report was to be made in reply to a request by Congressman Hamilton Fish of New York, who demanded to be fully advised of the facts respecting the break up of Negro combat organizations.

Congressman Fish had written to the Secretary: "I have been informed that several Negro Tank Destroyer Units, which underwent training at Fort Hood, TX, have been broken up and the entire personnel transferred to quartermaster trucking companies.

"I have also been informed that numbers of enlisted men of the 931st were transferred to the quartermaster service organization under order, August 16, 1943.

"More recently, the Negro press carried an article sent from an advanced Pacific base by Fletcher P. Martin, that the crack 24th Infantry Regiment, fully equipped and prepared for any eventuality is performing duties at docks and supply dumps while awaiting possible assignment to combat. Twenty-five months have past since this outfit embarked from California for the South Pacific."

In his reply to Congressman Fish, Secretary Stimson stated the Army General Staff view that Negroes were "unable to master techniques of modern war." He also stated that the 930th and 931th Field Artillery units performances were "unsatisfactory for overseas services." However, on one occasion, a LTG Ben Lear had commended the units for mastering the techniques of mechanical firing.

Representative Fish, who had commanded Negro troops in World War I, read the Secretary's Communication on the floor of the House and sharply rebuked the Secretary for his views.

The implication that Negroes were "too dumb to fight" caused William L. Dawson, the only Negro member of Congress at the time to assail the Secretary, stating "that Secretary Stimson should quit immediately... for he is either woefully ignorant on the matter of Negro troops or is purposely carrying out the pattern of fascist elements within the military establishment, whose purpose is to discredit Negro fighting men of this nation."

Perry Howard, the Negro Republican National Committeeman of Mississippi, in a letter to Congressman Fish, called Secretary Stimson's assertions "Pure Bunk", and urged "Keep up the good work."

Negro Democratic leaders met in Pittsburgh and adopted a resolution condemning without reservation the maltreatment, discrimination and segregation of Negro men and women in the armed services of the United States. A mass meeting in Chicago, sponsored by the National Negro Council and the Chicago Committee of 1000, adopted a resolution calling the statement of Secretary Stimson "unfounded and utterly false" and called on President Roosevelt to oust the Secretary.

The editor of the *Pittsburgh Courier* charged, "The diabolical activities of some brass hat in strategical positions within the military establishment of the Nation is sabotaging the real American program of the President, robbing the Nation of services of thousands of first class fighting men and causing the deaths of hundreds of white boys, who must fill the front lines in the place of Negro boys, ready, and eager to do their best if given the chance."

Meantime, on October 13, 1943, each Service Command was directed to establish special aviation cadet examination boards at the reception centers. The establishment of the boards proved to be the answer to the Air Force's recruiting problem. They not only eliminated the number of unqualified candidates, which ran as high as 65 percent, but accelerated the recruiting program. The establishment of special aviation cadet examination boards at the reception centers created another problem that affected the development of the 477th. The new recruitment program supplied more pilots and aircrew trainees than needed. The problem now became one of curtailment to forestall an unnecessary backlog of cadets. During the manpower crisis, the Air Force was reluctant to use its allotted monthly quota to recruit black youths. Now, black youths were faced with the curtailment problem.

On November 18, 1943, the War Department decided to cut back the number of men recruited as aviation cadets so as not to exceed the annual training rate set for 1944 of approximately 60,000 pilots. To curb the number of qualified applicants, the mental and physical qualifications were raised for aircrew training, effective February 10, 1944. On November 30, the War Department decided to reduce the monthly quota of officers training in grade to 200 men.(15) It directed that officers applying for aviation training in grade be required to pass the aviation cadet qualifying examination and that stanine scores be adjusted to assure that only 200 officers would be accepted for training. There were a number of officers, naming a few, John Hurd, who transferred from the cavalry, Charles *Hatch* Hunter, Wilson Savoy, and Elmore Kennedy, who transferred from the Infantry, were trained in grade and assigned to the 477th.

In early January 1944, the military Personnel Division of the War Department reported that the backlog of aircrew trainees were large enough to suspend recruitment until December 1944. On February 22, the Adjutant General directed all service commanders to suspend the recruitment of aviation cadets from the Army Ground and Services Forces, and to refuse applications from officers and enlisted men to transfer to the Air Force for aircrew training. The following week the ruling was extended to include Air Force personnel, and in late March 1944, the recruiting of civilian volunteer inductees was stopped and the enrollment of 17 year old youths was temporarily halted.

In April 1944, the War Department announced that 36,000 men waiting to be called for aircrew training were not needed. This announcement was very discouraging to many black youths. It appeared that the 477th would never be organized. It was rumored at Tuskegee that the training program would be drastically curtailed. However, addressing graduating Class-44-C in March 1944, COL Parrish stated that it was the last of the smaller classes, that "future classes will be much larger." He had just received notice from the

War Department that black applicants 18-26 years of age could, through voluntary induction and Army Air Corps officers and enlisted men returning from combat, be eligible for aircrew training.

COL Parrish and black youths soon learned that the picture was not as it appeared. The Air Force, in order to forestall the acceptance of white youths for training, began using stanine scores to limit the flow of candidates. Stanine scores had been used prior to this time only as a means of selecting potential trainees and to help determine whether trainees selected for aviation training were best qualified to be bombardiers, navigators, or pilots. Stanine scores were now to be revised upward to admit fewer cadets into the training program.(16)

On July 2, 1942, when the use of stanines were adopted, it was directed that all men assigned to navigation training would be required to have a stanine score of five or better. On November 28, 1943, a stanine score of three was made a perquisite for bombardier and pilot training.

In late 1943, it was observed that 79.3 percent of black youth scores fell in the stanine group of IV and V, in contrast to 14.6 percent for white applicants. There was a demand for black pilots to serve as replacements for the fighter units in combat and for the organization of the 477th Bombardment Group. To meet the demand for the black units, black youths were accepted for pilot and bombardier training with stanine scores of not less than four and not less than five for navigator training.(17) On the other hand, there were more qualified white applications, pilots and crewmen than needed. To curtail the number of white applicants, a stanine score of six or better was required for pilot and bombardier training and not less than seven for navigator training.(18)

Naturally, the different standards for accepting blacks and whites for pilot and aircrew training brought complaints from white applicants and training school instructors. For example, on October 20, 1943, the first class of black trainees for the 477th, known as Squadron #10, arrived at Hondo Field, Texas. The Squadron led by cadet Walter H. Arrington immediately began 18 weeks of intensive training. Near the end of its training, the class of 24 cadets flew a navigation training mission to New York City. En route, the Squadron flew first to Kansas City, where it was greeted at a luncheon, attended by Assistant Secretary of War McCloy and Truman Gibson.

They then traveled to Chicago and Pittsburgh where they made brief stops before continuing their flight to New York. There they were welcomed by a huge crowd at La Guardia Airport and after a brief ceremony traveled in a motorcade to City Hall where they were welcomed by Mayor Fiorello La Guardia and other city officials.

The cadets of Squadron #10 were graduated and commissioned on February 26, 1944. In addressing the graduates, COL George B. Dany, the Commanding Officer of Hondo Field, remarked, "By your extremely fine attitude, determined efforts, military discipline and bearing, and accomplishment on the athletic field and scholastic attainment, you have contributed immensely to the fine performance of this class. You have established a record for future Squadrons to aspire to achieve."

Despite the praise of COL Dany, there was criticism of the cadets by the instructors at Hondo. Four classes of navigators trained at Hondo. After the third class was graduated, a report was made. The report read, "The morale of Negro cadets is as high as any group of cadets on the field. There have been very few cases of animosity toward Negro cadets from white cadets... In the opinion of their instructors it is difficult and perhaps unfair to compare the Negro cadet in his ground and air work with the white cadet. Class 44-11-9B was equal to the average white classes in flying and considerably above average in ground school. A great deal of additional effort, however, was expended by their instructors in order to master even the smallest details of ground school work.

"With class 44-20-N-9, a pronounced diminution in the quality of work has been observed and there is every reason to believe that the explanation lies in the native quality of the students, not in the quality of the instructors... Of the 32 cadets who entered with the class, ten had stanine scores of four, five had stanines of five, eleven had stanine of six, two had stanines of eight, and one had a stanine of nine. Thus, only six of the 32 have stanines of seven or above and no white cadet is accepted for navigation training unless his stanine is seven or more.

"Men with stanines of seven or above are doing work that compares well with accepted, standard work. The others are noticeably slower in learning and a great deal slower in retaining the material. In the opinion of their instructors, these men will, inevitably, be less proficient navigators than the average white graduates... Instructors all agreed, however, that no cadets, whether white or colored, with stanine scores below seven should be accepted for navigation training."(19)

Gordon Boyd, a native of Baltimore and a graduate of the Bombardier-Navigator School at San Angelo, commenting on the report of the instructors at Hondo Field, said, "I can't refute the instructors, because I was not one of those who received training at Hondo. I will say this. All of us who were sent to the various training schools, were highly motivated. Our stanine scores might not have been equal to that of the white trainees, but we had more determination to achieve and excel, and that's what counts. I know at San Angelo, while the white cadets socialized, we stayed with the books. It was nothing exceptional to the white fellows, but to us, it was an opportunity no black youths had ever been given. Of course, the white cadets wanted to qualify, but it was no big thing for them; they took it for granted that they would graduate and be commissioned."

Even though black youths were accepted with lower scores than white youths, their training at Tuskegee compared favorably with that of white youths. For example, by February 1944, the cadets primary training classes of the 66th Flying Training Detachment at Tuskegee Institute had received, for six consecutive times, the Eastern Flying Training Command scholastic honor. Class 44-D that was graduated from primary school in November 1943 won third place honor. In the five previous classes, 43-J, 43-K, 44-A, 44-B, and 44-C, two of the classes won first place honors.

The cadets that received pilot training at Tuskegee also did well in flying and gunnery. In November 1943, the Tuskegee graduating class, in competition with graduating classes from bases throughout the country, excelled. In the meet held at Eglin Field, pilot cadet Othel Dickson won the honor of being the best pilot aerial gunner of the Eastern Flying Command and won third place in the national competition. In fact, going into the final round of competition, Dickson was far ahead of all competing cadets, but unfortunately his gun sight failed, just at it appeared he would win the honor of being the top cadet of the Air Force.

Cadet Dickson's performance overshadowed the performance of his classmates, who also won honors. All but two members won expert ratings in gunnery and those two qualified as sharp shooters. Other graduating classes competed favorably in competition at Eglin Field. Class 44-E that was graduated on March 1, 1944, set a record in the competition. The entire class received ratings of expert.

The graduates of Hondo Field navigation training school were sent to Roswell Army Air Field for bombardier training where they qualified and became the first black dual-rated officers of the Air Force.

The bombardier-navigation training program was moved to Midland Field, Texas in early 1945. Approximately 53 cadets in the first class were graduated on December 27, 1945, 50 in the second class, and 30 cadets and four student officers in the third graduating class of January 27, 1946. The training was then moved to San Angelo Field, where it remained until the bombardier-navigation training program was terminated.

While the bombardier and navigators were in training, 84 cadets and four officers, namely LT Leonard E. Williams, Louis H. Anderson, Robert S. Peyton and Coleman H. Young were sent on May 27, 1944 from Tuskegee to Tyndall Field, FL, to qualify as gunners for the 477th. Meantime in April 1944, the War Department announced that eight experienced Negro mechanics were in training on the flight line at Mather Field, CA, as the nucleus of the all-black maintenance unit for the 477th. The eight mechanics were T/SGT George B. Agard, William P. Jones, William H. Bently, Robert E. Kirtley, Arthur W. Freeman, Dennis H. Hunton, and SGT Daniel H. Fields. All of the men had been trained at Chanute Field, as single-engine mechanics and sent to Tuskegee in the fall of 1942. At the completion of their training at Mather Field, they were sent to Inglewood, for additional training at a school operated by the makers of the B-25. A second detachment of eight mechanics was sent approximately the same time from Tuskegee to the Army Air Force mechanic training school at Lincoln. Upon the completion of their training the trainees were sent to an advance mechanic center in Buffalo. While the mechanics were in training a detachment of trainees was sent to Scott Field, for radio technician training.

When General Arnold ordered the 477th activated, trained and sent overseas, the operational date for the 477th was set as July 1944. The Training Command, however, concluded that Tuskegee could not train enough twin-engine pilots to meet the operations day date. It requested that Tuskegee be relieved of the responsibility of training all types of pilots. It stated that Tuskegee was incapable of training sufficient pilots to furnish replacement pilots for the fighter units in combat and train enough twin-engine pilots to enable the 477th to meet the operation date. The Training Command predicted that at the present production rate the organization of the 477th would be delayed until July 1945. It requested that black cadets be accepted for training at white pilot training schools. The War Department rather than granting the request, canceled the 477th operational date on November 15, 1943, and directed that all black pilot training continue at Tuskegee.

Despite the limited number of air cadets recruited throughout most of 1943, Tuskegee managed to maintain a backlog of pilot and aircrew trainees. This was due mainly to the small number of qualified cadets called to fill the training school vacancies.

By the spring of 1944, however, there developed a shortage of cadets for pilot training at Tuskegee. The effort to train pilots and supply trainees for the bombardier-navigator schools quickly exhausted the backlog of cadets. It became very difficult to fill the pilot training classes at Tuskegee. To make matters worse, the Air Corps made it more difficult to recruit cadets by raising the stanine score from four to five for black applications while activating three new squadrons for the 477th. It activated the 617th on April 13, 1944, the 618th on May 15, and the 619th on May 24, 1944.

General Parrish (ret), later recalling the experience, said, "It was very frustrating for me to maintain the training program. I made trips to the Pentagon to discuss the problems, and received praise for the work I was doing; but, no help. There was one high-ranking official, that always had some prejudicial remarks about Blacks--the young men who were preparing to sacrifice their lives for their country. It was very disgusting to me to think a man of his position was so ignorant. It got to be sickening to me to be in his presence."

The shortage of cadets became so acute at Tuskegee that enlisted men, who could qualify for pilot training, were encouraged to apply. One of them accepted for training was George Bell. He had washed out of pilot training just before graduation day because of a physical disability. He was now found physically fit, reinstated and successfully completed the pilot training course.

Non-rated officers at Tuskegee, namely, LT George Hubbard, Nathaniel Goins, Orville E. Lewis, James S. Moseley, Robert J. Randall, Raymond E. Tinsely, David E. Woody, and Claude M. Dixon were also accepted for pilot training. Likewise, the men who had earned commissions as bombardiers and navigators and found to be qualified were accepted for pilot training. This gave some of these men the distinction of being among the few triple-rated flying officers of the Army Air Force. In addition, many of the veteran fighter pilots--as Deiz, Sheppard, Curtis, Govan, Daniels, Melton, Walker, McGee and many more--elected to qualify as bomber pilots and serve with the 477th. They were battle-hardened veterans who loved flying, had lost the fear of death, and were willing to volunteer for combat with the 477th. Some of these men had already completed two tours of combat and were now volunteering for a third combat tour.

By early 1945, the pilot training crisis at Tuskegee began to subside when the Air Force terminated its bombardier and navigator training programs, and the cadets unable to complete their training were returned to Tuskegee and given pilot training.

In February 1945, applications were again accepted from men in the Ground and Services Forces. To further alleviate the pilot shortage, the Eastern Flying Training Command lowered the black cadet stanine score requirement from five to four. These actions ended the cadet shortage and a large number of cadets were accepted for twin-engine pilot training to accelerate the organization of the 477th Bombardment Group.

Top: Members of the first AAF Class joined by young admirers at Hondo Army Air Field, Texas. Bottom: LT Cyril Burke and F/O Daniel Keel receive their wings at Midland Army Air Field.

Formation of Black Cadets at Hondo Army Air Field.

Cadets May, Trotter, and Evans at Midland Army Air Field.

Mayor Fiorello LaGuardia greeting Hondo Army Air Field flyers.

Standing: F/O Levert V. Middleton, Bombardier Navigator; 2nd LT Eugene Henderson, Co-Pilot; 1st LT Henry P. Hervey, Pilot. Sitting: SGT Charles Jones, Tail Gunner, PVT Frank Hector, Radio Operator, Gunner; FFC John E. Starks, Engineer, Gunner.

Chapter 20
Drawing The Battle Line At Freeman Field

When COL Parrish took over the command at Tuskegee, the morale of the base personnel was very low, because of the racial friction in the area of the base. COL Parrish immediately set about to address the problem with the idea of making the base so self-sufficient and attractive that there would be little need for implementing his program. To accomplish this goal, he appointed MAJ Fred Minnis as the base Education Recreation and Morale Officer.

When the first class of pilots completed its primary training at Tuskegee, it was sent to Tuskegee Army Air Field. A short time later, after the cadets began flying training, COL Parrish was transferred to Tuskegee Army Air Field as Director of Training. CPT Williams was also transferred from the 66th Primary Training Detachment, stationed at Tuskegee Institute, to Tuskegee Army Air Field and assigned as Physical Fitness Officer.

Williams not only developed physical fitness activities for all military personnel on the base, but developed morale-building activities such as football, basketball, baseball and tennis teams that competed on college level.

MAJ Minnis, however, was responsible for the educational, recreational and morale-building activities. Like Williams, he was a very dedicated, energetic and enervated officer who participated in the planning of entertainment and recreation facilities as well as in developing interesting and enjoyable activities to promote the use of the facilities, with programs for pocket billiard, bowling, and other games and entertainment activities.

Tuskegee was a small air base compared to others, but it appeared to have had as many men with special talents. MAJ Minnis encouraged those with special talents to share them with their fellow airmen, with civilian organizations of the area, as well as with airmen at the other bases.

One of the most talented airmen was T/SGT James C. Mosley, a native of Muskogee, OK, an accomplished piano-player and composer; he helped to organize an orchestra that provided music for entertainment and dances, and gave piano recitals on and off base.

MAJ Minnis also encouraged the development of more cultural programs. For example, he got CPT Ulysses G. Lee, former Professor of English at Howard University, and Corporal John Lucas, a classical pianist, to give regular Sunday afternoon music programs featuring the classical recordings by great artists. They often also featured the Post Chapel Choir which sang religious songs and spirituals, and CPT Drye with his post band who entertained with marching and patriotic music.

MAJ Minnis provided the post theatre with the latest movie films and a variety of nationally known celebrities and entertainers as Ella Fitzgerald, Lena Horne, Louis Armstrong, Jimmie Lunceford, Willie Bryant, Huber Jasper, Joe Louis, Sugar Ray Robinson, including famous Negro poets as Langston Hughes and Sterling Brown.

Frequent dances and entertainment for the Non-Commissioned officers and enlisted men were also sponsored by MAJ Minnis. Young ladies from the area colleges, such as Talledega, Tuskegee Institute, and Atlanta University were invited, provided with transportation and given overnight quarters.

Although the officers enjoyed the entertainment, their activities centered mostly at the officers club, which was administered by a board of officers. The most popular activity for the officers was the Sunday evening dance termed *The Blue Hour*. The music was provided by SGT Busby, who often featured LT Ira O'Neal as a "sit-in" on drums, and other officers and their lady friends who took turns as vocalists.

By late 1943, Tuskegee had truly developed into a place of excitement, with the morale, on the whole, having improved considerably. It became a place where young black men and women, military and civilians, caught up in the excitement and glamour of military flying, worked to make, what the War Department termed, "The Experiment"--a success, while, at the same time, making life enjoyable as never before afforded to black Americans.

In spite of the pride of seeing young black men fly military aircraft for the first time, and the lively and entertaining activities of the base, and in spite of all the efforts by COL Parrish to provide the best for the personnel of the base, Blacks still were not satisfied. There lingered, in the minds of those who had come from areas where racial distinction was less obvious and discrimination and segregation was less enforced, a feeling that they were being quarantined, that Tuskegee as a symbol of one of the "hot beds" of racial hatred and intolerance. It was obvious to many that no amount of pleasure on the base could minimize Blacks' desire to be respected and treated as other American citizens.

On November 15, 1943, the first class-43-J, twin-engine pilots, consisting of LT Herman Campbell, Perry E. Mason, Henry F. Flecher, Perry E. Hudson, Haldene King, Harvey N. Pinckney, Jerome D. Spurling, William D. Toppins, and Leslie A. Williams were graduated and were immediately transferred to Mather Field for transition training to fly the B-25 Mitchell Medium Bomber. While training there, other twin-engine pilots were sent to Douglas Field, AZ for similar training. Three of these were sent to Douglas: F/O Edward Harris of Pittsburgh, LT Edward Dixon of Lynn, MA, and Claude C. Davis also of Pittsburgh.

These hostile conditions, in the area of Tuskegee and in the entire South, caused many of the airmen to wish for transfer to other areas of the country, many opting for California considered more liberal believing that it did not enforce its segregation and discrimination policies as rigidly as the southern states. Naturally, the twin-engine pilots were happy on being sent to California.

When the pilots arrived at Mather Field, they were cordially received and accepted by the white pilots. However, this quickly changed when COL Ralph Cousins visited the base. On observing black and white officers eating and socializing in the same officers club, he recommended that a separate mess hall and officers club be established for black and white officers.

The pilots quietly accepted the segregation, because they realized that the training they were receiving was very important to them for the continuation of the bombardment program; they were also aware that upon completion of the training, they would be sent to Selfridge Field. They decided to continue the training, but agreed that at Selfridge, they would challenge any attempt to segregate them.

Although the training of twin-engine pilots started at Tuskegee in September 1943, the 477th was not activated until January 1944, when COL Robert R. Selway was appointed its commanding officer. A native of Wyoming, and a West Point graduate, he had commanded and prepared the 332nd for combat. When COL Davis, Jr. took over command of the 332nd and leading it overseas into combat, COL Selway was also assigned the task of preparing the 477th for combat.

Although COL Selway was a great organizer and combat instructor, his attitude toward Blacks was similar to that of COL Cousins, who started the segregation of black pilots at Mather Field. Soon after the pilots arrived at Selfridge, the enlisted men informed them of COL Selway's segregation practices. The pilots decided that they would not tolerate any discriminatory practices and agreed to challenge COL Selway, regardless of the outcome of a confrontation.

It was observed that an officers club was being hastily constructed for them. Instead of using the club prepared for them, the officers made application for membership in the old established club used by white officers. All of the applications were disapproved.

The disapprovals made the black officers more determined to challenge COL Selway's segregation policy, contending that Blacks were citizens of the United States under a Constitution that guaranteed them the same rights and privileges as other Americans, that it was the responsibility of the Federal Government to enforce those laws which protected the rights of the citizens.

The officers were aware that Army Regulation A-R 210-10 specifically stated that all officers clubs would be opened to all officers. With this in mind, when the officers attempted to enter the officers club, they were told by base Commander COL William L. Boyd in the presence of the Provost Marshal that black pilots were not welcomed and, therefore, access was being denied.

On being informed of the confrontation, COL Selway, the next morning, called an assembly, informing the officers that they were henceforth neither to enter the club nor make applications for membership.

General Frank O. Hunter, Commanding General First Air Force, was also informed of the confrontation, prompting him to make a special visit to Selfridge Field. He called an assembly, at which he stated that "the War Department was not ready to recognize Blacks on the social level equal to white men; that it was not time for Blacks to fight for equal rights or personal advantage; they should prove themselves in combat first." He then remarked that "there will be no race problems here, for I will not tolerate any mixing of the races and anyone who protests will be classed as an agitator, sought out, and dealt with accordingly." He urged COL Boyd to "stand firm" and later in a conversation with General Giles of the Air Staff, he commented on his segregation stance: "I didn't condone it; I ordered it."(1)

The Air Corps defended COL Boyd and praised him as being "well qualified and especially selected for the duty." It reported that a gym, service club and officers club were in process of being constructed and efforts were being made to implement expressed War Department's policy concerning equality of treatment of all military personnel. It related that it had established as a cardinal policy, "explicitly and definite direction" that recreational and social activities on each base, where colored and white troops are stationed jointly, should be so provided and handled as to avoid charges of discrimination or prejudice toward members of either race.

Faced with pressure from some congressmen and black leaders, the War Department instructed the Air Force Inspector to appraise the situation and to make recommendations. The Air Inspector appointed General Benjamin O. Davis, Sr. and COL Harvey Shoemaker to make the investigation. They reported that COL Boyd had forbade the black officers to use the officers club and used insulting language in conveying his views on the subject to a black officer. They charged that LTC Charles Gayle, the commander of the 553rd, a squadron activated to furnish trained combat replacement for the 332nd, had threatened the black officers under his command--that, "he would court martial for exciting a riot, the first man who stepped into the officers club."(2)

In his report to the War Department, the Air Inspector stated that since the officers club was closed after the confrontation, the problem was resolved, concluding that LTC Gayle mishandled the matter, but that COL Boyd was impartial, rational and made himself accessible to the black personnel on the base. He also reported that Army Air Corps leaders believed that the main source of racial unrest stemmed from the city of Detroit, that "Detroit has always been a center of racial activities and the communist elements are particularly active among Negroes at present." They further believed that the black press was attempting to start racial incidents and that it was playing up events at the base. The Inspector recommended that the 477th be moved from the area and from exploitation by the press, suggesting that the 477th be relocated in an area so remote that mail could be censored to prevent adverse criticism from reaching the United States.

Truman Gibson, in a letter to Assistant Secretary of War John J. McCloy, stated that Michigan had a Civil rights law, that black officers had used the club without incident in the past and considering the fact that black officers had been stationed at Selfridge for more than a year, it was only recent that efforts were made to provide them with a separate club. He charged that black living quarters were inferior and unsatisfactory, pointing out that the War Department had not always enforced its policies which were often vague and ambiguous; therefore, the Air Force was able to get by with a minimum initiative on the whole issue of equal treatment.

General Arnold agreed with the recommendation of the Air Inspector, favoring moving the 477th to Antiqua or Saint Lucia in the Caribbean, but realizing that the decision was to be made by the Secretary of State. He recommended that a detailed study of the problem be made for the Secretary, suggesting the reports should emphasize the influence of local agitation in the city of Detroit and their adverse affect on training and discipline, with a recommendation that, any location selected, must have a minimum interference so that the pilots of the 477th could be properly trained for combat.

During the summer and fall of 1944, a series of articles appeared in the *Pittsburgh Courier*, a popular black newspaper. The articles expressed the discontent of the members of the 477th at Godman Field, emphasizing their appeal to be moved from the South. The author of the article was Tom Young. Not satisfied with just publicizing the plight of the 477th, he proceeded to give publicity to the conditions at Tuskegee. On September 16, 1944, there appeared an article by an anonymous "Jack Day" titled, *The Inside Story of Tuskegee*. Highly colored with mockery, it basically expressed vividly the practices at Tuskegee as Blacks saw them.

Most of the material for the article was supplied to Young by his friend, LT Emory Smith, a graduate of Howard University. Smith had attended the Adjutant's General School, Fort Washington, MD, before being sent to Tuskegee and assigned as Assistant Personnel Officer, Post Headquarters.

Although COL Parrish was more tactful in handling the racial and social problems at Tuskegee than COL Kimble, he made no substantial changes in the operation of the base. There still remained numerous practices that tended to cause resentment by the black personnel.

When it was decided that a segregated base would be established for Blacks, high Army officials tried to explain their actions. They contended that the humiliation and possible maltreatment black cadets would face at unsegregated Army Air Force Schools would hinder them in developing the self confidence and initiative necessary as pilots.

When the construction of Tuskegee began, it was foreseen that a number of experienced white officers and enlisted men would be needed at the base until Blacks were sufficiently trained to operate the base. With this in mind, plans were drawn that provided for separate quarters and separate mess for white and black personnel.

It was then realized, by those who argued against the establishment of a segregated base for Blacks, that the Army, rather than shelter black soldiers from the humiliation and practices that tended to make them feel inferior, had deliberately planned such a program. Judge Hastie wrote, regarding the contemplated set-up at Tuskegee: "I protested against the segregation within the segregated training center. I pointed out that if the white officers and enlisted men wanted such segregation they were obviously unfit to train Negroes. Moreover, the psychological effect upon Negro officers and enlisted men was bound to be catastrophic. My representations were unavailing and the plan of racial segregation within the post was carried out."

Blacks were also told in the establishment of Tuskegee that black officers and enlisted men would replace the white personnel as rapidly as possible. Plans were made for the early graduates of the flying school to replace the white flying instructors and black non-rated graduates from various Officers Candidate Schools would replace the white non-rated officers. Yet, almost throughout the entire existence of the base, very few replacements were made, though there were numerous Blacks qualified for each position of the field. Black officers for the most part were relegated to positions that gave them little chance for promotions. While black officers were denied equal opportunities for service and advancement, they witnessed rapid advancement of young white officers, who were often less qualified.

In the spring of 1944, COL Parrish called an assembly to introduce the officer personnel of the field. He began by jokingly informing those assembled that he hated to disappoint them, but he was not being transferred. He received overwhelming applause of approval. In spite of the gripes, most of the personnel wanted him to remain at Tuskegee. It appeared that most of the personnel believed he meant well, but his hands were tied by the long social tradition of the country and more directly by high officials of the Pentagon. However, there were assistants galore, assistant to the assistant Mess Officer, assistant to the assistant Supply Officer, assistant to this, to that, and even an assistant to a makeshift position of the Post Beautification Officer. There were so many, in fact, that it was actually humiliating. Those who had gone through the rigors of training at the various officer training schools felt useless and despondent. Even though hundreds of able-bodied men were sitting around at Tuskegee doing practically nothing, the Army was in dire need of men on the battlefield. But it was Air Force policy to send all black graduates from the various officers training schools to Tuskegee.

The odious practices reached such proportions that LT James S. Mosley of Philadelphia felt it necessary to submit a letter of resignation while still in pilot training. The resignation read as follows: "Not believing in war primarily, I relinquished any rights I might have had, as a citizen, to adhere to this ideal by submitting to the draft. In doing so, I compromised certain ideals which I considered fundamental in human relations. In return for this compromise, along with thousands of others, I sincerely anticipated correspondingly progressive advances in policy and practice, relative to the treatment of minority segments of the Army, the Negro soldier, specifically.

"The war aims were directed primarily at uprooting the evil of man against man. These evils were described under varied titles, Nazism, Fascism, etc. Notwithstanding, I find many of the basic evils of the two aforementioned conditions existing within the structure of our Army. Worse, there is no definite move under way for the abolition of these practices. Namely, the establishment of segregation and the accompany evils of discrimination, which literally divides the Army into a caste system. Proof that it is discriminatory as well as segregated is found in the fact that it is Army policy never to have members of the non-white Army command units of the white. Though the antithesis is so frequent as to become odd indeed to find even a non-white in command of a non-white unit.

"These discriminatory practices together with the failure of the army to provide protection for personnel in hostile communi- ties... has led men to ponder seriously the cause for which so many sacrifice so much."

Many members of the 99th and the 332rd found Tuskegee a very disheartening place when they returned from combat. Though they had risked their lives fighting for their country, they were given no assignments to keep them occupied. Even COL Roberts, who had commanded the 99th and the 332nd in combat, met with the same degrading treatment. Even though he was quite capable as a leader, administrator and combat pilot, he was assigned as Bachelor Quarters Officer, a position that the lowest non-commissioned officer could have held.

COL Parrish was deeply disturbed by the article published in the *Pittsburgh Courier*. Later, he revealed that he and his Public Relations Officer made a special visit to the office of the *Pittsburgh Courier* to voice their complaint to the editor. The editor, however, informed them that since the article had already been published, there was nothing he could do.

COL (now General, ret.) Parrish, recalling his experience at Tuskegee, said he felt he was unjustly criticized by the writer for the *Pittsburgh Courier* and some who had served with him at Tuskegee, relating that he permitted the relatively few white officers to live off-base because he was determined to avoid friction between the races. He believed that if white officers had been made to live on the base there would have been trouble. As to the allegations that the white officers received promotions quickly, he stated, "they received promotions only when required by regulations." In fact, he stated "most of the white officers believed that they were being punished by being sent to Tuskegee," and he added, "that in some respect they were." They believed that they could advance quicker in combat or at larger bases where there were more positions to be filled and many more promotions. He revealed that two of his best flying instructors were sent to Tuskegee as punishment for infractions at another base. Then, there were two other men who demanded that they be transferred. He was reluctant to let them leave until they threatened to cause trouble. Rather than have them face a court martial, he sent them away.

COL Parrish said that the main gripe of the white officers was that at Tuskegee they had no social life, there being few white women in the area. They did have a little place where they could socialize, but that it was not much of a place.

He related that it was very difficult finding assignments for the veterans. The position assigned LTC Roberts was a perfectly legitimate position held by high ranking officers at other fields. He also stated that he already had more officers than positions, that before the veterans returned; they had a choice of going to Waltersboro, SC to help train replacements for the 332nd; instead, they elected to return to Tuskegee. "I had to find some assignment for them, it was required, and I did the best I could."

The publicity given the plight of the 477th prompted Truman Gibson to visit Godman Field. He reported that the morale of the men was exceedingly low, due partly to the fact that all supervisory personnel were white and that there was little contact between the command and the black officers. He related that racial lines were sharply drawn and that supervisors held their positions merely because they were white and not because of any superior ability or training.(4)

Godman Field proved to be too small to accommodate the 477th and its support units. In addition, it lacked adequate recreation facilities. Fort Knox had the facilities, but permitted the black personnel of Godman Field to use only the Post Exchange and a section of the segregated theatre.

The continuous complaints about poor facilities at Godman Field and those of the near-by town led the Air Force to transfer the 477th between March 2 and March 7, 1945 to Freeman Field.

There were two officers club buildings at Freeman Field. Although the War Department directive of August 1944 prohibited the segregation of recreation facilities, it did stipulate that facilities could be designated for units and organizations. However, there was Army Regulation 210-10 that stated that all officers at an Army Post had the right to membership in all officers clubs. COL Selway ignored the Army Regulation and took advantage of the loop hole in the directive of August 1944 that sanctioned the designation of facilities for units and organizations.

On March 10, 1945, General Hunter and COL Selway devised a plan designating one of the clubs for Blacks, and agreed not to mention color in connection with their plan. Meanwhile, the black officers were using the facilities of the club used by white officers, causing COL Selway to call and discuss the problem with General Hunter.

He informed the General that he thought it would be best to close the club until a decision was made on the legality of the separate club. General Hunter advised him to "stand firm", that he would be delighted for them to commit enough action "for he could court martial some of them."(5)

On April 1, 1945, COL Selway issued a directive stating his policy relative to the designation of clubs. A few days later, on April 5, the combat training squadron, the administrative unit of the 477th arrived from Godman Field. On being informed of COL Selway's directive, the men let it be known that they would disregard it and would use the club designated for whites.

COL Selway was informed that the members of the 477th would attempt to enter the club, ordering the Provost Marshal to station guards at the front door of the club, and to lock all other doors.

The officers arrived as anticipated, and, on attempting to enter, were challenged by the guard whom they pushed aside and entered the club. On refusing to leave when ordered, the Provost Marshal placed 36 officers under arrest.

Alfred McKenzie, one of the officers who was arrested, said, "Now we realized that this was not a matter of a prejudice individual or local prejudice, but an Army Air Force policy. We decided to continue the challenge and took turns in the challenge."

The continuous challenge prompted COL Selway to close the club and request legal experts from the First Air Force Headquarters at Mitchell Field, NY to assist him in preparing charges against the challenging officers.

The legal experts decided that the directive of April 1 was inexact and ambiguous in the meaning and purpose. COL Torgils Wold, the Air Inspector, confided that the order was quite obvious to separate colored from white officers, in regard to certain base facilities. Instead of denouncing the directive, he recommended that another directive more concise and clear be prepared in the form of "a base regulation" to effect the degree of separation desired.

COL Selway, with the help of General Hunter, prepared a base regulation as suggested. On April 9, 1945, the members of the 477th were given the newly prepared regulation, titled "Assignment of Housing, Messing, and Recreation Facilities for Officers, Flight Officers, and Warrant Officers." In preparing the regulation, COL Selway assigned all trainees assumed to be black to one club and all supervisory personnel, assumed to be white to the other club. He overlooked the fact that some of the black officers of the 477th, such as Chaplains and Surgeons were not trainees, and therefore qualified for membership in the white club.

F/O McKenzie said "that the regulation completely segregated us from all of the facilities used by the white officers. We were instructed to sign that we had read and understood the regulation. We responded by stating, that we did not understand the regulation, so they deleted the word "Understand". We were instructed to sign that we had read the regulation, but when we refused to sign, 101 of us were placed under arrest and marched between lines of heavily armed guards to C-47 transport aircraft, waiting to fly us to Godman Field.

"When we arrived at Godman Field, we were housed in specially prepared barracks that had flood lights installed on and around the buildings. It was like a Nazi prison camp. We could expect such treatment from the Germans or Japanese, but here was our own country, for which we were preparing to fight and die for, treating us in such a manner. Anyway, we learned where the first line of battle was and we were more determined to fight any attempt to segregate us. We all agreed that if the 477th were sent overseas, some of us wouldn't return, and since none of us knew who would be the victims, all of us should take the risk right here at home, at least we would be dying for our rights as human beings."

On April 14, General Roy Owens, the Deputy Chief of Staff, informed General Hunter that a meeting between the Secretary of the Air Force, Robert Lovett, and General Giles, Kuter, and Timberlake, a decision was made to return the 477th to Godman Field within a few days and that the replacement to General Selway was discussed. A week later, General Owens informed General Hunter that General Giles had recommended and Marshall approved the release of the 101 officers under arrest in quarters and charges would be dropped against all but three officers. Each of the officers, however, would be given an administrative reprimand. The three officers accused of forcing their way into the officers club were to be brought to trial and the 477th returned to Godman Field. General Hunter requested that COL Selway remain as commander of the 477th "to avoid giving Blacks the idea that they had got another one."

Meantime, the arrested officers, led by a young labor leader from Detroit, Coleman Young (the future Mayor of Detroit), were making plans for their defense. As they debated and vented their anger, one officer, William T. Coleman, a law student from Philadelphia, sat alone and listened.

When the talk subsided, he arose and said, "I have been sitting here listening to a bunch of damn dummies, planning how to get all of us hanged or sent to prison for life. Now, if you don't know what you are doing, you better ask someone. You are not challenging a Colonel or General; you are challenging the War Department--the United States government. Believe me, they are just waiting for you to make one mistake--one mistake, and they will be on you like a bunch of tigers."

One of the officers sarcastically remarked, "If this gentleman is so smart, smarter than all of us dummies, I am sure he will advise us, as to what we should do to save our necks." Another officer remarked, "If you don't know it, he was a Philadelphia law student before entering the service. We all know that Philadelphia lawyers have a reputation for knowing everything about the law."

McKenzie related that LT Coleman, whom they nicknamed *Bumps*, later served as Secretary of Transportation during President Ford'a administration. Anyway, LT Coleman replied, "If you guys listen to me and don't go too far, everything will be all right. Don't worry, I'm going to get you out. Just follow my instructions. I will draft a letter and I want each of you to copy the letter and submit your letter to the commanding officer at Freeman Field." The letter read:

SUBJECT: Request for Individual Counsel
TO: Commanding Officer, Freeman Field, Indiana
I, being advised of my right to individual counsel and being, at present, in arrest by your order at this station, pending preferment and processing of charges against me, herewith and hereby request to be represented by counsel as follows, and I do further request that the below named counsel be granted permission to see me without further delay, for the purpose of adequately preparing my defense. Military Counsel: 1st Lieut. Edward K Nichols, Jr., Regional Hospital, Ft. Knox, Kentucky
Civilian Counsel: William H. Hastie, Esq., Dean of Howard University Law School, Washington, DC

The officers were held under arrest for 12 days before a General from Fort Knox arrived. After talking to the men, he informed them that the charges against them were dropped and that they were free to leave the barracks. The three officers accused of resisting arrest by the Provost Marshal, however, were referred for trial by Court Martial.

General Hunter assigned COL Davis, Jr. and nine other black officers to sit as a General Court Martial. The members realized that by appointing COL Davis to supervise the court martial was not only embarrassing and frustrating to him, but surmised that an unfavorable decision might jeopardize his army career.

COL Davis was quickly changed by the defense and dismissed as a member of the court. The three officers being tried, LT Shirly R. Clifton of Camden, NJ, Marsden A. Thompson and Roger C. Terry both of Los Angeles, were charged with refusing to obey the order of a superior officer by entering the officers club and mess hall and refusing to obey when ordered into arrest. LT Clifton and Thompson were acquitted of both charges, but Terry was found guilty of refusing arrest and was fined 50 dollars for three months. The other arrested officers of the 477th received letters of reprimand from COL Selway, which read:

On or about 11 April 1945, at Freeman Field, Seymour Indiana, you displayed a stubborn and uncooperative attitude toward the reasonable efforts of constituted authority to disseminate among officers and flight officers of the command information concerning necessary and proper measures accepted in the administration of the officers club at this station. This action on your part indicates that you lack appreciation of the high standard of team work expected of you, as an officer of the Army of the United States, and a failure to understand that you should conduct yourself at all times so as to be a credit and source of pride to military service. In these respects, you have failed definitely in your obligation to your command and your country. It is hoped and expected that you will consider this reprimand as a stern reminder of the absolute requirements of prompt and willing compliance with the policies and superior authority, and that there will be no repetition of such regrettable action on your part. This reprimand will be made part of your official record, you will acknowledge receipt by endorsing hereon.

In reply to COL Selway's reprimand, a number of officers submitted the following letter:

For the record, the undersigned wishes to indicate over his signature, his unshakable belief that racial bias is Fascistic, un-American, and directly contrary to the ideals for which he is willing to fight and die. There is no officer in the Army who is willing to fight harder, or more honorably for his country and the command than the undersigned. Nor is there an officer, with a deeper respect for the lawful orders of superior authority. The undersigned does not expect or request any preferential treatment for the tenure of his service, but asks only protection of his substantial rights as a soldier and as an individual, the same identical opportunities for service and advancement offered all other military personnel, and the extension of the identical courtesies extended all other officers of the Army.

Meantime, the McCloy Committee at the War Department was studying the events at Freeman Field. On May 19, it met to consider the report and recommendations of the Inspector General. After reading the report, the Committee decided that the separation of the officers club and facilities was not in accord with existing regulations.

On June 4, 1945, Secretary McCloy, in a letter to Secretary of War Stimson, pointed out that the issue at Freeman Field was whether or not a Post Commander had the authority to exclude individuals because of race from using recreational facilities on any Army Post.

He stated that the Army Air Force suggested that the Army return to a policy of separate but equal facilities, that what he stated would be a reverse of the position taken by the War Department in the Selfridge Field case and in his opinion would be a step backward.

The widespread publicity given the Freeman Field confrontation and pressure from black and white leaders moved the War Department to pressure the Air Force to settle the issue. The Air Force responded by removing COL Selway and appointing COL Davis on June 21, 1945, to command the newly activated 477th Composite Group. The new Group, when completed, was to consist of two bomber squadrons and one pursuit squadron of the 332nd. The other two squadrons of the 332nd were to be retained as reserves.

LTG Eaker, who had become the Acting Commanding General of the Army Air Forces, flew from Washington, DC to Godman Field to install COL Davis in his new position. The other officials participating in the ceremony were BG Davis, Sr. of the Office of the Inspector General, European Theatre of Operation, BG Glenn, of the War Department and Mr. Truman K Gibson, Jr., the Civilian Aide to the Secretary of War.

General Eaker, in his address to the large crowd that had gathered for the ceremony, said, "It was upon my recommendation and insistence that COL Davis is to take command of this Group because of the excellent work I saw him do overseas." He revealed that General MacArthur, when asked whether he would accept the 477th in the Pacific, replied, "I'll take anybody willing to fight the Japs."

General Davis, Sr., speaking to the members of the 477th, said, "The Department is sparing no pains to give to you the advantages of experience. Your new commanding officer, COL Davis, and the officers accompanying him from his former assignment are men fresh from the European combat zone. Nearly all of them have not only been in combat but they have been awarded decorations for meritorious service performed in combat.

"The *Jap* is a rough soldier and in most cases he has to be killed. To the veterans of World War I, who may be with you now and have not had combat experience in the present war, I would like to say that the experience of the soldier of the present war is far different from that of yours.... The only people who know how to fight this war to the best advantage are the people who have had actual combat experience with the enemy. I wish to congratulate you on the calibre of the officers to be assigned to you. They have the confidence of the Department and the respect of the men they have fought with and against. I urge you to give them your wholehearted loyalty, support, and maximum effort to bring about a victory."

The great surprise came on July 1, 1945, when COL Davis was appointed commanding officer of Godman Field. This gave him the distinction of being the first Negro to command an Army Air Force base in the United States. He assumed the new command with the same enthusiasm and confidence that he portrayed in his command of the 99th and the 332nd. Immediately, he sat about to build up Godman Field by soliciting experienced ground officers and enlisted men from Tuskegee Army Air Field. To strengthen the 477th, he also had a large number of veteran pilots at Tuskegee transferred to Godman.

The takeover of the 477th and Godman Field, ironically, came at a time when officials of Tuskegee Army Air Field were planning the Field's fourth anniversary celebration. COL Parrish took the opportunity to express his delight in the progress made at Tuskegee. In an article published in the Base newspaper, *The Hawk Cry*, he wrote:

When we celebrated our third anniversary last year, we were very hopeful of an early victory in Europe. Those hopes were based more on our desire than on the military; so it seemed to many that victory was long delayed. We are now hopeful of an early final victory, but our progress at this station is designed for an extended effort. We now have more pilots in training than ever before.

We have supplied all the rated personnel and many others for an entire new unit preparing for action in the Pacific. We have already enrolled in training sufficient pilots to maintain this unit through the entire year of combat operation.

We, at this station, have started so many new and different jobs that it is difficult now to understand there are no new jobs to attack. We have still a job to finish in order to supply the men required to keep in action the units we have already created. We have many other services to perform as we have in the past, including the training of men on the job who will eventually use their skills and experience gained here for the benefit of other units all over the world at present and eventually in the peace at home.

We have done a much bigger job than anyone could possibly predict four years ago. It is up to us now to finish that job with ever-increasing efficiency and make some contributions through every individual stationed here to the future welfare of a peaceful and united nation.

The fourth anniversary celebration was planned to be the largest celebration in the history of the base, and turned out to be much larger than anticipated. COL Davis started the celebration by praising COL Parrish for his broad shoulders and his contribution to the war efforts by "carrying out the War Department's Experiment far beyond the experimented state." Dr. Frederick D. Patterson, President of Tuskegee Institute, COL Eugene Dibble, Director of Tuskegee Veterans Hospital and MAJ H. C. Magoon, Commander of the Primary Training Detachment at Tuskegee Institute, also praised COL Parrish for the "wonderful job he had done in the training of black combat pilots."

COL Davis, in his address, remarked, "I am very proud to have been at one time part of this training center and am deeply grateful for all that I have learned here.

"It would be relatively easy to heap praise upon praise for your accomplishments. It should state that a very definite and concrete contribution to the War effort has been made here at Tuskegee. Fortunately, this is completely unnecessary, for, the men whom you have trained here have produced an indelible record reflecting the accomplishments of Tuskegee. It is a record written in blood of our own and that of our enemies, in Italy, France, Greece, Yugoslavia, Albania, Bulgaria, Hungary, Austria, Czechoslovakia, Poland, and Germany. It is a record that stands on its own, and empty words would not add to it.

"All Americans hate war; it is basic American philosophy not to seek war, but to prevent it. This has been true from the shot heard around the world at Lexington to the treachery of Pearl Harbor. It is also true, and I am proud to say, that whenever there has been war, American Negroes have been more than willing to carry out their share. Bunker Hill, San Juan, the Argonne Forest, Bataan, and the shores of Normandy are all drenched with the blood of Negroes who have made the supreme sacrifice for the right to be called Americans without qualifications."

In February 1945, Roosevelt, Churchill and Stalin met in a conference at Yalta. During the meeting, Stalin agreed to the terms of a secret agreement stipulating that Russia would declare war on Japan three months after Germany surrendered. On July 26, 1945, officials of Great Britain, China and the United States met at Potsdam, Germany and issued the Potsdam Declaration demanding that Japan accept an unconditional surrender ultimatum. Japan refused, and on August 6, the first atomic bomb was dropped on the Japanese city of Hiroshima.

The bomb had more destructive power than 20,000 tons of TNT and more than 2,000 times the power of the largest bomb previously used in the war. The bomb destroyed approximately 60% of Hiroshima--an area of two and a half miles in diameter was completely destroyed. It is estimated that 130,000 persons were either killed, badly injured or reported missing. Two days after the bomb on Hiroshima, Stalin declared war on Japan and launched a powerful offensive against Japanese forces in Manchuria.

In Spite of Russia's declaration of War and the great destruction of Hiroshima, the Japanese government was still reluctant to accept an unconditional surrender. On August 9, 1945, the United States released a second atomic bomb--this time on Nagasaki. With a destruction comparable to that of Hiroshima, it brought quick action. On August 10, Japan announced that it would accept the Potsdam terms, provided that the surrender would not be construed to "compromise any demand which prejudices the prerogatives of his majesty as a Sovereign Ruler."

The Allies replied that "from the moment of surrender, the authority of the Emperor and the Japanese government to rule the state shall be subject to the Supreme Allied Commander, who shall take such steps as he deems proper to effectuate the surrender terms."

Fearing other bombs would be dropped, the Japanese accepted the surrender terms on Tuesday, August 14, 1945. That evening at 7:00 P.M., President Truman announced over radio that the Japanese had surrendered, and declared a 48 hour holiday for the nation.

The two-day holiday just about closed down operations at Tuskegee. The airmen and civilian workers spent the days enjoying the facilities at Tuskegee. But the celebration reached its climax with the arrival of *Lucky* Millinder and his orchestra on August 15, and entertained perhaps the largest gathering ever at the Post Amphitheater.

The mood of jubilation, however, did not last long. Now, both airmen and civilian employees were faced with reality. They were aware that the war had ended and that the base would probably be closed. This meant that not only the pleasure of Tuskegee would end, but many of their jobs would also be terminated. Most disturbing, however, was the thought that after four years of war, Blacks had gained practically no respect and acceptance by whites, that the law of the land, which sanctioned discrimination and segregation, still prevailed.

The opposition to the segregated base at Tuskegee reached its climax in late 1945, when President Patterson of Tuskegee Institute requested the War Department to consider other locations for a peace time base for Negro Airmen. In a telegram to the Chief of Staff at the War Department, he advised:

"Acting on advice which I regarded as reliable and personally believing that participation of Negroes in the Army Air Force could be encouraged and effectively aided by the use of the splendid facilities and relationships developed during the war at Tuskegee Army Air Field, I suggested to you that tactical reserve units for peace time be based at the government owned and operated field.

"Information now received indicates objection by an important percentage of Negro flying officers to basing of such tactical units at the field.

"I, therefore, withdraw my suggestion that this be done. I do not believe that the best interest of the Negro in the Army Air Force will be served if the Group were stationed in the community with the personnel of the said group displeased with the location."

In spite of all efforts by COL. Parrish to divorce the national racial problem from the operations at Tuskegee, he continued to be harassed by the racial problem. He observed the frustrations and impatience of Blacks with the progress made in race relations and the growing belligerent attitude of Blacks toward the government they believed had no intention of abrogating its segregation and discrimination policies. However, despite the growing militancy on the part of Blacks, COL Parrish moved ahead with his training program. On October 16, 1945, Tuskegee graduated its smallest class 45-G. It was divided almost equally between cadets and student officers. Most of the student officers had been commissioned as navigators and bombardiers and now were awarded a third rating.

The graduation speech was delivered by Dr. Edwin R. Embree, President of the Rosenwald Foundation. He was brought to the base in a B-25 flown by John Daniels, a veteran combat pilot. The selection of Dr. Embree by COL Parrish appeared to have been designed to bring a special message to the Blacks.

Dr. Embree began sketching the progress Blacks had made through persistence and competence. He warned against intolerance and the common fault of minority groups who fight among themselves as well as against each other. He continued,"I am not going to glorify the brave deeds of war. You know America is proud of you. Instead, I want to think out with you, soberly and frankly, how you and we may work out our problems in building the fully democratic America we both want...

"You have a special responsibility to your group and to the nation.

"To win the home-front, peace time battle of democracy, even wise and more courageous leadership will be required of you specially trained men than would have been needed in war in foreign fields. You need especially three qualities: perseverance, competence, and cooperation.

"This country is still far from a full-functioning democracy. But we have been moving steadily if slowly toward that goal for 300 years. But arrogance and intolerance are rising too. Opposing the fresh urge to democracy is the angry determination to maintain a master race, a master class, a mastery of vested interest.

"To win the home-front, peace-time battle of democracy, even the wise have been trodden upon... Instead of fighting for equality, they struggle for the privilege of trampling on someone else...

"A Negro fascist is just as ugly as a white fascist... We are not going to get democracy in America so long as each group strives for special advantages for itself. We are not going to break the tough wall of segregation and discrimination unless all groups unite in behalf of full participation in all phases of American life by all of the people."

In July 1945, some members of the 99th returned to the States and were assigned to the 477th. MAJ William A. Campbell, who had commanded the 99th overseas, was reassigned to the 477th. The remaining squadrons of the 332nd, led by LTC Roberts, arrived at Pier 15, Staten Island, aboard the *USS. Levi Woodbury* on October 17, 1945. Here the members of the Group were heartily received by a crowd who had gathered to welcome them. As soon as disembarkation was completed, the 322nd was sent to Camp Kilmer, New Jersey, where it was deactivated. A large percentage of its enlisted personnel was discharged while the remainder was given extended leave before being reassigned to new stations. Most of the officers were reassigned either to Tuskegee Army Air Field or to Godman Field.

COL Davis reassigned a large percentage of the experienced staff personnel of the 332nd to responsible positions at Godman Field. MAJ Edward Gleed, who had served as the Commander of the 301st and as Operations Officer for the 332nd, was assigned as Operation Officer for the 477th. MAJ Elmer Jones, who had served as Commander of the 523rd Air Service Group that supported the 332nd in combat, was assigned as Commander of the 387th Service Group, a support group for the 477th. MAJ Thomas J. Money was assigned as Executive Officer, and CPT Omar Blair was assigned as Commander of the Material Squadron of the Service Group.

COL Davis also appointed CPT Charles I. Williams to command the 617th, Elmore Kennedy to command the 618th, J. H. Williams, the 602nd Air Engineer Squadron, and Elizabeth C. Hampton, the 118th WAC Squadron.

When the war ended, Tuskegee continued its pilot training program for those classes already in training. However, On June 29, 1946, the last class of pilots 46-C, namely Charles W. Allen, George E. Bell, William C. Carter, Conrad Cheek, Jack Chin, Edward Drumond, James W. Allison, Claude A. Rown, and Nicholas S. Neblett were graduated and assigned to the 477th.

Shortly after the last class was graduated, Tuskegee was placed on inactive status. Many years later, General Parrish, reminiscing his experiences during the war, said, "I believe the closing of Tuskegee was one of my most frustrating experiences. When Tuskegee was ordered inactivated, COL Davis was informed that any personnel he needed could be acquired from Tuskegee. COL Davis immediately made request for all of my experienced personnel. I immediately began to complain to COL Davis and to Air Force officials that I needed my experienced personnel if I were to dismantle the base. 'You know,' he said, 'it is almost as big a job to deactivate a base as to activate a base. There was all the paperwork to be processed, the inventories to be made, the supplies, equipment, machines, vehicles and airplanes to be shipped out; and finally, the dismantling of the buildings.' It was frustrating to even think of the job without experienced help. Anyway, the Colonel and I worked out an agreement, and things worked out fine. I was transferred to the Army War College at Maxwell Field, AL before the job was completed. COL Donald McPherson, who succeeded me, completed the job."

* * *

At the concluding banquet of the 1995 National Convention of the Tuskegee Airmen held in Atlanta, GA, National President Roger C. *Bill* Terry finally received a resolution from Rodney A. Coleman, Assistant Secretary of the Air Force for manpower, reserve affairs, installations and environment acquitting him of any wrong doing while at Freeman Field. Additionally, the Service restored all the rights, privileges and property Terry had lost due to that conviction. The reading of the Resolution drew a thunderous applause amidst copious tears of joy. Thus, another injustice has been rectified.

(A list--of those pardoned in 1995 by General R. Fogelman, Chief of Staff USAF--can be found in the Appendix. See also the chapter, "To Do Battle", in which the complete transcript of LeRoy Battle is reproduced).

Atlanta, GA August 12, 1995, Roger C. Terry, President of the Tuskegee Airmen, is surrounded by Colonel Caso, Frank *Fuzzy* Hector, and admirer, celebrating the vindication of over one hundred Tuskegeeans who had held fast against segregation and racism, photo courtesy of Sylvia Freeman.

Top: MAJ Mattison, CPT Temple, LT Stewart, LT Harvey and LT Alexander. Bottom: LT George G. Turner, LT Clinton E. McIntyre, LT George B. Choise, (Unknown), F/O Clifford C. Mosley, F/O Harold B. Maples, LT Henry T. Holland.

Chapter 21
Integrating the Air Forces

On September 2, 1945, aboard the battleship Missouri anchored in Tokyo Bay, high Japanese officials surrendered, bringing World War II to an end. General Benjamin O. Davis, Jr., recalling the end of the war, said, "When it was announced that Japan had surrendered, I felt sorry for the men of the 477th. I wanted the war to end, because of the unnecessary bloodshed and deaths; but the men had trained so hard and sacrificed so much in preparation for combat, I was somewhat disappointed because I wanted to lead them into combat. They were so disappointed because they really wanted to get in combat to prove they were a competent combat unit. They were a damn good group of men; they had pride. I wanted to lead them, because I knew they were well trained for combat and would make a good showing. They were just unfortunate not getting into combat and as a result received little recognition for all of their efforts."

General Parrish also had faith in the members of the 477th. He said, "You know, we spent a lot of money and time training those men. When they left Tuskegee for combat training, there was no doubt in my mind that they would be successful. We had all of those men trained and ready for combat, but they wouldn't send them overseas when they were not really needed. At one point in the war in Europe, they were short of bomber pilots and they used volunteer fighter pilots to fly the bombers on missions. Imagine pilots with practically no experience in flying bombers, taking a crew of men on a combat mission! Fighter pilots and bomber pilots are two different breeds. They are trained for the type of flying and fighting they are to do. A fighter pilot is usually the dare-devil type of fellow, with quick reflexes, able to maneuver a plane instantly in any direction. He does his own shooting in combat and is responsible for his own life.

"I was trained as an attack pilot. Attack pilots come closer to the fighter pilot. Bomber pilots are altogether different. They are trained to take bombers up with heavy loads and a crew of men. They depend on their gunners to fight off enemy fighters or shoot them down. Now there is not too much maneuvering they can do; so they must be trained to fly more or less straight ahead, regardless of the opposition, with the hope and confidence that the gunners will do their job. It seemed to me foolish and careless with men's lives to send bomber crews on missions with inexperienced fighter pilots, especially when we had so many men well trained for the job."

Immediately following the cessation of hostility, the War Department began to analyze the problems it had encountered during the war. It concluded that the racial belief of white Americans that Blacks were inferior was so deeply ingrained in American society that it was necessary to develop a postwar era racial policy for the Armed Forces. It was realized that there was a growing militancy on the part of Blacks to challenge both military and civilian authorities. It was also realized that the war had weakened all of the United States allies, except for Russia. It was known that Russia, with her communistic ideology, was both strong and aggressive. It was feared that in case of a war with Russia, the division and hostility between the races would be detrimental to the war effort.

The presentation for the development of a post-war policy actually began before the war ended. On September 1, 1944, Assistant Secretary of War McCloy sent a memorandum to the Advisory Committee on Negro Troops Policy requesting a study be made that would insure a definite workable postwar policy.

A study was made and in May 1945, the Secretary submitted the study to the Army Air Force, requesting the Air Force prepare an evaluation of the performance of Blacks during the war and make recommendations for the use of Blacks in the postwar era. The Secretary suggested that all communications relating to the survey be classified as *Secret* and that Colored Personnel were not to know the survey was being made. It was feared that should black leaders and the black press learn of the survey, they would use it to put pressure on the military.

In compliance with the Secretary's directive, each Air Force set up a board to evaluate the Blacks under its command.

In the fall of 1945, the reports and recommendations were submitted to the War Department. The Surveys as a whole were critical of Blacks. Most of the commanders reported on the inability of Blacks to adjust to training, especially training that required skill and the ability to think fast. They reported that Blacks were best qualified to perform jobs requiring manual abilities rather than thought. The First Air Force, commanded by General Hunter, however, was by far the most critical.

It appeared that General Hunter and COL Selway used the survey to strike at the black airmen of the 477th that had challenged them during the war. COL Selway, who wrote the report for the General, criticized the members of the 477th for their leisurely pace in meeting the minimum standards of proficiency. He charged that, unlike white airmen, Blacks required longer periods of training, achieved a lower proficiency, lacked pride, initiative and discipline, were afraid of combat, lacked the sense of responsibility and the qualification for leadership. He stated, "the performance of the 332nd during the period of organization and training was approximately equal to the poorest of a comparable white unit." He blamed black leaders, organizations and the black press for urging black soldiers "to seek to gain social positions in the army which they do not have in civilian life and which is contrary to the customs and social usage of the country as a whole." He concluded that there was no practical use for Blacks except in a service capacity.(1)

COL Selway's report was so critical of Blacks that COL Louis Nippert, a staff officer, was assigned the task of requesting base commanders to submit evaluations of black troops, and preparing a summary report from the evaluations for General Arnold.

The evaluations by the base commanders were almost unanimously for segregation. COL Parrish was one of the few white men at that time who dared to express the conviction that Blacks should be accepted and treated as first class citizens. He stated that Tuskegee graduates met all Army Air Force standards; that all the planes were serviced by black mechanics and all of the administrative work was performed by Blacks. He commented:

"It is a discouraging fact that officers of the Army Air Force, whose scientific achievements are unsurpassed and whose scientific skill is unquestioned in mechanical matters and in many personal matters, should generally approach the problem of races and minorities with the most unscientific dogmatic and arbitrary attitudes.... Whether we like or dislike Negroes and whether they like us, under the Constitution of the United States, which we are all sworn to uphold, they are citizens of the United States having the same rights and privileges of other citizens and entitled to the same applications and protection of the laws."(2)

In the conclusion of his report, COL Parrish wrote: "Either the Constitution and the laws must be changed or we must make some adjustment rather than defensive bewildered evasions, at least where the officers are concerned. Negro officers should be assigned, according to qualifications, or dismissed. They cannot forever be isolated so that they will always be non-existent at meal time or at night. This has nothing to do with social problems or marriage, but only with a place to eat and sleep, and occasionally relax. The more rapidly officers in the Air Corps learn to accept these practical matters, as many of us have learned already, the better the position of everyone concerned. The answer is wider distribution, rather than greater concentration of Negro units, officers--and trainees."(3)

On September 17, 1945, COL Nippert submitted his Summary Report, reporting that black aviation cadets stanine (aptitude) scores had been lowered beyond what was justified to obtain any number of black pilot trainees and that training time for Blacks as considerably longer than for whites. Black officers were "below average in common sense, practical imagination, resourcefulness, aggressiveness, sense of responsibility, and in their ability to make decisions."

The report contributed to the disorder and confrontation initiated by Blacks, to the unwillingness of Blacks to accept segregation both on and off bases and Blacks' insistence on equal opportunity. It recommended equal training and opportunity in the postwar era, but at segregated facilities. It suggested that Blacks be assigned separate units, not to exceed the size of a group and that recreation and social activities be separate in accordance with local customs of the surrounding communities. It also recommended that employment of Blacks should not exceed 10 percent of the total personnel of the Army Air Force.

While COL Nippert was making his investigation, an investigative board appointed by the War Department began its own investigation. The board of four generals, chaired by General Alvan Gillem, was asked by the Secretary of War to prepare a policy for the use of black manpower by the services during the postwar period. It was directed to develop a program by which the country could derive the maximum efficiency from the full authorized manpower in the event of war.

During the summer of 1945, the Gillem Board convened, and a number of black and white leaders were called to testify.

The black leaders who testified were almost unanimously for integration. Dr. Frederick D. Patterson, President of Tuskegee Institute, one of the men instrumental in establishing the black pilot training program, recommended the employment of Blacks solely on ability, while Walter White, Secretary of the NAACP urged the board to end segregation because it was inefficient and caused racial frictions. Judge Hastie, charged that there had been a tendency to magnify the difficulties which integration might raise. He advised the board not to be concerned with civilian attitudes, because they need not "prevail over army policy." Army integration, he stated, would be less difficult than civilian, because of military training and discipline.

General Benjamin O. Davis, Sr. was the most militant and outspoken of those who testified. He stated that Blacks had been misassigned because of segregation. He charged that the Army was more concerned about eating and billeting than military effectiveness, and commented that the dichotomy between American ideals and practices must negatively impress foreign people such as the French, Russians and Brazilians.

Truman Gibson was of the opinion that full integration would not work. He suggested that select black individual servicemen be treated as individuals rather than as Blacks. He recommended a flexible policy and the maintenance of separate black platoons, companies and battalions within larger white organizations.

White military leaders were almost totally against the use of Blacks in combat roles. Again COL Parrish was the exception. He told the board that the Army had created resentment and precipitated the formation of groups of agitators. He asked the board to avoid the use of the controversial term "integration" and try simply to speak of assignments by qualifications. He stated that Blacks wanted only equality of opportunity and of individual treatment. However, despite the fact COL Parrish had more direct contact and knowledge of Blacks, civilian and military, than any of the other white military leaders, he was virtually ignored.

General Carl Spaatz, who had succeeded General Arnold as Commanding Chief of the Army Air Force, stated that the most carefully selected black air crewmen and pilots could not form an outfit of better than average efficiency. He doubted that the individual black could stand the pace of being integrated into white crews. He admitted that some Blacks had command ability, but was against them commanding white troops. He favored segregated training schools for black pilots and the use of black technical specialists at white installations if there were enough of them to have their own mess and barracks.

General Ira Eaker, who had become the Deputy Commanding General of the Air Force and the chief of the Air Staff, was one of the most vehement opponents of integration. During the war, he had solicited the service of COL Davis and the members of the 332nd to carry out his plan of close support for bomber crews, when white commanders and pilots refused. Now that the war was over--and Blacks may have perhaps saved his career, General Eaker turned his back on them. Of all people, he refused to accept black pilots on an equal basis with white pilots, contendending that blacks and whites "do not do their best work when so integrated", and that integration might cause difficulty in recruiting white volunteers. He expressed the opinion that the War Department should not conduct social experiments; that black officers would not be commissioned on merit if competing with white candidates; that Blacks should be promoted to staff jobs required by the size of black units, but should not be in command of white servicemen. He further stated that Blacks should not be permitted to attend white flying schools because they require more training time than whites, and would not graduate in a school run by white standards.(4)

General Dean C. Strother, who commanded the 15th Air Force Fighter Wing, under whom the 332nd served in combat, was equally prejudicial toward Blacks and against integration. During the war, he praised the pilots of the 332nd and awarded the Group with one of the highest honors, *The Presidential Unit Citation*. Now, he charged that the 332nd was never decorated because it was not good enough and that the 332nd was inferior to all of the white units in the theatre. He stated that with the exception of COL Davis, the officers of the Group lacked leadership, initiative, aggressiveness and dependability.

Despite the adverse appraisal of Blacks and the objections to integration by Army Air Force and other service, the Gillem Study recommended the peacetime utilization of Blacks in proportion to the population of the United States and the use of Blacks on a broader professional basis; it also recommended that combat and service units be organized from black manpower to meet the requirements of training and expansion. It further recommended that qualified individuals be utilized in appropriate special overhead units, that all officers be accorded the same rights, privileges, and opportunities for advancement.

The report took the Selfridge and Freeman fields confrontations in consideration when it stated that, "at mixed bases the War Department's policy regarding use of recreational facilities, and membership in officers clubs, mess, and similar social organizations be continued and made applicable in the post-war army." The board advised many officials that, "We must strive for improvements in the quality of the whole." "Blacks," it stated, "are no small part of the manpower reservoir... They are ready and eager to accept full responsibility as citizens and should be given every opportunity and aid to prepare themselves for effective service in company with every other citizen who are called to service."

The Board stated that it realized that American society was mainly segregated and that Blacks were looked upon with low esteem by white Americans, but it was necessary that white Americans be convinced that integration was best for all Americans. It advised officials of the services that, "Courageous leadership in implementing the program is imperative. All ranks must be imbued with the necessity for straightforward, unequivocating attitude towards the maintenance of a forward thinking policy... Vacillation or weak implementation of a strong policy will adversely affect the Army. The policy which is advocated is consistent with the democratic ideals upon which the nation and its representative Army are based."

Most of the military leaders refused to believe that the proposal by the Gillem Board was necessary and felt that the proposal was too advanced by calling for changes too rapidly. Army General Daniel Noce expressed the sentiment of most military officials when he wrote, "For the present and foreseeable future, social intermingling of Negroes and whites is not feasible. It is forbidden by law in some parts of the country and not practiced by the great majority of the people in the remainder of the country... To require citizens while in the Army to conform to a pattern of social behavior different from what they otherwise follow would be detrimental to the morale of white soldiers and would tend to defeat the effort to increase the opportunities and effectiveness of Negro soldiers. It would be a mistake for the Army to attempt to lead the nation in such a reform as social intermingling of the races.(5)

General Eaker, speaking for General Spaatz and himself, said, "We should not organize certain types of units for the sole purpose of advancing the prestige of one race, especially when it is necessary to utilize those units up to strength... The Army Air Force believes that the difficulties of the Colored problem will be with us as long as any extensive race prejudice exists in the United States. The real solution to the problem lies in the overall education on this subject, otherwise it will put itself in a position of stimulating racial disorders rather than overcoming them..."(6)

While the argument over integration of the service and the extent Blacks were to be used in the postwar Army, the 477th continued its training. However, it suffered from the shortage of personnel because many of its trained and experienced men were voluntarily leaving the service.

On March 13, 1946, the 477th and its support units were transferred from Godman Field to Lockbourne. The move was not welcomed by many of the white citizens of Columbus. The publicity given the Freeman Field confrontation caused the Group to be labeled as a "bunch of trouble makers."

COL Davis made aware of the attitude of the citizens of Columbus, immediately organized a program to establish a good working relationship with the citizens of Columbus. Blacks and whites of the city were invited to the various entertaining activities of the base, to witness flying exhibitions and to participate in the Field Day and other sport activities.

In many respects, Lockbourne became an extension of Tuskegee Army Air Field. In fact, when Tuskegee was closed, a sizeable number of men with special talents were sent to Lockbourne. It was here that the first postwar entertainment units sponsored by the USAF was organized. Much of the credit for the unit was due to the musical and organizational ability of LT Alvin Downing, who had served at Tuskegee as assistant band leader; on being transferred to Lockbourne, he was assigned as a Special Service Officer.

In the summer of 1947, Downing conceived the idea of stimulating the morale of the troops at Lockbourne by presenting a series of talent shows. Each week a different squadron was assigned the responsibility of entertaining the other squadrons. This proved to be so successful that Downing decided to adopt a variety show, titled *Operation Enjoyment*; it had been conceived by PFC Calvin Manuel, a professional actor before entering the service. He had not only acted in plays, but danced and played drums with symphony orchestras and jazz bands.

The first presentation of *Operation Enjoyment* was so successful that a second was requested. In August 1948, COL Joseph F. Goetz, Chief of the entertainment section of the USA.F., visited Lockbourne. COL Davis invited him to attend the show. COL Goetz was so impressed with the show that he persuaded the Air Force to sponsor it on a tour of bases throughout the United States.

The show was renamed *Operation Happiness*". After two months of reorganizing and rehearsing, it was presented with LT Daniel Chappie James as Emcee.

"Operation Happiness was a fun-packed and enjoyable show of dancing, comedy, magic acts, jazz, swing, and symphonic music.

"The star of the show was PFC Manuel, who performed in five different acts as a singer, dancer tap dancer, and comedian. The show also featured Wac Evelyn Matthews, who sang "I'll Close My Eyes", accompanied by an airmen chorus. She was followed by an airmen chorus called "The Skylanders", and a WAC dance group called the "Lockettes". The show also featured WAC SGT Verline Jones, who sang "Stormy Weather", WAC Rebecca Gilbert, who performed a Top Hat White Tie dance, PFC Ivory Mitchell, who gave piano renditions in jazz, swing and the classical *Warsaw Concerto.*

The show also consisted of a rendition of "Run Joe" by LT James, a magic act by SGT Crawley, a Jitterbug drill team led by SGT Charles Cook, a tap dance team consisting of PFC Manuel and SGT Gilbert, who tapped to the tune of "Tea For Two". Lastly, SGT Bill

Chatman sang "It's Magic", and the show ended with a thrilling piano battle between PFC Mitchell and LT Downing. In the finale, the entire cast, accompanied by the Lockbourne base band, sang the Army Air Corps song, "Into The Wild Blue Yonder".

After performing at a number of bases, the show was performed at a USAF World Wide Personnel Conference in Orlando, FL. It was such a hit that installations throughout the United States, Europe, and the Far East requested its performance. Changes, however, had been in the making for some time that would end the show.

On July 1, 1947, the 477th was inactivated and the 332nd was reactivated. Approximately one month later, on August 15, another change was made when the 332nd was reorganized and designated as the 332nd. While these changes were being made at Lockbourne, Congress was considering making the Army Air Force an independent branch of service. In July 1947, it passed the National Security Act which established the United States Air Force.

The newly-created US Air Force, however, still held to the basic doctrine of separate but equal rights. The organization of the US Air Force proved to be very difficult because it came at a time when large numbers of experienced men were leaving the service. It was especially true for the black units at Lockbourne, because the experienced personnel could not easily be replaced. The black training program at Tuskegee had been terminated and the segregated policy of the Air Force precluded the assignment of white personnel to the undermanned units at Lockbourne. It was alleged that there was a strong desire by some Air Force officials to let the organization at Lockbourne "die from the lack of personnel". MG Paul Williams, the Commander of the 9th Air Force, under whom Lockbourne Air Base operated, was in favor of maintaining the black units. He expressed satisfaction with the black units and stated that the "record of the parent units including the 477th was known to every student of World War II, and if for only political reasons, the 332nd Wing had to be maintained, even if it had to operate with reduced staff."

The problem of post-war policy for the use of Blacks was finally resolved by President Truman, concerned with the increasing number of incidents in which the rights of minorities were violated. On December 5, 1946, he created the President's Committee on Civil

Rights "to determine in what respect current law enforcement measures may be strengthened and improved to safeguard the rights of people".

In October 1947, the Committee released its famous report entitled, "To Secure These Rights". Among its many recommendations, the Committee urged Congress to pass legislation to end immediately all discrimination and segregation in the Armed Services.

President Truman responded to the recommendations by submitting to Congress on February 2, 1948, a "Special Message on Civil Rights". In addition he recommended ten specific objectives which he felt Congress should enact into legislation. He stated, "During the recent war and in the year since its close, we have made progress towards equality of opportunity in our armed services without regard to race, color, religion or national origin. I have instructed the Secretary of Defense to take steps to have the remaining instances of discrimination in the armed services eliminated as rapidly as possible. The personnel and practices of all the services in this regard will be made consistent."

President Truman's Civil Rights Bill brought a storm of protest from southern Congressmen causing a revolt in the Democratic Party. On April 8, 1948, Representative William Colmar, from Mississippi, addressed Congress: "... for the first time in the history of the country, the United States has asked Congress to enact such a devastating, obnoxious, and repugnant program on the people of that section and their Jeffersonian conception of democracy as this so-called civil rights program. No President either Democrat or Republican has ever seen fit heretofore to make such recommendations.

"And what, I ask you, my colleagues, has this message of our President, calling for the enactment of the program accomplished to date? So far as I have been able to observe, its accomplishments have been two-fold: First, it has inflicted an apparently fatal blow, not only to the unity of the party, but to the unity of the country, at a time when that unity is so highly desirable in a fight to the death with the enemy of free men... communism; secondly, it has encouraged the arrogant demands of these minority groups to whom it was designed to appeal. Witness, Mr. Speaker, the sorry spectacle of an erstwhile Pullman Porter, William Randolph (A. Philip Randolph), a Negro labor leader, defiantly telling the membership of a committee of this

Congress that unless segregation in the armed forces should be abolished that he will call upon the Negroes of this country to ignore the call of their country in the event of a war with Russia. Such ingratitude, such arrogance, such treason can only be attributed to such political bargaining as this proposed program."(7)

The failure of Congress to enact any part of his civil rights program led President Truman to issue two executive orders. On July 26, 1948, he ordered that "All personnel actions taken by Federal appointing officers shall be based solely on merit and fitness; and such officers are authorized and directed to take appropriate steps to insure that in all such actions there shall be no discrimination because of race, color religion, or national origin."

On the same day, President Truman issued a second order, which was designed to desegregate the armed services.

EXECUTIVE ORDER 9981

Establishing the President's Committee On Equality of Treatment And Opportunity In the Armed Forces.

WHEREAS it is essential that there be maintained in the armed services of the United States, the highest standards of democracy, with equality of treatment and opportunity for all those who serve in our country's defense:

NOW THEREFORE, by virtue of the authority vested in me as President of the United States, and as Commander in Chief of the armed services, it is hereby ordered as follows:

1. It is hereby declared to be the policy of the President that there shall be equality of treatment and opportunity for all persons in the armed services without regard to race, color, religion, or national origin. This policy shall be put into effect as rapidly as possible, having due regard to the time required to effectuate any necessary changes without impairing efficiency or morale.

2. There shall be created in the National Military Establishment an advisory committee to be known as the President's Committee on Equality of Treatment and Opportunity in the Armed Services, which shall be composed of seven members to be designated by the President.

3. The Committee is authorized on behalf of the President to examine into the rules, procedures and practices of the Armed Services in order to determine in what respect such rules, procedures and practices may be altered or improved with a view to carrying out the policy of this order. The Committee shall confer and advise the Secretary of Defense, the Secretary of the Army, the Secretary of the Navy, and the Secretary of the Air Force, and shall make such recommendations to the President and to said Secretaries as in the judgement of the Committee will effectuate the policy hereof.

4. All executive departments and agencies of the Federal Government are authorized and directed to cooperate with the Committee in its work, and to furnish the Committee such information or the services of such persons as the Committee may require in the performance of its duties.

Meantime, despite the bickering over the use of black troops and integration, COL Davis kept his training program moving. The 477th trained and participated creditably in war games at Myrtle Beach, Turner Field, and Fort Knox. When the 477th was deactivated, and the 332nd was activated, the training programs continued with amazing success, despite the shortage of flying personnel. For example, on July 1948, a formation of 36 planes of the 332nd--led by MAJ William Campbell, accompanied by veteran combat pilots, Edward C. Gleed, William T. Mattison, Joseph Elsberry, and Richard Harder--took off from Lockbourne and flew to Stewart Field. The trip was made to participate in a ceremony held at the New York International Airport in celebration of the opening of an International Air Exposition.

After a brief stop at Stewart Field, the formation flew to Philadelphia, where it joined other participating units, then proceeded to New York where it thrilled a huge crowd with flying demonstrations.

In mid August 1948, the 332nd began preparation for a war maneuver termed *Operation Combine,* which was to be drawn from all of the services. They were scheduled to demonstrate for military observers and officials from Argentina, Ecuador, China, England, France, Canada, Puerto Rico, Brazil, Mexico, Turkey, Switzerland, and the Philippines.

The air units were to demonstrate the techniques of dive-bombing: laying smoke screens as cover for ground troops, bomber escort, and dropping Napalm bombs in simulated attacks on enemy strongholds.

After several months of preparation, the 332nd flew to Eglin Field for the war game. However, before the war game started, the pilots of the 332nd encountered a humiliating incident. Spann Watson, one of the veteran combat pilots who participated in the war game, recalled: "Bill Campbell led our formation of 48 P-47 down to Eglin Field. I can't recall the exact date. Anyway, the following day, COL Davis, his co-pilot, CPT Dudley Watson, and LT Collier, the base Public Relations Officer, arrived in a C-47.

"Before the game started, we were briefed that there would be a three-minute interval between each attacking unit. Bill, however, was advised that he should disregard the three-minute time lapse and follow closely behind the 20th from Shaw Field and to use the 20th I.T. P. (Initial Target Point) to attack the targets.

"As you know, Bill is usually a calm, unexcitable fellow, but at that suggestion, he blew up. He said, 'I'll be damned if we will follow any unit closely and use its attack point. Who do you think we are? We know what to do and we will do it our way. We will establish our own point of attack'. Well, we did it our way and did better than any of the other groups. We never did see any of those jokers again. Can you imagine them trying to treat us as nobodies. Some of us were seasoned combat pilots, second to none. Pilots like Bill Campbell had served two tours of combat, having fought almost from the beginning of the North African Invasion until the end of the war.

"We had flown every type of combat mission, dive-bombing, bombing, strafing, air-sea rescue, convoy protection, ground troop support, road blocks, railway interdictions, escorted bombers to supply the partisans and rescue pilots and crewmen shot down. We were the work horses. We had fought in every campaign from the battle of Pantelleria to the end of the war. Now those jokers were trying to tell us that we might misjudge and drop a bomb on the observers. We weren't about to let them humiliate us as they did the 477th. The 477th was sent down to Turner Field to participate in a maneuver. Every bomber group except the 477th was given live ammunition. The 477th was given *dummy bombs*; that is, practice bombs. It was the most humiliating thing I ever witnessed."

In October 1948, President Truman created "The Committee on Equality of Treatment and Opportunity". It was popularly known as the Fahy Committee, taking the name of the chairman, Charles Fahy. The Committee was created to supervise the implementing and the monitoring of Executive Order 9981.

The first meeting of the Committee with the President was held on January 12, 1949. In addressing the Committee, President Truman informed the members that he was not interested in better treatment or fair treatment, but equal treatment in the government service for everyone, regardless of race or color. He stated that he wanted the spirit as well as the letter of his order carried out, assuring the Committee that what he had ordered was not a publicity stunt, that he wanted concrete results. This was the man that Blacks respected as a Congressman for his liberal views, the man who, in 1939, as a Senator, had sponsored Chauncey Spencer's flight from Chicago to Washington, DC to dramatize the ability of Blacks to fly aircraft if given the opportunity. He not only issued an executive order decreeing equal treatment for all Americans, but provided for monitoring its implementation. Secretary of Defense James Forrestall informed the President that the Air Force had a very progressive plan to integrate.

The Secretary of the Air Force, Stuart Symington, concurred by stating that "We have a fine group of Colored boys. Our plan is to take those boys, break up that fine group, and put them with other units themselves and to go right down the line all through those subdivisions one hundred percent."(8)

While Secretary Symington expressed enthusiasm for the Air Force plan to integrate, many Air Force officials and some of the personnel at Lockbourne objected to the plan. Secretary Symington was informed that there was solid opposition by Air Force officers against integrating blacks and whites in the same units. He was told that Air Force officers, particularly Southerners, believed that the departure from the past practices would cause riots, disruptions and desertions. Secretary Symington was determined, however, to carry out President Truman's Order, ordering the Air Force generals not to frustrate integration. If anyone didn't agree with the policy, then he should resign, now. He remarked: "We don't want to do it halfway... integration is the right thing to do morally... the right thing to do legally... the right thing to do militarily... Furthermore, the Commanding Chief said that this should be done..."(9)

General Strother, later expressing his views of the proposal to COL Gropman, an Air Force historian, said "I thought we were rushing into it... I think they rushed into it too fast, they almost ruined the service... Most of the Air Force staff also thought that the Air Force was rushing into integration... Truman put out a damn flat order and the Air Force ran with it. Being good soldiers, we did the best we could with what we had."(10)

When the War Department announced that Lockbourne would be de-activated and its personnel integrated into white units, there were many Blacks who were not optimistic as to the actual plans of the War Department for Blacks. Many, who knew about the wholesale discharge of Blacks after World War I, and the treatment of Blacks in the armed services prior to World War II, surmised that it was the beginning of a movement to discharge Blacks from the Army Air Force. It was said that, from the beginning of the country, Blacks have readily accepted the fact that this is their country and have been among the first to volunteer in times of national crisis. In each of the wars the United States had to fight, Blacks had been denied the opportunity to serve until the shortage of manpower or initial failures made it necessary. Nevertheless, in spite of the heroic performances of Blacks in wars, they were not granted the right to remain in service after the wars ended.

Some of the airmen at Lockbourne believed that the same policy was being carried out regarding to Blacks of the Air Force. It was pointed out that the only black bomber group had already been disbanded, that practically all of the navigators, bombardiers, gunners, and pilots of the group were either discharged or transferred to the fighter units. They complained that, now under the proposed integration program, the only all black Air Force Group and Army Air Base were to be de-activated. They concluded that they, like their forefathers who fought all of the other wars, were not wanted in the peacetime service.

There were Blacks who felt that integration would not work because the Air Force was not ready for integration, contending that the integration of Blacks into white units would only result in another form of segregation and discrimination, surmising that only a few Blacks would be permitted to remain in service. Those few, they reasoned, would be relegated to the lowest position and given little opportunity for advancement and leadership. It was also said that even COL Davis, who had proved his ability as a soldier and leader, would meet the same fate. COL Davis, however, was more optimistic.

He pointed out that the job of commanding the 99th and the 332nd in combat was made difficult by the segregation policy of the War Department. While in combat, he often found himself short of replacements. A large number of his men were required to fly more than 100 missions while white pilots were being sent back to the United States upon completing 50 missions. At the same time, while he was in dire need of replacements, many white organizations had more pilots than they could use. Even then, he could not draw from those organizations to fill his shortage. This factor more than anything else kept the morale of his pilots low.

Recognition of the ability of black pilots also came slowly. Soon after the 99th entered combat, its pilots were unjustly criticized for not shooting down enemy aircraft they did not contact. COL Davis, relating the experience of the 332nd in combat, said, "At first we were called upon to fly important missions because high Air Force commanders had little confidence in us. When white crewmen returned from missions after missions and praised us for our 'Close Support' and requested that we fly as escort on other missions, we began to gain recognition as a competent outfit. Soon we began to get more missions and later we were treated as any other outfit."

During the period of May 2-12, 1949, a team selected from the 332nd represented Lockbourne in a National Gunnery meet, held at Las Vegas. The team consisted of CPT Alva Temple, LT James Harvey, Harry Stewart, and Halbert Alexander, who served as a "spare" or replacement pilot.

In the completion, each pilot of the competing teams was required to compete in five different events: Air to Air gunnery at 10,000 and 20,000 feet altitude, rocket firing, strafing, dive-bombing, and skip bombing. The average score of the three pilots that comprised a team represented the team's score. The 332nd team won first place in the conventional fighter aircraft class, second place in panel strafing, and CPT Temple won second place in the individual pilot competition.

The success of the 332nd at Las Vegas came at a most opportune time. The Air Force had been urged by the Fahy Committee to submit a plan for desegregation. The Air Force responded by submitting a plan, which was approved by the Fahy Committee.

Shortly after receiving the approval, the Air Force announced that "qualified Negro personnel may be assigned to fill any vacancy in the

Air Force organizations or installations without regard to race." Following this announcement, on May 11, 1949, a screening board headed by COL Davis began screening individually all of the personnel of the base. On June 1, 1949, Lockbourne was de-activated and its personnel assigned to bases throughout the world.

The men proved to be competent pilots in spite of the hardship encountered both in administrative and combat units. COL Parrish, in discussing the success of the flying school, said, "How good were our pilots? We heard the question so much we could hear it in our sleep. How good is any pilot? Our men were good enough to graduate from any flying school in the country... We made sure of that... and working together we proved it. We emphasized that a pilot or a man of whatever color, size, or shape is just as good as he proves himself to be. Men, and particularly pilots, have to be considered as individuals. We have had some of the worse pilots in the world right here and we have had and still have some of the best. In the first place, they flew and fought as men. They may have been classified as Negroes, and abused as Negroes. They may have had pretty good alibis for being failures if they wanted to use these alibis, or they may have been proud of their group as the only one like it in the world, as they had a right to be. But when the test came, they had to fly and to fight just as men--American men against a common enemy."

Shortly after the war ended in Europe, and before the battle over integration began, General Eaker, in praising the Tuskegee Airmen, said, "They carried out the missions assigned to them and they have destroyed enemy aircraft both in the air and on the ground. By their efforts and performances, they have won a place on the great Air Force team. They came on the hard way."

The Tuskegee airmen later learned that they had been only tokenly accepted on the "great" Air Force team, and that they were still subjected to discrimination and segregation.

FIFTEENTH AIR FORCE - BOMBER WINGS
ESCORTED BY THE 332nd FIGHTER GROUP DURING WORLD WAR II

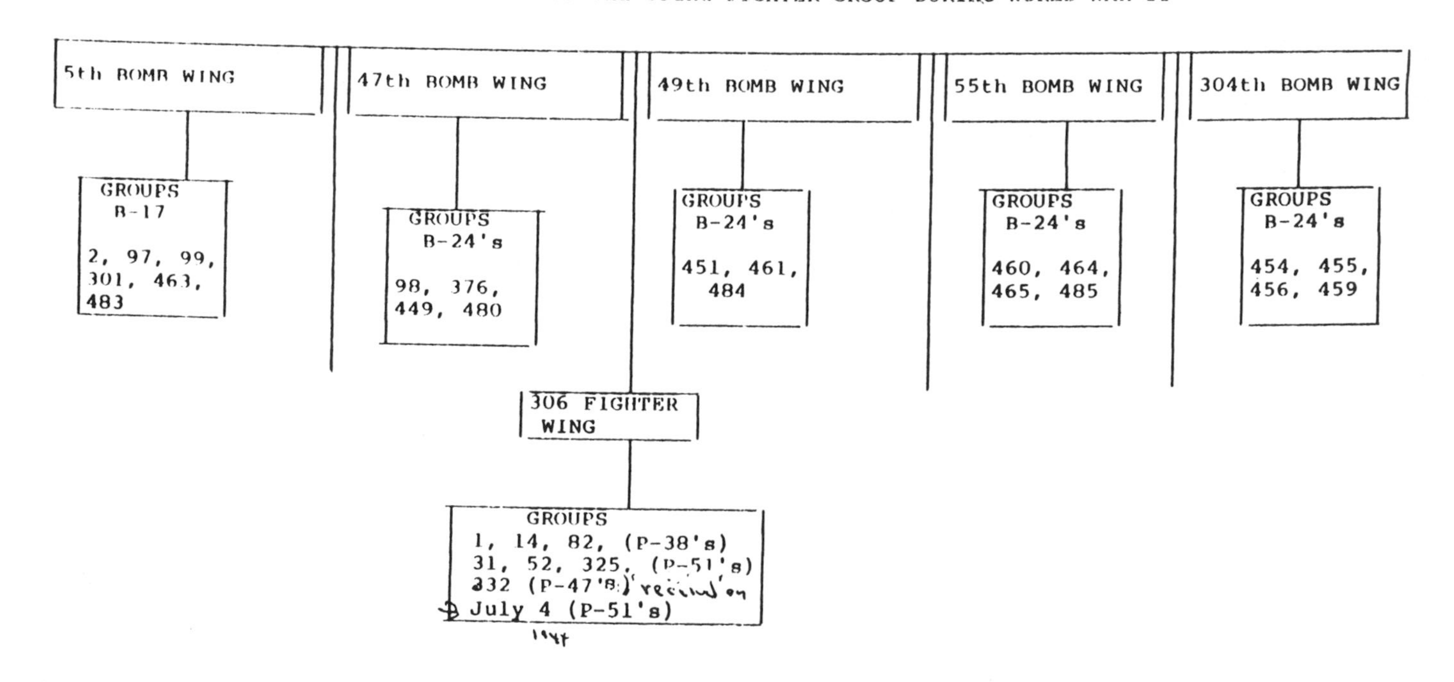

Chapter 22
They Changed A Nation

Integration programs progressed beyond the hope of the most optimistic proponents of integration. To a large extent, those who were reassigned to white units were received at their new bases as American soldiers and given assignments according to their abilities. Black officers and enlisted men were given the same privileges as whites and treated as individuals rather than as a race.

Black pilots were not only integrated into white organizations, but some were assigned as instructors of cadets. The work of CPT Vernon V. Haywood, LT Lewis Lynch, Henry B. Perry and John Whitehead at William Army Air Force Base, is an example of the acceptance of Blacks at a once segregated base. These men fought with the 332nd during World War II. When Lockbourne was deactivated, they were given instructions in flying jet planes and later assigned as cadet instructors at William Air Base.

The war in Korea also revealed the success of the integration program. Many of the former members of the 99th and the 332nd distinguished themselves. It was estimated that about 21 black pilots and hundreds of enlisted men were employed in the Korean War. LT James Harvey, Jr., one of the first jet pilots to see action in the war, was a former member of the 99th. His squadron commander, MAJ Williams of Texas, commented to a War Correspondent that, "Harv is one of the best officers I've ever had, and as a man, I don't think I've ever known one I respect more... He's a fine pilot, dependable in every way. As to his being a Negro, the only trouble we've ever had about that was when some stupid GI made tactless remarks about his race in his presence. The rest of the pilots wanted to take those men apart, but Hav just shrugged it all off... We have two Negro pilots in our Group, and both of them are among the most popular men in the outfit." The other pilot was reported as LT Edward P. Drummond of Philadelphia, a graduate of the last class that trained at Tuskegee Army Air Field 46-C.(1)

Braddord Laws, Far East Correspondent for *The Afro-American*, writing from Korea, commented: "Here in Korea as throughout the entire US Far East Air Force, colored personnel have long been assigned according to their skill and abilities... The Air Force exhibited the true democracy that colored Americans have longed to see in action. There are colored section chiefs, Non-Coms, chief clerks, radio operators, airplane technicians, etc., working together in a common cause--freedom."(2)

Some of the men who served under COL Davis criticized him because they felt his standards were too rigid in combat. They related that while white pilots did nothing but fly combat missions, they (the pilots of the 332nd) were required to keep their areas clean, their clothes cleaned and pressed, and remain tidy at all times. Some jokingly said that COL Davis never could forget his West Point training--that he was a soldier 24-hours a day, "even while asleep".

The men who served in Korea in integrated units gave credit to COL Davis for much of their success. CPT Charles W. Dryden, a veteran combat pilot of the 99th, related to a correspondent in Korea that the rigid training they received under COL Davis fitted them for integration, "by making us toe the mark in every detail". He further stated they were prepared for anything from precise army social courtesies to combat flying.

Another veteran combat pilot related to the same correspondent, "We used to think sometimes that our subordinates and superiors were incompetent. We used to say that we just aren't ready yet, but we were living in a little closed room and did not know what went on in the rest of the house. Now the men can compare and they all have the highest regard for COL Davis, who flew according to the rule, but who was most fair."(3)

LT Harvey, expressing his view on the success of the integration program, said, "It is not necessarily the individuals who make for social prejudice; it is the environment they live in.

"I know that the pilots of my outfit won't change when we get back. They know me, and I think they like me for what I am. But the folks back home: will they let those men continue to be my friends back in the States? It will be pretty hard to do, a rough thing to buck, I'm afraid.

"One thing I am sure of, none of these boys here in this outfit would ever let me down in any way. Perhaps my wife and I can't go out to the restaurants or hotels with them in some parts of America, not because they don't want to, but because of the long-standing prejudices and customs that are hard to go against. Still, I feel I could count on everyone personally."(4)

Although integration was hailed during the Korean War as being successful, not long after the war ended black servicemen began to complain. Those who had served during the period of total segregation found the integrated service more aggravating. They complained that they were not only ostracized in social and recreational activities, but were relegated to the menial jobs and often subjected to derogatory remarks. Even four star General Daniel *Chappie* James had been a victim of such remarks.

General James, who had served at Tuskegee during World War II, had distinguished himself by bravery in combat during the Korean War. When the war in Korea ended, *Chappie*, a Major, and a highly respected combat pilot, was assigned with some of his comrades to a fighter group stationed at Westover Field, MA. Somehow, his friends arrived at Westover before he arrived. They were greeted by their new commander, LTC Coleman. While welcoming the pilots, LTC Coleman informed them that he expected a *pickaninny* to be assigned to the Group, but they need not worry, "just ignore him, because I'm going to get rid of him as soon as possible."

The pilots who had served with *Chappie* and respected him as an outstanding and courageous fighter pilot were shocked. When *Chappie* arrived at the base, he was immediately informed of the remark, and was hurt and embarrassed. He loved flying as much as anyone and to be a fighter pilot was his ultimate dream. He wanted nothing more than to continue his service career. But the more he thought about the remark, the angrier he became. He stormed into the commander's office and announced, "I am that 'pickaninny' that you are expecting. I don't want to be in your damn group." He moved within striking distance of the commander and said, "If you want to get rid of me as soon as possible, why not start now. I would like for you to strike me for I can break every bone in your body." Challenged by perhaps one of the largest fighter pilots he had ever seen (six feet four inches and 230 pounds), LTC Coleman appeared shaken and remained silent.

Chappie was transferred to Otis Air Force Base on Cape Cod, MA. There he was later promoted to the rank of full colonel. Sometime later, while traveling aboard a commercial plane, he spied LTC Coleman sitting not far from him. This time, *Chappie*, with his usual broad, friendly smile, greeted Coleman and pleasantly thanked him for the transfer to Otis Field and for his promotion.

The incident involving General James is an example of humiliation reported by other black servicemen, especially those of lower rank. Although Blacks had been integrated into white organizations with surprisingly little friction, they were still faced with the long-standing prejudices on and off bases. They not only faced these prejudices and abuses in the United States, but overseas as well.

It took the efforts and determination of a former Tuskegee airman to address the problems of black servicemen. He was Representative Charles Diggs. When Diggs was elected to Congress in 1953, there were only two other Blacks in Congress: Adam Clayton Powell, who had no military service, and William L. Dawson, who had served in World War I. Diggs had the most recent service as an officer in the Army Air Force, and was familiar with the treatment of Blacks during World War II. In fact, he was very lucky in not being killed while in service at Tuskegee. On a trip to Opelika, AL, he made the mistake of addressing a white bus driver as *buddy*. The driver whipped out a pistol from his belt and threatened to kill Diggs. The driver remarked, "If you weren't wearing that uniform, I would blow your brains out for calling me *buddy*. I'm not your buddy!"

Upon entering office as a Congressman, Diggs decided that one of his projects would be to see that black servicemen would be fairly treated. In 1959, after visiting bases in Asia, with *Chappie* as his aide, Diggs reported that he had found conditions similar to that in Europe, and that President Truman's Executive Order 9981 had not been fully implemented, due to the rigid segregation of communities outside the military installations. He reported that the housing problems for Blacks overseas were as severe as those in the United States, although much of the housing was subsidized by the services. He asked that sanctions be placed on proprietors who discriminated against Blacks.

Shortly after Diggs began his investigations, he was besieged with complaints from servicemen relating mistreatment. In 1960, after receiving a complaint of off-base mistreatment of Blacks at Maxwell Field, Diggs referred the complaint to the office of the Inspector General. In reply to Diggs, the IG stated that the Air Force was most interested in the health, welfare, security and morale of all of its personnel, and believed in equal opportunity, but that in this matter, the Air Force authority was restricted to the limits of its jurisdiction. "Beyond those limits," the Inspector General wrote, "Civilian jurisdiction prevails, as determined by civic laws and local customs... There is little basis to expect that any member of the Air Force will receive more favorable treatment from the civilian community than he receives as a civilian under the same circumstances. Nor does the Air Force have authority to use any measure of force or coercion to change or influence local law or custom which does not agree with official Air Force policy."(5)

The Inspector General's reply made Diggs more determined to fight for the rights of black servicemen. He continued to prod military leaders and base commanders to take positive actions to stop the mistreatment of black servicemen and their families on and off bases. Base commanders, however, responded almost unanimously that they had no authority to act against off-base mistreatment of black servicemen.

Although Dr. Martin Luther King Jr., whose protest marches against the ugly racial practices won support from many national leaders and organizations, he was unable to gain the support of the law makers of the country. Congressmen avoided him as if he were a coral or copperhead snake. For example, in 1963, Dr. King and four of his colleagues, Reverend Jesse Jackson, Ralph Abernathy, Hosea Williams and Andrew Young visited Capitol Hill three days with the hope of meeting with Senators Jacob Javits of NY, George McGovern of SD, and Ross Bass of TN, with the hope of persuading them to introduce and push for the passage of some form of Civil Rights legislation to protect the rights of Blacks. After three days of visits and getting the run-around by the staffs of the senators, Dr. King was able to meet with Senator Javits and McGovern in their private hideaways at the Senate Office Building. This was accomplished only by the help and arrangement of Robert Parker, the head waiter of the Senate Dining Room.(6)

It took Congressman Diggs to spark the movement that caused President Kennedy and Congress to act. Diggs inadvertently started the action that culminated in the passage of the Civil Rights Act of 1964. The Act not only officially granted equal opportunity and treatment to servicemen, it also included all of the Blacks of the United States.

In February 1962, Congressman Diggs wrote to Secretary of Defense, Robert McNamara, stating that he had received in a period of 60 days over 250 complaints of abuses and discrimination against black servicemen. He called to the attention of Secretary McNamara his letter of August 1961, in which he had demanded that a "Citizen Committee be appointed to investigate the current status of integration in the Armed Forces." He submitted with his letter a summary of the racial incidents which occurred primarily off-base.(7)

Representative Diggs' letter was brought to the attention of President Kennedy, who, on June 24, 1962, appointed a Citizen Committee, asking the Committee "to look into the general problem of equal opportunity for members of the Armed Forces and their dependents in the civilian community, particularly with regard to housing, education, community events and other activities.(8)

The Citizen Committee, later known as the Gesell Committee, consisted of seven men (four whites and three Blacks), and chaired by Gerhard A. Gesell from whom the Committee derived its name. The three black members were Nathaniel Colley, John Sengstacke, and Whitney Young. In addition to Chairman Gesell, the white members were Joseph O'Mears, Benjamin Muse, and Abe Fortas.

When the Gesell Committee completed its work, it submitted a report to the President, who informed the Committee that it would receive immediate attention from the Secretary of Defense.

The Committee found in its investigation that most Base Commanders contended that off-base discrimination and segregation of Blacks were not the responsibility of the military and that commanders had no legal right to interfere in the off-base activities of local communities.

The Committee recommended that Commanders use all means available to eliminate segregation and discrimination in the near-by communities. It further recommended that if no improvements were observed, then all of the personnel of the bases or installations be restricted to patronize only those establishments which were open to all servicemen and their dependents without regard to race or color. Moreover, the Committee recommended that the bases or installations be moved to other localities if the hostile conditions continued to exist.

The Committee made other recommendations which included:

1. That complaints by Blacks be privileged and Service Regulations should prohibit the disclosures of such communications without the serviceman's consent.
2. A specially appointed Equal Opportunity Monitoring Office with access to Commanders be used at each base to receive complaints, discuss the complaints with the commanders and help commanders resolve the complaints.
3. Commanders be graded on their success in the performance of this duty.
4. Blacks be appointed to serve on the promotion boards, and all evidence that might cause bias selections of candidates for promotion be deleted from their records before consideration.(9)

On July 26, 1963, Secretary McNamara responded to the Committee's report by issuing a directive that adopted the main recommendations. The directive, titled "Equal Opportunity in the Armed Force", instructed the Services to issue appropriate manuals and regulations to implement equal opportunity. The directive also established a Civil Rights Office within the secretariat.

The most objectional part of the directive, for many commanders, was that which read, "Every military commander has the responsibility to oppose discriminatory practices affecting his men and their dependents, and to foster equal opportunity for them, not only in areas under his immediate control, but also in near-by communities... In discharging that responsibility a commander shall not, except with prior approval of the Secretary of his military department, use the off-limit sanction in discrimination cases arising within the United States."(10)

Many military commanders expressed opposition to what they considered involving the military in enforcing and coercing civilians to respect the civil rights of Blacks.

Meantime, the increased demonstrations by Dr. King and the accompanying violence in 1963 caused President Kennedy great concern. He decided that new laws were needed to enforce the rights of Blacks, hoping that those laws would put an end to the demonstrations and violence. The President asked Congress to enact a Civil Rights Act which would give Blacks the legal status of first class citizens. However, on Friday, November 22, 1963, the President was assassinated in Dallas. Nevertheless, Lyndon Johnson, who succeeded Kennedy, stirred the Civil Rights legislation through Congress; and on July 2, 1964, he signed it into law.

With the passage of the Civil Rights Act, base commanders' tasks of prohibiting discrimination and abuses against Blacks should have been less difficult. The law forbade racial discrimination in publicly-owned and operated facilities, and in most privately-owned places of public accommodations such as hotels, motels and theatres. The law also gave the Attorney General of the United States authority to begin civil rights actions on behalf of the victims of discrimination. It also forbade voting registrars from discriminating against prospective black voters, and created a commission to investigate alleged racial discrimination by employers and labor unions.

Secretary McNamara, in a letter to the Services, advised that the Civil Rights Act of 1964 was an immensely important and historic expression of the nation's commitment to freedom and justice... that the Civil Rights Act had special meaning for members of the armed forces, all of whom had already given a personal commitment to defend freedom and full justice in their own country.

McNamara further stated that the, "President has made it very clear that he expects each Department to move with dispatch within the area of concern, developing programs and policies which will give full impact to the Civil Rights Act."

"In the Department of Defense this means primarily the vigorous, determined, sensitive commitment by military commanders to a program of fostering and securing equal opportunity for all their men, and their families off-base as well as on..."(11)

The Air Force responded to Secretary McNamara's letter immediately by publishing a revised and expanded Air force regulation 35-78. The revision stated:

It is the policy of the Air Force to conduct all of its activities in a manner which is free from racial discrimination, and which provided equal opportunity and treatment for all uniform members irrespective of their race, color, religion, or national origin...

Discriminatory practices directed against military personnel all of whom lack a civilian's freedom of choice in where to live, to work, to travel and sped his off-duty hours, are harmful to the military effectiveness.(12)

The revised Regulation published on August 19, 1964 was effective not only in the United States, but world wide. Commanders were made responsible for processing complaints of discrimination to the Attorney General. Moreover, the revision provided that all servicemen, regardless of race, color, religion and national origin "be afforded equal opportunity for enlistment, appointment, advancement, professional improvement, promotion, assignment and retention."

With the new revisions, it appeared that the Air Force was serious in providing for equal opportunity and treatment for black servicemen. Actually the revised regulation was designed only for the purpose of giving the Secretary of Defense the impression that the Air Force was willingly carrying out his mandate. The revised regulation not only failed to carry a provision for monitoring its implementation by base commanders, but forbade base commanders to use sanctions against local communities without prior approval of high Air Force officials, and then only after all reasonable alternatives had failed.

By 1965, the one group created by the War Department to aid in fostering equal opportunity and treatment, "The Equal Opportunity Group", had been so downgraded that it consisted of only one officer with no clerks. As a result, the base commanders, left on their own to implement the Secretary of Defense policy and Air Force Regulation 35-78, exerted little efforts or initiative to provide equal opportunity and treatment for Blacks.

It took a riot at Travis Air Force Base to shake up the War Department and the Air Force. The riot was actually only one of a number that had occurred at various installations throughout the country and overseas, but it was the most intense.

The Travis riot began between one black and one white soldier at a Non Commissioned Officers club party. When the word spread that the fight was in progress, white and black airmen from near-by barracks rushed to the scene of battle. They joined the fight and chaos spread to other areas of the base. The riot, which began on May 17, lasted four days, requiring water from high pressure fire hoses to disperse the airmen. More than 70 civilian policemen were brought in from the near-by communities to help restore order.

The Travis riot was actually caused by tensions sprouting from un-addressed grievances. Blacks had for sometime complained that they received harsher punishment for similar offenses for which white airmen received only reprimands or counseling. They were disturbed by the practice of discrimination in duty assignments, promotions and leave, and were angered because of base commanders' refusal to place off-limit restrictions on an apartment complex whose owner refused to rent to Blacks. They claimed too that the Base Exchange and the civilian office were discriminatory to them and their families in their hiring practices.(13)

The riot brought quick response from the Air Force. The Equal Opportunity Group, which had been operating in the Pentagon with only one officer, was expanded and placed within the Directorate of Personnel Planning, and a new Social Action Directorate was created within Headquarters of the Air Force to monitor all social problems, and specifically that of race relations, drug abuses, alcoholism, and human relations.

To expedite the new Air Force policy, social action programs were established on all bases and mandatory race relation courses became a requirement for all Air Force personnel. The courses were designed to help black and white servicemen learn to communicate across the racial and ethnic barrier, which had existed for generations; and familiarize white servicemen with contributions made by Blacks and other minorities to the nation. Noteworthy, a similar recommendation had been made by General Benjamin O. Davis, Sr. as early as

September 1942. At that time, however, the War Department turned down his proposal.

The Travis riot not only caused the Air Force to promote better race relations, it also caused all of the Services to become more active in this endeavor. Shortly after the riot, an All-Service Investigating Task Force was appointed to research the race problem and General Lucius Theus, a former Tuskegee airman, was appointed to head the task force. General Theus' service career is a good example of what any American, regardless of race, color or nationality, can accomplish if he or she has a positive attitude, the determination to achieve, the willingness to apply himself or herself, the willingness to sacrifice, and of course, to be blessed with a little luck.

General Theus was born in Madison County, TN on October 11, 1922; as an infant, he moved with his parents to Illinois, where he was graduated from Community High School, and in December 1942, was inducted into the Air Corps as a private and sent to Keesler Field. There he advanced to the rank of First Sergeant before being accepted for officers training at Maxwell Field. He was graduated second in his class, and in January 1946 was sent to Tuskegee Air Field where he was assigned as squadron adjutant. To those who had been at Tuskegee for sometime, Theus caught attention by his friendliness, unusual politeness and quiet and courteous manners. Unlike most youngsters called to service, Theus refused to allow the Service to interrupt his education. After serving at Tuskegee a short time, he was reassigned to Lockbourne Army Air Force Base, where he was assigned as Statistics Control Staff Officer. He continued his education and in 1956 was graduated from the University of Maryland with a degree of Bachelor of Science. The following year, he received a master's degree in business administration from George Washington University, and in 1969 successfully completed an advanced management program at Harvard University Graduate School of Business Administration. All of this was accomplished while serving intermittently at the Pentagon.

General Theus' service career kept him equally busy. When Lockbourne was closed, he was transferred to Erding Air Depot, Germany, where he served as an Analysis and Presentation Officer and Commander of Statistic Control Flight. In 1952, he was assigned to the office of the Deputy Chief of Staff, Comptroller, Headquarters, US Air Force, as Chief of the Materiel Logistics Branch.

In October 1957, General Theus was assigned to Headquarters Central Air Materiel Forces Europe, Chateauroux Air Base, France. Then, after assignments in Greece, Vietnam and several air bases in the United States, he became a distinguished graduate of the Air War College and the Industrial College of Armed Forces and a graduate of the Armed Forces Staff College Statistical Officer School.

He returned to the Pentagon and was assigned to the office of the Comptroller of the Air Force as a data automation staff officer in the Directorate of Data Automation.

In July 1971, General Theus was appointed Director of Management Analysis, Office of the Comptroller of the Air Force, and Assistant Director for Social Action, Headquarters USAF. In June 1972, he was appointed Director of Accounting and Finance, USAF, and Commander of the Air Force Accounting and Finance Center, Denver. Of these, perhaps not the most glamorous but one of the most important and respected positions in the US Air Force was the position of paymaster for the entire US Air Force.

The All-Service Investigating Task Force headed by General Theus recommended that a Defense Race Relation Institute (DRRI) be established to train instructors in the teaching of race relations at the base level to all servicemen. This was the idea of General Davis Sr. that had been incorporated into the recommendations of the Gesell Committee and went ignored. This time, however, the Air Force approved the recommendation and published a new Regulation 50-26, titled, "Education and Race Relation."

The new regulation was described as "intended to improve and achieve equal opportunity within the United States Air Force and to eliminate and prevent racial tension, unrest and violence." The purpose of the course of study was stated "to broaden the ability to communicate across racial and ethnic barriers, to heighten the awareness of the minority contribution to American history, and to assure all personnel that the Air Force was serious about improving race relations.(14)

The program called for the establishment of a one hour course in race relationship. All base personnel would be required to attend the classes during duty hours beginning with the highest ranking officers and airmen. The regulation also required the establishment of formal race relation courses at all military schools. It stipulated that all servicemen sent to the Defense Race Relation Institute to train to be instructors were to be volunteers.

Shortly after the Defense Race Relation Institute began operating and the services began conducting race relation course, Richard Nixon became President. He appointed Melvin Laird as his Secretary of Defense.

Laird decided to continue the affirmative action program, and to address the grievances expressed by black servicemen. The Gesell Committee had noted in its report that *de facto* segregation still existed on bases, a phenomena which commanders chose to ignore. Laird decided to address this problem. He appointed a bi-racial task force to study the administration of justice.

The task force reported that it found two forms of racial discrimination existed, intentional and systematized. The intentional was described as individual bias that affected Blacks as individuals negatively. The systematized discrimination was more complex and was described as neutral practices or policies which disproportionately impact harmfully or negatively on minorities."

The first problem considered by the task force was the implementation of military justice. Blacks had repeatedly charged that base commanders had imposed punishments on them for offenses for which white servicemen received only counseling or reprimands. The task force found that Blacks had received a disproportionately number of confinements, received more non-judicial punishments than white servicemen for short term absence without leave and were more inclined to receive dishonorable discharges if found guilty of some offenses. The task force concluded that those servicemen who performed the less satisfying or menial jobs were more likely to commit offenses to cause punishments than those with more satisfying and challenging jobs. It reasoned that since Blacks on the whole had been deprived of equal education in the past, they scored low on the aptitude test, and as a result were assigned to the less satisfying jobs. The task force recommended that the Department of Defense give consideration to a national movement to improve and upgrade educational opportunities for Blacks.

The task force made several more recommendations to promote equal opportunity and treatment for Blacks. It recommended that the position of Deputy Assistant Secretary of Defense (Equal Opportunity) be upgraded to Assistant Secretary, and an equal opportunity staff be added to both the Inspector General and the Judge Advocate General offices. It further recommended that a course in military discrimination be added to the curriculum of the DRRI and that the Armed Forces qualification test program be re-evaluated and re-constructed to include the personal interest and preference of individuals as a criteria for determining specialties. The task force also suggested that personnel be periodically rotated out of menial jobs, that is, the less satisfying jobs, and that the dress standard be relaxed. Finally, it recommended that a "Specific punitive article prescribing discriminatory acts and practices be included in the Uniform Code of Military Justice in order to provide a more visible focus on detection and elimination of discrimination."(15)

Since President Truman issued his executive order that provided for the integration of the services, the Air Force had been publishing progressive directives and regulations that made it appear that it was serious about integrating the service and providing equal opportunity and treatment. However, in all of the directives and regulations, it candidly stopped short of making their implementations mandatory. Base commanders were more or less left to use their own discretion, and as a result, in the matter of race relation very little progress was made. In fact, the Air Force did only what it was ordered to do by the Department of Defense. Now, under pressure from the Department, it was forced to give substance to its directives and regulations. The Department of Defense directed that all Armed Force commanders appoint an equal opportunity officer and that all officers be rated on their equal opportunity participation. Most important to Blacks, it forbade all military personnel to lease or rent housing which was not opened to all service personnel and their families.

There was another equally important problem black servicemen faced. As early as 1949, when it was announced that Blacks would be integrated into white units, the subject of promotions and assignments was raised. Many of the black officers at Lockbourne expressed objection to the plan, because they believed that the few Blacks permitted to remain in the service would be so overwhelmingly out-numbered by whites that Blacks would be given little opportunity for promotions and no opportunity for leadership over whites.

In the early 1960s, the Gesell Committee, fearing the possibility of bias in the promotion of Blacks, recommended that Blacks also be assigned to the promotion boards, suggesting that white board members, who had experiences with black officers and enlisted men, should be selected. Moreover, it recommended that all racial data, including photographs, be removed from the folders of those under consideration for promotions.

These recommendations brought a storm of protest not only from the Services, but from Congressmen and white civic leaders. They charged that the provisions to remove racial information and photographs of those under consideration for promotion would deny "essential information to promotion boards". White servicemen expressed concern that black servicemen might be given preferential treatment. In competition for promotions, Blacks would be in a favorable position to receive the promotions. Air Force officials questioned whether the promotion standards would be lowered by promoting personnel for reasons other than experience and qualifications.

Despite the protest, Secretary Laird was convinced that to truly integrate the Services, the attitudes of white servicemen toward Blacks had to be changed. He reasoned that slavery, and the long standing segregation and discrimination policy and practice that followed, had distorted the image of blacks in the minds of whites to such an extent that whites knew very little about the true nature of black people. Generations of whites had grown up in an America that had relegated Blacks to an inferior role in American society. Every facet of American society had been geared to make Blacks feel and conduct themselves as inferiors and whites feel and conduct themselves as superiors to blacks. Generations of brainwashing had so distorted the minds of most whites that they believed that Blacks could not perform on a level with them and were surely incapable of holding responsible leadership positions.

Secretary Laird realized that the existing promotion system, the long chain of whites eligible for the promotions and the lack of qualified Blacks eligible for the promotions, would preclude Blacks from being promoted to leadership positions for generations to come.

To expedite his integration program, Laird decided to adopt an affirmative action program. Education improvement classes were organized for black servicemen. Blacks were either given specialty training on the bases or sent to specialty schools. Black officers who showed command potentials were sent to the Air Force University, the Air War College or the Air Force Command and Staff College. Likewise, servicemen in other branches of service were given the same opportunities to qualify for promotions, and those who qualified were given preferential treatment in the promotions. Blacks were promoted on all levels from the lowest position of leadership, from Private First Class, to that of the highest position of general.

Naturally, the preferential treatment given Blacks caused resentment and protest by white servicemen. However, Secretary Laird looked upon his plan as only a temporary measure to break the barrier between the races. He knew that the overwhelming number of whites eligible for the promotions precluded any sizeable number of Blacks being promoted for generations. Yet, it was urgent that the image of Blacks be changed in the minds of white servicemen if any progress in race relations were to be made. To expedite his plan, he believed it necessary to promote Blacks on all levels of leadership to quickly show white servicemen that Blacks could perform efficiently, if given the proper training and equal opportunity. This, Secretary Laird believed, was the only way that white servicemen would learn to respect Blacks and the only way that total integration of the services could be achieved. It was this action on part of Secretary Laird that finally brought total integration of the services and the implementation of the Civil Rights Act of 1964. It was this action that gained for the Tuskegee Airmen official acceptance on the great Air Force team--a team that they had been an integral part of since World War II but never accepted as members of that team.

LTC Edward C. Gleed (retired), one of the most decorated pilots and leaders of the 332nd, conveyed to a friend, "When we were in training at Tuskegee and in combat, we never gave it a thought that we were making history. All we wanted was to learn to fly as Army Air Corps pilots, fight for our country and survive." Yet, in spite of that simple desire, the Tuskegee Airmen made history--a history that will forever stand out boldly in the annals of the United States.

The demonstrations of courage and effectiveness in combat by members of the 99th Fighter Squadron, the 332nd Fighter Group, and the 477th Bombardment and Composite Groups changed the image of Blacks in the eyes of high governmental and military officials. Thus, through their efforts, the Tuskegee Airmen opened the door of opportunity for black youths who aspire for Air Force, Aero-Space, and other service careers. More important for all the Blacks of this nation is the fact that the Tuskegee Airmen, working independently but in conjunction with the efforts of civil Rights leaders such as Supreme Court Justice Thurgood Marshall and Dr. Martin Luther King, Jr., changed this nation. They brought more respect, better treatment and more opportunities for Blacks; more importantly for all Americans, the Tuskegee Airmen placed the freedom train, for the first time in the history of the nation, on designated tracks provided by the framers of the Constitution--a Constitution all Americans revere as a symbol of the equality of individuals, of freedom and of respect for all people regardless of race, color, nationality or religious practices and beliefs. The questions are: Will the citizens of this great nation permit the bigots and demagogues to de-rail this train, or, will they, with ever vigilance and demand, assure that this train will continue on its journey as a beacon of hope for people of all lands, who love and cherish freedom and democracy, but still are denied such blessing?

Major General Lucius Theus.

General Daniel C. James.

Chapter 23
Stories of Prisoners of War

To fall in the hands of the enemy and to become a prisoner of war is a hectic experience. Not that all prisoners were treated inhumanely; they were not. But, no matter how humanely a prisoner was treated, he lived in anticipation of the worst that could happen to him.

One day at Tuskegee, I talked with a few men who had experienced the German prison camp. To see these men, jolly and seemingly in excellent health, one would never suspect they had braved the deprivations of German prison camps. However, as I listened to them relate their varied experiences, I realized that the Germans treated prisoners of war as prisoners and not as gods or "little bad boys" as we Americans treated captured German soldiers.

LT Alexander Jefferson, one of the smallest pilots of the 332nd and perhaps of the entire US Army Air Force, was one of these men who experienced the war as a prisoner. It was August 12, 1944, three days before D-Day in southern France when he and several other members of the 332nd fell victim to Nazi guns. On that day, the 332nd was assigned to destroy radar stations on the coast of France in preparation for the invasion of ground troops. Upon arrival over the target area, the group encountered heavy and accurate flak and machine gun fire. But in spite of the heavy and concentrated enemy fire, the group went in to dive bomb and strafe its targets. At this point, LT Jefferson began his story:

"I started my dive at 15,000 feet and headed straight in for the station. But when I got about 200 yards from the target, a 20mm shot burst through the floor of my cockpit. Immediately, my plane burst into flames. I kept my control, however, rolled my plane to the left, pushed forward on the stick, and fell out of my plane at about 600 feet. I landed about 200 feet from the target and was immediately picked up by the Germans and taken to the headquarters of a flak battalion.

"Just before my ship was hit, CPT Robert H. Daniels' ship was also hit by a 20mm shell. The burst ripped his plane practically apart and sent it spiraling into the water below. But somehow, Daniels managed to get out of his plane before it sank. He was later fished out of the water by the Germans and the next day brought into headquarters. Frankly, it made me feel much better to have some one I knew with me. You know, misery loves company.

"On the morning of August 14, about 4 o'clock, we were taken by two guards to Toulon and later to Marseilles. There, we were put on a train, which was packed with German civilians and soldiers.

"When we arrived at Orange, the tracks were bombed out so we hitch hiked to Lyon. I noticed, as we were going along, that the Germans were moving all types of equipment and vehicles out of the Rhone Valley. Incidentally, the train was strafed once by a P-38 while we were on the way to Orange. The strafing was ineffective, but it forced everybody to jump off the train into the ditches. I also saw B-25s bomb Valence and, about 45 minutes before reaching Lyon, B-24s bombed the industrial plants of the city.

"The ride from Lyon up to Frankfurt was uneventful except for curious glances from the people. Probably many of them had never seen Negroes before; so naturally they were curious to get a good look at us.

"We passed through Belfort, Mulhouse, Freiburg, Karlsruhe, and Mannheim before reaching Frankfurt. At Frankfurt, we were placed in solitary confinement and later interrogated. The most startling thing about the interrogation is that the interrogators seemed to know more about my outfit than I did. I was shown a booklet, compiled on the 332nd Fighter Group. It contained the names and addresses of nearly all the graduates of Tuskegee, pictures of classes, and approximate dates the pilots arrived overseas. The only thing they didn't seem to know was the number of missions I had.

"We stayed at Frankfurt for three days and were then shipped to Wetzlar, about 75 miles from Frankfurt. Here we got the benefit of the American Red Cross for the first time. We were allowed to take shower baths, given clean bedding and clothing, and given our first hot meal, which consisted of oatmeal, German bread, cocoa, and powdered eggs.

"We stayed in Wetzlar only two days. Then, with about 300 other prisoners, we were crowded on a train and for four days and four nights traveled. We were taken off the train at Sagan and held at Stalag Luft III for six months.

"At Stalag Luft III, ten officers lived in a room about 16 x 16 feet. We did our own cooking and made our own implements from cans received in Red Cross parcels. But in spite of the hardship of prison life, the morale of the prisoners was rather high. Most of my room mates were Southerners: two from Georgia, three from Alabama, two from FL, one from Missouri, and one from Michigan. Although I was a Negro, they treated me as one of them. Each man performed a duty, and each day we combined our rations, cooked it together, and shared equally.

"Stalag Luft III was divided into five sections with approximately 2,000 men in each section. Altogether there were about 10,000 prisoners. Every morning at 6:30 we were called out to answer roll call.

"The Red Cross parcels, received usually once a week, came in very handy. They not only supplemented the German rations, but often were the only food we received. In the latter part of September, each prisoner's ration was cut to half a parcel because the German transportation system was under constant bombardment. This cut in ration hurt us tremendously but we managed to make out.

"For amusement and to help pass away time, we played various games, presented camp shows, and read books from the large library which had been built up by previous prisoners. Two plays that were presented while I was at Stalag Luft were, *The Philadelphia Story* and *Kiss and Tell*. They were interesting.

"Saturday night, January 29, 1945, we received orders that we were going to move. This hasty movement was probably due to the fact that the Russian troops had advanced from Warsaw within 30 miles of the camp. We could hear the roar of the big guns.

"The forced march from Stalag Luft III at Sagan was no fun. We marched a distance of about 85 kilometers in bitter cold weather. We were guarded by Volksturm guards made up of old men. There were about two and a half feet of snow on the ground and the temperature was about ten degrees below zero. I saw four guards fall out from exhaustion. No one seemed to pay much attention to them and they probably froze to death. Fortunately for us, when we got ready to move the Red Cross gave us new shoes, heavy socks, gloves, scarfs, and new overcoats.

"When we reached Spremberg we were placed in box cars, 60 men to a car. For three days and nights we traveled southward through Dresden, Chemnitz, Plauen, Nurnberg, and finally ended up in Moosburg. Here we were held at Stalag 7-A. The conditions at Stalag 7-A were deplorable. We lived in tents about 40 feet wide and 100 feet long. We slept on the ground as comfortably as possible, but had one faucet for approximately 400 men. The only satisfaction we had was the Red Cross kept us from starving by sending us parcels regularly.

"Our last few months at Moosburg were spent in almost agony. The intense sweating out what the Germans were eventually going to do with us was torture. We knew the Americans were coming, and feared the Germans might shoot us rather than let us be rescued by the Allies. We also feared that we would be caught in the midst of a battle between the Americans and the Nazi guards. We watched B-17s bomb Munich one day. It was really a wonderful sight, but after that we feared that we would be victims of such a raid.

"Incidentally, Richard Macon was also shot down the day I was shot down. I met him two days later, but when we arrived at Sagan we were separated. When I arrived at Moosburg, I learned that LT Woodrow Morgan, Hatchcock, and Wilbur Long were there, but we were in different sections and couldn't see each other.

"We stayed at Moosburg until the Third Army arrived and liberated us on April 29, 1945. However, we remained in camp for a week or so; then we were taken to Strasbourg in trucks. Here we boarded a C-47 and were flown to Le Havre, France. We stayed at camp *Lucky Strike* for approximately five days, then boarded ship for our voyage back to the States. Daniels and I arrived in the States on June 2, 1945, happy that we were safely home again."

After listening to LT Jefferson's interesting narrative of his life as a prisoner of war, I wandered into the pool room at Tuskegee Air Base where I found LT Long, a small, slender, light-complexioned, quiet sort of fellow, offering to play me a game. As we shot pool, I began to ask questions about the mission on which he was shot down and became a prisoner of war.

"Well," he said, "I guess you have heard my story many times. I was one of the fortunate pilots who got shot down and was lucky enough to get back home. Anyway, it was an escort mission to Blechhammer about 150 miles east of Berlin. I was hit over the target by flak. My canopy was damaged, my coolant system messed up, and I received several minor injuries.

"Immediately after regaining my composure, I checked over my plane. Figuring that I was not too badly damaged, I decided that I would try to make it back to the base. Several members of my flight warned me that my ship was damaged severely and that I should leave my ship.

"Meantime, I was unaware that I was flying in the wrong direction. CPT Daniels (John) directed me on course, but a little later my engine began to freeze up, so I made preparations to bail out. But when I attempted to release my canopy, I found it was damaged. I informed CPT Daniels I could not release my canopy, so I would have to crash land. He instructed me to find a field and land, that he would pick me up. I found a field that looked rather clear from a high altitude. But as I approached the field for a landing, I found it had many obstacles. Skimming over tree tops and dodging through spaces between trees, I finally hit the ground and began skidding. From this time on I remember nothing about my landing.

"When I regained consciousness, I was running with a large gathering of civilians chasing me. I remembered I had a pistol on me. I also remembered that I had been briefed that pilots caught by the enemy with fire arms were severely beaten and often killed. Therefore, I threw my pistol away. I was overtaken and beaten by the angry mob. However, a group of soldiers arrived in time to save me. The solders tried to question me, but I couldn't understand them. A kid who could speak English came up and acted as interpreter. The soldiers searched me and found my extra clip of ammunition. They inquired as to what I did with my gun, where I was from, etc. When they finished questioning me, they took me to a small town where a doctor bandaged up my nose, which had been split open, probably by my gun sight when I crashed.

"Shortly afterwards, a Hungarian colonel arrived and endeavored to interrogate me. He, unable to speak English, and I, unable to speak Hungarian, could not understand each other. The Colonel then changed to German. I studied German before entering the Army, so I was able to understand him. I learned that I was in Hungary. When the Colonel asked me questions that I didn't wish to answer, I pretended that I couldn't understand him.

"I was told by the Colonel that I was going to be sent to a hospital for treatment. To my surprise, I was placed in solitary confinement. The next day I was taken to another garrison and again placed in solitary confinement.

"Five days later I was carried to Budapest and placed in a hospital for treatment for two weeks. But at this time, the Allies began their campaign against the city. This angered the Nazis and they took me out of the hospital and threw me in solitary confinement. The following day, I was interrogated. I was asked a few questions which I refused to answer. I told the interrogator I could give him only my name, rank, and serial number. Seeing that he was making no headway, the interrogator told me that I didn't know any more than he. Walking to a desk he pulled out a book entitled the 332nd Red Tails. This book contained practically the history of the group from its activation at Tuskegee.

"After I had been interrogated, I was placed in a garrison with some more prisoners. I was approached by an inmate dressed as a prisoner. He was particularly interested in Russia. I told him that I never had any contact with the Russians and knew very little about them.

"Finally the inmate revealed that he had lived many years in America. He stated he knew how Negroes were treated in the United States, but couldn't understand why Negroes were so faithful to such a country.

"I asked him why they were so hard on the Jews, who wanted life, liberty, and happiness like other people. He responded that the Jews had sold Germany out after the last war, and that they had hoarded all the capital of Germany. I inquired as to why they attacked Poland and occupied all the smaller countries of Europe. He maintained that the Germans were the underdogs of Europe, that they were allowed to travel through only one street of Poland to get to Danzig, and the

Poles, backed up by France and Britain, made fun of them. He also alleged that the Germans were not treated fairly in sharing the markets of the world like other countries.

"He was interested in knowing what the United States was planning to do with Germany should she win the war. He had heard that the United States planned to divide Germany into two or three smaller countries. I told him that I was only an ordinary soldier and knew nothing of the plans of the United States.

"The next day I was put on a box car with a group of prisoners and sent to Stalag Luft III. Here I met Floyd Thompson and Lewis C. Smith. I also learned that several other members of the 332nd were also imprisoned here, but since this camp was divided into several compounds, each surrounded by high barbed wire fences, we never met while there.

"On July 29 we were marched out of Stalag Luft III. After a forced march of 75 or 80 kilometers we were placed on a train and shipped to Moosburg. We remained here until April 29th when we were liberated by the Third Army.

"One morning I ventured over to LT Harold Brown's room to chat with him. I found Brown still in bed though it was nearly eleven o'clock. Brown, a rather nice looking youngster, appeared too young to be a veteran combat pilot. Although always pleasant and friendly, his mannerism gave him the appearance of a spoiled only child. Brown and I talked for a while about various things, but finally we got around to the usual subject of combat. 'You know,' he said, 'we had a lot of good pilots in the 99th, but in my opinion our squadron commander, MAJ Campbell, was the best pilot of the Squadron and Group. He loved to fly and was a damn good pilot. He had so much nerve! He led so many missions COL Davis grounded him. I'll never forget the mission he led when I went down.

"'On March 14, 1945, we went on a strafing mission to strafe enemy railroads between Brux and Stety. I flew MAJ Campbell wing that day. Anyway, we were strafing a railroad when we spotted a locomotive. One by one we peeled off from formation and dived down on the locomotive that was steaming down the tracks trying to outrun us. I went in with my guns opened up, but I had my mind so set on hitting my target I allowed my plane to come too close to the locomotive. As I pulled up, the locomotive exploded. My ship was severely damaged. I managed to climb up to approximately 20,000 feet and headed for Yugoslavia, friendly territory. En route my ship began to act up. I tried to keep it under control, but after falling to about 14,000 feet I decided to jump.

"'I landed on a snow covered mountain slope between a group of tall pine trees. I received a few minor lacerations, otherwise I wasn't hurt. Immediately upon hitting the ground I decided to get out of the area as quickly as possible, because I knew someone must have seen me bail out and would investigate.

"'I started out with the idea of reaching Yugoslavia. After walking for approximately 20 minutes I was picked up by some civilian policemen and turned over to some German soldiers.

"'The next morning I was put on a train and carried to a small town about 45 kilometers from where I was captured. That evening, I was taken out of jail, put on a bus and carried to a private Air Field. I remained there eight days. During my stay there a bomber crew joined me. Four days later we were placed on a train and sent to Regensburg and from there to Nurnberg.

"'We were interrogated at Nurnberg and again put on a train headed for Frankfort on the Main. However, due to the destruction of the rail system by the Allies, we were forced to return to Nurnberg. On my return to Nurnberg I met LT Lincoln Hudson, who had been shot down on March 23. The same evening I was carried across town and placed in a German prison camp called Stalag Luft III. A few days later, Hudson joined me. While there, I met LT Iles and Gorham.

"'Early in April the Germans decided to move the personnel of the camp because Allied Forces were closing in fast. We were marched about 150 kilometers to Moosburg where we were imprisoned at Stalag Luft VII-A. I met several officers of the 332nd here. They were: LT Lloyd S. Hatchcock of Peoria, IL, who was shot down over Rome in June, 1944; Robert H. Daniels Jr., who was shot down over Toulon in August, 1944; Kenneth I. Williams, who was shot down over Athens; Wilbur F. Long, shot down over Blechhammer in September, 1944; Carrol S. Woods, shot down over Athens, Greece, on October 6, 1944; CPT Armour McDaniel, shot down over Berlin on March 24, 1945; Walter McCreary, shot down over Hungary; Robert B. Gaither, shot down over Budapest, Hungary; Richard

Macon, shot down over Montpelier, France; Thurston L. Gaines, Jr., shot down over Nurnberg; Clarence N. Driver, shot down over Linz on March 25, 1945; Woodrow F. Morgan, shot down over Rome; Alexander Jefferson, shot down over Toulon, France; and Newman Golden, shot down over the Alps near Linz, Austria, on March 20, 1945.

"My interrogation at Nurnberg revealed how thoroughly the German Intelligence Department gathered information. The interrogators knew practically everything about the 332nd except the range of the P-51 we flew. After telling me the history of my squadron the interrogator remarked: 'Brown, I hear that CPT Toppins has returned from his leave and has resumed flying. He was lucky in shooting down several of our planes. This time we intend to sack him up.

"'Tell me, Brown, why are you fellows so willing to fight for the United States? I know how colored people are treated in the United States and especially in the South. We are considered enemies of the United States, and you fellows are dying for the United States, yet our boys receive better treatment in the United States than you. I can't understand you fellows!'"

One of my acquaintances at Tuskegee was LT Newman C. Golden. He was inducted into the army at Patterson Field, on October 14, 1942. He applied for cadet training and was sent to Tuskegee where he was graduated as a Flight Officer and sent overseas as a replacement for the 99th on January 25, 1945. While flying his 13th mission on March 20, 1945, his plane developed engine trouble. In the words of Golden: "I bailed out about 50 miles west of Linz, Austria. When I pulled my chute I became entangled in the cord and received a very bad injury to my left knee. I was unable to walk. After lying on the ground for about ten minutes I saw a small child playing nearby, so I yelled at him. He ran home and a little later returned with his parents, who disarmed me and carried me to their farm house. Here I was held until some soldiers arrived and carried me off to jail. After two days I was sent to Nurnberg, Germany. I stayed at Nurnberg a week then was moved to Stalag Luft VII-A at Moosburg. I remained at Moosburg until April 29, 1945, when I was liberated by General Patton's Third Army, 14th Armored Division."

Top: Four Astronauts: COL Guion S. Bluford, Dr. Ronald E. McNair, COL Frederick D. Gregory, and LTC Charles F. Bolden. Bottom: COL McPhearson, A. Cisco, L. Jackson, H. Baugh, *Ace* Lawson, Dempsey Morgan, and L. Turner.

Chapter 24
Leaders of Men

COL Benjamin O. Davis

No doubt the most outstanding member of the 99th and the 332nd was COL Davis Jr., born in Washington, DC. After completing high school, he entered Western Reserve, but later transferred to the University of Chicago. His impressive record there led Oscar Depriest, former Republican Congressman of Illinois, to appoint him to West Point Military Academy. In June 1936, he was graduated from West Point with the distinction of being the first Negro to graduate from that institution in 47 years.

After a short assignment at Fort Bennings, he was transferred to Tuskegee Institute to teach military science and tactics. This assignment lasted until the spring of 1941 when he was sent to Fort Riley to become military aide to his father, BG Davis, Sr. This assignment was also brief. In July 1941, he was accepted as a cadet by the Army Air Force and sent to Tuskegee for pilot training.

Upon receiving his wings as an Air force pilot in March 1942, he was assigned to the newly activated 99th. On August 27, he was elevated to the command of the 99th, and in April 1943, he carried the squadron overseas. His assignment with the 99th was terminated in September 1943, when he was recalled to the States to assume command of the 332nd. He led the 332nd overseas in January 1944, and commanded it until hostilities in Europe ceased.

In June 1945, COL Davis returned to the United States and on July 21 was appointed to command the newly activated 477th Composite Group which consisted of two bomber squadrons and one fighter squadron. A week later, on July 1, he became the first Negro to command a military post in the United States, when he assumed command of Godman Field. On March 13, 1946, the entire personnel of Godman Field was transferred to Lockbourne Army Air Base, and COL Davis was appointed to command the base. Here the 477th Compsite Group was reorganized into the 332nd Fifth Group on May 1, 1946. A few months later, on August 15, the 332nd Fighter Group was reorganized into the 332nd Fighter Wing and operated as such until July 1949 when Lockbourne was deactivated and its personnel integrated into white organizations throughout the world.

Following the close of Lockbourne, COL Davis was sent to the Air War College. Upon completion of his studies, he was assigned to the office of the Deputy Chief of Staff for Operations, Hq. USAF, where he served in various capacities. In November 1953, he completed training at the advanced Jet Fighter Gunnery School, Nellis AFB, and was assigned as commander of the 51st Fighter Interceptor Wing, Far East Air Force, Korea. Eight months later, he was appointed Director of Operations and Training, Far East Forces, Japan. While serving in this position, he was promoted to BG in 1954.

In 1955, he assumed the position of Vice Commander of the 13th Air Force. When the Chinese communists began shelling the nationalist China islands of Quemoy and Matsu, General Davis was assigned the additional duty of Commander of Air Task Force 13 (Provisional) and sent to Formosa to plan the defense of Formosa.

In April 1957, he was sent to Germany as Chief of Staff, 12th Air Force USAFE. When the 12th was returned to the States in December 1957, he was assigned as Deputy chief of Staff for Operations, Hq. USAFE. In this position, he was promoted to Major General.

COL Davis returned to the States in July 1961 and became the Director of Manpower and Organization DCS/Programs and Requirements, Hq. USAF, Pentagon. His next assignment was that of Assistant Deputy Chief, Programs and Requirements, a position that brought him a promotion to LTG on April 30, 1965. Shortly after, he was reassigned as Chief of Staff for the United Nations Command and US Forces in Korea. Two years later in August 1967, he assumed command of the 13th Air Force at Clark Air Base in the Philippines. The following year, he was assigned as Deputy Commander in Chief, Middle East, Southern Asia and Africa south of the Sahara.

COL Davis retired on February 1, 1970. For his outstanding service, he was awarded the Air Force Distinguished Service Medal, Army Distinguished Service Medal, Silver Star, Legion of Merit with two oak leaf clusters, Distinguished Flying Cross, Air Medal with four clusters, Air Force Commendation Medal with two oak leaf clusters, and the Philippines Legion of Honor.

LTC George Spencer Roberts

Next to COL Davis and one of the men mostly responsible for the success of Negro airmen in combat was LTC Roberts. *Spanky*, as he was known by his comrades, was born and reared in Fairmount, West Virginia. He attended West Virginia State where he earned a private pilot's license under the civilian aviation program. Roberts was a member of the first class to be commissioned at Tuskegee and, shortly after receiving his wings, was appointed as Commanding Officer of the 99th. In August 1942, COL Davis took over the command of the 99th and Roberts became the squadron's operation officer. When COL Davis returned to the States in September 1943, to command the 332nd, Roberts again assumed command of the 99th. On June 9, 1945, Roberts was elevated to the command of the 332nd Fighter Group. This job was administrative in nature because the war in Europe was over and little flying was being done. He brought the 332nd back to the States in October 1945, and saw it deactivated at Camp Kilmer.

CPT Charles B. Hall

Perhaps CPT Hall of Brazil, IN, received more fame as a pilot than any Negro other than COL Davis. Before entering the Army, Hall was a student at Illinois State Teachers College. Like thousands of young men, he gave up his studies to enlist in the Army. He was accepted for aviation cadet training in 1941 and was commissioned with the fourth class graduated from Tuskegee.

On July 2, 1943, he destroyed a Focke-Wulf 190 over Castelvetrano. This gave him the honor of being the first Negro to destroy an enemy aircraft in aerial combat. For this accomplishment, he was personally congratulated by General Eisenhower, Allied Commander in Chief, MG Doolittle, Commanding Officer of the 8th Air Force, General Spaatz, Commander of the United States Strategic Air Force, and Air Marshal Cunningham of the Royal Air Force. On landing at the field, General Eisenhower said, "I want to see the pilot who shot down that Jerry." This was a great honor for a youth who only a few years before was studying to be a teacher.

Success and more glory, however, were in store for Hall. On January 28, 1944, while leading a flight of eight planes on patrol in the Anzio area, a flight of enemy aircraft was encountered. Hall destroyed two of the enemy aircraft. For this feat, he was awarded the Distinguished Flying Cross. His citation read as follows:

12th Air Force--Charles F. Hall
Captain, Air Corps--79th Fighter Group
For extraordinary achievement while participating in aerial flight as pilot of a P-40 type aircraft.
On 28 January 1944, while leading an eight plane patrol over Anzio, Italy, Captain Hall sighted six FW-190 and ME-109 preparing to strafe Allied ground troops. Attacking so aggressively that he completely disorganized the enemy formation, Captain Hall shot down two enemy aircraft and his comrades destroyed two FW-190s and dispersed the remainder without loss or damage to the P-40s. On many missions throughout the Sicilian and Italian campaign, his steadfast devotion to duty and outstanding proficiency as a combat pilot has reflected great credit upon himself and the armed forces of the United States.

Although Hall gained fame practically over night, he remained modest and regular. One night while we were lounging around *shooting the breeze*, I asked Hall if he intended to write about his experiences in combat.

"No", he replied. "Frankly, I don't think I have done anything unusual. True, I shot down a few enemy planes, but compare my score with that of many white pilots, especially those pilots who flew for the 8th Air Force. They frequently encountered enemy aircraft and gained many victories. The only reason I received so much publicity was because I am the first Negro to have shot down an enemy plane in aerial combat. You know, there were many whites who thought Negroes could not master swift moving planes under combat conditions. When I shot down a plane they were surprised, and it changed their minds. Furthermore, I wouldn't feel right if someone writes about me and ignores the hundreds of other fellows who did as much as I did to make the 99th Fighter Squadron and the 332nd Fighter Group successful in combat."

MAJ William A. Campbell

There were many pilots of the 332nd who praised MAJ Campbell as the best flight leader of the group. Everyone who flew with him respected him for his aggressiveness and bravery. Campbell, a tall, slender, jovial lad, was one of the local boys at Tuskegee. He was born and reared at Tuskegee Institute only ten miles from the flying field. After completing high school at Tuskegee, he enrolled at Tuskegee Institute, where he received a degree of Bachelor of Science in Business Administration. He enlisted in the Army as an aviation cadet in February 1942, and won his wings on July 3, 1942. He was assigned to the 99th and in April 1943 was sent overseas with the Squadron.

After completing his tour of duty, Campbell returned to the United States on December 8, 1943. After a short stay at home, he became bored with inactivity and requested more combat duty. He returned to combat and, shortly after rejoining the 99th, was made its commanding officer. In his new assignment he displayed leadership and bravery that brought him a promotion of Major.

At the completion of his second tour, Campbell was credited with 106 combat missions. He was awarded the Distinguished Flying Cross with one oak leaf cluster and the air medal with nine clusters. Even then he was neither tired of fighting nor satisfied to rest on his laurels. When COL Davis requested volunteers to aid him in leading the 477th into combat against the Japs, Campbell was among the first to volunteer. However, the war in the Pacific ended before the 477th could be sent overseas and Campbell thereby lost the chance of fighting the Japs.

CPT Edward L. Toppins

One cannot speak of the merits of Negro airmen in World War II without mentioning CPT Toppins. He was born in Mississippi. At an early age, he moved with his parents to San Francisco. After completing his elementary training he entered Los Angeles Junior College, from which he was graduated. While still a student at the University of San Francisco, Toppins learned that the Army Air Force was accepting Negroes as cadets. He applied for cadet training at Tuskegee Army Air Field.

While in training as a cadet, Toppins cracked up a trainer plane that put him in a hospital for several months. Many less stout hearted men would have given up the idea of winning wings, but not Toppins. He was determined to become a pilot and returned to flying. On

September 6, 1942, Toppins was commissioned as a 2nd LT in the Army Air Corps.

Toppins was one of the first four replacement pilots to join the 99th in combat. As a member of the 99th and the 332nd, he flew 141 missions over Pantelleria, Sicily, Southern France, Germany, Austria, Yugoslavia, Greece, Bulgaria, Poland, Czechoslovakia, and Romania. He was officially credited with destroying four enemy aircraft in aerial combat and one probable. For this he was awarded the Distinguished Flying Cross, the Air Medal with five clusters, the E.T.O. ribbon with seven battle stars, the American Defense, and the Victory Medal.

If there ever was a pilot who was confident in his ability to shoot down any enemy pilot daring to do battle with him, it was Toppins. Whenever he flew he was out to shoot down an enemy plane. The Germans learned this after he had shot down several of their planes. LT Harold H. Brown, a member of the 99th, who was captured by the Germans upon crash landing in enemy territory, related that German intelligence officer promised that Nazi pilots would get Toppins if it was the last thing they did. In spite of this promise, Toppins completed his tour and returned to the States.

At Tuskegee, Toppins, relating his most memorable mission, said: "One day we were assigned to fly an escort mission to Austria. My flight consisted of LT Leonard Jackson, Alva Temple, Heber Houston and myself. On arriving over Lake Balaton, we found the sky covered with clouds of varying layers. This was excellent cover for attacking enemy aircraft. We were flying P-51s.

"Shortly afterwards, we observed some enemy aircraft dodging into some clouds above us and at a distance. Immediately we dropped our wing tanks and I led the flight to investigate three ME-109s that had been cavorting high above us since we entered enemy territory.

"The investigation turned into a 30 minute chase, something unusual in aerial combat. Starting at 25,000 feet with everything to the fire wall, we slowly closed in on them, both in altitude and distance, despite their 10,000 feet altitude advantage. At 41,000 feet with us just out of range, Jerry decided he could not out climb us and decided to try and outdive us. The superiority of our ships was so evident that I designated a target for each member of the flight as we jockeyed for position on their tails. Two of the three were confirmed victories and the other a probable. LT Leonard Jackson was credited with one enemy plane and I the others. Having flown the P-40 during most of my tour of duty it was a great thrill to fly a ship which gave me such an overwhelming mastery of the engagement."

CPT Wendell C. Pruitt

There came to Tuskegee in the early part of the war a tall, handsome, Indian featured youngster who was eager to become a pilot. Like all other cadets, he worried from day to day that he would be "washed out". Months passed and he gained more and more confidence in his ability to fly. Then came graduation day and, finally, combat. Soon his uncanny ability to maneuver his plane became so noticeable by other pilots of the group that he became the envy of those who flew with him. This pilot was CPT Pruitt of St. Louis.

Pruitt seemingly was cut out for flying. He took chances that the boldest and most experienced pilots dared not take. Even professional acrobatic pilots were cautious in performing stunts that Pruitt did nonchalantly. He scraped roofs of buildings with the wheels of his plane while flying at a very fast rate; slow rolled his plane so close to the deck that his wings missed the ground by only a few inches. Pruitt seemed to have little or no premium on his life. He attacked a group of enemy planes with the same lack of caution that he attacked a single enemy ship. CPT Archer, who often flew as wingman for Pruitt, and a very good pilot in his own right, often related this story of how he almost met death trying to follow Pruitt.

"One day after registering five victories between us, Pruitt and I went home feeling very good. On approaching the base we decided to do a little acrobatics. It was the custom of the pilots of our group to perform a slow roll over the field when they gained victories. Anyway, we buzzed the field twice. Then we decided to make a victory roll. It is almost a habit for all pilots to make a slow roll from the left. Pruitt was left handed and did his rolls from the right. I did not think of this and followed Pruitt in almost on the deck. As he rolled his plane to the right I, by habit, rolled mine to the left. My plane slid under Pruitt's plane while I was upside down. My prop stalled and as I fell out of my roll my plane's wing missed the ground by only a few inches. I was through for that day and today consider myself one of the luckiest pilots in the world."

It was alleged by members of 332nd that not long after the group arrived overseas, CPT Pruitt, together with CPT Archer, Haywood, and Alfonso W. Davis. Jr., were reported to COL Davis for performing acrobatics over Naples. COL Davis did not approve of his pilots performing acrobatics because he was short of pilots and felt that acrobatics were too risky. He therefore, upon receiving the report, ordered CPT Gleed, the 302nd Squadron Commander, to court martial the men. CPT Gleed, however, informed COL Davis that he could not willingly court martial the pilots because he felt acrobatics were good practice and useful to combat pilots. Shortly after this reply, CPT Gleed was relieved of his command and assigned to the North African Ferry Command as a test pilot. When this assignment was completed, Gleed returned to the group and was appointed by COL Davis to one of the highest positions in the group, Group Operations Officer.

CPT Pruitt completed 70 combat missions before returning to the States. He was credited with three aerial victories and shared in the sinking of an enemy destroyer. For this he was awarded the Distinguished Flying Cross and the Air Medal with six oak leaf cluster. Upon his return to the United States, he was also honored by the Mayor of his home town, who proclaimed December 12, 1944, "CPT Wendell O. Pruitt Day".

Death overtook Pruitt on Sunday afternoon, April 20, 1945, when his trainer plane crashed a few miles from Tuskegee Army Air Base. Although most of his comrades had witnessed many pilots meet the same fate they could hardly believe that this had happened to Pruitt. The only conclusion they could draw was that PVT Edward N. Thompson of Miami, who was also killed, became nervous and froze the stick when Pruitt attempted a slow roll on deck.

Father Andrews, who officiated at Pruitt's funeral, gave a fitting epitaph of this hero when he remarked: "CPT Pruitt is dead, but the fruits of his life will be multiplied over the earth. He was a student, a man who used his intellectual abilities to achieve. All of us could learn from Wendell Pruitt the necessity of labor to accomplish our goal. We knew him as an interesting and unassuming young man, daring but not bold; vigorous and energetic, but not offensive; a good citizen, a good friend, and a devout Catholic. We needed a modern hero for us to pattern our lives so God called him home."

Andrew D. Turner

When it became known that Negroes were to be accepted for pilot training, air minded youths throughout the United States rushed to make application. One of such men was Turner, *Jug* as he was known by his comrades. He was born in Washington, DC, January 6, 1920. After completing his elementary training at Deanwood Elementary School, he entered Dunbar High School. Here he began to manifest the leadership ability which he carried into military service. Upon graduation from Dunbar, his classmates inserted the following poem in the class year book which most nearly described this youth:

He stands for truth and high ideals,
His versatility reveals
He's good in any field.

Turner was commissioned at Tuskegee on October 9, 1942. In March 1943, he was transferred to Selfridge Field and assigned to the 100th of the 332nd. In July 1943, he was appointed operation officer of his squadron, a position he held until July 23, 1944. On this date he was appointed Commanding Officer of the 100th, succeeding CPT Tresville, who failed to return from a mission.

MAJ Turner completed 69 combat missions during his overseas service. In recognition of his outstanding achievement in aerial combat against the enemy in the North African and Mediterranean Theatres, he was awarded the Distinguished Flying Cross on July 10, 1944. He was also awarded the Air Medal with four oak leaf clusters and a certificate of valor by the Commanding General of the 15th Air Force. As a member of the 332nd, he was also awarded the Presidential Citation, and credited with participating in seven campaigns, including the Rome-Arno, Southern and Northern France, Balkans, Germany, the Appennines, and the Po Valley.

At the conclusion of the European War, MAJ Turner volunteered to assist COL Davis in leading the 477th into combat against the Japs. He returned to the United States on June 10, 1945, and reported for duty as Deputy Group Commander of the 477th on July 17, 1945.

The war with Japan terminated before the group could be sent into action against the Japs. However, he remained at Godman Field and moved with the 477th to its new home at Lockbourne on March 13, 1946.

On May 1, 1946, the 477th Composite Group was reorganized into the 332nd Fighter Group. The 100th was reactivated and MAJ Turner was again appointed its leader. A few months later, on August 15, the Group was reorganized into the 332nd Fighter Wing and MAJ Turner was appointed Operation and Training Officer. Like numerous combat pilots, MAJ Turner fought throughout the war without a serious accident only to lose his life on a routine training flight. On September 18, 1947, MAJ Turner's plane collided in mid air with a plane piloted by LT Hall. Both pilots were killed. Thus ended the career of one of the most outstanding leaders of the 332nd.

MAJ Lee Rayford

One of the most decorated Negro pilots of the United States Army Air Force was MAJ Rayford of Ardwick, MD. He was born in April 1918 in West Chester, PA, and was enrolled in the graduate school at Howard University when the war began. On September 30, 1941, he enlisted in the Air Corps and was commissioned as a second lieutenant on May 20, 1942. Rayford was sent overseas with the 99th. Upon the completion of his tour of duty, he returned to the States. He was reassigned to the 332nd and appointed Operation Officer of the 301st. Shortly after the group was sent into combat, Rayford was elevated to the command of the 301st. He completed 90 missions in his two tours of combat. For his outstanding service he was awarded the Distinguished Flying Cross, the Air Medal with six oak leaf clusters, the Purple Heart, the Order of Yugoslavia Partisan Red Star, the American Defense Medal, and the Victory Medal.

Edward C. Gleed

On the afternoon of November 25, 1942, a tall, slender cadet stood beside a fighter plane on the runway at Tuskegee. As Gleed listened attentively to an instructor, a large gathering of spectators formed on the edge of the runway to watch what was to be the first attempt of a Negro to fly the P-39 Airacobra. This plane differed from the conventional fighter plane in that it had tricycle landing gears.

For an hour the instructor went over the procedures of flying the plane with the young cadet. Then the cadet climbed into the plane and started the engine. A few minutes later, the plane raced down the runway and an outburst of applause went up from the spectators as the plane rose swiftly into the air.

The young pilot maneuvered his ship over the field for 40 minutes; then he pointed his spiral-nosed plane towards the ground and came in for a landing. In his first attempt to land, he overshot the runway. He circled the field and tried a second landing. This time, he made a perfect three-point landing. The cadet who flew this historic mission was Gleed.

Gleed was born and reared in Lawrence, KS. Upon completion of high school, he enrolled at the University of Kansas. Here he successfully completed his studies. With the ambition to become a lawyer, he entered Howard University Law School. By this time the war was in full force. Unable to place his personal ambition above his country, he left school and enlisted with the 9th Cavalry, which was then stationed at Fort Riley. His knowledge of law brought him back to Washington, DC, where he was assigned to the Military Intelligence Department. The desire for action and excitement would not let him be satisfied with this assignment. He made application for pilot training and was sent to Tuskegee for training. Here he almost immediately showed aptitude and ability to fly. When the Air Force decided to test the ability of Negroes to fly the new P-39 Airacobra, Gleed, as a cadet, was chosen to make the experimental flight. After graduating as a 2nd LT, he was assigned to the 332nd. Later he was appointed as Squadron Commander of the 301st Fighter Squadron. Shortly after entering combat, and upon the request of General Strother of the 15th, he was relieved of his command and sent on detached service to North Africa as a test pilot. Upon his return to the 332nd, he was appointed Group Operation Officer, holding this position until he returned to the United States at the conclusion of the war.

Gleed, like many of his comrades, could not remain idle. He volunteered for more combat service and was assigned as Operation Officer of the 477th, which was scheduled to fight the Japs. However, the war in the Pacific ended before the 477th could be sent overseas. In March 1946, the 477th was moved to Lockbourne where the group was reorganized. Gleed maintained his position as operation officer in the new organizations and served efficiently until the 332nd was deactivated in July 1949.

CPT Robert B. Tresville

The early death of CPT Tresville perhaps robbed the 332nd of one of its most promising leaders. CPT Tresville was born on May 9, 1921, at the Station Hospital, Fort Huachuca, AZ, where his father, an army band leader, was at the time stationed. Shortly after his birth, his father was transferred to Fort Bennings, GA, where he became director of the famous 24th Infantry Band.

From the time he was old enough to stand alone and go with his father to look at the big guns at Fort Bennings, young Treville's every move was in the direction of a military career. He had hardly finished elementary school at Columbus, GA, when his father sent him to Germantown to enter high school where he was graduated in 1938 with honors. He entered Pennsylvania State College in September. After one year, he was appointed by Congressman Arthur Mitchell to the United States Military Academy at West Point.

While at West Point, he applied for pilot training. He was sent to Tuskegee Army Air Field, where he won his wings in January 1943. Upon receiving his wings, he went back to West Point and received his commission as 2nd LT in the Regular Army of the United States.

When the 332nd went overseas in January 1944, CPT Tresville was sent with them as Group Commanding Officer of the 100th. Before he was reported missing on June 24, Tresville had completed 23 missions, and on each he displayed leadership and courage which won the admiration of all who flew with him.

General Daniel *Chappie* James, Jr.

One of the most outstanding graduates of Tuskegee was *Chappie*. He was born in Pensacola, FL, February 11, 1920, graduated form Washington High School in 1937, and enrolled at Tuskegee where he received a Bachelor of Science degree and completed a Civilian Pilot Training course in 1942. He was employed as a civilian pilot instructor in the Army Air Cadet Program at Tuskegee until January 1943 when he was accepted into the cadet program. He was commissioned as a 2LT in 1943 and assigned to the 477th at Selfridge.

In September 1949, he was appointed to command the 12th Fighter Bomber Squadron at Clark Field, and in July 1950, he was sent to Korea where he flew 101 combat missions. This was followed by many important assignments, commanding the 437th and 60 fighter Interceptor Squadrons, served a tour with the Air Staff Division, and in July 1960, he was sent to England to command the 81st Tactical Fighter Wing. There he also served as commander of the 92nd Tactical Fighter Squadron and Deputy Commander of Operations before returning to the States in 1964 to serve as Director of Operations of the 4453rd Combat Training Wing at Davis-Monthan AFB.

In December 1966, General James was sent to Thailand, where he became the Deputy Commander for Operations and later became the Vice Commander of the 8th Tactical Fighter Wing. He flew 78 combat missions in North Vietnam, many in the Hanoi-Haiphong area, including participation in historical Bolo Mig sweep in which 7 Mig21 were destroyed, the highest total of any mission during the Vietnam war.

On return to the States, he was assigned as vice Commander of the 33rd. In August 1969, he was reassigned as Commander of the 7272nd at Wheelus AFB, Lybia.

On March 31, 1970, Secretary of Defense Laird appointed him as Deputy Assistant Secretary of Defense (Public Affairs) and concurrently was promoted to Brigadier General. In 1972, he was promoted to Major General; the following year, he was promoted to Principal Deputy Secretary of Defense (Public Affairs), and was appointed Vice Commander of the Military Airlift Command with Hq. at Scott AFB. He was promoted to LTG on September 1, 1974, and to the rank of General (four stars) on August 29, 1975. His last assignment was that of Commanding Chief of the North American Air Defense Command (NORAD). He retired on February 2, 1978, and died on February 25, 1978.

Spann Watson

I know of no one who has been more helpful to me in writing my book than Spann Watson. In fact, I know of no one who has played a more significant role in perpetuating the story of the Tuskegee experiment and encouraging minority aviation and aero-space.

Spann was born in Johnston, South Carolina and moved to Lodi, N.J. with his family in April, 1927. After graduating from Hackensack High School, he enrolled at Howard University where he studied mechanical engineering. He began his aviation training at Howard University in 1939 by enrolling in the College Pilot Training Program, and continued that training at Tuskegee Institute when, in 1941, he was accepted for pilot training by the Army Air Corps.

During one of his training flight, Spann's engine broke down, and was forced to an emergency landing. Luckily, he saw a corn field and was able to land in it without too much difficulty. To his amazement, many farmers rushed to see the landing, amazed that a black man piloting the plane. Sometime earlier, another pilot--a white man--had also made an emergency landing in exactly the same field. Spann asked them for their assistance, and soon, with their help, he was ready for the take-off, except that there were several high poles standing in the way down the field. "Those supposed *Red Neck* farmers," he said, "got their sons and friends together, and quickly cleared the field of those poles, and I was able to take off without incident. I still remember the looks on their faces when they first saw me, and how delighted they were to see me in the air. They were as amazed as I was happy gaining altitude."

He was graduated in July, 1942, assigned to the 99th Fighter Squadron and sent into combat with the original Squadron committed to combat. He flew over seventy combat missions over North Africa, Sicily and mainland Italy before returning to the States.

Spann remained in Service at the end of World War II, served in numerous capacities and achieved the rank of Lt. Colonel before retiring in 1965 with 23 years of service.

After retiring from the Air Force, Spann was employed by the Federal Aviation Administration as an equal opportunity specialist. Throughout his career, Spann provided counsel and assistance to hundreds of military personnel and government employees. He also has been instrumental in helping minority youths gain employment, including 483 airline attendants, and has been responsible for more than thirty youths gaining appointments to the three Service Academies.

Spann Watson has received numerous awards and honors for his achievements. In 1970, he was the recipient of the Transportation

Department Award for his exceptional service toward the achievement of equal opportunity. In 1985, he was elected to the presidency of the 2000 member of the Thomas W. Anthony Chapter of the Air Forces Association serving Andrew AFB and Prince George's County, MD. In 1987, he was awarded the National Coalition of Black Federal Aviation Employee C. Alfred C. Anderson Award for his special assistance in helping minorities and women gain employment in the aviation industries. In 1990, he was honored as an "Elder Statesman of Aviation" by the National Aeronautic Association and in 1991 was elected to the Board of Directors of the National Aeronautic Association. He was also honored in 1991 as the recipient of the BG Noel F. Parrish Award presented by the Tuskegee Airmen, Inc. and awarded National Headquarter's Air Force Association President's Citation. Then in 1992, the Dade County Airport Authority of Miami, FL, and the 4th Air Wing, US Air Force, located at Seymour Johnson AFB in Goldboro, NC, honored him for this contribution to military and civilian aviation.

Clarence Lucky Lester

One of the most outstanding pilots of the 332nd Fighter Group was Clarence "Lucky" Lester. He was such an outstanding combat pilot that he is permanently featured at the Air and Space Museum in Washington, DC

Lester was born on February 8, 1923 in Richmond, Virginia, but reared in Chicago. He enrolled at Virginia State College, where he was a star football player. When World War II broke out, he enlisted in the Army Air Corps in July 1943, and was accepted for pilot training at Tuskegee. He was graduated from the pilot training program in December 1943 and assigned to the newly activated 100th Fighter Squadron.

Lester was sent overseas with the 100th Fighter Squadron and completed ninety combat missions. The highlight of his combat tour was on July 18, 1944 when he shot down three enemy aircraft in less than five minutes.

Relating his victories, Lester said, "It was a clear day when we took off from an airfield at Ramitelli, Italy. We were flying P-51 Mustangs. Our mission was a rendezvous over northern Italy's Po Valley at 2,500 feet with B-17 Flying Fortress enroute to bomb an airfield in southern Germany. Our mission was to escort the bombers to the target and back, providing protection from enemy aircraft.

"The rendezvous was made on time at 25,000 feet. The other squadrons of the 332nd, the 99th, 301st, 302nd started close cover at 27,000 feet. My squadron, the 100th Fighter Squadron, was flying at 29,000 feet when bogeys were spotted above us. We were flying a loose combat formation 200 feet apart and zig, zagging. On spotting the enemy aircraft, our flight leader commanded hard right turn and punch tanks, this is drop external wing tanks to prepare for battle. One of our members called that he could not get one of his two tanks off. After his call, we never saw him again.

"I saw a formation of ME 109s straight ahead and I closed in about 200 feet and started firing. Smoke began to pour from the aircraft and a little later it exploded. I was going so fast I was sure I would hit some of the debris from the explosion, but luckily I didn't.

"As I was dodging pieces of the enemy aircraft, I saw another ME109 to my right, all alone on a heading 90 degrees to mine, but at the same altitude. I turned onto his tail and closed in to about 200 feet while firing. I noticed the aircraft began to smoke and almost stopped. I was going so fast I overran him, but noticed a blond pilot parachute from his burning plane.

"I was alone and looking for my flight mates when I spotted a third ME 109 flying very low about 1000 feet above the ground."

Lester remained in service when World War II ended. He served a tour in Occupied Germany and a tour in Korea before being assigned to Howard University as an Associate Professor of Air Science. He also served a tour in Alaska and other assignments within the United States.

In addition to being awarded the Distinguished Flying Cross and the Air Medal with nine oak leaf clusters, he was awarded the Legion of Merit. Lester served 28 years with the Air Force before retiring, dying of cancer in March 1986 and was buried in Arlington Cemetery.

COL Elwood T. Driver

One of the most outstanding Tuskegee Airmen was Elwood Thomas Driver, addressed by his fellow airmen as "Woody". He was born on August 20, 1921 in Trenton, NJ, one of four children born to Robert Thomas Driver and Susan Morris Driver of Gloucester,

Virginia. Driver graduated from Trenton Central High School and won a scholarship to Rutgers University. He had to turn down the scholarship, however, because it did not include room and board. Determined that he would continue his education, he stayed home and worked to pay expenses while attending Trenton State Teacher's college. He was graduated in 1942 with a Bachelor of Science degree. Later, he continued his education at New York University, earning a Master's degree in Safety Engineering.

After graduating from Trenton State College he applied for the Naval Academy. He ranked number one on the entrance examination but was turned down because of his color. Not one to be discouraged, Driver enlisted in the Army Air Corps and was sent to Tuskegee Army Air Field for pilot training. He was graduated in October, 1942 with class 42-I and assigned to command the newly activated 100th Fighter Squadron. However, in August 1943, he was sent to Licata, Sicily as a replacement pilot with the 99th Fighter Squadron. He flew 124 combat missions and was credited with shooting down a German FW190 while flying his P-40 aircraft over Anzio Beach.

On the completion of his tour of combat, he returned to Tuskegee and was assigned to head the academic ground school when its director, Major Harold Martin of Washington, DC was killed in a plane crash near Reidville, N.C. He held this position until the base closed in 1946.

Driver continued service with the Air Force. From 1949 to 1953, he served in the Office of Air Safety, Pentagon, Washington, DC as assistant Director of Safety, Far East Air Logistic Forces, Japan, and Aircraft Mission, Korea. From 1956-1958 he commanded Show Air Base, Japan.

Driver returned to the United States in 1958 and was assigned as Personnel Officer and Executive Officer, Field Training Wing at Chanute Air Force Base, IL, retiring on October 31, 1962 wherein he moved to Riverside, CA, where he was employed as Chief of Safety for the Minuteman Missile at North American Aviation.

In July, 1967, Driver was sent on loan to the US Government National Highway Safety Administration in Washington, DC. In 1978, he was appointed by President Carter as a Board member and Vice Chairman of the National Safety Board, serving in that capacity until 1981 when he became a self-employed consultant for the Institute for

Safety Analysis, located in Rockville, MD. Driver died on March 26, 1992.

Woodrow W. Crockett

Woodrow W. Crockett was born in Texarkana, AR and attended Dunbar High School and Junior College in Little Rock, AR. He joined the US Army as a private in August 1940. Competition within the 349th Field Artillery (Heavy-155 millimeter gun), the Blacks' first field artillery unit in the Regular Army, resulted in SGT Crockett being selected as the Model Soldier of the Regiment. He was subsequently assigned to the Tuskegee Army Air Field in August 1942 as an aviation cadet.

LTC Crockett graduated as a pilot, single-engine, in Class 43C on March 25, 1943 and was commissioned a Second Lieutenant in the US Army Air Corps. He was a member of the 100th Fighter Squadron, 332nd Fighter Group, also known as the *Red Tails*. He flew 149 combat missions during a 15 month tour of duty in Italy during World War II. Fifty missions constituted a tour of duty. In 1952 and 1953 he flew 45 combat missions in Korea as a jet combat fighter pilot, while assigned to a staff position that did not require combat flying.

He has occupied various positions during his 30 years of military service, including Squadron and Group Operations Officer, Flying Safety Officer, Squadron Commander, and Radiological Safety Officer (RSO) on an atomic bomb test in the Southwest Pacific in 1951. In the latter position, Crockett was a member of a B-17 crew and was airborne during each atomic blast. He was also a member of a small group who were authorized to visit "Shot Island" (site of the bomb explosion) the day before and the day after each test shot. He was the Assistant Test Director for the 106 Category II Test Program at Edwards Air Force Base, CA in 1958 and also for the Category III Test Program at McGuire Air Force Base, NJ, in 1959-1960. Crockett has a Mach 2 card, dated June 2, 1959, having flown the F-106 Delta Dart at twice the speed of sound, that is at 22 miles per minute. In September 1967, LTC Crockett flew Mach 2 in a West German built F-104 Star Fighter, while assigned to the NATO in Oslo, Norway.

A graduate of the US Air Force Command and Staff College, LTC Crockett received many awards during his military service including the Distinguished Flying Cross, and two Soldier's Medals for bravery, awarded for extricating pilots from burning fighter aircraft in 1944 in Italy and 1953 in Korea. Additional medals awards to him are the Air Medal with four oak leaf clusters, the Meritorious Service Medal, the Army Commendation Medal, and the Air Force Commendation Medal with one oak leaf cluster. He attained the highest aeronautical rating in the military command pilot in March 1958. LTC Crockett served in an Air Staff Officer position for the National Guard Bureau at the Pentagon for more than 10 years. Governor Orval Faubus awarded him the Arkansas Traveler Award on January 5, 1967. In 1970, he retired from the Air Force as a Lieutenant Colonel after 28 years on flight status, with 20 years of jet experience, approximately 5000 hours of flying time and 520 in combat. He piloted the P-39, P-40,P-47, P-51 Mustang, the F-80 Shooting Star, the F-86 D/L-All Weather Intercepter, the F-106 and the B-17.

LTC Crockett was inducted into the State of Arkansas Aviation Hall of Fame on October 15, 1992.

Vernon Vincent Haywood

No doubt Vernon Haywood was one of the men who made the Tuskegee Experiment, a success story. He was born October 4, 1920 in Raleigh, NC., where he attended the public schools of North Carolina and was a student at Hampton Institute, VA when World War II began.

Haywood entered the service as an aviation cadet in August, 1942 and was commissioned a Second Lieutenant by the Army Air Corps in April, 1943. He was sent overseas with the 332nd Fighter Group and served as Flight Commander, Operation Officer and Squadron Commander of the 302nd Fighter Squadron. He completed 356 combat hours in 70 combat missions. He returned to Tuskegee in 1945 and became the Assistant Director of the Instrument Training School. When Tuskegee closed, he was transferred to Lockbourne Air Base.

In 1949, he entered the Jet Pilot Training Instructor Program, Williams Air Force Base, AZ and at the completion of the course was assigned as Assistant Section Commander and Section Commander of the 3525th Pilot Training Wing.

Haywood served in the Far East, with the 35th Tactical Fighter Wing at Chitose, Johnson and Yokata Air bases, Japan at Clark Air Force Base, 13th Air Force, Philippines, and Saigon, Vietnam, Headquarters, MACV.

On returning to the United States, Haywood was assigned to Kirkland Air Force Base, as Director of Operation and Training, 34th Air Division. His other assignments included, Director of Safety 64th Air Division, Stewart Air Force Base, NY, Director of Operations 4453 Tactical Training Wing, and Special Assistant to the Commander, Military Aircraft Storage and Disposition Center, Davis Monthan Air Force Base, AZ. He retired in October, 1971 as a Command Pilot with 29 years of military service with more than 6000 hours flown mostly in Fighter Aircraft.

COL Charles E. McGee

COL Charles E. McGee is one of the few pilots of the US Air Force credited with fighting in three wars: World War II, Korea, and Vietnam. McGee was born in Cleveland, OH, on December 7, 1919. He enlisted in the US Army on October 26, 1942 and was sent to Tuskegee Army Air Field for pilot training. He was graduated with Class 43-F on June 30, 1943 and sent overseas with the 302nd Fighter Squadron of the 332 Fighter Group then commanded by CPT Edward C. Gleed. He flew 136 combat missions with the 332nd Fighter Group and was promoted to Captain. He completed his combat tour on November 17, 1944 and returned to the States on December 1, 1944 with four of his comrades, namely, Weldon Groves, Dempsey Morgan, Lawrence Wilkins and Willard Woods.

On his return to Tuskegee, he was given Twin-Engine training and assigned as a Twin engine Instructor, a position he held until Tuskegee Air Field closed in 1946.

COL McGee remained in service at the end of World War II. At the closing of Tuskegee Army Air Field, he was sent to Lockbourne and assigned as Base Operation and Training Officer. In 1948, he attended and completed an Aircraft Maintenance Technical Course at Chanute Field, and was assigned to the 301st Air Refueling Wing, Smoky Hill Air Force Base, KS.

When the Air Force was integrated, he was sent first to March Field, CA and later to Clark Field, Philippines Island. He flew P-51 aircraft during the Korean War, as a member of the 67th Fighter-Bomber Squadron. He was credited with 100 missions, awarded the DFC, Air Medal and promoted to Major.

After completing his combat tour, he returned to Clark Field and took over the command of the 44th Fighter-Bomber Squadron and flew the P-80 Jet aircraft.

In 1953 McGee attended the Air Force Command and Staff School, Maxwell Air Base, AL. At the completion of this course, he held several assignments with the Air Defense Division that qualified him to fly the F-89 Interceptor and brought him a promotion to LTC.

In 1959, McGee was promoted to Regular US Air Force Officer and sent to Italy to command the Luigi Bologna Sea Plane Base and the 7230th Support Squadron in conjunction with NATO deployment of the Jupiter missile.

In 1962, McGee served at Minot Air Force Base, ND and at Richard-Gebuar Air Force Base, MO. In 1967 he completed tactical Reconnaissance and RF flight training and appointed to command the 16th TAC Recon Squadron, Tan Son Nhut Air Base. He flew 172 missions during the Vietnam War and was awarded the Legion of Merit and other air medals.

After his tour in South Eastern Asis, McGee was assigned as a Liaison Officer serving USAEUR and the 7th Army in Germany. He was promoted to Colonel and completed his tour in Europe with the 50th Tac Fighter Wing as Chief of Maintenance.

McGee returned to the United States in 1971 and was assigned as Director of Maintenance Engineering, Air Force Communications Service and Commander of the 184th Air Base Wing and Richard-Gebaur Air Force Base, MO. He was awarded the Legion of Merit oak leaf clusters. McGee retired on January 31, 1973 as a command pilot with 6,308 flying hours.

COL McGee's military decorations include the Legion of Merit with one oak leaf cluster, Distinguished Flying Cross with two Oak Leaf Cluster, Bronze Star, Air Medal with 25 Oak Leaf Clusters, Army Commendation Medal, Presidential Unit Citation, Korean Presidential Unit Citation, and the Hellenic Republic World War II Commemorative Medal and several more campaign and service ribbons.

COL John B. Roach

Born in Boston, MA in 1925, COL Roach received his pilot training and his aeronautical experience as an Air Force pilot and as an inspector in the Federal Aviation Administration.

He is an original Tuskegee Airman having graduated in 1945 from the Army Air Corps pilot training program at Tuskegee Army Air Field, Tuskegee, AL. He then served with the 477th Composite Group at Godman Field, KY under the command of COL Benjamin O. Davis, Jr.

Following separation from active military service in 1946, John attended and graduated from Boston University's College of Industrial Technology. He continued his military career in the U.S. Air Force Reserve flying fighter and transport aircraft. He advanced to the position of Deputy Group Commander for Operations prior to his retirement.

In 1969 John was employed by the Federal Aviation Administration as an Air Carrier Operations Inspector. He progressed to the positions of Chief Inspector at the FAA Boston (Logan Airport), Massachusetts Office, Chief Inspector at the FAA Pittsburgh (Greater Pittsburgh Airport) Pennsylvania office, Chief of the FAA New England Region Flight Standards General Aviation & Air Carrier Branches and to the position of Deputy Regional Director of the FAA's New England Region.

John possesses an FAA Airline Transport Pilot's certificate with ratings in the Convair 240/340/440 the Boeing 727 and the NA B-25. Additionally, he is a licensed Airframe and Powerplant Mechanic, and a licensed Flight Engineer with Turbojet rating. He has qualified in 45 different types of military and civil aircraft.

John is married, and he and his wife Ethel have two daughters, Lorraine and Carolyn. He retired from the FAA in 1983 and from the USAFR in 1985. Presently, he travels throughout the United States on speaking tours on behalf of the Tuskegeean history.

Veteran Tuskegee Pilots attend reunion in Tuskegee, in 1977. Left to right: Alva Temple, Lowell Steward, Four Star General Daniel *Chappie* James (names of other two gentlemen unknown).

The late, Charles E. Francis, with his son, daughter-in-law and grandchildren (1987).

Top left: Former pilot with 99th, Dr. Curtis C. Robinson and Mrs. Florie Robinson. Top right: Former test pilot for the 99th, Wylie Selden and wife June at a celebration party at Howard University. Bottom: Colonel William Campbell at the 1987 San Francisco TAAF Convention.

Chapter 25
The Unsung Heroes

Even the most versatile writer would find it impossible to relate adequately the part played by all the members of any particular outfit. There are almost as many stories of bravery as there are pilots in combat organizations. Yet the fact that most of these stories will never be written is no indication that the pilots who made these stories were not as important to the success of their outfits as those who received the publicity. Many of these men were the backbone of their organizations and were considered by their comrades as the most capable and dependable pilots of their outfits. Unfortunately, however, these men failed to register popular victories and as a result received little recognition outside their outfits.

Willie Fuller

The highly popular victory of the Air Force in conquering the island of Pantelleria without the use of the ground forces is one of the highlights of World War II. It was the first time in history that the Air Force had completely subdued a territory. The battle of Pantelleria had still another highlight. It was the first time Negro airmen fought against the enemy. Although the 99th as a squadron was credited with playing a significant role in subduing the island, little is known of the individual pilots whose bravery brought the Squadron success in its first campaign. One of these pilots was LT Fuller, born on August 2, 1919 in Tarboro, NC. After completing high school, he enrolled at Tuskegee Institute. He was a student there when construction began on the new Tuskegee Army Air Base. Thrilled over the new opportunity offered to Negro youths, he applied for cadet training. He was accepted as a cadet and on August 5, 1942, was commissioned and assigned to the 99th. In April 1943, he was sent overseas where he completed 70 missions before returning to the United States.

Walter I. Lawson

LT Lawson was another pioneer of the 99th, who received very little credit for the part he played in carrying the battle to the enemy. Lawson was born in Chancellor, VA, on November 7, 1919. He attended Hampton Institute in Hampton, Virginia, for three years and a half before entering the Air Corps on November 23, 1941. He was sent to Tuskegee where he won his wings on August 5, 1942. Lawson was sent overseas with the first group of pilots of the 99th. In combat he distinguished himself as one of the most aggressive and daring pilots.

James T. Wiley

There was also among the first group of replacements for the 99th, a young and unusually neat fellow whose reticent and dignified manner caused his friends to nickname him *The Little Flower*. This young pilot hailed from Pittsburgh. Wiley was actually born in Bransville, IN, on August 2, 1918, but claimed Pittsburgh as his home when he matriculated at the University of Pittsburgh. He was awarded a Bachelor of Arts Degree from the school in 1940. He entered Carnegie Institute of Technology following his graduation and was a student there when he was accepted as an Air Corps cadet on February 2, 1942. Wiley was commissioned at Tuskegee Army Air Field on July 3, 1942. On April 16, 1943, together with four replacement pilots (LT Mills, Toppins, Morgan and Gibson), Wiley arrived overseas and joined the 99th. He was one of the five pilots selected by COL Davis to make the initial flight of the 99th against the enemy. He completed 85 missions before returning to the States on May 31, 1944.

Once back, Wiley was reassigned to Tuskegee. Here he was made a cadet instructor. Because his experience as a combat pilot made him more valuable to the 477th, an all Negro group scheduled for combat in the Pacific, Wiley was later sent to Douglas Field, AZ, and given transition training as a bomber pilot. When this training was finished, he was sent to Godman Field where he joined the 477th. The war in the Pacific ended before the 477th could be sent overseas and Wiley lost the chance to engage the Japs in combat.

Louis R. Purnell

There were few pilots of the 99th and the 332nd who saw more combat duty than CPT Purnell of Snow Hill, MD. He studied for three years at Lincoln University in Pennsylvania before enlisting as a cadet in the Air Corps. He was commissioned at Tuskegee on July 3, 1942, and assigned to the 99th. Purnell was sent overseas with the 99th and fought four months before being sent back to the States to join the 332nd which was about to make its debut in combat. Upon joining the 332nd, he was given the administrative position of Assistant Group Operations Officers. Administrative duty, however, did not appeal to him and shortly after the Group entered combat, he requested flying duty. He completed 88 missions with the 12th and 15th Air Forces. For his outstanding bravery and devotion to duty, he was awarded the Distinguished Flying Cross and the Air Medal with eight oak leaf clusters.

Alva Temple

The 332nd, like the 99th, had many pilots who did not receive the publicity they merited. One of these pilots was CPT Temple of Carrolton, AL. Temple, a slender, raw-boned youth, was perhaps the quietest member of the group. Temple loved to fly and was always willing to make a mission though he realized the risk involved. In combat, he flew most of the time as wing-man for CPT Toppins, one of the group's most aggressive and popular pilots. This gave Temple very little opportunity to shoot at enemy aircraft. In spite of this, Temple won respect as a very competent pilot. Whereas Toppins was colorful, aggressive, and daring, Temple was reliable, dependable and unexcitable. He gave Toppins the confidence that he was invulnerable in attacks from the rear. This confidence enabled Toppins to take chances that he otherwise would have been hesitant to take, and as a result Toppins scored several aerial victories.

Heber Houston

Like CPT Temple, LT Houston of Detroit was also a very dependable pilot. He entered combat with the 99th in the early part of the war and flew over 75 missions before returning to the States. Though he received little popularity outside his own outfit, there was no question as to his bravery and ability as a fighter pilot. For example, in three days of fighting over the Anzio beachhead, he was forced to hitch hike back to the base two times. On the first day his carburetor went bad. This forced him to belly land on an emergency strip. The following day his plane again developed engine trouble and again, rather than lose his ship, he belly landed in a field. In spite of his bravery, however, Houston returned to the States and was received as just another pilot.

Alton F. Ballard

As a leader, CPT Ballard was excelled by very few members of the 332nd. He was born in Pasadena, CA. He attended elementary and high school in that city and was a junior at Santa Barbara State College when the United States went to war with Germany.

Ballard was accepted as an aviation cadet in April 1942, and was sent to Tuskegee where he won his wings on April 30, 1943. He was assigned to the 301st in January 1944, and was sent overseas.

In combat, he displayed leadership that brought him promotions to 1st LT in July 1944, and CPT in January 1945. He flew 89 missions over Italy, France, Hungary, Yugoslavia, Greece, Romania, and Germany. He was awarded the Distinguished Flying Cross, the Air Medal, and the E.T.O. Ribbon.

Wilson Eagleson

In the early part of the war, when the 99th was being highly criticized for its failure to shoot down enemy aircraft, there arrived overseas a group of eager replacement pilots who boasted they would show the older members of the Squadron how to shoot down enemy aircraft. Naturally, these arrogant newcomers antagonized the older members of the 99th. The older members, however, were quite willing to wait and watch this cockiness get knocked out of these "eager beavers" by the rigors of combat.

Among this group of replacements was a soft spoken but loquacious pilot who seemed more arrogant than the others. He had come overseas to shoot down enemy aircraft and nothing would stop him. This young pilot was LT Eagleson of Bloomington, IN.

Only seven days passed before Eagleson's ability as a combat pilot was put to a test. On the afternoon of January 27, 1944, he was flying as a wingman for CPT Lawrence when a flight of enemy planes was sighted over the Anzio beachhead. In the battle that followed, LT Eagleson scored his first victory.

In relating the mission, Eagleson said, "It was about my fifth mission. It was to Anzio Beachhead. At that time, the 99th was attached to the 79th fighter Group. For over a period of nine months the Squadron had been on strafing duty, but had never encountered enemy aircraft. Each day it seemed that the Germans would bomb between missions. That is, as soon as the 99th would bomb between missions. That is, as soon as the 99th would leave an area, the Germans would come in and bomb. On this particular mission we were late arriving over the target. We arrived in time, however, to observe the Germans making their run to bomb. We were flying P-40s and realized that we could not head off the Germans who were flying much faster planes. We decided to stay up about 10,000 feet and wait until the Germans finished bombing, then as they pulled up out of their dives we pounced upon them. This we did, and when the time came for us to make our attack I followed CPT Lawrence. However, CPT Lawrence was so eager to make the kill he overshot the aircraft he selected to attack. The enemy fell in behind Lawrence and opened fire on him. But while the enemy pilot was busy trying to shoot CPT Lawrence down I pulled up behind him and began to fire. After a few bursts the enemy plane began to smoke. A few more bursts caused it to fall off and head down to the ground. I followed the falling plane and continued to fire on it until it was hardly one hundred feet above the ground."

A week later on February 7, 1944, LT Eagleson scored another victory for the 99th. Three Focke-Wulf 190s were sighted by his flight on a patrol mission over the Anzio area. This patrol consisted of CPT Leonard Jackson, and LT Mills, Knighten and Eagleson. The Germans attempted to flee, but Eagleson and his comrades were not to be denied victories. In spite of their comparatively slow planes, they gave chase and destroyed the entire group of enemy aircraft.

Harry A. Sheppard

When the War Department announced that it was accepting Negro youths in the Air Force, Sheppard was one of the first to volunteer. Sheppard was born in New York City on October 24, 1917. He enrolled in the school of Technology at City College following his graduation from Jamaica High School. He abandoned his studies in electrical engineering to enlist in the Air Force on April 1, 1944. Sheppard was sent to Chanute Field Air Force Technical School for mechanic training. Upon completion of his training as a mechanic, he was sent to Tuskegee with the first group of enlisted men assigned to the 99th. Sheppard was not satisfied with being just a mechanic. He applied for pilot training and was accepted as a cadet in October 1942. On May 28, 1943, he was commissioned and assigned to the 302nd fighter Squadron which was then stationed at Oscoda, MI. In January 1944, he was sent overseas with the 332nd. He flew 87 missions with the 12th Tactical Air Force and 36 missions with the 15th Strategic Air Force before returning to the United States. Sheppard not only did his share in combat flying but served as Engineering and Technical Supply Officer in combat. He was awarded the Distinguished Flying Cross and the Air Medal with oak leaf clusters.

Gordon M. Rapier

CPT Rapier was born in Chicago, but his family moved to Gary, IN, when he was very young. He was a student at the University of Chicago when the war began. He enlisted in the Army at Fort Wayne, IN, on December 12, 1944. Rapier joined the 301st in Ramitelli, Italy on August 14, 1944, and flew 60 missions before returning to the States in October 1945. Rapier was awarded the Air Medal with five clusters, the Distinguished Flying Cross, and the Unit Citation Ribbon.

Charles F. Jamerson

Jamerson was born in Louisiana, but moved to California at an early age. After completing high school, he entered San Jose State College and was an engineering student when the war began. He enlisted in the Air Force at March Field on April 1, 1941, and was sent to Tuskegee. On March 25, 1943, he was commissioned and assigned to the 332nd. Jamerson was sent overseas with the 332nd in January 1944, and was assigned to the 99th. He flew 78 missions with the 99th and was credited with damaging a jet plane in a running battle in which he chased the German aircraft within ten minutes of Berlin.

Leonard F. Turner

LT Turner was also one of the many unfortunate pilots who fought gallantly as a member of the 332nd but received little publicity because he failed to register an aerial victory. Turner was born in Washington, DC. After graduating from Dunbar High School, he enrolled at Howard University. He entered cadet training in June 1942, and was graduated on June 20, 1943. Upon receiving his commission he was assigned to the 301st Fighter Squadron and sent overseas with the 332nd Fighter Group. Turner flew 70 missions before returning to the States in December 1944. LT Turner was awarded the Distinguished Flying Cross, the Air Medal with four oak leaf clusters, and the European Campaign Ribbon with four battle stars.

John H. Leahr

Born in Cincinnati, OH, Leahr attended Wilberforce University two years, then transferred to the University of Cincinnati. But the desire to fly forced him to leave school and make application for pilot training. On July 28, 1943, Leahr was commissioned at Tuskegee as a fighter pilot and assigned to the 301st. He was sent overseas with the 332nd in January 1944, and flew 72 missions before returning to the States on January 25, 1945.

Lowell C. Steward

CPT Steward was one of the most loquacious and "happy-go-lucky" pilots of the 332nd Fighter Group. But the fact that he was awarded the Distinguished Flying Cross, the E. T. O. Ribbon with four battle stars, and the Air Medal with four oak leaf clusters is ample proof that he took his flying seriously. Steward was born in Los Angeles where he attended school and was graduated from college with a Bachelor of Arts degree in Physical Education. On July 28, 1943, Steward was commissioned as a 2LT in the Air Corps at Tuskegee and assigned to the 100th Fighter Squadron of the 332nd. He entered combat with the 332nd Group in January 1944, and completed 46 missions. CPT Stewart returned to the United States in March 1946, and was reassigned to Tuskegee as a cadet instructor.

Lemuel Rodney Custis

One of the original pioneers was born on June 4, 1915 and attended the public school of Hartford, CT. After graduating from high school, he enrolled at Howard University, Washington, DC, where he was awarded a Bachelor of Science Degree in 1938.

He applied for pilot training, was accepted as an Army Air Corps cadet and sent to the newly activated Tuskegee Army Air Field. He began pilot training in July, 1941 as a member of the first class of black youths accepted for pilot training by the Army Air Corps. He was graduated in March, 1942 as a second lieutenant.

Custis was sent ovrseas in April, 1943 as a member of the original 99th Fighter Squadron that entered combat operation in North Africa. His military decorations and awards include the Distinguished Flying Cross, the Air Medal with oak leaf clusters, the African, Sicilian and Italian campaign medals and he is also credited with one aerial victory and two probables.

After leaving the service, Custis attended the University of Connecticut Law School and later joined the State of Connecticut Tax Department. In 1975, he was promoted to the position of Chief of Sales Tax, a position he held until retiring on June 30, 1980 with 32 years of service.

James B. Knighten

In every organization there are alawys those who seem to have the knack of seeing the brighter side of life. They are the un-official morale builders of their outfits. They are just as valuable as guns and ammunition. They make the darker moments brighter and kept life in their organizations during the most adverse times.

The 99th Fighter Squadron and the 332nd Fighter Group were fortunate in having such individuals. One of these unforgettable characters was LT James B. Knighten, born on December 11, 1919 in Tulsa, Oklahoma. He attended elementary school in Tulsa, and after having completed secondary school, he matriculated at Dillard University in New Oreans where he earned a degree of Bachelor of Arts. He was accepted in the cadet corps on August 2, 1941 and was sent to Tuskegee. On May 20, 1942 he was commissioned as a 2LT in the Air Corps and assigned to the 99th Fighter Squadron.

Knighten was sent overseas as a member of the original 99th Squadron. Even before entering combat, he won the respect of his comrades by his bold and daring flying and his keen sense of humor. He seemed to see everything and could make the most simple and ordinary things appear interesting. He was a man among men. Most of the time he could be found surrounded by a group of his friends who listened attentively while he talked.

Perhaps Knighten's most outstanding attribute was his uncanny ability to grasp foreign languages. The first night overseas, while his comrades slept, Knighten ventured into the city of Casa Blanca. The next morning when they awoke, he surprised them with his newly acquired vocabulary, which made him the envy of all.

Any place the 99th Squadron went Knighten was the first to meet the people and learn their language and customs. How he learned the languages so quickly amazed everyone. He acquired a vocabulary in one day that took the average fellow several weeks to acquire. Naturally, with this ability, Knighten became one of the most popular pilots of the Squadron.

Willie Ashley.

It is impossible to speak of morale builders without mentioning LT Willie Ashley, of Sumter, South Carolina. He was really a comical fellow. Even the simplest fact took on a hilarious aspect when stated by Ashley.

My knowledge that there was such a character as Willie was gained at the Post Theatre at Tuskegee. One day the theatre featured a reel on "the 99th Squadron in combat." One scene showed Ashley and a few of his friends hovering around a fire built on a snow covered runway, somewhere in Italy. Ashley was wrapped in a large bear-skin coat, the heavy combat boots. Even with the seemingly roaring fire, Ashley appeared half-frozen. The thought of this big fellow trying to squeeze into the cockpit of a small fighter plane was enough to put the entire audience in an uproar.

Ashley returned to Tuskegee Army Air Field upon completing his tour of duty. There was never a dull moment throughout his stay at Tuskegee. His stories of combat made him the ideal of the "bull sessioners", and seemed to derive unusual delight in telling about his first combat mission. While breezing along towards home "fat, dumb and happy," Ashley noticed, the ship began to behave in a peculiar fashion, and he thought it was due to an unusually large number of air pockets. Glancing back at this moment, he was startled to see flak bursting all around him, and his tail being eaten up by that flak. He started a zig zag course to avoid being hit; but, each time he zigged it seemed he zagged it instead, and never did he pray so quickly and so earnestly. Evidently, his prayers were answered for he returned to the base in one piece, though soaking wet from prespiration.

At Tuskegee, Ashley occupied a room in the Bachelor Quarters. His best friend, LT Willie "Drink" Hunter was quartered only a few doors away, and the two became one of a kind. There was no peace the whole time they were in the barracks. They talked, joked and sang. But, once airborne, they put aside their the happy-go-lucky attitude; they took their flying seriously.

Willie flew a total of 77 combat missions during his 14 months combat tour. At the end of the war, he left the service and enrolled at the University of Omaha, where he earned a Bachelor Degree in Biology. He then worked seven years as a Railroad Mail Clerk while continuing his education. In 1958, he was awarded a Master of Science Degree in Micro-Biology, and, in 1962, he was awarded a PhD in Radiation Biology. He retired from the US Government in 1976 and was employed by Howard University as Associate Professor of Biology, a position he held until June, 1983. Ashley died of cancer in 1984 and was buried with full military honors in Arlington Cemetery.

Spurgeon Ellington

One of the most unforgettable characters I have ever met was Lieutent Spurgeon Ellington. If there was ever a proud man, it was Ellington. He was not only proud of being a pilot, but proud in general. To him, there was only one person--Ellington. He figured he could out-talk and out-smart anyone. Needless to say, he also pictured himself as "God's gift to women."

Ellington got the opportunity to show his ability to outwit others while at Tuskegee. On a weekend flight to his home town, Winston-Salem, NC, he decided to "buzz" the town. He flew down the main street "on deck", that is, close to the ground. He was reported for this and later court martialed at Tuskegee.

Everything went Ellington's way at the early stages of the trial. The jury, made up of his friends, were prejudiced in his favor. No one could neither positively identify Ellington as the pilot of the low-flying plane, nor give the exact identification number of the plane. The only evidence against Ellington was that he was scheduled to be in the vicinity of Winston-Salem that day.

As the trial progressed, it was almost decided that there was insufficient evidence to convict him. Just at this time, Ellington decided that he would demonstrate his ability to outwit his accuser. However, while trying to make his accuser appear ridiculous, he gave himself away, and the same jury made found guilty and fined him.

Perhaps it was Ellington's showmanship and ego that largely accounted for his success in combat. He could not conceive of any German pilot capable of shooting him down. On the other hand, to maintain the respect of his comrades, he had to be daring and aggressive. This won him the Distinguished Flying Cross and the Air Medal with four oak leaf clusters.

On December 10, 1945, Ellington was killed in a plane crash near Atlanta, GA. The plane, piloted by LT Richard W. Hall, another combat pilot, crashed while making an approach for a landing at the Atlanta Airport. Thus the career of one of the most unforgettable characters of the 332nd Fighter Group ended.

Maceo A. Harris

On November 20, 1944 the 332nd Fighter Group lost one of its most colorful members, when LT Maceo A. Harris of Boston failed to return from a mission over Germany. Proud, high spirited and loquacious, Harris was, none the less, the type of man one would love to be with on the battle field or on "Main Street." His thoughts seemed to cover everything and he loved to convey them to others. Whenever his buddies were depressed or lonely, they could find relief when Harris was around. Always starting his conversation with his popular phrase "My wife will never understand," he would keep his friends laughing and listening for hours.

Perhaps Maceo, as he was known by the fellows, loved clothes better than anything else. He was particular about his appearance and remained tidy and dressed up at all hours under the most adverse conditions. He dressed for a mission with the same care that one would for a parade. He was a morale builder, an important man to a combat outfit.

Captain Cassius A. Harris, III

One of the officers who played a most important part in the success of Tuskegee Flying Training Program was CPT Cassius Harris, a native of Philadelphia. CPT Harris attended Temple University in Philadelphia from 1938 to 1939, then transferred to West Virginia State College where he was a member of the first class of Negroes to receive a CPT rating as an air amphibious pilot. Later he was assigned to Tuskegee Army Air Field where, after being sent to the Pratt Whitney Engine School in Hartford, CT, he was assigned as Engineering Officer of the Basic Flight Training Squadron at Tuskegee. It was due to his experience and knowledge that the mechanics at Tuskegee were so successful.

Captain Samuel Curtis

Curtis was born on October 16, 1919 in Charlottesville, Virginia, the son of Golden and John Curtis. He received his elementary and high school education in Yeadon, PA. Following the bombing of Pearl Harbor, he was drafted by the army and sent to Fort Lee, Virginia. He applied for pilot training, was accepted and sent to Tuskegee Army Air Field. He was graduated in August, 1943 and assigned to the 100th Fighter Squadron of the 332nd, earning the Distinguished Flying Cross and Air Medal with oak leaf clusters.

On returning to the States at the end of his combat tour, he qualified and served as an twin-engine instructor at Tuskegee Army Air Field and as a Squadron Commander at Lockbourne Air Force Base.

Curtis left the Service at the end of World War II, but was recalled to active duty at the outbreak of the Korean conflict. He was assigned as Wing Operation Officer with the 123rd Fighter-Bomber Squadron stationed in Kentucky.

On his return to civilian life, Curtis was graduated from the Pennsylvania Museum College of Art, and later earned a Master's Degree from Temple University's Tyler School of Fine Arts and a Doctor's Degree from New York University in 1974.

Meantime, he had joined the faculty at Chaney State College in 1956 and served as Chairman of the Department of Art and as Director of Instructional Television and Educational Media.

Curtis exhibited paintings in Philadelphia and New York and was awarded several prizes for his work. He died on January 14, 1989 at his home in Buena, NJ and was buried at Philadelphia Memorial Park in Malvern.

LTC Herbert E. Carter

One of the men who played a very important part in the success of black pilots during World War II was Herbert E. Carter. Born on September 27, 1919 in Amory, MS, he attended the public schools of Mississippi. After graduating from high school, he enrolled at Tuskegee Institute.

When World War II broke out and, on learnig about the preparations for constructing an Air field at Tuskegee for training black youths by the Army Air Corps, he was thrilled. He made application, was accepted and was graduated a member of the fourth class 42-F.

Carter was sent overseas as the Engineering Officer of the original 99th Fighter Squadron. It was his responsibility to see that the planes were kept in tip top shape for combat duty. In addition to holding the position of Aircraft Maintenance Officer, he flew 77 combat missions.

Carter remained in service at the end of World War II. At Godman Field and Lockbourne, he served as Group Maintenance Officer from 1945-1948. Meantime in 1945, he attended the North American Aircraft Maintenance School and in 1948 attended the Air Force Tactical School, Tyndall Air Force Base, FL and the Aircraft Maintenance Officers School, Chanute Air Force Base, IL. In 1959, he attended the Command and Staff School and in 1960 completed a Jet Aircraft Qualification Course at Randolph Air Force Base, Texas.

Carter continued a very busy career with the Air Force. From 1950 to 1955, he served as Professor of Air Science and Commander of the Air Force ROTC detachment at Tuskegee Institute. From 1955 to 1959, he served as Deputy Director Military Advisory Group to German Air Force, a position in which he was a pilot instructor and technical training officer for the German pilot conversion program, for T33 Jet aircraft to F and RF-84 Jet aircraft. From 1959 to 1963, he served as Chief of Maintenance, 328th Fighter Wing, Richards-Gebaur AFB, Missouri for T-33 and F-102 Fighter Interceptors. From 1963 to 1965, he served as Chief of Maintenance, 27 Fighter Interceptor, Loring AFB, ME and Director of Air Defense Command's F-106 severe climatical operations project. He returned to Tuskegee Institute. And, from 1965 to 1969, he served as Professor of Aerospace Studies.

Carter retired from the Air Force as a LTC and was employed first by Tuskegee Institute as Associate Dean of Student Services and later as Associate Dean of Admissions and recruiting.

LTC Hiram E. Mann

Among the many unsung heroes of the 332nd Fighter Group was Hiram E. Mann, born in New York city on May 23, 1921. When World War II began, like many other black youths, on learning about the Tuskegee Experiment that offered Army Air Corps pilot training to black youths, he made application. He was accepted, and, on the completion of his training, was graduated as a member of one of the most outstanding classes, 44-F to be graduated and commissioned at Tuskegee. He was assigned to the 302nd Fighter Squadron of the 332nd Fighter Group and sent to combat with the Group.

When the war in Europe ended Mann joined the 477th Composite Group, which had been organized under COL Davis, Jr. at Godman Field, and later moved to Lockbourne Air Force Base. After the 477th was deactivated, he served at several Air Force Installation and advanced in rank to LTC. His last military assignment was with the Air Force Academy as Admissions Counselor.

LTC George E. Hardy

George has seen action in three wars, having flown missions in Europe, Korea and Vietnam. His decorations include The Distinguished Flying Cross, the Air Medal with eleven (11) Oak Leaf Clusters, and the Commendation Medal with one (1) Oak Leaf Cluster.

A native of Philadelphia, PA, George lives in Framingham, MA with his wife Katharine, six children and eight grandchildren. He graduated from New York School of Technology, and Air Force Institute of Technology.

George entered Aviation Cadet Training at Tuskegee in 1943, graduating as pilot in 1945. Assigned to the 99th Fighter Squadron, 332nd Fighter Group in Italy, he flew 21 combat missions. In 1947, he was discharged at Lockbourne Army Air Field, where in 1947, he was recalled to active duty. In 1949, he went to Guam, and in 1950, he flew 45 combat missions over Korea in B-29 aircraft. In 1964, he was transferred to Hanscom Air Force Base, MA. In 1970, he was transferred to Vietnam as a pilot in AC-119K Gunships, and served as Operating Locating Commander at Udorn Air Base, having flown 70 combat missions. Having returned from Vietnam, LTC Hardy retired from the Air Force in November 1971.

2LT LeRoy A. Battle on leave in Brooklyn, NY with his mother (left) and his aunt. LeRoy is not wearing an Officer's uniform as it had not yet arrived. Photo courtesy of LeRoy Battle, Sr.

Chapter 26
To Do Battle

A native of New York, LeRoy Battle Sr. became involved with music when he was about ten years old as a member of the Boy Scouts' Drum and Bugle Corps. He became steeped in music while attending Alexander Hamilton High School for boys in Brooklyn, where he won a scholarship to study with Saul Goodman, who was New York Philharmonic's concert master and premiere timpanist. This budding career, however, suddenly was interrupted on August 25, 1943 when he was inducted in the service at Camp Upton, Long Island.

He went to Keesler Field, MS for Basic Training, then to Tuskegee Institute for Air Cadet Training, then to Tyndall Field in Florida for Gunnery Training; then to Midland Field in Texas for Bombardier Training; to Freeman Field and to several other camps and fields, eventually returning to Tuskegee for Pilot Training, and finally to Maxwell A.F.F. for discharge on October 13, 1945.

At Freeman Field, he was ordered into arrest by order of COL Robert S. Selway, for having fought to gain access to the all-white Officers Club.

Following is the declassified, newly released full transcript of his testimony given to COL John A. Hunt:

Q Will you please state your name, rank, organization, serial number, station and duty?

A LeRoy A. Battle, 2nd Lieutenant, AC, 0-2075525, 118th Army Air Forces Base Unit, Squadron E; my duties are bombardier.

Q We officers are down here at the direction of the Secretary of War to make an investigation that was requested in a letter written to The Inspector General and signed by yourself and 100 other officers. Are you familiar with the letter to which I am referring?

A Yes, sir.

Q In taking testimony to find out the facts desired by the Secretary of War, we ordinarily take in under oath. Now, we would rather have all testimony under oath because most of it is, and we would like your testimony to carry as much weight as the testimony of other people and a simple statement does not carry as much weight, but I am putting that up to you. You may make a statement under oath or not under oath, as you see fit. Are you willing to make the statement under oath?

A Oh, yes, sir, anything I say would be the truth.

(The witness was sworn.)

Q As you are now a witness under oath, I am going to read the 24th Article of War to you, which reads as follows:

*Article 24. Compulsory Self-Incrimination Prohibited. -- No Witness *** before any officer conducting an investigation, shall be compelled to incriminate himself or to answer any question the answer to which may tend to incriminate him, or to answer any question not material to the issue when such answer might tend to degrade him.*

Do you understand?

A May I ask some questions about that, sir?

Q Yes.

A In other words, if any questions come up that might in the case of a court-martial or anything tend to incriminate, I can keep from answering that?

Q I shall keep you posted all the way through this as to your rights, and if I ask a question that is liable to incriminate you, I will indicate that you don't need to answer.

A Yes, sir.

Q But this has nothing to do with a court-martial. As far as I know, there is going to be no court-martial. I don't know anything about that at all. We know certain allegations were made in the letter that you signed, and that is the thing that I am out here to investigate.

A Yes, sir.

Q Now, I would like to have you tell me in your own way what it was that occurred at Freeman Field that made you feel it necessary to request, along with 100 other officers, that an investigation be made.

A Well, I will just tell you what happened to me personally on the night when we hit the field.

Q All right.

A I went to a show, I did, and after that I went down to the club.

Q What was the date?

A Well, the same day we went to the field. I think it was the 5th.

Q The 5th of April?

A That's right, sir. Well, after the show, I went down to the club, to the Officers' Club, and there I was met by a first lieutenant, the OD, and he told me if I stepped over the threshold I would be put under arrest.

Q Were you alone?

A No, sir, there were a couple of others with me. I don't know how many. There were just a group of us, and we asked him why we were put under arrest. He said he just was acting under orders. So we went in anyway, and we went inside, and a Major came out -- I can't recall his name -- but he told us that we would be under arrest in our quarters. Well, the next day, several others went down there too -- that is what I was told -- and I think altogether about somewhere between fifty and sixty of us were put under arrest in quarters.

Q You say you believe that was on the 5th of April?

A That's right.

Q You went there and you were told that if you entered that Club you would be placed under arrest, is that right?

A Yes, sir.

Q And the following day, you again went to the club?

A No, I didn't go. Some other officers went.

Q I see.

A And the whole issue was that there was two clubs on the field, and I didn't think that they didn't want us to use that club and -- well, I can't see why. From what I understand about Army Regulations, there is only supposed to be one club on the field available to all officers.

Well, we were held under arrest for, I think it was a day and a half, and then the OD, he came around and told us that we were out of arrest. Well, no orders came out or anything about placing -- giving us a release or anything. It was just by word of mouth. Well, what we were trying to put across, that club that they gave us up there was originally a noncommissioned officers' club, and, well, we felt that this club should be for the use of the noncommissioned officers because they have a multitude of them up there and we would be depriving them of their recreational facilities, especially when there is another officers' club on the field. That is about all I can think of. It was just an issue of the clubs there that caused all the trouble.

A Colonel came down from the Inspector General's Office, I think, Sunday, and he questioned us about it and said that no charges would be preferred against us.

Q He said that no charges would?

A That's right?

Q That was The Air Inspector, wasn't it?

A It may have been. I thought he was from the Inspector General. It may have been the Air Inspector, I don't know.

Q You were pretty intent upon seeing that Army Regulations 210-10 were complied with by the Commanding Officer, is that right?

A Well, isn't that right according to Army Regulations 210-10 concerning clubs, that there should be one on the field available for the use of all officers?

Q Yes, that's right. Now, what you were after was having that regulation complied with, is that correct?

A Yes, sir.

Q Do you know of other Army Regulation that required that a proper order be complied with?

A I don't understand you, sir.

Q Well, it seems as though you picked out one Army Regulation and you wanted the Commanding Officer to comply with that by opening up Officers' Club No. 2 to the colored officers. That is what you wanted, isn't it? You wanted the Commanding Officer to obey that regulation, isn't that right?

A Well, in my opinion, how I felt, there shouldn't be any issue over a club at all on a field where all officers are concerned.

Q Well, I would like to talk about regulations now. What you wanted was to get that regulation complied with so that you could use Club No. 2?

A Yes, sir.

Q Regulations and orders in the Army require that the order of a superior officer be obeyed unhesitatingly and without question. Did you know about that?

A Yes, sir.

Q How would you expect justice to be done if you tried to get the Commanding Officer to comply with one regulation when you violate another regulation? You see, you were violating a direct order. I don't mean you personally, but the officers of your group violated an order that was in existence here signed by the Commanding Officer, isn't that true?

A What order was that, sir?

Q The order telling them that they should use Officers' Club No. 1 and not Officers' Club No. 2. That was one order, and another one was conveyed to you, as you have just testified, by two officers at the club when you were there. You were told that you were going to be put under arrest by order of the Commanding Officer if you went into the club, isn't that correct?

A Yes, we were told we would be put under arrest.

Q Yet you did violate the order and you were placed under arrest, isn't that true?

A Well, that wasn't in the form of an order. That was just a statement by them, sir.

Q You didn't understand it to be an order?

A No, sir.

Q A superior officer told you that that was the case and that you would be arrested if you went inside. That didn't indicate to you that you were not supposed to go in, is that it?

A Well, he didn't explain anything, sir.

Q He just told you that you weren't supposed to be there and that you were arrested if you went in, and in spite of that you did go in?

A Yes, sir, but he also said, sir, that there was an order, a memorandum put out, and it should have been read to us before we left this field, and there was no order read to our group about it.

Q Then you just did not believe him when he told you that. You thought he was lying to you?

A No, not lying. I just didn't understand it.

Q You understood his words, of course?

A Yes, sir, I understood what he said.

Q And he informed you that there was an order requiring that you remain out of that club?

A No, he didn't say there was an order. He said I should have -- I'm trying to get the right words -- he implied there was a memorandum which should have been read to us concerning clubs and recreational facilities. That's all he knew about it.

Q All right. Now, you say you were released from arrest verbally by the Officer of the Day?

A That is correct.

Q Tell me the circumstances that led to your present arrest. How did that come about?

A Well, it was the next day, we were called down to the Orderly Room by Captain Chiappe. He was CO, and there he had, I think it was Memorandum 85-2.

Q Base Regulations 85-2?

A Base Regulations 85-2.

Q Was that read to the officers?

A That was read to us.

Q What did you understand by that orders?

A Well, I just didn't understand why they made that.

Q Let me put it this way. Did you get the idea, after the order was read to you, that you were to be denied access to certain buildings that were assigned to base personnel, instructors and command personnel?

A Well, in that order, I knew that -- I think that it didn't include Club No. 2.

Q Did you understand that that particular base regulation designated a certain club building for use by the base, supervisory, instructor and command personnel?

A It designated some buildings for them to use.

Q Paragraph 3b reads: "Base, Supervisory, Instructor and Command personnel will use the quarters, messing, recreational facilities as follows:" and then it lists various buildings, including Club Building No. T-930. Did you hear that part of it read?

A Yes, sir.

Q Did that mean to you that the permanent party personnel would use Club Building T-930 and that it was assigned for their use? Did you understand that?

A Well, that includes -- let's see, Captain Chiappe -- he is in the training, sir.

Q Yes, he is included in supervisory, instructor and command personnel. Let me say this again. The order reads that base supervisory, instructor and command personnel will use the quarters, messing, recreational facilities that are listed there. Among the various buildings listed in Club Building T-930. Now, was it your understanding that the personnel mentioned there was to use Club No. 2, which is T-930?

A Well, that is what the order reads there.

Q You understood that much of the order, is that right?

A Yes, sir.

Q Then did you read or hear this, "Officer, Flight Officer and Warrant Officer personnel undergoing OTU, Combat Crew and Ground and Air Replacement Training will use the housing quarters, messing, recreational facilities as follows," and then it lists those facilities, and also that they will not enter buildings or use tennis courts listed in paragraph 3b, except on official business. Did you understand that part of it or did they read that to you?

A Well, that is one of the parts I don't understand.

Q Well, if I say you are an officer undergoing training and that you were not to enter Club Building T-930, would you understand it?

A Well --

Q Would you understand that you were to remain out of Club Building T-930?

A Well, I don't understand why, sir?

Q I'm not talking about why. Do you understand from the language in here that you are not supposed to enter Building T-930?

A I don't understand why, sir.

Q If I told you that I did not want to you enter that closed door over there, would you know what I meant?

A Well, yes, sir.

Q As your superior officer, if I ordered you not to leave this building, would you understand what I meant?

A Yes, sir.

Q If I told you that, as your commanding officer, I forbade you to enter that building across the street, would you know what I meant?

A Yes, sir.

Q And if I were at Freeman Field and told you that Building T-930 was assigned to other personnel and that you were not to enter it, would you understand what I meant?

A Well, no, sir.

Q All right. Now, go ahead and tell me what happened after this was read to you on the occasion that you mentioned a little while ago. Were you asked to sign that at that time?

A Yes, sir.

Q Did you sign it at that time?

A No, sir.

Q When you were asked to sign it the first time, were you alone?

A No, sir, we were all in a room, sir.

Q When you say "we," who do you mean?

A Well, the whole CCTS.

Q Officers, warrant officers and flight officers of the CCTS?

A That's right.

Q Go ahead and tell me some more about it. What happened at that meeting? Who was there? Who was conducting it? Was it Captain Chiappe?

A Yes, sir.

Q Was there any other officer there from the base?

A Well, I saw a lieutenant colonel there. I don't know his name.

Q What did they do?

A Nothing. He just asked us to sign it.

Q The lieutenant colonel read it, is that right?

A Captain Chiappe read it.

Q After they asked you to sign it, what happened? Did they go out of the room and come back later to see if you had signed it?

A Well, I think he gave out copies of it and told us to read it, and if we understood it, to sign it.

Q Did he give you any time to consider it?

A He gave us about ten minutes, I think.

Q How did he do that? Tell me what he said when he gave you ten minutes. Did he stay there with you?

A We stayed there in the room where we were. Nobody would leave the building and we would have, I think it was ten minutes, I don't know. Anyway, he designated the time.

Q You mean he gave a certain length of time in which you were to sign it?

A That's right, sir.

Q Did he remain in the room with you all during that ten minute period?

A Well, he was practically -- it was one long building. I think he went through the door, and I don't know, they were smoking, I think -- that's about all, just waiting for us to sign it.

Q I wonder if they might have told you to think it over or talk it over and decide whether you were going to sign it or not, or something of that sort; is that what they did?

A I don't know. I don't recall his exact words.

Q Did they threaten you at all?

A Threaten -- no, I don't think they threatened us.

Q At any rate, he came back at some little time later, and after the lieutenant colonel and Captain Chiappe came back in, did they ask you if you were ready to sign it or if you would sign it?

A He asked if anybody had signed it, and something like if anybody signed it to bring the papers forward. I don't think anybody came forward.

Q Were you called in at any time later and talked to about signing that order?

A Yes, sir.

Q When was that?

A It was about three hours later.

Q It was the same day, is that right?

A Yes, sir.

Q What happened then? Were you called in alone or was the whole group called in together?

A He called everybody in singly.

Q Were you called in singly?

A Yes, sir.

Q When you were called in, what did they tell you?

A Let's see -- he asked me to read it.

Q To read Base Regulation 85-2

A That's right. Then he crossed out something down there.

Q Was it your understanding?

A It was after the Colonel's signature. He said he would cross it out and asked me would I be willing to sign it then.

Q Here is a copy of Base Regulation 85-2 (handing same to witness). Will you show me on there what he crossed out?

A I think he crossed out this here (indicating).

Q The whole line?

A I wouldn't know. He made a mark on there and said something about crossing out that and he asked me would I be willing to sign.

Q Could it have been just the words "and fully understand?"

A It may have been. It may have been more.

Q You are not sure of what he did cross out?

A It included "understand," I know.

Q Do you know who questioned you at that time?

A Captain Chiappe.

Q Did Captain Ochs, the Base Legal Officer, question you?

A I was questioned by Captain Ochs some night later. I don't remember what night it was.

Q Was it a different day entirely?

A Yes, sir.

Q Were you talked with on three different occasions about signing that order?

A No, it was two.

Q Are you sure that Captain Ochs wasn't there at the same time that Captain Chiappe asked you those questions?

A If he was, I didn't see him.

Q Do you know Lt Kinder?

A No, sir.

Q Do you feel, when they were talking to you the second time when they had you in there alone, that they were trying to put something over on you?

A I don't think I can make any statement on that.

Q Did they explain that it was a pretty serious offense to refuse to obey a direct order from a superior officer?

A Yes, sir.

Q Did they indicate that if you did sign this you would not be in the position of disobeying an order?

A Would you repeat that?

Q Did they indicate that if you did sign it you would not be in the position of having disobeyed a lawful order?

A I don't know, sir.

Q You don't understand what I mean?

A If I did sign it, what?

Q If they ordered you or gave you a direct order, as I understand Captain Chiappe did, to sign it and you signed it, you would not be disobeying an order, would you? You would be obeying it, wouldn't you?

A That's right.

Q If you did what they told you to do?

A That's right.

Q But, if you don't do what they tell you to, then you are disobeying a direct order, is that right?

A That's right.

Q Now, do you think that they had some wrong purpose in asking you to sign that order?

A I have no statement to make, sir.

Q What is that?

A I haven't any statement to make there, sir.

Q Getting back to the fact that you signed this letter, dated 6 April, and addressed it to The Inspector General in Washington, you indicated in the letter discrimination through the means of an order which was wrong and which was a subterfuge, and a violation of Army Regulations 210-10. In connection with that allegation in that letter, is there anything further that you want to give for consideration by higher authority in connection with this investigation?

I will put it a little more simply. You have made a charge of unfair treatment in this letter which you signed.

A Yes, sir.

Q We have talked about it. Now, do you wish to make any further remark in support of the charge you made in the letter?

A Yes, sir. It is about -- well, sir, may I ask a question. You said before that there wouldn't be any court-martial or anything.

Q What's that?

A You said before that there wouldn't be any court-martial.

Q No, I did not. I said that I didn't know. I don't know of any court-martial. I have seen no court-martial order.

A Well, I prefer that anything else I say -- you see, what I don't understand is our position now, sir. That is what has got me confused, our being in arrest down here at Godman.

Q Well, remember, to begin with, I told you to be very careful and that you don't have to answer any question if you think it will incriminate you. If you have additional charges to make or additional explanation to make in connection with the letter, which will not incriminate you, and I don't see how it would incriminate you, then you are at liberty to go ahead and help to sustain the case that you make in the letter, but if you feel that the thing you would like to say would lead to trouble directed toward you, then, of course, you need not answer and should not answer, but if you can put anything into the record in further support of the things said in the letter, or further allegations, you are at liberty to do so as long as they are true and they can't be used against you.

A Well, isn't there an Article of War, a statement I think that -- I don't know which one it is, it may be the 24th -- about signing or making any statement that are degrading to an officer.

Q Well, that Article of War that I read to you is to the effect that you need not answer any question the answer to which would incriminate you; neither need you answer a question the answer to which would tend to degrade you, unless that answer is material to the issue, in which case you would be required to answer it, but I am not going to require you to answer any question.

A And this Base Order 85-2 came out the night after we went to the club too, sir.

Q After that?

A The night after I went to the club, this 85-2 came out. Now, if there wasn't any order out on it before, why should they put one out after we went to the club.

Q Well, there was; there were two orders out before to that effect.

A Well, shouldn't we have been notified to at least one of them.

Q You should have been notified. There is no question about that, because if an order isn't brought to your attention, you can't obey it, and that is the very reason they wanted your signature on there, to satisfy the Commanding Officer that this order was known to you, do you see?

A Well, in this 85-2, what is the Army Air Forces standards governing the control and curfew of personnel?

Q I take it by that they mean that on certain posts, certain buildings for quarters, certain buildings for recreation, certain buildings for school and certain buildings for messing are set aside for the permanent base personnel and that certain other buildings are set aside for the training personnel. We find that in all posts, whether they are Air Corps or otherwise, and that appears to be what they refer to as to their standards. Usually, the personnel that remains more or less permanently at a post are given somewhat better accommodations than the transitory personnel, and that is true in all posts in the Army, and I presume that that is what they are referring to there. At any rate, they say that in accordance with their standard procedure they are hereby designating certain buildings for personnel undergoing training and certain other buildings for the remaining personnel of the base.

A Well, what is the standard. Is it an order that comes out?

Q It may be a custom of the service. However, you put yourself into a bad position here of quibbling over words. It was not necessary that you understand this, but since the Commanding Officer had ordered that every officer, white or colored, acknowledge receipt of it, it was incumbent upon every officer, white or colored, to obey the order and acknowledge receipt of it. Now, in your case they told you that you might cross out the words about understanding and just certify that you had read it. You didn't have to certify that you understood it. You merely had to certify that you had read the order so that the Commanding Officer would know thereafter whether or not you were familiar with the Base Regulation. Does that explain your question?

A Well, I heard what you said, sir, but I still don't understand that letter.

Q I know it would be beyond my power to make you understand it further because that is as clearly as I can explain it. However, is there anything else that you would like to bring up in connection with this alleged discrimination?

A I would like to ask you, sir, about the noncommissioned officers' club. If we use that, they won't have a club, would they?

Q I don't know. It is the Commanding Officer's right to designate what the buildings on his post will be used for. That is the right of every commanding officer, and he apparently wanted you officers in training to have a club facility as good as the officers of the base and the permanent base personnel. As I understand it, the building that was assigned to you, regardless of what its former use was, was fully the equal and in some respects superior to the club that was assigned to the base personnel. That, of course, has nothing to do with whether you are right or not to disobey that order. That doesn't make any difference. If it had been any other building that had been turned over and assigned to you for club purposes, that had no effect whatever on whether it was right or not to disobey an order to acknowledge receipt and reading of an order. Is there any other question that bothers you?

A Yes, sir. It is about our status here.

Q That I don't know. We were not sent here to investigate that. We are here in compliance with this request, and your status here, as far as I know, is that you are in arrest in quarters, and I have seen the orders and they appear to be all quite regular, and you are in arrest in quarters.

A What I want to know is about that we also were told we aren't allowed to have visitors, military or civilian. Now, just how does that stand with officers arrested in quarters?

Q The Commanding Officer may establish such a condition if he wishes. Presumably he has a reason for it. I don't know. As we understand it, unauthorized personnel did get in and mingle with the officers at Freeman Field. That is known, of course, as a fact. They were people who were not even in the military service, and they repeatedly attempted to get in by violating post orders, and obviously they do not want unauthorized personnel in here. That order may have been to prevent that, I don't know, but the Commanding Officer has that privilege, and if he did issue such an order, I have seen no evidence of it except verbally.

A Well, he didn't put it in writing. We were just told by the Major.

Q What Major?

A I don't know his name, but I think his branch of service is in the military police, and he told us we wouldn't be able to have any visitors, military or civilian.

Q We are going to look into that, but we can't give you anything on that now, because we don't know anything about it. We have seen nothing on it and I can't answer your question beyond the answer that I have given you.

A Well, what about our counsel to represent us. We are allowed to choose our own, aren't we?

Q Well, you have no occasion to have counsel, as far as I know. You have not had any charges preferred against you, have you?

A Well, I can't understand this. How long are they going to keep us under arrest? How long have they got the right to keep us under arrest?

Q If they keep you under arrest, they are supposed to prefer charges against you within ten days or as soon thereafter as they can, and if not, then to release you, but there is no specific number of days within which they must do it. However, the outcome of this investigation has to be known before they will know whether to prefer charges against you or not, but if they prefer charges against you they are required to give you counsel, and if you don't like that counsel then you can call for any additional counsel through him that you want.

A And they can come on the field, is that right?

Q Oh, yes. They will then be given authority to come and represent you at the trial, but remember, we don't know that there is any trial. That is something that is beyond us. We have come down here from Washington to investigate the charges made in your letter, which is an entirely different thing, you see.

A Well, it has been over a week now since we were just punt under arrest, and then moved down here, and nothing has been said to us either pro or con.

Q I imagine that they will do nothing unless our investigation of your charges has been completed.

A Yes, sir.

Q That is something I don't know about. We are not investigating that matter. Is there any other question that you have?

A No, sir, I have nothing else to say.

Q Since I have been here tonight, I was handed a letter, dated 14 April 1945, Subject: "Limits of arrest in quarters," addressed to all officers names in paragraph 19, Special Orders No. 87, Headquarters, Freeman Field, 12 April 1945, in which it states the limits of arrest for you and the other officers under arrest, and grants you, in response to a request, as I understand it, the use of the gymnasium, and has at the bottom an acknowledgment that each officer has read and understood the foregoing order, which he was supposed to sign. Were you asked to sign that acknowledgement, or do you know about that?

A Yes, sir, I know that.

Q Were you asked to sign this acknowledgement?

A They wanted us to sign.

Q Who wanted you to sign that?

A Colonel Selway sent it down, I think.

Q Who?

A I think Colonel Selway sent it down.

Q Yes.

A I don't know. It is signed by Colonel Selway.

Q It is signed by Major McDowell.

A I mean by order of Colonel Selway.

Q That's right. Was it your understanding that you were supposed to sign in the blank space opposite your name to indicate that you had read it and understood it?

A Yes, sir.

Q Did you decline to sign it, or did you sign it?

A I didn't sign it, sir.

Q Did you tell anybody that you would not sign it?

A No, sir.

Q You just declined to sign it?

A Yes, sir.

Q Do you know whether any of the officers did sign it?

A I don't know, sir.

Q Well, that is all that I have, unless you want to state something else about this.

A I would like to add something more, sir.

Q Yes.

A Just what I said, if that is an order of our status, we would like to include that we shouldn't have any visitors, military or civilian.

Q This is limits of arrest.

A That's right, sir.

Q That indicates the areas. It has nothing to do with visitors.

A Well, I mean, that is our whole status of arrest there, sir.

Q As I understand it, what you are implying is that you based your having declined to sigh this on the fact that nothing was said about visitors, is that right?

A That's right.

Q Is there anything else?

A No, sir.

Q All right; that's all. Thank you.

(Witness excused)

(For a complete list of those arrested, see Disciplinary Action in Appendix).

The above transcription speaks for itself. It should serve as a sobering reminder of ways of maintaining and enforcing segregation, and how everyone is robbed both in the meaning and in the basic rights inherent in "We, the people..."

Following his discharge, LeRoy Battle enrolled at the Julliard School of Music. Thereafter, he enrolled at Morgan College, graduating in 1950 with a Major in Instrumental Music. He received his Master of Education in 1961 from the University of Maryland. Now a retired educator, he continues with his music, More importantly, he continues to speak against racism, whatever the form.

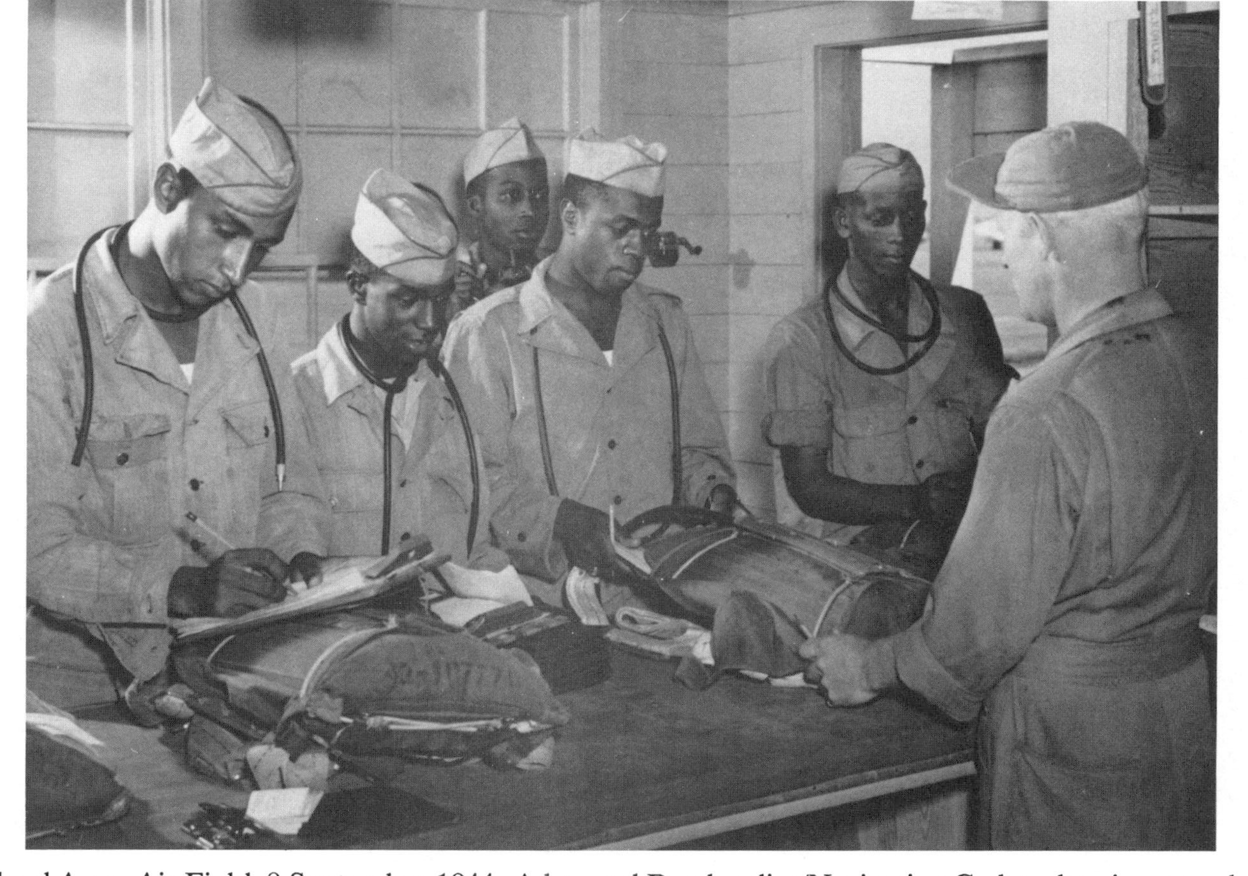

Midland Army Air Field, 8 September 1944--Advanced Bombardier/Navigation Cadets drawing parachutes for a night mission. From left to right: Robert S. Lawrence, Benjamin J. Williams, Ivan G. Bynoe, LeRoy A. Battle, and Robert A. Lee, photo courtesy of LeRoy Battle, Sr.

Top: Airplane Armorer, SGT Conway Waddy at an air base in Italy.
Bottom: The author, Charles E. Francis, in 1944.

Chapter 27
The Enlisted Men

The story of the Tuskegee Airmen would be incomplete if the enlisted men were not given recognition for the part they played. Though they played the less glamorous role, without a doubt, they played a major role in the success of the Tuskegee Experiment.

When it was proposed that a black Army Air Corps squadron be activated, General Arnold argued against it, stating that perhaps black youths could be trained as pilots in 18 months, but it would take years to train enlisted men as mechanics, especially keeping within the frame work of the separate-but-equal doctrine.

General Arnold was not alone in his thinking. General Parrish, in relating his experiences at Tuskegee, recalled a visit to the base by an official from the government of India. The official was interested in developing an Indian Air Force to participate in the war. He had gone to England with the idea, but was turned down by British Air Force officials. He was told that even if they were able to train pilots in a short time, it would take years to train the mechanics to service the planes. They stated that before this could be accomplished, the war would be over.

The visitor was amazed to see the black mechanics servicing the planes. He was more amazed after questioning the men and learning that most of the mechanics had been in service only a year. Before entering the service most of these men were farm workers. The Indian remarked to COL Parrish, "Now I am going back to England and tell those English men that they told me a damn lie."

Despite General Arnold's conviction, the War Department, pressured by black and white leaders and directed by President Roosevelt to accept black youths for pilot training, decided to activate a 99th Pursuit Squadron. Black colleges, namely, Tuskegee Institute, Morehouse, Hampton, NCA & T, Fisk, West Virginia State, Delaware State, and Howard University were requested to encourage students to apply for training as pilots, aviation mechanics and technicians. This resulted in a large number of the pioneering classes of mechanics and technicians being college men, all of whom tested for their mechanical aptitude. Many qualified for pilot training but chose to accept training in the less glamorous technical jobs.

On March 15, 1941, the Adjutant General's office constituted the 99th Pursuit Squadron and ordered its activation at Chanute Field. On March 22, 1941, the 99th was activated and a cadre of 14 black non-commissioned officers from the 24th and 25th Infantry Regiments were sent to Chanute Field to help in the administration and supervision of the trainees. A white officer, CPT Maddux, was assigned as the first commander of the 99th Fighter Squadron.

While the enlisted men at Chanute were in training, five black youths were admitted to the Officers Training School at Chanute Field as aviation cadets. They were: Elmer D. Jones, Dudley Stevenson, and James Johnson of Washington, D.C, Nelson Brooks of Illinois, and William R. Thompson of Pittsburgh. These successfully completed their training and were commissioned as the first black Army Air Corps officers.

Contrary to the belief of General Arnold, the enlisted trainees completed their training in eight months. On November 7, 1941, Special Order # 263, Chanute Field read:

P-29 Pursuant to authority contained in immediate action letter W.D. the Adjutant General's Office--Subject troops of the 99th Pursuit Squadron and its supporting Air Base Detachment dated November 3, 1941, the 99th Pursuit Squadron A.C. Colored Unit and its Support Air Base Detachment of approximately 400 enlisted men is transferred from Chanute Field to Maxwell Field at the earliest practical date, for temporary change of station pending completion of facilities at Tuskegee, Alabama this unit will be moved to that place for permanent change of station.

On November 10, a detachment of 49 men were sent from Maxwell to Tuskegee to help in the activation of the base. Prior to the arrival of these men, 31 enlisted men had arrived at Tuskegee from Fort Custis, as the cadre for the 318th Air Base Squadron. It was activated in January 1942 under the command of LT Fred Minnis.

Ralph Jones, one of the original members of the 318th, related, "I was drafted on October 16, 1941, and I was among the enlisted men selected to go to Tuskegee Air Base.

"We arrived in a train at the little station called Cheehaw in Alabama, which described the place quite adequately. From Cheehaw we were trucked to the base... really what was to become the base, for on our arrival we immediately dubbed it tent city. There were no permanent buildings for the army personnel and the air strip was still under construction. It was about November 10 when a cadre from Chanute came to tent city... There was no race problem because all whites lived in the town; they didn't even take their meals at the base."

Robert Pitts, one of the enlisted men trained at Chanute and sent to Tuskegee, related, "A few members of the administrative personnel journeyed to Tuskegee to get the offices ready. I was one of those in the group, and my first time at Tuskegee was quite a shock. There was nothing but tents available to us. Captain Davis and the other flying cadets were occupying tents in a near-by area. I can remember staring in awe as CPT Davis put the other cadets through their military routine.

"Our time was taken up because the offices upon the hill were beginning to take shape, and we had to set them up as fast as the rooms were completed. The leader of our group was Thomas J. Money, who came from Camp Walters. Like myself, he was regular army, having enlisted. As we proceeded to develop the administration, the base began to grow. By living adjacent to the cadets, we were able to watch their development. We saw the air base grow into the home of the 99th and the 332nd."

COL Frederick Kimble, who assumed command of Tuskegee Army Air Field soon after its activation, best described the dedication of the pioneers of the base in a speech to Class 42-E in December 1942. He remarked, "November 8th of last year marked the opening of flying operations of this field. The flying area proper from which ships could take off and land was a small flat, roughly between what is now the north-south runway and west of the north-west-south-west runways. All of the troops were under canvas in the vicinity of gate number one. The first paved runway, the north-south-east was opened at the end of the year and at the same time the ships were moved over to the main area in the northeast end. The field was so muddy that some of them were taken into the air and flown across... The first class of graduates did all of its flying on this field on one runway, regardless of the wind. Cross wind landings were habitual. It cannot be said that anyone relished this handicap, but there was never a word of complaint...

"Motors were changed not in hangers as today, but with movable tripods in the open. Frequently the work was carried on in the rain. As you know, footing is insecure in this area after much water has fallen, but the work went on."

Every organization must have good leaders and dedicated workers if it is to survive and prosper. Tuskegee was very fortunate in having had dedicated and efficient pioneers. By their dedication and effectiveness, they not only gave the base and the black pilot training programs a good start, but set a standard for others who followed. There were pioneer mechanics such as:

M/SGT Harry Williams

A native of Cleveland, he attended the Cleveland East Technical School where he starred in football and track. SGT William was accepted by Miami University of Ohio to study architecture and was graduated with a B.S. degree. He was employed as a teacher at Cleveland High School when inducted into the Service in February 1941 and sent to Chanute for basic training. Upon the completion of his basic training, he was accepted for mechanic training, and upon completion of that training was sent to Tuskegee where he became a line chief for all AT-6 and P-40 aircraft.

M/SGT James Blackstone

A native of Annapolis, MD, SGT Blackstone was another of the outstanding mechanics. He not only served as a Crew Chief and Line Chief, but was assigned as an instructor of aircraft mechanics.

T/SGT Harold Garibaldi

No doubt, Garibaldi was one of the most gifted of the mechanics at Tuskegee. Born and reared in Los Angeles, he enlisted in the Air Corps in April 1941 and was sent to Chanute with the first class of black trainees. He was graduated as the most outstanding student mechanic in the entire school. At Tuskegee, he served as Crew Chief for AT and BT aircraft before being promoted to the highest position on the flight line as Technical Airplane Inspector. In this position, he and his assistant, Bernard Brown, were responsible for the maintenance of all aircraft at Tuskegee.

M/SGT Earl Ausby

Hailing from Portsmouth, Virginia, SGT Ausby dropped out of Union College, enlisted in the Air Corps and was sent to Chanute as a mechanic trainee. Upon the completion of his training, he was sent with the first class to Tuskegee, where he was assigned as a BT aircraft mechanic.

S/SGT James Atchison

Having worked as a carburetor specialist at McClelland Field, CA before being inducted into the service in October 1942, SGT Atchison arrived at Tuskegee on October 9, 1942, and was immediately sent to Curtiss-Wright Airplane factory in Buffalo to study P-40 type engines. He returned to Tuskegee and was appointed crew chief for single engine aircraft. He was sent into combat with the 332nd and served as crew chief for P-40, P-39 and P-51 aircraft.

S/SGT Albert H. Brown

There were a number of outstanding mechanics employed at Tuskegee, who were not considered among the pioneers; nevertheless, they performed equally efficiently. One of these was SGT Brown from Pittsburgh. He arrived at Tuskegee in February 1943, after completing a mechanic course at Shaw Field, South Carolina. He served as Crew Chief, and received a rating of excellent for three consecutive months by the base inspector.

In the pilot training program there were other specialists who played significant roles. There was SGT Kenneth White of Brooklyn, who enlisted in the Air Corps on April 1, 1941 and went to Chanute where he completed a course in Armament. He applied for pilot training, was accepted, eliminated and assigned to the Ground School as an instructor of armament, gunnery, aircraft recognition and aero-dynamics.

Another eliminated cadet was SGT Thomas B. Hopkins from Pasadena. He was sent to the Air Force Photographic School at Lowery Field, CO. He was graduated as a specialist in aerial photography and gunnery. He returned to Tuskegee and served as NCO (Non Commissioned Officer) in charge of all phases of gunnery.

Then there was M/SGT John A. Calloway, a native of East Orange, NJ. He enlisted in the Air Corps in 1941 and was sent to Chanute Field, where he finished second in his class as a welder. At Tuskegee, he was assigned to the Inspection Department. His job consisted of making continuous airplane and technical inspections.

Everyone who trained as a pilot is familiar with the Link Trainer, popularly termed as "flying under the hood". This training was a necessity for pilots, because they often had to fly at night or during daylight hours often running into heavy cloud covers. Pilots without this training were in danger of becoming lost and crashing. The NCO in charge of this training was S/SGT Edward Guillard. He had completed a link training course at Chanute and an Advance Instrument Course at the Advanced Instrument Flying School at Bryan Field, Texas.

There were other enlisted men who played important roles in the pilot training program, namely S/SGT Robert Wilson of Chicago, who was studying aeronautics at Chicago Technical School when drafted into service; he was the NCO in charge of instrument training. T/SGT Harold Hilton, Joseph C. Mills, and Luther Pugh, radio mechanics and operators, who taught the cadets radio code and aerial communication; T/SGT William H. Killings of Akron, Ohio, was the NCO in charge of their Air Inspector's office, and T/SGT Rudolph Jeter, a native of Philadelphia and a graduate of West Virginia State University served as chief weather observer.

The enlisted men were also the backbone of the base operation and administration. At Tuskegee the top enlisted man was SGT/M Allen L. Searcy from Mt. Pleasant, Texas. He was a student at Tuskegee studying agriculture when he decided to volunteer for service in the Air Corps. After completing his basic training, he was sent to the clerical school at Chanute and after the completion of his training was sent to Tuskegee in November 1941. In August 1942, he was promoted to Sergeant Major. In this position he became the

NCO in charge of all personnel affairs and classification of those assigned to the base.

Another important enlisted man was T/SGT James B. Oliver, the NCO in charge of the Administrative Inspector's Office. A native of New York City, he was a graduate of Northwestern University School of Journalism and had earned a M. A. Degree from Boston University. He was also a graduate of the Army Air Force Clerical and Administrative Inspectors School. The Quartermaster Department was headed by SGT Richard A. Myers of Charleston, South Carolina, who was a student at Allen College when drafted. The *laundry* section was administered by S/SGT Albert D. Clark of Fayette, MS. He was a graduate of Alcorn College and was the principal of Walthall County Training School, Tylertown, MS when drafted.

One of the few white enlisted men assigned to Tuskegee was T/SGT Frank Levenson. He was a graduate of Boston University School of Finance and at Tuskegee served as technical assistant in the finance office. Of course, there were many more leaders and pioneers who helped make the Tuskegee Experiment a success story. Men such as PFC Elwood E. Peterson of Brooklyn served as section chief of the Personal Affairs office. T/SGT Pable Diaz Albortt from Puerto Rico was NCO in charge of the Special Service office. SGT Caulton Mays of Detroit, a graduate of Wilberforce University, headed the production section; SGT Leon Smith was the editor of the base newspaper. SGT Cecil D. Nelson and William (Bill) Chase were columnists and cartoonists for the base newspaper. And SGT Rudy Sable from New York was NCO in charge of the physical fitness department.

The enlisted men assigned to Godman and Lockbourne with the 477th and the men who served in combat with the 99th and the 332nd carried on the spirit of excellence--all started at Tuskegee. M/SGT Alexander Buchannon, one of the mechanics sent overseas with the 99th related, "A few days before we left Tuskegee for combat, COL Parrish delivered a farewell address. He told us to stick together, one for all and all for one, and if we did that, we were sure to be successful. We did exactly what COL Parrish advised, officers and enlisted men. We enlisted men were determined to do our share. COL Davis didn't know it but we enlisted men were determined to see that he always had sufficient planes for his missions. Sometimes we would find that we didn't have necessary parts. A few of us would jump into a jeep or truck and travel to a supply depot or other bases to acquire the parts. We begged, borrowed, bartered and sometimes had to go into other groups wrecked plane lots at night and salvage parts with a flashlight and moonlight.

"Often engines of our planes had to be changed or overhauled, or planes returned from missions so badly damaged they looked like they were ready for the junk yard, but in a few hours or days, they were back in service."

M/SGT Fred Archer, armament specialist, said, "I don't think any other Air Force group stuck together as a team like we did. The officers and enlisted men worked and socialized as a family. After every mission the pilots would spend time briefing us as to what happened on the missions. CPT Hannibal Cox practically lived in our area. I believe he had as many personal friends among the enlisted men as he had officer friends. Then there was *Gene* Carter, a pilot with the 99th; he was a pilot and mechanic. He loved to fly and work on planes. When he wasn't flying missions, he would spend his time on the flight line with us, servicing the planes."

Both General Davis, Jr. and Parrish praised the enlisted men for their contribution to the war effort. After the war, when an investigation was being made to evaluate Blacks for post-war service, General Parrish reported that, "all of the mechanical work at Tuskegee was done by black mechanics without the help or supervision from white mechanics and likewise all of the administrative work was done by Blacks." General Davis stated, "I had a good group of enlisted men to work with me throughout the war. They all knew their jobs and gave their best. When it was decided to integrate the services, I had no trouble finding jobs for the enlisted technicians and mechanics. I received more requests for them than I could supply."

George Watson, Sr.

George was born in Wildwood, NJ on August 10, 1920. He graduated from Lakewood High School in 1941 after four seasons as a quarterback and end on the football team.

On February 25, 1942, he volunteered for the U.S. Army, and following a short stay at Fort Dix, NJ, he was one of many selected and sent to Tuskegee as the first recruits to help form the 99th, the

100th, the 301st and the 302nd Pursuit Squadron, making up the 332nd Fighter Group and the 96th Air Service Group. George, therefore, is one of the original Tuskegee Airmen.

George served in Italy, Germany, england, Turkey and Iran. In Italy, he served with the 332nd Fighter Group. He was with the 332nd Fighter Wing when segregation ended in the Air Force. After 26 years of service, he retired from McGuire Air Force Base, NJ, as an aircraft and missile electrician.

While in the service, George was the first African American Recruiter for the Army and Air Force in Trenton, NJ from 1951 through 1955. As a civilian, he spent 15 years with the New Jersey Bell Telephone Company as a frameman and Telephone Installer.
He is the recipient of numerous awards both from the military and civilian, including the Air Force Outstanding Unit Award with one Bronze Oak Leaf Cluster, the European-African-Middle Eastern Campaign Medal with two Bronze Service Stars, the World War II Victory Medal, the Key to the city of Tuskegee, AL, the NAACP Lifetime Award, and the Community Service Award for Outstanding Contributions to the African-American Community. He is also the founder of the American Legion Chapter named after Captain Robert B. Tresville.

Married for over 50 years, George lives happily with his wife Juanita Jackson. They have two sons, one daughter and three grandchildren.

Italy 1944--Tuskegee Airmen Ground Support. Courtesy of George Watson, Sr.

Italy 1944--SGT George Watson, Sr. with an Italian boy who could have been yours truly-- (that is, Colonel Caso, who, as a boy posed for many such pictures). Courtesy of George Watson, Sr.

James A. Hurd, Pilot 477th, and Crew.

Left to right--top row: Luther A. Goodwin, John Rector, Robert C. Brown, Augustus Brown, James A. Hurd. Bottom row: Warren E. Henry, Russell C. Nagle, Frederick Samuels, Paul C. Bonseigneur, (unknown).

CPT Herbert Carter and LT Wiliam W. Green, veteran combat pilots of the 99th and 332nd.

Left to right: Dual-rated Pilot-Navigator Officer LT Turner, LT McIntyre, LT Choise, LT William Williams, LT C.C. Moseley, LT Maples, and LT H.J. Holland (September 1945 by J.S. Mosley).

Chapter 28
A Forgotten Lonely Eagle

After some fifty years later, another hero (practically forgotten in the annals of our Tuskegeean history) has come forth to join our earthly and spiritual world. LT James Albert Calhoun, winner of the Air Medal, with eleven missions under his belt and two downed enemy aircraft to his credit, is also the recipient of the Purple Heart. With his death properly recorded, the US government mailed the American Flag together with the Purple Heart to his wife, Mrs. Grace Carlsen Calhoun. Unfortunately, the correspondence did not reveal the location of the burial site, though it indicated Italy.

Buried somewhere in a foreign land, his grave unknown to relatives and friends, the marble cross bearing the name of "James A. Calhoun 2LT 100 FTR SQ 332 FTR GP Connecticut Sept 8 1944" was finally discovered in 1995 among the thousands of graves in the Sicily-Rome Cemetery, outside of Nettuno, Italy. How the discovery came about is in itself worthy to tell in that, in spite of its brevity, it generates wonderment and a rumble of goose pimples at the same time.

Robert Royster, husband of Jean Calhoun, prodded by their children, on learning that his work buddy, Theodore Carmone was visiting Italy, asked him to see if he could find his father-in-law's grave. Mr. and Mrs. Carmone, whose ancestors live in that general area, made a special effort to visit the various military cemeteries around Anzio. On discovering the large cemetery at Nettuno, and on asking for the list of the more than 8,000 buried soldiers, they discovered the names of LT Calhoun. Rushing to the grave site, to their amazement they saw the cross of his friend's fallen hero. After taking a few quick snapshots, Mr. and Mrs. Carmone rushed to the nearest telephone to relay the information. Mr. Royster, immediately called his wife Jean, who in turn called her children and her brothers, thus ending a fifty year-old search for their loved one. Now that the two families--the Carmones and the Roysters--are friends, the

Roysters have planned to make a pilgrim to Nettuno where they will hold an appropriate religious service. By so doing, they will have gained peace of mind and of heart for themselves, and will have restored another fallen hero to the great Pantheon of the Lonely Eagles.

James Albert Calhoun was born on March 3, 1917 in Deluthe, MN, to a Cherokee mother and an African American father. As a student at Bridgeport, CT's Central High School, he met and fell in love with Grace Carlsen and were married after senior graduation in 1935. In the years that followed, they had three children: James (1936), Jean (1938), and Raymond (1941).

LT Calhoun was a well-liked young man in his community. Known for his sense of humor and intelligence, he supported his family by working as a janitor at the Bullard Company in Bridgeport. Realizing, however, that a black man's future without a college degree would be a bleak one, and, in any event, not having the money to pursue it, and because he was fascinated with planes, he joined the Air Force with the hope of becoming a fighter pilot.

On March 28, 1943, he left his family and joined the Tuskegee Airmen in Alabama, where he graduated with the class of 44C and the 100th Fighter Squadron, 332nd Fighter Group. Shipped overseas, he quickly proved his skill as a talented pilot. In eleven missions, he got two kills, for which he received the Air Medal on July 9, 1944. On his last mission, however, while strafing in the Balkans, he was hit and went down, thus receiving his Purple Heart.

Now, after 50 long years of diligent and untiring search, the young and old Calhouns and Roysters (joined by other friends and relatives) will be traveling to Italy for the first time to pay tribute to a true American hero. And finally, after all this time, his portrait was presented at the 1996 National Convention of the Tuskegee Airmen's Lonely Eagle ceremony where a candle was lit in his honor.

After his name was called, the flame was put out on earth and rekindled skyward in the Pantheon of the great Lonely Eagles spirits.

James A. Calhoun, "To My Darling" Wife.

LT Calhoun (left rear, right of pole) and his fellow classmates.

Top: The Cross (*photo courtesy of T. Carmone*). Bottom: The Purple Heart bespeaks of heroism.

Appendices

Footnotes

Chapter 1

1. Record of Public Relation Office, Tuskegee Army Air Field
2. Lee, Ulysses, G., *The Employment of Negro Troops in World War II*, US Printing Office, Washington, DC 1965, p. 55
3. Ibid, p. 56
4. Ibid
5. Ibid
6. Ibid, p. 59
7. *Congressional Record* House pp. 7666-8. June 21, 1939, also Lee op cit p. 60
8. Ltr. AG to Rep. William H. Larrabee (Indiana), December 21, 1939, AG 291.21
9. Congressional Record. House. June 21, 1939 O. p. 7667
10. Congressional Record. Senate. 1040. p. 671
11. Ibid
12. Ibid
13. Congressional Record. Selective Compulsory Military Training and Service, Hearing. on H.R. 10132, 76th Congress, 3rd Session. p. 587
14. Lee. p. 72
15. Congressional Record. Senate. August 26, 1940. p. 10888
16. Lee, p. 73
17. Public Law 783, 76th Congress, 16 September 1940
18. Lee, p. 74
19. *The Crisis* LXVII, November 1940; also, Lee, pp. 74-75
20. Lee, p. 75
21. Ibid, p. 76
22. Congressional Record, 86, pp. 13610-13827, Hastie William H. *On Clipped Wings* }Published by National Association of Colored People, 1943
23. Ibid

24. Lee, p. 81
25. Hastie
26. Ibid
27. Ibid
28. Release No. 3--Selective Service Headquarters, Washington, DC, March 25, 1941

Chapter 3

1. COL Benjamin O. Davis, Jr., Press Conference at Pentagon, September 10, 1943

Chapter 5

1. Pyle, Ernie, *Brave Men*, p. 16
2. Ibid, p. 20
3. Dean, Fred M., COL, "The Luftwaffe At Bay", *Air Force*, October 1943, p. 6-7, 56

Chapter 6

1. Craven, W.E. & Cate, J.L., *The Army Air Force in World War II*, Vol II, pp. 492-494
2. Ringold, *Salerno* Air Force, pp. 28-35
4. Record, 33rd Fighter Group
5. Record, 99th Fighter Squadron
6. Pyle, p. 161
7. Butcher, *My Three Years with Eisenhower 1942-1945*, p. 59
8. Lee, op. cit. pp 453-454
9. *Time* Magazine, September 20, 1943

Chapter 7

1. Mathews, "Road of Mud, Fatigue, and Glory"
2. Pyle, p. 233
3. Lind, *The Falcon*
4. *Composite Record*, 79th Fighter Group

Chapter 8

1. Norstad, *Airlock in Italy*, pp. 31-35
2. Second Report, pp. 45-6
3. Norstad, p. 35

Chapter 10

1. Coffey, *Decision Over Schweinfurt*, p. 222
2. Ibid, also Craven, pp. 841-49
3. Coffey, pp. 222-228
4. Ibid
5. Interview, General Benjamin O. Davis, Jr., May 1985
6. Lee, pp. 518-19
7. Ibid

Chapter 12

1. Norstad, pp. 31-35

Chapter 13

1. Craven, pp. 640-646
2. Record of 332nd, Entry 7
3. Ibid

Chapter 14

1. Commanger, *The Story of the 2nd World War*, p. 438
2. Craven, p. 412
3. Ibid, p. 413
4. Ibid
5. Record 332nd

Chapter 17

1. Craven, p. 412
2. Record 332nd
3. Craven, p. 471

Chapter 18

1. Eisenhower, *Crusade In Europe*, p. 410

Chapter 19

1. Osur, *Blacks in the Army Air forces During World War II*, also, Lee, p. 579
2. Lee, p. 176
3. Craven, Vol VI. pp. 78-96

4. Ibid, p. 490
5. Ibid, p. 438
6. Ibid, p. 491
7. Ibid, p. 494
8. Ibid, pp. 549-556
9. Ibid, p. 486
10. Ibid, p. 516
11. Lee, p. 462
12. Craven, p. 134
13. Ibid, pp. 521-526
14. Lee, p. 465, also, Craven, pp. 521-22
15. Craven, p. 521
16. Ibid, pp. 464-465
17. Lee, p. 464
18. Craven, pp. 550-56
19. Lee, pp. 464-5

Chapter 20

1. Osur, p. 57
2. Ibid, p. 55
3. Ibid, p. 56
4. Ibid, p. 113
5. Ibid, p. 114

Chapter 21

1. Gropman, *The Air Force Integrates 1945-1964*
2. Ibid, p. 45, also Parrish, "History of the 2143rd..."
3. Ibid, p. 46
4. Ibid, p. 54-55
5. Ibid, p. 57, also, Alvan, "Board Papers"
6. Ibid, p. 58
7. Congressional Record, 80th Congress, Vol 93, April 8, 1948
8. Truman, *Public Papers*
9. Gropman, p. 91
10. Ibid, p. 91

Chapter 22

1. *Ebony* Magazine, October 1952, p. 22

2. *Afro-American*, October 31, 1950
3. Ibid, November 29, 1950
4. *Ebony*, October 1950, p. 25
5. Gropman, pp. 157-158
6. Parker, *Capitol Hill In Black and White*, p. 114
7. Diggs Folder Carton 8
8. Kennedy, *Public Papers of the President*
9. Gropman, pp. 172-180
10. Ibid, pp. 179-180
11. Ibid, p. 199
12. Ibid, pp. 200-201
13. Ibid, pp. 215-216
14. Ibid, p. 217
15. Ibid, p. 219

References

Primary

1. *Congressional Record* Senate Committee on Military Affairs, Hearing on H.R. 3791, 76th Congress, 1st Session, Washington, DC, March 7, 1939
2. *Congressional Record* House, 76th Congress, 1st Session, June 21, 1939
3. *Congressional Record* Senate, Selective Compulsory Military Training, 76th Congress, Vol. 86, Part 10, August 26, 1940
4. *Congressional Records*, 1947-1949, House, 1963-1965
5. *Federal Register*, Public Papers, Harry S. Truman, Govt. Printing Office, Washington, DC, 1948
6. Truman, Harry, S., *Public Papers of the President of the US*, January 1 to December 31, 1948, US Govt. Printing Office, Washington, DC, 1964
7. *Second Report of the Commanding General of the Army Air Forces to the Secretary of War*, February 27, 1945, US Govt. Printing Office, Washington, DC
8. *Third Report of the Commanding General of the Army Air Force to the Secretary of War*, November 12, 1945, US Govt. Printing Office, Washington, DC
9. *Secretary of Air Force Papers*, Record Center, Suitland, MD, Group 340
10. ----- Group 330
11. *The President's Committee on Civil Rights*, "to Secure These Rights", Govt. Printing Office, Washington, DC
12. Kennedy, John, F., *Public Papers of the President of the United States*, Govt. Printing Office, Washington, DC, 1962-1963
13. The President's Committee on Equality of Treatment and Opportunity in the Armed Forces, *Freedom to Serve*, Govt. Printing Office, Washington, DC

14. War Department Bureau of Public Relation, *Releases 1941-46*
15. *Special Orders*, Tuskegee Army Air Field, 1941-46
16. *Special Order* No. 338, Selfridge Field, MI, 20 December 1943
17. National Archives Record Center, Suitland, MD, Records of Group 18, Entry 7, as follows:
    a. 99th Fighter Squadron
    b. 332nd Fighter Group
    c. 33rd Fighter Group
    d. 79th Fighter Group
    e. 86th Fighter Group
    f. 24th Fighter Group
    g. 52nd Fighter Group
18. Parrish, Noel, F., *The Segregation of Negroes in the Army Air Force* (unpublished), Air Command and Staff School Research Study, Maxwell Field, AL, 1947
19. Gillem, Alvan, C. Jr., *Papers*. US Army Military History Research Collection, Carlisle Barracks, PA
20. Hastie, William H., *On Clipped Wings* NAACP, October 1943

Secondary

1. Butcher, Harry, C., CPT USNR, *My Three Years with Eisenhower*, Simon and Schuster, New York, 1946
2. Coffey, Thomas M., *Decision Over Schweinfurt*, David McKay Inc., New York, 1977
3. Commager, Harry S., *The Story of the Second World War*, Little Brown & Co., Boston, MA' 1945
4. Craven, Wesley & Gates, J.L., *The Army Air Forces in World War II*, Volumes I, II, II, IV, University of Chicago Press
5. Dalfiume, Richard M., *Desegregation of the US Armed Forces: Fighting on Two Fronts: 1939-1953*, University of Missouri Press, Columbia, MO, 1969
6. Eisenhower, Dwight D., *Crusade In Europe*, Doubleday & Co. Inc., Garden City, New York, 1948
7. Forrester, Larry, *Fly For Your Life*, Banton Book, Inc., New York, 1978
8. Franklin, John H., *From Slavery To Freedom: A History of Negro Americans*, Vintage Press, New York, 1969

9. Galland, Adolf, *The First And The Last*, Bantan Book, Inc., New York, NY, 1978
10. Gentile, Don S., *One Man Air Force*, L. B. Fischer Publishing Corp., NY
11. Infield, Glenn, *Big Week*, Pinnacle Books, Inc., Los Angeles, CA, 1974
12. Gropman, Alan, *The Air Force Integrates 1945-1964*, Govt. Printing Office, Washington, DC, 1978
13. Harrison, Gordon A., *Cross Channel Attack*, Govt. Printing Office, Washington, DC, 1951
14. Howe, George F., *Northwest Africa: Seizing the Initiative in the West*, Govt. Printing Office, Washington, DC
15. Lee, Ulysses G., *The Employment of Negro Troops*, Govt. Printing Office, Washington, DC, 1966
16. Lincoln, Eric C., *The Negro Pilgrimage In America*, Bantan Books, New York
17. Lind, Ragnor G., *The Falcon, Combat Story of the 79th Fighter Group*, F. Bruckman, Munich, Germany, 1946
18. Maurer, *Air Force History*, Washington, DC, 1969
19. -----, *Air Force Combat Units of World War II*, Franklin Walls, Co., New York, NY 1963
20. Murray, Florence, *The Negro Handbook*, Wendell Malliet & Co., New York, 1942
21. Myral, Gunnar, *An American Dilemma: The Negro People and Modern Democracy*, Harper and Brothers, New York, 1944
22. Osur, Alan M., *Blacks in the Army Air Forces During World War II*, Govt. Printing Office, Washington, DC, 1977
23. Parker, Robert, *Capitol Hill in Black and White*, Dodd, Mead & Co., New York, 1968
24. Parks, Gordon, *A Choice of Weapons*, Berkeley Publishing Corp., 1965
25. Pyle, Ernie, *Brave Men*, Henry Holt & co., New York, 1944
26. Silvera, John, *The Negro In World War II*, Military Press, Inc.
27. Stillman, Richard J., *Integration of the Negro in the US Armed Forces*, Frederick A. Praeger Co., New York, 1968
28. White, Walter, *How Far The Promised Land?*, The Viking Press, 1956

Other Sources:

1. Personal Interviews--Members of the 99th Fighter Squadron, the 332nd Fighter Group, and the 477th Bombardment and Composite Group
2. Personal Interviews with General Benjamin O. Davis, Jr. and Noel F. Parrish
3. Biographical Survey, Pilots of the 99th Fighter Squadron, the 33rd Fighter Group, the 477th Bombardment and Composite Group, and Tuskegee Army Air Field's Base Complement
4. Personal Interview, BG Benjamin O. Davis, Sr.
5. Temple, Alva (CPT), *Diary*, (unpublished)
6. Thomas, Edward (CPT), *Diary*, (unpublished)
7. Personal Interviews, Watson, Spann, COL
8. *Blacks in Aviation 1995*, Gary J. Dellapa

Newspapers & Periodicals

Afro-American, 1941-51
Pittsburgh Courier, 1941-51
Norfolk Journal and Guide, 1941-51
New York Times, 1942
Time Magazine, September 1943
Air Force 1942-46
Washington Post, June 20, 1975
The Lantern, May 27, 1949 (Lockbourne Air Force Base)
Wing over Tuskegee, Tuskegee Institute
The Hawk Cry, Tuskegee Army Air Field

COMBAT RECORD OF NEGRO AIRMEN

June 9, 1945

	DESTROYED	DAMAGED	TOTAL
Aircraft (aerial)	111	25	136
Aircraft (ground)	150	123	273
Barges and Boats	16	24	40
Box cars	58	361	619
Buildings-Factories	0	23	23
Gun Emplacements	3	0	3
Destroyers	1	0	1
Horse Drawn Vehicles	15	100	115
Motor Transports	6	81	87
Power Transformers	3	2	5
Locomotives	57	69	126
Radar Installations	1	8	9
Tanks on Flat Cars	0	7	7
Oil-Ammunition Dumps	2	0	2

Total Missions	12th Air Force	1267
Total Missions	15th Air Force	311
Total Sorties	12th Air Force	6381
Total Sorties	15th Air Force	9152
Grand Total Missions		1578
Grand Total Sorties		15533
Total pilots sent overseas		450
Total pilots graduated at Tuskegee		992

Awards:

Legion of Merit	1
Silver Star	1
Soldier Medal	2
Purple Heart	8
Distinguished Flying Cross	95
Bronze Star	14
Air Medal and Clusters	744

*Final total of
Distinguished Flying Crosses awarded to
Negro pilots estimated at: 150

RECORD OF ENEMY AIRCRAFT SHOT DOWN BY NEGRO PILOTS

1. LT Clarence W. Allen, Mobile, AL—1 FW 190 shared with CPT Baugh (Jan. 28,1944)
2. CPT Lee Archer, New York City—1 ME 109 (July 18, 1944); 1 ME 109 (July 20, 1944--unofficial); 3 ME 109s (Oct. 13, 1944)
3. LT Willie Ashley, Sumpter, S. C.—1 FW 190 (Jan. 27, 1944)
4. LT Charles Bailey, Punta Gorda, Florida—1 FW 190 Jan. 27,1944); 1 FW 190 (July 18, 1944)
5. CPT Howard L. Baugh, Petersburg, Va.—1 FW 190 shared with LT Allen (Jan. 28, 1944)
6. LT Ruall W. Bell, Portland, Oregon—1 FW 190 (March 31, 1945)
7. F/O Charles V. Brantley, St. Louis, Missouri—1 Jet ME 262 (March 24,1945)
8. LT Thomas P. Braswell, Buford, Georgia—1 FW 190
9. CPT Roscoe Brown, New York City—1 Jet ME 262 (March 24, 1945)
10. LT John F. Briggs, St Louis, Missouri—1 ME 109 (August 24, 1944)
11. CPT Charles M. Bussey, Los Angeles, California—1 ME 109 (June 9, 1944)
12. LTC William A. Campbell, Tuskegee Institute, AL—2 ME 109s (March 31, 1945)
13. LT Earl Carey, St Louis, Missouri—2 ME 109s (April, 1945)
14. CPT Lemuel R. Custis, Hartford, Connecticut—1 Macchi 205 (Jan. 27,1944)
15. CPT Alfonso W. Davis, Omaha, Nebraska—1 Macchi 205 (July 16,1944)
16. LT John W. Davis, Kansas City, Kansas—1 ME 109
17. LT Robert Die, Portland, Oregon—1 FW 190 (Jan. 27, 1944); 1 FW 190 (Jan. 28, 1944)
18. CPT Elwood T. Driver, Trenton, NJ—1 FW 190 (Feb. 5,1944)
19. LT Wilson V. Eagleson, Bloomington, Indiana—1 FW 190 (Jan. 27,1944); 1 FW 190 (July 20, 1944)
20. LT John E. Edwards, Steubenville, Ohio—2 ME 109s (April 1, 1945)

21. CPT Joseph D. Elsberry, Langston, Oklahoma—3 FW 190s (July 12, 1944); 1 FW 190 (July 20, 1944)

22. F/O James Fischer, Stoughton, MA ME 109 (April 1, 1945)

23. LT Frederick Funderburg, Monticello, Georgia—2 ME 109s (June 9, 1944)

24. MAJ Edward C. Gleed, Lawrence, Kansas—2 FW 190s (July 27, 1944)

25. LT William W. Green, Staunton, Virginia—1 Macchi 205 (July 16, 1944); 1 ME 109 (July 26, 1944 shared with Lieut Groves); 1 ME 109 (Oct. 13, 1944)

26. CPT Claude B. Govan, Newark, New Jersey—1 ME 109 (July 27, 1944)

27. LT Alfred N. Gorham, Waukiska, Washington—2 FW 190s (July 27, 1944)

28. LT Weldon Groves, Edwardsville, Kansas—1 ME 109 (July 26, 1944 shared with Lieut Green)

29. CPT George Gray, Welch, West Virginia—1 ME 109 (Oct. 4, 1944)

30. CPT Charles B. Hall, Brail, Indiana—1 FW 190 (July 2, 1943); 1 FW 190 and 1 ME 109 (Jan. 28, 1944)

31. LT James L. Hall, Jr., Washington, DC—1 ME 109 32. LT Richard W. Hall, Albany, Georgia—1 ME 109 (July 27, 1944)

33. LT Milton Hayes, Los Angeles, California—1 ME 109 (Oct. 4, 1944 shared with CPT Perry)

34. LT Jack Holsclaw, Spokane, Washington—2 ME 109s (July 18, 1944)

35. LT William Hill—1 ME 109 (August 23, 1944)

36. CPT Freddie Hutchins, Donaldsonville, Georgia—1 ME 109 (July 26, 1944)

37. LT Thomas W. Jefferson, Chicago, Illinois—2 ME 109s (April 26, 1945)

38. CPT Melvin T. Jackson, Warrenton, Virginia—1 ME 109 (June 9, 1944)

39. CPT Leonard M. Jackson, Fort Worth, Texas—1 FW 190 (Feb. 7, 1944); 1 ME 109 (July 26, 1944); 1 ME 109 (July 27, 1944)

40. LT Carl E. Johnson, Charlottesville, Virginia—1 ME 109 (August 6, 1944); 1 Reggiane 200,1 (July 30, 1944)

41. LT Langdon E. Johnson, Ramp, West Virginia—1 ME 109 (July 20, 1944)
42. LT Felix Kirkpatrick, Jr., Chicago, Illinois—1 ME 109 (July 27, 1944)
43. LT Earle R. Lane, Wickliffe, Ohio—1 Jet ME 262 (March 24, 1945)
44. LT Jimmie Lanham, Philadelphia, Pennsylvania—1 ME 109 and 1 Probable (April 26, 1944)
45. CPT Clarence Lester, Chicago, IL—3 ME 109s (July 18, 1944)
46. F/O John H. Lyle, Chicago, IL—1 ME 109 (March 31, 1944)
47. LT Walter Manning, Philadelphia, PA—1 ME 109 (April 1, 1945)
48. CPT Armour G. McDaniel, Martinsville, Virginia—1 ME 109 (July 20, 1944)
49. CPT Charles E. McGee, Champaign, Illinois 1 ME 109 (Oct. 4, 1944)
50. LT Clinton B. Mills, Durham, North Carolina—1 FW 190 (Feb. 7, 1944)
51. LT Harold Morris, Portland, OR—1 ME 109 (April 1, 1945)
52. CPT Walter J. Palmer, NY City—1 ME 109 (July 18, 1944)
53. CPT Henry Perry, Thomasville, Georgia—1 ME 109 (Oct. 4, 1944 shared with LT Milton Hayes, Los Angeles, California)
54. LT William S. Price, Topeka, KS—1 ME 109 (Feb. 1, 1945)
55. CPT Wendell O. Pruitt, St. Louis, Missouri—1 ME 109 (June 9, 1944); 2 ME 109s (OCt. 12, 1944)
56. LT George M. Rhodes, Brooklyn, New York—1 FW 190 (August 12, 1944); 1 ME 109 (Oct. 4, 1944)
57. LT Daniel L. Rich, Rutherford, NJ—1 ME 109 (March 31, 1945)
58. CPT Leon C. Roberts, Pritchard, Alabama—1 FW 190 (Jan. 27, 1944)
59. LT Roger Romine, Oakland, California—1 ME 109 (July 18, 1944); 1 ME 109 (July 26, 1944); 1 ME 109 (Oct. 13, 1944)
60. LT Richard A. Simons, White Plains, New York—1 ME 109 (April 26, 1945)
61. CPT Lewis C. Smith, Los Angeles, CA—1 ME 109 (Jan. 27, 1944)

62. LT Luther H. Smith, Jr., Des Moines, Iowa—1 ME 109 (July 17, 1944); 1 ME 109 (Oc 13, 1944)

63. LT Robert Smith, Baltimore, MD—1 ME 109 (July 17, 1944)

64. LT Harry T. Stewart, Jr., Corona, Long Island—3 ME 109s (April 1, 1945)

65. CPT Edward Thomas, Chicago, Illinois 1 ME 109 (Oct. 4, 1944)

66. LT William H. Thomas, Los Angeles, California—1 ME 109 (August 24, 1944)

67. CPT Edward L Toppins, San Francisco, California—1 FW 190 (Jan. 27, 1944); 1 FW 190 (July 18, 1944); 1 ME 109 (July 20, 1944); 1 ME 109 (July 26, 1944)

68. LT Hugh Warner, New York City—1 ME 109 (July 18, 1944)

69. CPT Luke Weathers, Memphis, TN—1 ME 109 (August 23, 1944 shared with LT William Hill); 2 ME 109s (Nov. 16, 1944)

70. LT Shelby E. Westbrook, Toledo, Ohio—1 ME 109 (Oct. 4, 1944)

71. CPT Charles White, Oakland, CA—1 ME 109 (April 1, 1945)

72. CPT Hugh J. White, St. Louis, Missouri—1 ME 109 (March 31, 1945)

73. LT Lawrence D. Wilkens, Los Angeles, California—1 ME 109 (July 17,1944)

74. LT Bertram W. Wilson, Brooklyn, New York—1 FW 190 (March 31,1945)

75. LT Robert W. Williams, Ottumwa, Iowa—2 FW 190s (March 31, 1945)

Destroyer

Shared honor of destroying a Nazi Destroyer on July 25, 1944:

LT Gwynne Pierson, Oakland, CA.

CPT Wendell O. Pruitt, St. Louis, Mo.

PILOTS AWARDED THE DISTINGUISHED FLYING CROSS Unofficial List

COL Benjamin O. Davis, Jr., 1721 S. Street N. W., Wash., DC
MAJ George S. Robem, 317 Quarry Ave., Fairmount, WV
MAJ Lee Rayford, 1822 9th Street, N. W., Wash., DC
CPT Edward C. Gleed, 1721 Ohio Street, Lawrence, KS
CPT Jack D. Holsclaw, 2301 W. College Ave., Spokane, WA
CPT Arnold W. Cisco, 1129 Highland Ave., Alton, IL
CPT Joseph D. Elsberry, 1114 N. Washington, Langston, OK
CPT Claude E. Govan, 142 Somerset St., Newark, NJ
CPT Harold E. Sawyers, 1587 North Star, Columbus, OH
CPT Andrew D. Turner, 1000 Westford Place, N. E. Wash., DC
MAJ William T. Mattison, 2616 Park Place, N. W. Wash. DC
CPT Woodrow W. Crockett, 613 Vine Street, Little Rock, AR
CPT Lawrence E. Dickson, 220 W. 11th St., New York City CPT
CPT Samuel L. Curtis, 188 Fairview Ave., Yeadon, PA
CPT Lowell C. Steward, 1407 E. Wash., Los Angeles, CA
CPT Clarence W. Dart, Jr., 506 Dewitt Ave., Elmira, NJ
CPT Elwood T. Driver, 30 Fountain Ave., Trenton, NJ
CPT Alton F. Ballard, 372 E. Orange Grove Ave., Pasadena, CA
LT Felix J. Kirkpatrick, Jr., 4155 Prairie Ave., Chicago, IL
LT Richard Harder, 137 Renwich Place, Syracuse, NY
LT Milton S. Hayes, 377 La Salle Ave., Los Angeles, CA
LT Edward M. Thomas, 1245 W. 107th Place, Chicago, IL
LT Charles W. Tate, 1004 Decatur, Pittsburgh, PA
LT Herman A. Lawson, 204 White's Bridge, Fresno, CA
LT Lawrence D. Wilkens, 1355 E. 53rd St, Los Angeles, CA
LT Roger Romine, 829 36th St., Oakland, CA
LT Luther H. Smith, Jr., Des Moines, IA
LT William H. Thomas, 143 W. 6th St., Los Angeles, CA
LT Felix J. Kirkpatrick, Jr., 4155 Prairie Ave., Chicago, IL
LT William W. Green, Jr., 29 Park Boulevard, Staunton, VA
LT Lee A. Archer, Jr., 350 W. 1 19th St, New York City
LT Frank E. Roberts, 94 Harrison St, Boston, MA
LT George M. Rhodes, Jr., 331 Jefferson Ave., Brooklyn, NY
CPT Clarence D. Lester, 5321 Prairie Ave., Chicago, IL
CPT Melvin T. Jackson, Warrenton, VA

CPT Vernon V. Haywood, 902 Manley St., Raleigh, NC
CPT Dudley M. Watson, Frankfort, KY
CPT Gwynne W. Pierson, 865 45th St, Oakland, CA
CPT Milton R. Brooks, 411 Harrison St, Glassport, PA
CPT Luke J. Weathers, Jr., 601 South Lauderdale, Memphis, TN
CPT Freddie E. Hutchins, 208 N. Bowling St. Donaldsonville, GA
CPT Charles B. Hall, 80 S. 18th St., Terre Haute, IN
CPT Alfonso W. Davis, 2118 N. 29th St, Omaha, NB
CPT Edward L. Toppins, 1519 Baker St., San Francisco, CA
CPT Howard L. Baugh, 93 Lee Ave., Petersburg, VA
CPT Louis R. Purnell, Snow Hill, MD
LTC William A. Campbell, Tuskegee Institute, AL
CPT George Gray, 809 McDowell St, Welch, WV
CPT Albert H. Manning, 269 Cemetery St., Spartanburg, SC
CPT Wendell O. Pruitt, 4569 Garfield Ave., St Louis, MO
CPT Henry B. Perry, 519 N. Oak, Thomasville, GA
CPT Alva N. Temple, Carrollton, AA
CPT John Daniels, 15314 Vine Ave., Hartay, IL
CPT Willard L. Woods, 1906 S. Lauderdale, Memphis, TN
LT Norman W. Scales, 1107 Myrtle St, Austin, TX
LT Walter J. Palmer, 3762 Park Ave., New York City
LT Leonard F. Turner, 244 P St, N. W. Wash., DC
LT Dempsey W. Morgan, Jr., 6062 Calfax, Detroit, MI
LT Robert L. Martin, 560 Hill St., Dubuque, IA
LT Lawrence B. Jefferson, 1029 Sigsla, Grand Rapids, MI
LT John F. Briggs, Jr., 3651 Finney St., St. Louis, MO
LT Spurgeon Ellington, 1302 Highland Ave., Winston Salem, NC
CPT Leonard M. Jackson, 1200 Missouri Ave., Ft Worth, TX
CPT Robert J. Friend, Washington, DC
CPT Henry R Peoples, St Louis, MO
CPT Marion R. Rodgers, Detroit, MI
CPT Charles L. White, 4278 W. St. Ferdinand Ave., St Louis MO
LT Roscoe C. Brown, Jr., New York City
LT Earle R. Lane, Wickliffe, OH
LT William S. Price, Topeka, KS
LT Charles V. Brantley, St Louis, MO
LT Hannibal M. Cox, Jr., 6639 S. Rhodes Ave., Chicago, IL
LT Vincent I. Mitchell, 4468 Kentucky Ave., Mt. Clemens, MI

CPT Gordon M. Rapier, 2549 Madison St., Gary, IN
LT Thomas W. Jefferson, Chicago, IL
LT James Lanham, Philadelphia, PA
LT Thomas P. Braswell, Buford, GA
LT Shelby F. Westbrook, Toledo, OH
LT William H. Walker, Carbondale, IL
LT John W. Davis, Kansas Cit, KS
LT Quitman C. Walker, Indianola, MS
LT Heber C. Houston, Detroit, MI
LT Charles P. Bailey, Punta Gorda, FL
CPT Walter M. Downs, McComb, MS
CPT Clarence H. Bradford, St. Louis, MO
LT Reed E. Thompson, New Rochelle, NY
LT Gentry E. Barnes, Lawrenceville, IL
LT John E. Edwards, Steubenville, OH
LT Robert W. William, Ottumwa, IA
LT Bertram W. Wilson, Brooklyn, NY
LT Harry T. Stewart, Jr., 105-11 34th Ave., Corona, NY
CPT Emile C. Clifton, Jr., San Francisco, CA
CPT Theodore A. Wilson, 47 Patton Ave., N. E., Roanoke, VA

May 1949

Commanding Officer
Lockbourne Air Force Base
Columbus, Ohio
Greetings:

In my capacity as Governor of Ohio and individually, I desire to commend Captain Alva Temple of the 301st Fighter Squadron, LT Harry Stewart of the 100th Fighter Squadron and LT James Harvey of the 99th Fighter Squadron, who represented the 332nd Fighter Group in the Conventional Fighter Class of the Air Force National Fighter Gunnery Meet at Las Vegas Air Force Base, Nevada.

The winning of first place in open competition by your men situated at Lockbourne Air Force Base is a source of gratification to all people of Ohio, and will serve as an inspiration, particularly to the youth of this state.

Congratulations and best wishes.

Sincerely,
Frank J. Lausche

May 1949

CPT Alva Temple, 301st Fighter Squadron
LT Harry Stewart, 100th Fighter Squadron
LT James Harvey, 99th Fighter Squadron
Representing the 332nd Fighter Group

COMMENDATION

It is extremely gratifying to learn that the 332nd Fighter Group stationed at the Lockbourne Air Force Base won the first place in the Conventional Fighter Class of the Air Force National Fighter Gunnery Meet at Las Vegas Air Force Base, Nevada, recently. The 332nd Fighter Group is to be highly complimented on having officers of such high caliber and skill that bring renown and fame, not only to Lockbourne Air Force Base, but upon the City of Columbus and the State of Ohio as well. Truly, it is this type of achievement that is an inspiration for American youth and assurance to the people of this country of adequate protection in the event of an emergency.

Permit me as State Commander of the Air Force Association to personally commend CPTain Temple, LT Stewart and LT Harvey on their great achievement.

Yours very truly,
Fred M. Pickens
State Commander, Ohio Wing
Air Force Association

TWXs received by 332nd Headquarters: MAY 1949
From: Commanding General,
Continental Air Command,
Mitchell Air Force Base, N. Y.

My personal congratulations to members of the 332nd Fighter Group for taking first place in the Conventional Aircraft Class at the 1949 Annual Air Gunnery Meet held at Las Vegas Air Force Base.

* * *

From: Commanding General,
9th Air Force,
Langley Air Force Base, Va

Congratulations to members of the 332nd Fighter Gunnery Team for splendid showing in winning first place in Conventional Division of 1949 USAF Gunnery Meet at Las Vegas Air Force Base.

Lockbourne Air Force Base: MAY 1949
Columbus, Ohio
Subject: Letter of commendation
To: 332nd Fighter Group Detachment,
Las Vegas Air Force Base,
Nevada

It is with a great deal of personal pride that I commend the members of the 332nd Fighter Detachment which won the USAP Fighter Gunnery Meet for Conventional Aircraft at Las Vegas Air Force Base last week. Your team was composed of armament, maintenance, administrative, operations and pilot personnel, all of whom had to exhibit the highest type of cooperation, teamwork, and individual skill.

I add my congratulations to the many others you have received.

Benjamin O. Davis, Jr.
Colonel, USAP Commanding

TUSKEGEE HONOR ROLL

Men Lost in Training, Combat, and on Routine Missions

F/O William P. Armstrong, 93 Codling Street, Providence, RI. Shot down April 1, 1945 over Vienna, Austria.

F/O George A. Bates, 6231 Eberhart Ave., Chicago, IL. Killed in plane crash at Milstead, AL on April 26, 1946.

LT Richard H. Bell, 6535 Eberhart Ave., Chicago, IL. Died in training at Waterboro, KY on August 10, 1944.

LT Celsus E. Beguesse (MC), 910 South Walcott Ave, Chicago, IL. Died in plane crash at Tuskegee on May 19, 1946

LT Samuel A. Black, Plainfield, NJ. Bomber pilot. Died in crash at Madison, KY.

LT Linson Blackney, Weather Officer. Died when plane piloted by LT N. Hill spun into Lake Huron on June 16, 1943.

LT Fred L. Brewer, Charlotte, NC. Died when his plane spun in over the Alps.

LT Sidney Brooks, 3709 E. 142nd Street, Cleveland, OH. Killed on Aug. 19, 1943 in Sicily.

LT James E. Brothers, 5336 Kenwood Ave., Chicago, IL. Killed at Tuskegee in plane crash in May 1943.

Pvt Donald E. Brown, South Heren, MI. Died in plane crash at T.A.A.F. on May 19, 1946.

LT James B. Brown, Los Angeles, CA. Died on June 6, 1944 near Frosinone, Italy.

LT Roger B. Brown, Glencoe, IL. Died on June 14, 1944 in Italy while taking transition training.

LT Samuel Bruce, 319 12th Street, Seattle, WA. Died in battle of Anzio Beachhead on January 28, 1944.

LT James A. Calhoun, Bridgeport, CT. Reported missing on strafing mission in Sept 1944.

LT John H. Chavis, 324 Tarboro Street, Raleigh, NC. Spun into the Adriatic Sea.

CPT Arnold Cisco, 6049 Eberhart Ave., Chicago, IL. Died in plane crash at T.A.A.F. on May 19, 1946.

LT George Cisco, 1129 Highland Ave., Alton, IL. Died in plane crash at T.A.A.F.

LT James Coleman, Detroit, MI. Died shortly after VE-Day while practicing dive bombing in Italy.

T/Sgt. Coleman Conley, Birmingham, AL. Died on May 19, 1946 at Tuskegee in a plane crash.

LT Harry Jay Daniels, 1840 S. Keystone Ave., Indianapolis, IN. Missing in action on coastal patrol on February 23, 1944.

CPT John Daniels, Chicago, IL. Died on May 19, 1946 at T.A.A.F.

LT Luther R. Davenport, Loving, GA. Died at Oneida, TN in a plane crash.

CPT Alfonso Davis, 2118 North 29th Street, Omaha, NE. Killed in plane crash in Italy.

LT Richard Davis, Ft Valley, GA. Died in plane crash at T.A.A.F. on January 30, 1943.

Cadet Richard A. Dawson, 122 Shenandoa Street, San Antonio, TX. Died in training at T.A.A.F. on June 8, 1942.

LT Charles Warren Dickerson, 26 Winthrop Ave., New Rochelle, NY. Died in plane crash at Selfridge Field, MI.

LT Othel Dickson, 1430 O'Farrel Street, San Francisco, CA. Died in plane crash at Ramitelli, Italy on June 28,1944.

LT Alwayne Dunlap, Washington, DC. Died in battle of Anzio Beachhead.

LT Jerome Edwards, 902 Main Street, Steubenville, OH. Died in crash at Oscoda, MI.

LT Spurgeon Ellington, 1302 N. Highland Ave., Winston-Salem, NC. Died in plane crash near Atlanta, GA. on Dec. 10, 1945.

LT Maurice V. Esters, Box 17, Webster City, IA. Died in Italy in June 1944.

LT William J. Faulkner, Nashville, TN. Failed to return from mission over Southeastern Austria on November 7, 1944.

LT Samuel J. Foreman, Tulsa, OK. Reported missing in action over Europe.

LT Frederick D. Funderburg 191 18th Ave., Monticello, GA. Reported missing in bad weather over Linz, Austria, December 1944.

LT Howard C. Gamble, Charleston, WV. Reported missing over Europe.

LT Morris E. Gant, Chicago, IL. Failed to return from mission over the Adriatic Sea. Complained of gas shortage.

LT Clemenceau Givings, 100 E. Leigh Street, Richmond, VA. Killed in Italy on March 18,1944.

LT Walter S. Gladden, Providence, RI (Ground Officer). Killed at Lynchburg, Va.

LT Joseph E. Gordon, Brooklyn, NY. Died in the invasion of Southern France on August 12,1944.

F/O Robert A. Gordon, 26 South Cedar Street, Troy, OH. Died in plane crash at T.A.A.F. on May 19, 1946.

LT Milton R. Hall, 2324 West 9th Street, Owensboro, KY. Died in plane crash at Lockbourne, OH, on Sept. 18, 1947.

LT Richard W. Hall, Albany, GA. Died in plane crash near Atlanta, Georgia on Dec. 10, 1945.

LT Maceo Harris, 18 Lattimore Court, Boston, MA. Missing in action October 1944.

F/O Thomas L. Hawkins, Glen Ridge, NJ. Died March 7,1945 in Italy.

LT George Kenneth Hayes, 377 La Salle Ave., Los Angeles, CA. Died in plane crash near Birmingham, AL. on June 12, 1944.

LT Earl Highbaugh, 540 Udell Street, Indianapolis, IN. Collided near Foggia with plane piloted by LT Ramsey.

LT William E. Hill, 81 Boom Street, Narragansett, RI. Died at Oscoda, Michigan on Nov. 22,1943.

LT Nathaniel M. Hill, Washington, DC. Spun into Lake Huron near Oscoda, MI on June 16,1943.

LT Wendell W. Hochaday, 300 Whitehead Ave., Norfolk, VA. Died strafing in Munich area about Feb. 25, 1945.

LT Tommy Hood. Died when struck tree while strafing in Southern Germany.

LT Stephen Hotesse, New York City. Died in plane crash near Madison, KY.

F/O Sylvester H. Hurd, Jr., 102 138th Place, East Chicago, IL. Died in plane crash at Milstead, AL on April 26, 1946.

LT Oscar D. Hutton, Jr., Chicago, IL. Died when his plane was hit by belly tank dropped from another plane while on mission, July 18, 1944.

Cadet Horace E. Joseph, Jamaica, NY. Died in plane crash near Tuskegee Air Base in Sept 1943.

LT Wellington G. Irving, 299 Central Ave., Belzuni, MS. Lost in Kemton area on July 18, 1944.

LT Spencer P. Isabelle, 6250 Bromley Ave., Oakland, CA. Died at T.A.A.F. November 1945.

LT Samuel Jefferson, 2813 Ave. M, Galveston, TX. Died in action off coast of Corsica on June 22,1944.

LT Charles B. Johnson, 1544 North Gratz Street, Philadelphia, PA. Died in action off coast of Corsica on June 22, 1944.

LT Langdon E. Johnson, Rand, WV. Failed to return from mission to Southern France, August 12,1944.

LT Edgar Jones, New York City. Died on March 28,1944 in Italy.

F/O Robert M. Johnson, Pittsburgh, PA. Killed at Waterboro, KY. Collided with a B-24.

LT Oscar Kenny, P. O. Box 248 Tuskegee Institute, AL. Died in plane crash at T.A.A.F. on July 9, 1943.

LT Earl Eugene King, 16 Center Street, Bessemer, AL. Died in Martin Lake, Ala March 24,1943.

LT Edward Laird, 3229 7th Ave., Brighton, AL. Crashed on take off in Italy on June 28,1944.

LT Allen Lane, 205 Cherry Street, Demopolis, AL. Died on cross-country flight from Lockbourne, OH.

LT Carrol N. Langston, Jr., 6317 Lawrence Ave., Chicago, IL. Lost in Adriatic Sea on June 9, 1944.

CPT Erwin Lawrence, Cleveland, OH. Died Oct. 4, 1944 on mission to Athens, Greece.

LT Samuel Leftenant, Amityville, NY. Died in plane collision over Russian-held territory on April 12, 1945.

CPT Walter I. Lawson, Chancellor, VA. Died in 29 crash in Calif. in Feb. 1952.

LT Wayne Leggins, 242 East College Ave., Springfield, OH. Died in Italy in May 1944.

LT Walter P. Manning, 346 N. 42nd Street, Philadelphia, PA. Shot down over Vienna.

LT Andrew D. Marshall, 433 Salisburg Street, Wadesboro, NC. Missing in action over Greece in Dec. 1944.

LT Otis E. Marshall, 1439 Lippert Rd., N. E., Canton, OH. Died in plane crash at T.A.A.F. in Nov. 1945.

MAJ Harold Martin, Washington, DC. Killed near Reidsville, NC on March 23,1945.

LT Faythe A. McGinnis, 509 Hamp Street, Muskogee, OK. Died at Tuskegee on Sept. 12, 1942. Plane spun into Soughalachoe Creek, AL.

LT Vincent Jay Mason, 162 Taylor Street, Orange, NJ. Died at Selfridge Field, MI on March 17, 1944. Plane struck a garage and burst into flames.

LT George McCrumby, 806 Twonply Street, Ft. Wayne, TX. Failed to return to base after mission to Geata Point on Feb. 29, 1944.

LT Cornelius May, Nashville, TN. Died at Selfridge Field.

LT James McCullin, 3701 Enright Ave., St. Louis, MO. Died in battle of Pantelleria, July 1943.

A/C Rayrnond C. McEwen, 2439 Vincennes Street, Chicago IL. Died at T.A.F. Oct. 5, 1944.

LT Paul Mitchell, 808 Howard Rd. S. E., Washington, DC. Collided with LT Sam Bruce, Aug 1943.

LT Frank H. Moody, 93 E. 55th Street, Los Angeles, CA. Spun into Lake Huron, MI, April 1944.

LT Roland W. Moody, 187 Fayeweather Street, Cambridge, MA. Burned to death in tent in Italy when tank fell from a plane spraying the area for mosquitoes.

LT John Morgan, Cartersville, GA. Died in Italy, Jan. 1944.

LT Sidney Mosely, 1518 42nd Street, Norfolk, VA. Died at T.A.A.F. May 10,1943.

LT Andrew Maples, Jr., Box 403 Orange, VA. Missing over Italy June 26,1944.

CPT Mac Ross, Dayton, OH. Died in plane crash in Italy on July 12, 1944.

LT Neal Nelson, Amarillo, TX. Missing in Rome area on May 11, 1944.

LT Elton H. Nightengale, Tuskegee, AL. Missing in action on Nov. 27,1944.

LT Raymond F. Noches, Junction City, KS. Died on routine flight to Alabama in B-25.

LT Leland H. Pennington, Rochester, NY. Failed to return from mission to Yugoslavia. Suffered with appendicitis may have been cause of death.

LT Francis B. Peoples, 308 Rockspring Street, Henderson, NC. Died at Tuskegee on April 27, 1944.

LT Harvey N. Pinkney, Baltimore, MD. Died in plane collision at Lockbourne, Ohio in August 1948.

LT James Polkinghorne, Pensacola, FL. Missing in action on May 4, 1944.

LT Henry Pollard, 225 Madison Street, Buffalo, NY. Crashed near the Capodichino Airbase in Italy on May 22, 1944.

LT Driscoll Ponder, Chicago, IL. Failed to return from a mission; later returned to Group.

LT John H. Prowell, Jr., Lewisburg, AL. Missing in action near Salerno on May 24, 1944.

CPT Wendell O. Pruitt, 4569 Garfield Ave., St Louis, MO. Died in plane crash at Tuskegee in April 1945.

F/O Glen W. Pulliam (Navigator), Los Angeles, CA. Died in plane crash at Madison, KY.

LT Leon Purchase, 164 West 141st Street, New York City. Killed at Selfridge Field, MI on Nov. 19, 1943.

LT James C. Ramsey, Augusta, GA. Died in action near Foggia, Italy.

F/O Nathaniel Rayburg, Washington, DC. Killed at Selfridge Field, Mich. in Dec. 1943.

LT Emory Robbins, 738 Harguette Road, Chicago, IL. Missing in action in Italy.

LT Ronald Reeves, 2106 I Street, N. E., Washington, DC. Failed to return from a mission.

LT Robert C. Robinson, Asheville, NC. Failed to return from Yugoslavia on June 10,1944.

LT Cornelius Rogers, Chicago, IL. Missing on a mission to Yugoslavia on June 10,1944.

LT Roger Romine, 829 36th Street, Oakland, CA. Died in plane collision in Italy on Nov. 16, 1944.

LT Leon Roberts, 400 Murphy & McGee Street, Pritchard, AL. Died in action in Italy on July 11, 1944.

LT Paul C. Simmons, Detroit, Michigan. Killed at Selfridge Field, MI in Dec. 1943 when plane threw a rod.

LT Alfonso Simmons, Munerief Rd., Jacksonville, FL. Died in action on March 3,1945 in Northern Italy.

LT Sidat Singh, Washington, DC. Killed at Oscoda, MI on March 25, 1943.

LT John S. Sloan, 2817 South 6th Street, Louisville, KY. Shot down by flak on March 30, 1944 while dive bombing in the Cassino area, but survived.

LT Arnett Stark, Jr., Los Angeles, CA. Shot down by enemy plane on March 25, 1945.

F/O Charles W. Stephens, Monroeville, AL. Died in plane crash near Reidsville, NC.

LT Thomas C. Street, Springfield, NJ. Lost when plane spun into Adriatic Sea on March 23, 1945.

A/C Ross Stewart, Jr., Johnston, PA. Killed at T.A.A.F. with LT Brothers in May 1943.

LT Nathaniel C. Stewart, Philadelphia, PA. Injured at Selfridge Field, Michigan in Jan. 1944.

LT Roosevelt Stigger, 346 Damon Street, Jackson, MI. Lost on mission over the Adriatic Sea

LT Norvell Stoudmire, 4448 Ferdinand Ave., St Louis, MO. Died on March 31, 1944 when plane crashed into surf a few yards from shore in Italy.

LT John W. Squires, St Louis, Missouri. Killed near Pisa, Italy while buzzing the 92nd Division shortly after VE-Day.

Pvt. Reginald V. Smith, Ahoskie, NC. Killed at T.A.A.F. in plane crash.

LT Elmer Taylor, Pittsburgh, PA. Killed in Italy on June 2, 1944

CPT Edward M. Thomas, Chicago, IL. Killed at T.A.A.F. on May 19, 1946.

A/C Cleodis V. Todd, Berkeley, CA. Killed at T.A.A.F. in July 1944.

CPT Edward Toppins, San Francisco, CA. Reported died in plane crash in California.

CPT Robert Tresville, 6502 Musgrove Street, Germantown, PA. Missing in action on June 20,1944.

MAJ Andrew Turner, 1000 Westford Place N. E., Washington, DC. Killed at Lockbourne, Ohio on Sept. 18, 1947.

Pvt Edward N. Thompson, Miami, FL. Killed with CPT Pruitt at T.A.A.F. on April 15, 1945.

LT William Walker, Suffolk, Va. Killed at Selfridge Field, MI in 1943.

LT Johnson C. Wells, 44 Pine Street, Buffalo, NY. Killed at Selfridge Field, MI in Oct. 1943.

LT Walter Westmoreland, 375 Cain Street, N. E., Atlanta, GA. Shot down strafing near Lake Balaton on Oct. 13, 1944.

LT Leonard R. Willette, Belleville, NJ. Failed to return from mission over Germany on Sept. 22,1944.

LT Sherman White, Montgomery, AL. Killed in Italy on July 2, 1943.

LT LeRoy Williams, Roanoke, VA. Killed in collision with plane piloted by LT (Wild Bill) Walker in Nov. 1943.

Sgt Eli B. Williams, 911 9th Ave., Middleton, OH. Died in crash Sept 27, 1944 while flying with LT Luther Cartwright.

LT William F. Williams, Jr., 319-E. 121 Street, Cleveland, OH. Missing in action on July 21, 1944.

LT Robert H. Wiggins, Elmsford, NY. Killed in March 1945 on flight over the Adriatic Sea.

LT Frank N. Wright, 121 Cobat Ave., Elmsford, NY. Killed in March 1945 on mission over Europe.

LT James W. Wright, 70 Sylvania Ave., Pittsburgh, PA.

LT Deryl Wyatt, 405 South 14th Street, Independence, KS. Killed in Italy on April 17, 1944.

LT Albert L. Young, 590 South Wellington Street, Memphis, TN. Died in Italy when tried to land with an extra gas tank. Plane burst into flames.

LT Carl J. Woods, Box 177 Mars, PA. Killed in Italy.

Pvt Euclid R. Montgomery, Chicago, IL. Killed at T.A.A.P. on May 19, 1946.

MAJ William T. Mattison, Conway, AR and 2616 Park Place N. W., Washington, DC. Killed in plane crash near Toledo, OH on Jan. 28, 1951.

LT Ferrier H. White. Died April 15, 1945, Adriatic Sea near Ramitelli Air Force Base, Italy.

CPT Albert Manning, 435 19th Street, N. E., Washington, DC and Hartsville, SC. Killed in plane crash near Toledo, OH on Jan. 28, 1951.

A/C Judson West, Roxbury, MA. Killed at T.A.A.F. in Jan. 1944.

CPT George E. Gray, 809 McDowell St., Welch, WV and 637 Keefer Pl. N. W., Washington, DC. Missing in action in battle of Korea. Failed to return from a strafing in enemy territory on April 5, 1951.

S/Sgt Kenneth Austin. Killed in an F-82 jet plane at the National Fighter Gunnery Meet in May 1949.

SPECIAL ORDERS NO. 85
1 April, 1943
E-X-T-R-A-C-T

1. The 99th Fighter Sq with assigned Units (Personnel listed) are trfd fr this sta TAFS Tuskegee Ala to Camp Shanks NY and WP threto o/a April 3, 1943 reporting on arrival to the CO thereat for dy. Change of sta is permanent:

The movement of personnel of Units 2266 A, B & C, 99th Fighter Sq. AAF Serv Dot #99, Crd Dct (Avn) # 99, will be accomplished as indicated below:

Auth: Confidential Ltr 3AF 370(1-28-43) Hq 3 AF dtd Jan 31, 1943 Subject: "Movement Orders, Shipment 2288" and Secret Codo Message Hq 3 AF dtd Mar 26, 1943:

<u>BY GOVERNMENT RAIL TRANSPORTATION</u>

LTC BENJAMIN O DAVIS JR
CPT GOERGE S ROBERTS
1LT JAMES L JOHNSON JR
1LT GEORGE E PETTROSS
2LT GOERGE R CURRIE
CPT LEMUEL R CUSTIS
1LT HERBERT V CLARK
2LT WILLIE H FULLER
2LT LOUIS R PURNELL
1LT CLARENCE C JAMISON
1LT SIDNEY P BROOKS
2LT WILLIE ASHLEY JR
2LT JOHN W ROGERS
1LT CHARLES B AHLL
2LT GEORGE R BOLLING
1LT WILLIAM A CAMPBELL
2LT JAMES L MCCULLIN
CPT HAYDEN C JOHNSON
CPT MAURICE E JOHNSON
1LT HENRY M LETCHER
1LT BERNARD S PROCTOR
1LT ERWIN B LAWRENCE
1LT JAMES T WILEY
1LT ALLEN G LANE
2LT PAUL O MITCHELL
2LT GRAHAM SMITH
1LT CHARLES W DRYDEN
1LT LEE RAYFORD
2LT LEON C ROBERTS
2LT SPANN WATSON
2LT WALTER I LAWSON
2LT SAMUEL M BRUCE
1LT JAMES B KNIGHTEN
1LT SHERMAN W WHITE

FIRST PLATOON

1LT WILLIAM R TOHMPSON

MSG Newman, Asa V
SGT Turner, John H
PFC Anderson, Lucious
SGT Beavers, Morris S
CPL Wilson, Elmer H
CPL Singleton, Robert E
PVT Brown, Ernest
PVT Boisseau, Lawrence H
CPL Morgan, Amos
PVT Pickraum, Howard T
CPL Scruggs, Raymond
PFC Forche, Albert
PVT Bacon, Russell J
PFC Morris, Thomas
PVT Wright, Lawrence J
CPL Benson, William
CPL Pryor, Edward R
CPL Hammond, Nehemish
SGT Coleman, Elijah
CPL Peterson, Thomas
CPL Sharpe, Irvin
CPL Culp, Elliot C
TGT Jackson, James A
SGT Jordan, Oscar
SGT Morrison, William L
SGT Downs, Thomas
PVT McDonald, Charles E
SGT Reynolds, Russell W
PVT O'Steen, James E
SGT Archer, Fred
PFC Elliott, Kenneth E
CPL Alexander, Wardell P
CPL Grooms, George
CPL Ables, Robert H
SGT Smith, John L
CPL Mayers, Joseph F
SGT Chase, John M
PFC Blackwell, Redell
CPL Spooner, Joseph H
CPL Luck, John L
PFC Parks, Edward C
CPL Harding, Hiram M
CPL Brewer, Leonard R
SGT Gill, Thomas III
SGT Duncan, Leon N
SGT Charman, David B
SGT Burnley, Ralph A
SGT Butler, Charles M
PFC Brown, Alfred
SGT Laguna, Henry
CPL Grier, Arbor L
CPL Bigolow, Hubert
SGT Clark, Stocks
PFC Mungor, Fred
CPL Robinson, Shirley C
SGT Jordan, Stanley D
SGT Monroe, Randolph J

SECOND PLATOON

1LT DUDLEY W. STEVENSON

SGT Hordeaux, Clovis A
CPL Thurston, Reuben
SGT Davis, Charles
CPL Carter, Harold S
PVT Atkinson, James A
SGT Dancy, Isaiah
SGT Boone, Alexton S Jr
CPL Howard, Robert T Jr
CPL Hardesty, Herbert
CPL Gayles, Augustus W
SGT Holmes, Leo S
SGT Gail, George C
SGT Boykin, Lewmon H
CPL Reid, Sandy G
SGT Fisher, Morris T
CPL Hileygar, James
SGT Hinds, Charles M
CPL Fraser, Clarence E
CPL Brittian, Joseph
SGT Fawkes, William F
CPL Jackson, John J
CPL Bautista, Julio R
PFC Banks, Ernest H
SGT Simpson, William G
CPL Bullen, Eric A
SGT Swift, Nathan S
PVT Minon, Fred D
PVT Johnson, Jesse H
SGT Nichols, Herbert H
CPL Givens, Jackson
PVT Brown, Kermit E
CPL Jordan, Joseph T
SGT Goodson, Herbert L
SGT Smith, Paul E

THIRD PLATOON

1LT HERBERT E CARTER

SGT Crawford, Alexander
SGT Danby, Ellsworth H
SGT Kennedy, Charles W
SGT Stewart, Waddell H
SGT Watson, Vernon A
SGT Lovett, Julius G
SGT Grimes, Lionel E
SGT Hall, William C
SGT Pickett, Eugene
SGT Vaughn, Wiseamon
SGT Redmond, William N
CPL Gilliard, Robert A
SGT Moss, Paul E
SGT Gunn, Robert L
SGT Howard, Joseph C Jr
SGT McDowell, Daniel Q
SGT Williams, James
SGT Ransey, Jesse B
SGT Connally, Norris L
SGT Gary, James H R

SGT Bowden, Charles M
SGT Woodson, William D
SGT Lane, William B
SGT Combs, Thomas E
SGT Hull, Stennie C
CPL Rodgers, Elmer Jr
SGT McGuthrie, James O
SGT Johns, Milton E
SGT Searcy, Charles A
SGT Parks, Samuel F
SGT Barrow, Robert E
SGT Calland, Leonard A
SGT Cousins, Cecil A
CPL Freeman, Kenneth C
SGT Handy, James O Jr
SGT Edwards, McCary L
SGT Clarke, Clarence W
SGT Mitchell, Rufus C
SGT Cobb, William F
SGT Jones, Herman
SGT White, William P
SGT Smith, Charles T
SGT Hebb, George B
PVT Davis, Earvie
PVT Chapman, Robert J
PVT Lockhart, James A
SGT Warner, William O
CPL Robinson, James
SGT Hensley, Charles D
SGT Dillard, Earl D
SGT Graham, William T
SGT Lucas, Elliot W
SGT Helms, Robert L
SGT Hargrave, John L
SGT Corbin, Percy C
SGT Thomas, Abraham
SGT Dishman, Clarence S
SGT Jackson, James A
SGT Curl, Cecil P
SGT Garner, Glenn A
SGT Bills, Thomas J
SGT Qunder, Donald V
SGT Powers, Tom
SGT Boyer, Charles H
PVT Huff, Fluellen
SGT Accoo, William H
SGT Anderson, Lawrence A
SGT Perkins, Benjamin C Jr
SGT Short, Paul L
SGT Johnson, George D
CPL Taylor, Joseph A
CPL Kimes, Clarence
CPL Dunlap, Richard D
SGT Feaster, Charles P

FOURTH PLATOON

1LT CORNELIUS VINCENT JR

SGT Gary, Percy C
SGT Etheridge, Will
SGT Braithwaite, Oswald
PVT Shuford, Carlon
SGT Buchannon, Alex
CPL Lewis, Melvin J
SGT Jatt, Edsel A
PVT Gooding, Arthur L
SGT Anderson, James R Jr
SGT Carter, Carl
SGT Davis, Stephen M
CPL Rockett, Orville O

CPL Warren, Automo
PVT Cunningham, Howard
CPL Benniefield, Charles
SGT Jones, John E Jr
SGT Nelson, Herbert W
SGT Crumbley, Robert
CPL Watkins, Napoleon B
PFC Theriot, Warren
SGT Hart, Edgar N
PFC Teague, Roy
CPL Campbell, Donald G
SGT Davis, Joseph Jr
SGT McPhatter, Tearchie
SGT Anderson, Professor
CPL Crieghton, Daniel R
SGT Smith, Roscoe B
CPL Searly, Julius A
SGT Fraley, Herman L
SGT Marshall, Robert W
CPL Sawyer, Samuel W
SGT Watts, Cleveland H
CPL Williams, Jimmie L
CPL Brooks, Robert L
SGT O'Neal, James H
SGT Weir, Irvin
PVT Coleman, Herman
SGT Byron, Cyril O
PFC Sams, Samuel Jr
SGT Alexander, John P
PVT Jones, James W
CPL Pearl, Wilbur E
PFC Griffin, Wilmon
PVT Newsome, Robert
CPL McKinney, Wallace W
SGT Johnston, Otho L
CPL William, Alston
CPL McLeese, John C
CPL Ingram, Charles P
SGT Mofan, Robert
PFC Carriers, Aron
SGT Coiés, Leon W
PFC Quinonez, Nicholas P
PVT Jones, William J
CPL Bird, Raymond E
SGT Abrams, James
CPL DeGroat, John H
CPL Williams, Arthur T
SGT Wilson, Richard
SGT Bowden, Herman B
PVT Smith, Joseph B
SGT Thomas, Marshall Jr
CPL Johnson, Joseph B
CPL Roberts, Matthew
SGT Henderson, Samuel W
SGT Young, William H
SGT Stocker, Stnaley E
CPL Thompson, Edward N
SGT Coates, Clarence E Jr
PFC Jackson, Rubie
CPL Jackson, George W
SGT LaFleur, Wendell D
SGT Acree, Elmer R
SGT Harris, John H
PFC Carruth, Ceazer
PVT Donaldson, Clarence W
CPL Bertrand, Peter C

A.A.F. SERVICE DETACHMENT #99

CPT ELMER D. JONES JR.
1LT THOMAS N. MALONE JR.

FIFTH PLATOON

SGT Minor, Charles D
SGT Holmes, Hugh H
SGT Wormely, David N
SGT Devall, Leslie H
SGT Mumford, Nathan
SGT O'Neal, Harold
SGT Scott, Robert O
SGT Vaughn, Walter H
CPL Randolph, John J
CPL Squires, Fitz A
PFC Bryant, Richard
PFC Graham, Brew O
PFC Laguna, John M
PVT Cain, Harvey
PVT Loggins, Anron B
PVT Trollinger, Richard E
SGT Surcey, William S
SGT Nelson, Earnest F
SGT Brown, Edgar T
SGT Hartgrove, Edward M
SGT Norman, Andra
SGT Phillips, Eddie
SGT Tucker, Perry M
CPL Borders, John V
CPL Roulette, Roland R
PFC Boston, Herbert H
PFC Bush, Edward
PFC Green, James E
PFC Thompson, Lloyd F
PVT Hill, William
PVT Skinner, Louis W
PVT Young, John W

ORDNANCE DEDATHMENT (AVN) #99

2LT JAMES O FREEMAN JR

SGT Irving, Robert H
SGT Girardeau, English
SGT Dozier, Edward I
CPL Sampler, Marion

. . .

By order of LTC PARRISH:

CLYDE H BYNUM,
CPT, A.C.,
Adjutant

THE MEN—THE RECORDS
THE ORIGINAL 99th FIGHTER SQUADRON

Commanding Officer: LTC Benjamin O. Davis, Jr., Washington, DC (Pilot)
Operation Officer: CPT George Spencer Roberts, Fairmount, WV (Pilot)
Assistant Operation Officer: LT Erwin B. Lawrence, Cleveland, OH (Pilot)
Armament Officer: LT William R. Thompson, Pittsburgh, PA
Executive Officer: LT Henry M. Letcher, Jr., Washington, DC
Engineering Officer: LT Herbert Carter, Natchez, MS
Provost Marshal & Intelligence Officer: LT Cornelius Vincent, Boston
Ordnance Officer: LT George R. Curri, Los Angeles, CA
Communication Officer: LT Dudley W. Stevenson, Washington, DC
Assistant Intelligence Officer: LT James L. Johnson, Washington, DC
Adjutant: LT Bernard Proctor, Philadelphia, PA
Adjutant: CPT Hayden C. Johnson, Washington, DC
Flight Surgeon: CPT Maurice C Johnson, Washington, DC
Supply Officer: LT Benote H. Wimp, Chicago, IL
Personnel Adjutant: LT George Pettross, Washington, DC
Commanding Officer of service group attached to 99th: CPT Elmer D. Jones, Washington, DC
Supply Officer of service group: LT Thomas Malone, Detroit, MI

Pilots:

LT Lemuel R Custis, Hartford, CT
LT Clarence Jamison, Cleveland, OH
LT William A. Campbell, Tuskegee Institute, AL
LT Charles B. Hall, Brazil, IN
LT Paul G. Mitchell, Washington, DC
LT Sidney P. Brooks, Cleveland, OH
LT John W. Rogers, Chicago, IL
LT Walter I. Lawson, Newton, VA
LT James B. Knighten, Tulsa, OK
LT Willie Ashley, Jr., Sumter, SC
LT George R. Bolling, Phoebus, VA
LT Graham Smith, Ahoskie, NC
LT Louis R. Purnell, Snowhill, MD
LT James Wiley, Pittsburgh, PA
LT Willie H. Fuller, Tarboro, NC
LT Spann Watson, Hackensack, NJ
LT Lee Rayford, Ardwick, MD
LT James McCullin, St. Louis, MO
LT Sherman White, Montgomery, AL
LT Samuel Bruce, Seattle, WA
LT Leon Roberts, Pritchard, AL
LT Carter V. Herbert, Natchez, MS.
LT Charles Dryden, New York City, NY
LT Allen Lane, Demopolis, AL

Enlisted Men Airplane Mechanics:

M/Sgt Clarence W. Clarke
S/Sgt Charles Hensley
T/Sgt Ralph E. Jackson
Sgt Leon Coles
S/Sgt Milton R. Brooks
S/Sgt Leonard Calland
S/Sgt Robert J. Chapman
M/Sgt C. A. Bordeux
S/Sgt Thomas E. Combs
Sgt Robert Howard
S/Sgt James Gary, Jr.
S/Sgt Lewmon Boykin
S/Sgt Herman Jones
S/Sgt Thomas Gill
S/Sgt Elliott W. Lucas
Sgt Alexton Boone, Jr.
Sgt Julius C. Lovett
Sgt James A. Jackson
Corp James A. Lockhart
S/Sgt James Handy
Corp Leonard Brower
S/Sgt Alexander Crawford
S/Sgt Ellworth H. Dansby
S/Sgt Earl D. Dillard
S/Sgt Charles P. Feaster
S/Sgt Glenn A. Garner
T/Sgt James Anderson, Jr.
Corp John Turner
S/Sgt Charles Davis
Sgt Charles Ingram
S/Sgt Joseph T. Hamilton
S/Sgt Robert L. Smith
S/Sgt William O. Warner
Corp Paul E. Moss
(Armament)
(Parachute Rigger)

ORIGINAL 332nd FIGHTER GROUP

I HEADQUARTERS

Davis, Jr., Benjamin O., LTC, AC, Commanding
Beck, Franklin B., CPT, DC, Dental Service
Brooks, Nelson S., CPT, AC, Executive
Marchbanks, Vance N., Jr., CPT, MC, Medical (Flight Surgeon)
Perry, Cyrus W., CPT, CC, Chaplain
Banks, William A., 1st Lt., AC
Christmas, Joseph A., 1st Lt., AC
Harvey, Danzal T., 1st Lt, AC
Leonard, Wilmore B., 1st Lt., AC
McDaniel, Armour G., 1st Lt., AC
Money, Thomas J., 1st Lt, AC, Adjutant Personnel
Pitts, Robert G., 1st Lt., AC
Purnell, Louis R., 1st Lt., AC
Richardson, Roosevelt, 1st Lt, AC
Ross, Mac, 1st Lt, AC, Group Operation
Scurlock, Robert S., 1st Lt., AC
Ware, Ray B., 1st Lt, AC
Kelly, Jr., William A., 2nd Lt, AC
Richardson, Virgil J., 2nd Lt, AC
Simmons, Edward G., 2nd Lt, AC
Townsend, Prentice A., 2nd Lt., Ord., Ordnance
Womack, William M., 2nd Lt., AC
Edghill, Edward A., WOJO, AUS

OFFICERS: 100th Fighter Squadron
Anderson, Harry B., CPT, MC
Tresville, Robert B., CPT, AC, Commanding
Caesar, Richard C., 1st Lt, AC
Crockett, Woodrow W., 1st Lt, AC
Dickson, Lawrence E., 1st Lt, AC
Exum, Perq J., 1st Lt, Ord.
Jackson, Melvin T., 1st Lt, AC
Johnson, Morris T., 1st Lt, AC, Executive
Lumpkin, Theodore G., 1st Lt, AC

Mattison, William T., 1st Lt, AC, Asst. Operation
Pullam, Richard C., 1st Lt., AC
Ouick, John B., 1st Lt, AC, Chaplain
Turner, Andrew D., 1st Lt, AC, Operation
Briggs, John F., 2nd Lt, AC
Bowman, Henry P., 2nd Lt., AC
Curtis, Samuel L, 2nd Lt, AC
Ellington, Spurgeon N., 2nd Lt, AC
Givings, Clemenceau, 2nd Lt, AC
Hopkins, Moses, 2nd Lt, AC
Hall, Richard W., 2nd Lt, AC
Holsclaw, Jack D., 2nd Lt, AC
Jefferson, Samuel, 2nd Lt, AC
Johnson, Langdon E., 2nd Lt., AC
McCreary, Walter L., 2nd Lt, AC
Moore, Theopolis D., 2nd Lt, AC
Morgan, Dempsey W., 2nd Lt, AC
Mosby, Milledge J., 2nd Lt, AC
Nelson, Robert H., Jr., 2nd Lt, AC
Norris, Lester S., 2nd Lt, AC
Palmer, Walter J. A., 2nd Lt, AC
Taylor, George A., 2nd Lt, AC
Steward, Lowell C., 2nd Lt, AC
Stoudmire, Norvell C., 2nd Lt, AC
Washington, Alexander, 2nd Lt, AC
Williams, Craig H., 2nd Lt., AC
Woods, Carrol S., 2nd Lt, AC
Woods, Williard L., 2nd Lt, AC
Wyatt, Deryl, 2nd Lt, AC
Wyatt, William C., 2nd Lt, AC

OFFICERS: 301st Fighter Squadron
Captains:
Debow, Charles H., AC, Commanding
1st Lts.:
Byrd, Paul F., AC, Weather Officer
Daniels, Roland H., AC, Executive
Downs, Walter M., AC

Elsberry, Joseph D., AC
Govan, Claude B., AC
Rayford, Lee, AC, Operation
Scott, Samuel C., AC
Maples, Andrew, Jr., AC
Polkinghorne, James R., AC
Prowell, John R, AC
Waugh, Bascom S., MC, Flight Surgeon
Wilson, Commie, AC
2nd Lts.:

Ballard, Alton F.	AC	Fuller, Samuel L.	AC
Browne, Gene C.	AC	Hatchett, Morris M.	AC
Cabiness, Marshall S.	AC	Jefferson, Lawrence	AC
Cisco, Arnold W.	AC	King, Robert L.	AC
Dooley, Lawrence C.	AC	Langston, Carroll N	AC
Dunne, Charles A.	AC	Leahr, John H.	AC
Esters, Maurice V.	AC	McFatridge, James	AC
Foreman, Walter T.	AC	Lewis, Joe A.	AC
Faulkner, William J.	AC	Penn, Starling B.	AC
Rogers, Cornelius G.	AC	Turner, Leonard F.	AC
Sawyer, Harold E.	AC	Walker, Frank D.	AC
Taylor, Paulus C.	AC	Wiggins, Robert H.	AC
Taylor, Ulysses S.	AC	Williams, William F	AC

OFFICERS: 302nd Squadron
Captains:
Maloney, Arnold H., MC, Flight Surgeon
1st Lts.:
Beverly, John R., AC
Brooks, Milton R., AC
Burton, Chester R., ORD
Bullock, Benjamin F., AC
Davis, Alfonso W., AC
Gleed, Edward C., AC, Commanding
Haywood, Vernon, AC
Pruitt, Wendell O., AC, Operation
Punch, Vernon E., AC
Sheppard, Harry A., AC

Spencer, Roy N., AC
Watson, Dudley N., AC
Weathers, Luke J., AC
2nd Lts.:

Adams, Paul	AC	Archer, Lee A.	AC
Blackwell, Hubron	AC	Bussey, Charles N.	AC
Conley, James M.	AC	Green, William W., Jr	AC
Gordon, Elmer L.	AC	Groves, Weldon K.	AC
Haley, George J.	AC	Hunter, Willie S.	AC
Hutchins, Freddie	AC	Johnson, Everette W	AC
Kirkpatrick, Felix	AC	Lincoln, Vernon B.	AC
McGee, Charles E.	AC	Melton, William R.	AC
Mohr, Dean B.	AC	Moulden, William	AC
Romine, Roger	AC	Smith, Edward N.	AC
Smith, Luther H., Jr	AC	Taylor, Elmer W.	AC
Walker, James A.	AC	Westmoreland, Walter	AC
Wilkins, Larry D.			

EXTRA OFFICER PERSONNEL

2nd Lt. George E. Gray	AC
2nd Lt Charles F. Jamerson	AC
2nd Lt. John S. Sloan	AC
2nd Lt. Alva N. Temple	AC
2nd Lt. John Daniels	AC
2nd Lt John J. Suggs	AC
2nd Lt. William R. Bartley	AC
2nd Lt. Harry J. Daniels	AC
2nd Lt Joseph P. Gomer	AC
2nd Lt. Wayne V. Liggins	AC
2nd Lt. Clayborne A. Lockett	AC

REPLACEMENT PILOTS:

Adkins, Rutherford H. 2Lt.,	AC
Alexander, Robert, 2nd Lt,	AC
Alsbrook, William, 2nd Lt.,	AC
Anders, Emet R. 2nd Lt.,	AC
Andrews, Emet R., 2nd Lt	AC

Barnes, Gentry E., 2nd Lt.,	AC
Bailey, Henry, 2nd Lt.,	AC
Bolden, Edgar L., 2nd Lt.,	AC
Bonan, Leonell H., 2nd Lt,	AC
Bradford, Clarence, 2nd Lt.,	AC
Bratcher, Everett A., 2nd Lt.,	AC
Brooks, Milton R., CPT,	AC
Caldwell, Langston H., 2Lt.,	AC
Carl, Carey, 2nd Lt,	AC
Chandler, Robert C., 2nd Lt.,	AC
Charlton, Terry J., 2nd Lt,	AC
Chineworth, Joseph, 2nd Lt,	AC
Coleman, James 2nd Lt.,	AC
Cooper, Charles W.	FO
Cousins, William 2nd Lt.,	AC
Cox, Hannibal, CPT,	AC
Cross, William, Jr., 2nd Lt.,	AC
Darnell, Charles E., 2nd Lt.,	AC
Dart, Clarence W., Jr., CPT,	AC
Edwards, John E., 2nd k.,	AC
Edwards, William H., 2nd Lt.,	AC
Ellis, Carl F., 2nd Lt,	AC
Ellis, William, 2nd Lt.,	AC
Franklin, George E. 2nd Lt.,	AC
Fuller, Willie, 2nd Lt,	AC
Gaines, Thurston L., 2nd Lt,	AC
Garrison, Robert L., 2nd Lt,	AC
Glass, Robert H.	FO
Golden, Newman C., 2nd Lt.,	AC
Goodenough, Purnell J., 2Lt.,	AC
Gorham, Alfred M., 2Lt,	AC
Gould, Cornelius, 2nd Lt,	AC
Gray, Leo R., 2nd Lt.,	AC
Green, Paul I., 2nd Lt.,	AC
Greenlea, George B., 2nd Lt.,	AC
Harper, Samuel W., 2nd Lt.,	AC
Harris, Richard, 2nd Lt.,	AC
Halloman, William H., II, 2Lt	AC

Harder, Richard S., CPT,	AC
Hill, Charles A., Jr., 2nd Lt.,	AC
Hudson, Lincoln, 2nd Lt.,	AC
Isles, George, 2nd Lt.,	AC
Jackson, Frank A.	FO
Johnson, Conrad A., 2nd Lt.,	AC
Johnson, Robert C., 2nd Lt,	AC
Jones, Hubert, 2nd Lt.,	AC
Kimbrough, Benjamin R., 2Lt.	AC
Knighten, James B., 2nd Lt.,	AC
Lacy, Hezekiah, 2nd Lt.,	AC
Lawrence, Robert W., 2nd Lt.	AC
Lucas, Wendell, CPT,	AC
Lyles, John H., 2nd Lt.,	AC
Lyles, Payton H., 2nd Lt.,	AC
Lynch, George A., 2nd Lt,	AC
Lynch, Louis J., 2nd Lt,	AC
Mann, Hiram, 2nd Lt.,	AC
McCory, Felix M. 2nd Lt.,	AC
Merriweather, Elbert N., 2Lt,	AC
Mitchell, James, 2nd Lt.,	AC
Morris, Harold, 2nd Lt,	AC
Murdie, Robert J., 2nd Lt.,	AC
Newman, Christopher, 2nd Lt,	AC
O'Neal, Robert, 2nd Lt.,	AC
Oliphant, Clarence A., 2nd Lt	AC
Orduna, Ralph, 2nd Lt,	AC
Payne, Turner W., 2nd Lt,	AC
Pennington, Leland, 2nd Lt,	AC
Peoples, Henry R., 2nd Lt.,	AC
Pillows, Robert A., Jr., 2nd Lt	AC
Porter, John H., 2nd Lt,	AC
Rice, Price D., 2nd Lt,	AC
Robert, LeRoy, Jr., 2nd Lt,	AC
Robinson, Carroll, 2nd Lt,	AC
Robinson, Curtis, 2nd Lt,	AC
Ross, Washington D., 2nd Lt,	AC
Saunders, Pearlee, 2nd Lt.,	AC

Scales, Norman W., 2nd Lt., AC
Schell, Wyrian T., 2nd Lt, AC
Scott, Henry B., 2nd Lt, AC
Selden, Wiley W., 2nd Lt., AC
Sherrod, Earle S., Jr., 2nd Lt., AC
Simons, Richard A. 2nd Lt., AC
Smith, Eugene, 2nd Lt., AC
Spann, Calvin J., 2nd Lt., AC
Stanton, Charles R., 2nd Lt., AC
Stewart, Nathaniel C., 2nd Lt. AC
Tate, Charles W., 2nd Lt, AC
Thompson, Donald A. 2nd Lt. AC
Thompson, Reed E., 2nd Lt., AC
Thorpe, Richard E. 2nd Lt., AC
Verwayne, Peter C, 2nd Lt., AC
Washington, Samuel L., 2Lt, AC
Watts, Samuel, 2nd Lt, AC
Wheeler, Jimmie D., 2nd Lt., AC
White, Ferrier H. 2nd Lt., AC
White, Harold, 2nd Lt, AC
White, Joseph, 2nd Lt., AC
Whimey, Yenwith K., 2nd Lt., AC
Whittaker, Peter A., 2nd Lt. AC
Williams, Lawrence, 2nd Lt., AC
Williams, Robert W., 2nd Lt., AC
Wilson, Theodore A., 2nd Lt., AC
Wilson, Bertram W., Jr., 2Lt., AC
Wilson, James A., 2nd Lt., AC
Wilson, Myron, 2nd Lt., AC
Wright, Hiram, 2nd Lt., AC
Wright, Kenneth, 2nd Lt., AC
Young, Albert L., 2nd Lt., AC

TUSKEGEE ARMY AIR FIELD
Office of the Secretary
Tuskegee, AL

ROSTER OF GRADUATES Advanced Flying School 1942--1946 (Extracted from official Army Air Force documents).

CLASS SE-42-C Date of graduation: March 6, 1942

Benjamin O. Davis, Jr.	020146	CPT
Lemuel R. Custis	0441128	2LT
Charles DeBow	0441130	2LT
George S. Roberts	0441127	2LT
Mac Ross	0441129	2LT

CLASS SE-42-D Date of Graduation: April 29, 1942

Sidney P. Brooks	0789118	2LT
Charles W. Dryden	0789119	2LT
Clarence C. Jamison	0789120	2LT

CLASS SE-42-E Date of Graduation: May 20, 1942

James B. Knighten	0789449	2LT
George L. Knox	0789535	2LT
Lee Rayford	0789437	2LT
Sherman W. White	0789431	2LT

CLASS SE-42-F Date of Graduation: July 3, 1942

Willie Ashley	0789641	2LT
George R. Belling	0789961	2LT
William A. Campbell	0799453	2LT
Herbert E. Carter	0790454	2LT
Herbert V. Clark	0790455	2LT
Charles B. Hall	0790457	2LT
Allen G. Lane	0790458	2LT
Erwin B. Lawrence	0790460	2LT
Faythe A. McGinnis	0790462	2LT
Paul G. Mitchell	0790461	2LT
Louis R. Purnell	0790463	2LT
Graham Smith	0790465	2LT
Spann Watson	0790467	3d Lt.
James T. Wiley	0790469	2LT

CLASS SE-42-G Date Of Graduation: August 5, 1942

Richard Davis	0790935	2LT
Willie H. Fuller	0790934	2LT
Earl E. King	0790937	2LT
Walter E. Lawson	0791783	2LT
John W. McClure	0791538	2LT
Leon C. Roberts	0791539	2LT
John W. Roberts	0791540	2LT

CLASS SE-42-H Date of Graduation: September 6, 1942

Samuel W. Bruce	0792417	2LT
Richard C. Ceasar	0792418	2LT
Robert W. Diet	0792419	2LT
Joseph D. Elsberry	0792420	2LT
Wilmore B. Leonard	0792421	2LT
James L. McCullin	0792442	2LT
John H. Morgan	0792423	2LT
Henry B. Ferry	0792424	2LT
Edward L. Toppins	0792425	2LT

CLASS SE-42-I Date of Graduation: October 9, 1942

Marshall S. Cabiness	0792780	2LT
Elwood T. Driver	0792781	2LT
John A. Gibson	0792782	2LT
Nathaniel M. Hill	0792783	2LT
Herman A. Lawson	0792784	2LT
William T. Mattison	0792785	2LT
Price D. Rice	0792786	2LT
Andrew D. Turner	0792787	2LT

CLASS SE-42-J Date of Graduation: November 10, 1942

Howard L. Baugh	0793705	2LT
Terry J. Charlton	0793706	2LT
Jerome T. Edwards	0793707	2LT
Melvin T. Jackson	0793708	2LT

CLASS SE-42-K Date of Graduation: December 13, 1942

Edward C. Gleed	0794598	2LT

Milton T. Hall	0794599	2LT
Wendell O. Pruitt	0794600	2LT
Richard C. Pullam	0794601	2LT
Peter C. Verwayne	0794602	2LT
William H. Walker	0794603	2LT
Romeo L. Williams	0794604	2LT
Robert B. Tresville, Jr.	025761	2LT

CLASS SE-43-A Date of Graduation: January 14, 1943

Andrew Maples	0796264	2LT
George T. McCrumby	0796265	2LT
Armour G. McDaniel	0796266	2LT
Clinton B. Mills	0796267	2LT
Charles R. Stanton	0796268	2LT
Quitman C. Walker	0796269	2LT

CLASS SE-43-B Date of Graduation: February 16, 1943

Walter M. Downs	0797218	2LT
Claude E. Govan	0797219	2LT
William E. Graffin	0797220	2LT
James R. Pokinghorne	0797221	2LT
John H. Prowell	0797222	2LT
Roy M. Spencer	0797223	2LT
William H. Walker	0797225	2LT

CLASS SE-43-C Date of Graduation: March 25, 1943

Clarence W. Allen	0798941	2LT
LeRoy Bowman	0798942	2LT
Woodrow W. Crockett	0798943	2LT
Alfonso W. Davis	0798944	2LT
Lawrence E. Dickson	0798945	2LT
Alwayne M. Dunlap	0798946	2LT
Elmer L. Gordon	0798947	2LT
William M. Gordon	0798948	2LT
Charles F. Jamerson	0798949	2LT
Walter L. McCreary	0798950	2LT
Pearlee E. Sanders	0798951	2LT
Wilmeth W. Sidat-Singh	0798952	2LT

Lloyd G. Singletary	0798953	2LT

CLASS SE-43-D Date of Graduation: April 29, 1943

Paul Adams	0801160	2LT
Charles P. Bailey	0801161	2LT
James E. Brothers	0801162	2LT
James Y. Carter	0801163	2LT
Arnold W. Cisco	0801164	2LT
Wilson V. Eagleson	0801165	2LT
William J. Faulkner	0801166	2LT
Walter T. Foreman	0801167	2LT
Vernon V. Haywood	0801168	2LT
Heber C. Houston	0801170	2LT
Freddie E. Hutchins	0801171	2LT
Leonard M. Jackson	0801172	2LT
Sidney J. Moseley	0801173	2LT
Curtis C. Robinson	0801174	2LT
Harold E. Sawyer	0801175	2LT
Lewis C. Smith	0801176	2LT
Ulysses S. Taylor	0801177	2LT
Luke J. Weathers	0801178	2LT
Charles I. Williams	0801179	2LT

CLASS SE-43-E Date of Graduation: May 28, 1943

John L. Hamilton	0157607	2LT
John F. Briggs	0804546	2LT
Milton R. Brooks	0805477	2LT
Charles M. Bussey	0804548	2LT
Spurgeon N. Ellington	0804549	2LT
Maurice V. Esters	0804550	2LT
Clemenceau M. Givens	0804551	2LT
Joseph P. Gomer	0804552	2LT
George E. Gray	0804553	2LT
Langdon E. Johnson	0804554	2LT
Felix J. Kirkpatrick	0804555	2LT
Albert H. Manning	0804556	2LT
Oliver O. Miller	0804557	2LT
Dempsey W. Morgan	0804558	2LT

Harry A. Sheppard	0804559	2LT
Luther H. Smith	0804560	2LT
John J. Suggs	0804561	2LT
James A. Walker	0804562	2LT
Dudley M. Watson	0804563	2LT
Laurence D. Wilkins	0804564	2LT
Craig H. Williams	0804565	2LT

CLASSSE-43-F Date of Graduation: June 30, 1943

Milton R. Henry (SO-SC)	01636030	2LT
Robert R. Alexander	0805590	2LT
Alexander M. Bright	0805626	2LT
Weldon K. Groves	0805985	2LT
Herbert S. Harris	0806279	2LT
Richard H. Harris	0807096	2LT
Willie S. Hunter	0807097	2LT
Wilbert H. Johnson	0807098	2LT
Oscar A. Kenney	0807099	2LT
Hezekiah Lacy	0807100	2LT
Joe A. Lewis	0807101	2LT
Wayne V. Liggins	0807102	2LT
Charles E. McGee	0807103	2LT
Theopolis D. Moore	0807104	2LT
Walter J. Palmer	0807105	2LT
Virgil J. Richardson	0807107	2LT
Wiley W. Selden	0807108	2LT
John S. Sloan	0807109	2LT
Leonard F. Turner	0807110	2LT
Frank D. Walker	0807111	2LT
Johnson C. Wells	0807112	2LT
William G. Wilkerson	0807113	2LT
William F. Williams	0807114	2LT
Theodore A. Wilson	0807115	2LT

CLASS SE-43-G Date of Graduation: July 28, 1943

John Daniels	01106669	2LT
William B. Ellis	01637362	2LT
Lee A. Archer	0809236	2LT

Harry L. Bailey	0809237	2LT
William R. Bartley	0809238	2LT
Samuel L. Curtis	0809239	2LT
William W. Green, Jr.	0809240	2LT
George B. Breenlee, Jr.	0809241	2LT
Richard W. Hall	0809242	2LT
Jack D. Holsclaw	0809243	2LT
Daniel James, Jr.	0809244	2LT
John H. Leahr	0809245	2LT
Claybourne A. Lockett	0809246	2LT
James W. Mason	0809247	2LT
Eddie A. McLaurin	0809248	2LT
William R. Melton, Jr.	0809249	2LT
Robert H. Nelson, Jr.	0809250	2LT
Maurice R. Page	0809251	2LT
Cornelius G. Rogers	0809252	2LT
Edward M. Smith	0809253	2LT
Lowell C. Steward	0809254	2LT
Elmer W. Taylor	0809255	2LT
Alva N. Temple	0809256	2LT
Walter D. Westmoreland	0809257	2LT
Robert H. Wiggins	0809259	2LT
LeRoy S. Williams	0809260	2LT
Deryl Wyatt	0809261	2LT

HAITIAN AIR FORCE

Raymond Cassagnol	Unknown

CLASS SE-43-H Date of Graduation: August 30, 1943

Alton F. Ballard	0811173	2LT
Hubron R. Blackwell	0811193	2LT
Everett A. Bratchell	0811220	2LT
Harry J. Daniels	0811240	2LT
Andrew H. Doswell	0811246	2LT
Charles A. Dunne	0811277	2LT
Smith W. Green	0811280	2LT
William E. Hill	0811281	2LT
Lawrence B. Jefferson	0811282	2LT

Samuel Jafferson	0811283	2LT
Hubert L. Jones	0811284	2LT
William B. McClenic, Jr.	0811285	2LT
Sterling B. Penn	0811286	2LT
Leon Purchase	0811287	2LT
Roger Romine	0811288	2LT
Norvel Stoudmire	0811289	2LT
George A. Taylor	0811291	2LT
Charles W. Tate	0811290	2LT
Floyd A. Thompson	0811292	2LT
Carrol S. Woods	0811294	2LT
Willard L. Woods	0811295	2LT

HAITIAN Air Force

Alix Pasquet	None

CLASS,SE-43-I Date of Graduation: October 1, 1943

William N. Alsbrook	0814188	2LT
Cecil L. Browder	0814189	2LT
Gene Cole Browne	0814190	2LT
William Cross, Jr.	T61446	F/O
Purnell J. Goodenough,	0814191	2LT
George J. Haley	0814192	2LT
Maceo A. Harris, Jr.	0814193	2LT
Carl E. Johnson	0814194	2LT
Charles B. Johnson	0814195	2LT
Edgar L. Jones	0814196	2LT
Carroll N. Langston, Jr.	0814197	2LT
Cornelius F. May	0814198	2LT
Woodrow F. Morgan	0814199	2LT
Neal V. Nelson	0814200	2LT
Christopher W. Newman	0814201	2LT
Driscol B. Ponder	0814202	2LT
George M. Rhodes, Jr.	0814203	2LT
Washington D. Ross	0814204	2LT
Norman W. Scales	0814205	2LT
Henry B. Scott	0814206	2LT
Alphonso Simmons	0814207	2LT

Robert H. Smith	0814208	2LT
Edward Wilson Watkins	0814209	2LT

CLASS SE-43-J Date of Graduation: November 3, 1943

James B. Brown	0814825	2LT
Roger B. Brown	0814826	2LT
Herman R. Campbell, Jr.	0814041	2LT
Alfred Q. Carroll, Jr.	0814827	2LT
Clarence W. Dart	0814828	2LT
Charles W. Dickerson	0814829	2LT
Henri F. Fletcher	0814140	2LT
Ferry E. Hudson	0814818	2LT
Oscar D. Hutton	0814830	2LT
Haldane King	0814819	2LT
Edward Laird	0814831	2LT
Ivey L. Leftwich	0814832	2LT
Vincent J. Mason	0814820	2LT
Theodore H. Mills	0814933	2LT
Turner W. Payne	0814834	2LT

CLASS SE-44-A Date of Graduation: January 7, 1944

Clarence M. Driver	T61895	F/O
Charles H. Duke	0819455	2LT
Charles S. Jackson, Jr.	0819460	2LT
Alexander Jefferson	0819461	2LT
Robert L. Martin	0819462	2LT
Frederick D. McIver, Jr.	0819456	2LT
Robert O'Neil	0819463	2LT
Sanford M. Perkins	0819464	2LT
Frank E. Roberts	0819465	2LT
Arthur J. Wilburn	0819466	2LT

CLASS TE-44-A Date of Graduation: January 7, 1944

Charles H. Hunter (SO)	0367472	2LT
Frederick L. Parker, Jr	01166345	2LT
Leon L. Turner (SO)	0406744	2LT
Elliott H. Blue	0819446	2LT
Rolin A. Bynum	0819447	2LT

Virgil A. Daniels	T61867	F/O
Samuel W. Harper	0819448	2LT
Kenneth B. Hawkins	0819449	2LT
Andrea P. Masciana	0819454	2LT
William A. Rucker	0819450	2LT
Saint W. Twine, Jr.	T61710	F/O
Charles E. Walker	0819451	2LT
Clarence Williams	T61749	F/O
Herbert J. Williams	0819452	2LT
Eugene Winslow	0819453	2LT

CLASS SE-44-B Date of Graduation: February 8, 1944

Thomas P. Braswell	0821907	2LT
Robert C. Chandler	0821908	2LT
Emile G. Clifton, Jr.	0821909	2LT
Roger B. Gaiter	0821910	2LT
Thomas L. Gay	0821911	2LT
Cornelius P. Gould, Jr.	T62306	F/O
Joseph E. Gordon	0821912	2LT
Alfred M. Gorham	0821913	2LT
Richard S. Harder	0821914	2LT
Wilbur F. Long	0821915	2LT
Richard D. Macon	0821916	2LT
Frank H. Moody	0821917	2LT
Thomas G Patton	0821918	2LT
Marion R. Rodgers	0821920	2LT
Shelby F. Westbrook	0821921	2LT
Cohen M. White	0821922	2LT
Leonard R. Willette	T623O8	F/O
Kenneth I. Williams	0821923	2LT
Henry A. Wise	0821924	2LT

HAITIAN AIR FORCE

Ludovic F. Audant	Unknown

CLASS TE-44-B Date of Graduation: February 8, 1944

Louis G. Hill, Jr.	01573279	1st Lt.
Frederick P. Hicks	01030252	2LT

Charles D. Hill	0443955	2LT
Winston A. Adkins	0821901	2LT
Charles W. Diggs	0821902	2LT
William H. Farley	0821903	2LT
George B. Matthews	0821904	2LT

HAITIAN AIR FORCE

Felissier C. Nicolas	Unknown

CLASS SE-44-C Date of Graduation: March 12, 1944

Henry E. Rohlsen (SO)	0574092	2LT
Fred L. Brower, Jr.	0824827	2LT
Roscoe C. Brown	0824828	2LT
Walter R. Brown, Jr.	0824829	2LT
James Albert Calhoun	0824830	2LT
Vincent C. Dean	0824831	2LT
James L. Hall, Jr.	0824848	2LT
Herbert H. Heywood	0824833	2LT
Elbert Hudson	0824834	2LT
Andrew D. Marshall	0824835	2LT
Joseph L. Merton, Jr.	0824836	2LT
Rixie H. McCarroll	0824837	2LT
Elton H. Nightingale	0824849	2LT
John H. Porter	0824839	2LT
William S. Price III	0824840	2LT
Gordon M. Rapier	0824841	2LT
Roosevelt Stiger	0824842	2LT
William M. Wheeler	0824843	2LT
Charles L. White	0824844	2LT
Peter H. Whittaker	0824845	2LT
Charles T. Williams	0824846	2LT
Albert L. Young	0824847	2LT

CLASS TE-44-C Date of Graduation: March 12, 1944

Payton H. Lyle (SO)	01577497	1LT
Ahemed A. Rayner, Jr.	01043199	2LT
Charles E. Darnell	0824824	2LT
Reginald W. Hayes	0824825	2LT

Charles E. Wilson	T62O57	F/O

CLASS'SE-44-D Date of Graduation: April 15, 1944

Gentry E. Barnes	0828045	2LT
Ruall W. Bell	T62809	F/O
John H. Chavis	0828047	2LT
Hannibal M. Cox	0828048	2LT
Lewis W. Craig	0828049	2LT
Milton S. Hays	0828050	2LT
Charles Jackson	T62810	F/O
Major E. Jones	0828051	2LT
Earl R. Lane	0828052	2LT
Walter P. Manning	0828053	2LT
Vincent I. Mitchell	T62811	F/O
Roland W. Moody	0828054	2LT
Harold M. Morris	0828046	2d It.
Francis B. Peoples	0828055	2LT
Henry R. Peoples	0828056	2LT
Daniel L. Rich	0828057	2LT
Carroll H. Robinson	0828058	2LT
Ralph L. Turner	T62812	F/O
Jimmie D. Wheeler	0828059	2LT
James A. Wilson	0828060	2LT
Myron Wilson	T628O8	F/O
Vincent E. Williams	T62813	F/O
Carl J. Woods	T62814	F/O

CLASS TE'46-D Date of Graduation: April 15, 1944

Virgil Brashears	01313712	2LT
Augustus Cousins, Jr.	01307085	2LT
Harvey R. Alexander	0828041	2LT
Robert D. Anderson	0828034	2LT
William C. Coleman, Jr.	0828036	2LT
Martin L. Cook	T62816	F/O
Celostus King	0828038	2LT
George H. Kydd, III	0828043	2LT
Paul L. Moody	0828039	2LT
Lloyd R. Shultz	0828044	2LT

HAITIAN AIR FORCE

Eberle J. Guilbaud	1051F	

CLASS SE-44-E Date of Graduation: May 23, 1944

Wendell M. Lucas (SO)	0430199	1LT
George E. Cisco (SO)	01014831	2LT
Kenneth M. Wright (SO)	01031458	2LT
Richard H. Bell	0830780	2LT
Leonolle A. Bonam	0830782	2LT
Charles V. Brantley	T63110	F/O
James E. Chineworth	T63111	F/O
Harry J. Davenport, Jr.	0830784	2LT
John W. Davis	0830785	2LT
Samuel J. Foreman	T63112	F/O
Thomas L. Hawkins	T63113	F/O
Louis K. Harris	0830786	2LT
George K. Hays	0830787	2LT
Aaron Herrington	0830788	2LT
Earl B. Highbaugh	0830789	2LT
Wendell W. Hochaday	0830781	2nd Lt.
George J. Iles	0830790	2LT
Thomas W. Jefferson	T63114	F/O
Jimmy Lanham	0830791	2LT
Clarence A. Oliphant	0830792	2LT
Ralph Orduna	0830793	2LT
Robert A. Pillow, Jr.	T63115	F/O
James C. Ramsey	T63116	F/O
LeRoy Roberts, Jr.	0830794	2LT
Arnett W. Starks, Jr.	T631O9	F/O
William C. Walker, Jr.	0830795	2LT
Samuel W. Watts, Jr.	0830796	2LT
Robert W. Williams	0830797	2LT
Bertram W. Wilson, Jr.	0830798	2LT
Hiram Wright	T63117	F/O

CLASS SE-44-F Date Of Graduation: June 27, 1944

Robert W. Lawrence (SO)	01640660	2LT

Richard S. A. Armistead	T64272	F/O
Carl F. Ellis	0835324	2LT
Charles A. Hill, Jr.	0835325	2LT
Lincoln T. Hudson	0835326	2LT
Rupert C. Johnson	0835327	2LT
George A. Lynch	T64373	F/O
Lewis J. Lynch	0835328	2LT
Hiram F. Mann	0834329	2LT
James T. Mitchell, Jr.	T64247	F/O
Robert J. Murdic	T64275	F/O
Wyrian T. Schell	T6428O	F/O
Leon W. Spears	T64276	F/O
Harry T. Stewart, Jr.	0835330	2LT
Samuel L. Washington	T64278	F/O
Hugh J. White	0835331	2LT
Yenwith K. Whitney	T64279	F/O
Frank N. Wright	0835332	2LT
James W. Wright, Jr.	0835323	2LT

CLASS TE-44-F Date of Graduation: June 27, 1944

James Ewing, Jr.	T64271	F/O
William T. Jackson	T64269	F/O
Laurel E. Keith	0835319	2LT
Frank Lee	0835320	2LT
John R. Perkins, Jr.	T64270	F/O
John B. Turner	0835321	2LT
Rhobelia J. Turner	0835322	2LT

CLASS SE -44-0 Date of Graduation: August 4, 1944

George L. Ding	0835406	2LT
John E. Edwards	0835407	2LT
William H. Edwards	T64633	F/O
James H. Fischer	T64634	F/O
Thurston L. Gaines, Jr.	T64635	F/O
Robert E. Garrison, Jr.	0835408	2LT
Newman C. Golden	T64636	F/O
Leo R. Gray	0835409	2LT
Paul L. Green	0835417	2LT

Conrad A. Johnson, Jr.	0835411	2LT
Benny R. Kimnrough	0835412	2LT
John H. Lyle	T64638	F/O
Elbert N. Merriweather, Jr	T64639	F/O
Leland H. Pennington	T64646	F/O
Ronald W. Reeves	0835413	2LT
Maury M. Reid, Jr.	T64640	F/O
William E. Rice	T64641	F/O
Robert C. Robinson, Jr.	0835414	2LT
Calvin J. Spann	T64642	F/O
Thomas C. Street	0835415	2LT
Harold L. White	0835416	2LT
Joseph C. White	T64643	F/O
Robert E. Williams, Jr.	T64644	F/O

CLASS TE-44-G Date of Graduation: August 4, 1944

Claude C. Cavis (SO)	0441115	1LT
Harold H. Brown	0835405	2LT
James E. Brothers	T64623	F/O
Reginald A. Bruce	T64624	F/O
Edward T. Dixon	0835403	2LT
Edward Harris	T64625	F/O
Willard B. Miller	T64632	F/O
John W. Mosley	0835404	2LT
Ramon F. Noches	T64626	F/O
Maurice D. Pompey	T64627	F/O
Charles J. Qunader, Jr.	T64628	F/O
Harris H. Robnett, Jr.	T64629	F/O
James H. Shephard	T64630	F/O
Jesse H. Simpson	T64631	F/O

CLASS SE-44-H Date of Graduation: September 8, 1944

Albert J. Lieteau (SO)	01014240	1LT
Herbert C. Barland (SO)	01168159	2LT
Emet R. Anders	0838023	2LT
William P. Armstrong	T66139	F/O
Carl B. Carey	0838025	2LT
James Coleman	0838026	2LT

Charles W. Cooper	T66140	F/O
William M. Cousins	0838027	2LT
George E. Franklin	0838028	2LT
Morris E. Gant	T66141	F/O
George E. Hardy	0838029	2LT
William H. Holloman III	0838030	2LT
Stephen S. Jenkins, Jr.	0838031	2LT
Robert Montoe Johnson	T66142	F/O
Charles A. Lane, Jr.	T66143	F/O
Samuel G. Leftenant	0838032	2LT
Edward E. Manley	T66147	F/O
Samuel Matthews	T66144	F/O
Felix M. McCrory	0838033	2LT
Lawrence I. Miller	0838034	2LT
John W. Squires	T66145	F/O
Milton S. Washington	T66146	F/O
John L. Whitehead, Jr.	0838035	2LT

CLASS TE-44-H Date of Graduation: September 8, 1944

Luther A. Goodwin (SO)	01581149	1LT
James A. Hurd (SO)	01030158	1LT
John A. Hector (SO)	045317	1LT
Augustus G. Brown (SO)	01038394	2LT
Robert S. Brown (SO)	01048706	2LT
Paul J. Monseigneur, Jr.	0838036	2LT
Warren E. Henry	0838037	2LT
Russell C. Nalle, Jr.	T6615O	F/O
Frederick H. Samuels	T66149	F/O

CLASS SE-44-I-1 Date of Graduation: October 16, 1944

Cornelius D. Dowling (S)	01292319	2LT
Henry A. Hunter (SO)	01314639	2LT
Ferrier F. White (SO)	01824829	2LT
Rutherford H. Adkins	0838152	2LT
Thomas J. Daniels III	T66399	F/O
Edward D. Doram	0838164	2LT
Robert M. Glass	T66403	F/O
James H. Harvey, Jr.	0838153	2LT

Frank A. Jackson, Jr.	T66400	F/O
Theodore W. Lancaster	0838155	2LT
Charles E. Miller	0838156	2LT
Joseph M. Millett	0838157	2LT
Charles P. Myers	0838158	2LT
Richard A. Simons	0838159	2LT
Richard G. Stevens	0838160	2LT
Charles L. Stovall	0838161	2LT
Donald N. Thompson, Jr.	0838162	2LT
Richard E. Thorpe	0838163	2LT
Allen H. Turner	0838165	2LT
James W. Warren	T66402	F/O

CLASS TE-44-I-1 Date of Graduation: October 16, 1944

Paul T. Anderson (SO)	01294209	1LT
Harold E. Smith, Jr.(SO)	0420985	1LT
James R. Chichester (SO)	01312749	2LT
Charles H. Drummond, Jr.	01289402	2LT
Joseph E. Jenkins	01320946	2LT
James W. Brown, Jr.	0838166	2LT
William L. Cain	T664O4	F/O
Gamaliel M. Collins	T66408	F/O
Merven P. Exum	T66409	F/O
James L. Green	T66405	F/O
Silas M. Jenkins	0838168	2LT
Charles C. Maxwell	T66407	F/O
David J. Murphy, Jr.	T664061	F/O
Glenn W. Pulliam	T66410	F/O
Theodore O. Mason	0838167	2LT

CLASS SE-44-I Date of Graduation: November 20, 1944

Alvin J. Johnson (SO)	01169183	2LT
Halbert L. Alexander	0839082	2LT
William R. Alston	0839083	2LT
John J. Bell	T67141	F/O
Irvin O. Brewin	0839084	2LT
Julius W. Calloway	T67143	F/O
Russell W. Carpenter, Jr.	0839085	2LT

Tamenund J. Dickerson	T67144	F/O
Thomas Gladden	0839086	2LT
Vernon Hopson	T67146	F/O
Gaefield L. Jemkins	0839087	2LT
Andrew Johnson, Jr.	0839088	2LT
Louis W. Johnson	0839094	2LT
Willis E. Moore	0839089	2LT
Calvin G. Moret	T67147	F/O
Lincoln W. Nelson	0839090	2LT
Eugene G. Theodore	0839091	2LT
Leonard O. Vaughan	T67149	F/O
Reginald C. Waddell, Jr.	T67150	F/O
William M. Washington	0839092	2LT
Ralph D. Wilkins	0839093	2LT

CLASS TE-44-I Date of Graduation: November 20, 1944

Oscar H. York (SO)	0469633	2LT
Henry T. Fears	T67153	F/O
Bernard Harris	0839095	2LT
Donald A. Hawkins	T67134	F/O
Eugene R. Henderson	0839098	2LT
Charlie A. Johnson	T67159	F/O
Douglas McQuillan	T67155	F/O
Robert M. Parkey	T67156	F/O
Wayman P. Surcey	T67160	F/O
James V. Stevenson	0839099	2LT
Morris J. Washington	T67157	F/O
Raymond M. White	T67158	F/O
James W. Whyte, Jr.	0839096	2LT
Joseph H. Williams	0839097	2LT

CLASS SE-44-J Date of Graduation: December 28, 1944

Yancey Williams	0423693	1LT
Isham A. Burns, Jr.	0840202	2LT
Horace A. Bohannon	T67963	F/O
Henry C.I. Bohler	T67964	F/O
Lercy Bryant, Jr.	T67965	F/O
Lindsay L. Campbell	T67966	F/O

McWheeler Campbell	0840203	2LT
Robert A. Cloe	T67967	F/O
DeWitt Dickson	T67958	F/O
James W. Greer	T679G9	F/O
Eugene L. Guyton	T67970	F/O
James E. Harris	0840204	2LT
LeRoy Kirksey	T67977	F/O
Dempsey Nelson, Jr.	T67971	F/O
Melvin Parker	T67972	F/O
Frederick D. Pendleton	0840205	2LT
Clarence L. Shivers	T67973	F/O
Thomas W. Smith	T67974	F/O
William W. Stephenson, Jr.	T67975	F/O
Willie A. Williamson	T67976	F/O

CLASS TE-44-J Date of Graduation: December 28, 1944

Walter B. Herron (SO)	01311585	1LT
Walter H. Allen	T67978	F/O
Edwin T. Cowman	T67986	F/O
James E. Edwards, Jr.	T67979	F/O
Thomas M. Flake	T67980	F/)
Samuel C. Hunter, Jr.	0840206	2LT
Ivan J. McRae, Jr.	0840207	2LT
Flarzell Moore	T67981	F/O
John Ira Mulzac	T67987	F/O
John P. Qualles	T67988	F/O
Lawrence E. Roberts	0840208	2LT
Frederick E. Velasquez	T67982	F/O
William L. Williams, Jr.	T67983	F/O
Howard A. Wooten	T67985	F/O
Nasby Wynn, Jr.	T67984	F/O

CLASS SE-44-K Date of Graduation: February 1, 1945

Montro C. Askins	0841156	2LT
Lloyd W. Bell	0840735	2LT
Richard L. Biffle, Jr.	T68512	F/O
James E. Bowman	T68699	F/O
Lawrence A. Brown	T68700	F/O

Lloyd A. N. Carter	0841157	2LT
Lowell H. Cleaver	0841158	2LT
William A. Colbert, Jr.	T68701	F/O
Charles E. Craig	T68702	F/O
Joshua Glenn	T68703	F/O
Percy L. Heath, Jr.	0841159	2LT
William T. Henry	T68704	F/O
William H. Hymes	0841160	2LT
Bleacher A. Jones	T68706	F/O
Robert O. Merriweather	T68708	F/O
Ephraim E. Toatley, Jr.	0841161	2LT

CLASS TE-44-K Date of Graduation: February 1, 1945

Rayfield A. Anderson	0841162	2LT
Grover Crumbsy	T68711	F/O
Ollie O. Goodall, Jr.	T68713	F/O
Archie H. Harris, Jr.	0841163	2LT
Mitchell L. Higginbotham	0841164	2LT
Roger C. Terry	0841165	2LT
Haydel J. White	T68712	F/O

CLASS SE-45-A Date of Graduation: March 11, 1945

Vincent O. Campbell (SO)	0577285	2LT
Luzine B. Bickham	T68752	F/O
John Albert Burch, III	0841255	2LT
Ernest M. Cabule, Jr.	0841256	2LT
William J. Coleman	0841257	2LT
Edgar A. Doswell, Jr.	T68754	F/O
Clarence C. Finley, Jr.	0841266	2LT
Joseph E. Gash	0841258	2LT
Bertrand J. Holbert	0841259	2LT
Edward M. Jenkins	0841267	2LT
Robert Jones, Jr.	T68756	F/O
Wilber Moffett	T68757	F/O
Thomas J. Morrison, Jr.	0841265	2LT
Harry S. Pruitt	T68759	F/O
Marsille P. Reed	0841264	2LT
Clayo C. Rice	0841260	2LT

Eugene J. Richardson, Jr.	0841261	2LT
Alfred H. Smith	T68758	F/O
John B. Walker, Jr.	0841263	2LT
Harry P. Winston	T68760	F/O
Samuel L. Broadnax	T68753	F/O

CLASS TE-45-A Date of Graduation: March 11, 1945

Melvin A. Clayton	0841268	2LT
Herndon M. Cummings	0841277	2LT
William J. Curtis, Jr.	T68763	F/O
Charles J. Dorkins	0841269	2LT
Rutledge H. Fleming, Jr.	T68761	F/O
Charles S. Goldsby	T68764	F/O
Argonne F. Harden	0841270	2LT
James V. Kennedy, Jr.	0841271	2LT
Harvey L. McClelland	T68762	F/O
Alfred U. McKenzie	T68765	F/O
Luther L. Oliver	0841272	2LT
Herbert J. Schwing	0841273	2LT
Quentin P. Smith	0841274	2LT
Francis R. Thompson	0841275	2LT
Cleophus E. Valentine	0841276	2LT
Calvin T. Warrick	0841278	2LT

CLASS SE-45-B Date of Graduation: April 15, 1945

John H. Adams, Jr.	0842588	2LT
Clarence Bee, Jr.	0842579	2LT
Tilford U. Brooks	T69407	F/O
Clifton G. Casey	T69738	F/O
John W. Curtis	0842581	2LT
Richard G. Dudley	0842582	2LT
William L. Gilliam, Jr.	T69740	2LT
James W. Henson	0842583	2LT
Samuel R. Hughes, Jr.	T69741	F/O
William H. Knight	T69742	F/O
Clyde C. Long, Jr.	T69751	F/O
Humprey C. Patton, Jr.	T69743	F/O
Verdelle L. Payne	T69744	F/O

Robert F. Pennington	T69745	F/O
Robert B. Porter	T69746	F/O
William S. Powell, Jr.	T69747	F/O
George B. Purnell	T69748	F/O
Lloyd L. Radcliffe	0842584	2LT
George H. Sheats	0842585	2LT
Burl E. Smith	0842586	2LT
Paul Tucker	T69749	F/O
Robert H. Winslow	0842587	2LT
Charles H. Winston, Jr.	T69750	F/O

CLASS TE-45-B Date of graduation: April 15, 1945

LeRoy Criss	T69752	F/O
Russell F. Desvignes	T69753	F/O
Eldridge E. Freeman	T69754	F/O
Theopolis W. Johnson	0842589	2LT
Lowell H. Jordan	0842590	2LT
George G. Norton, Jr.	T69755	F/O
James E. Taylor	T69756	F/O

CLASS SE-45-C Date of Graduation: May 23,1945

Terry C. Bailey	T69972	F/O
Ralph V. Clabor	0842879	2LT
Earl N. Franklin	0842880	2LT
George W. Helem	0842881	2LT
Arthur N. Hicks	0842882	2LT
William D. Holman	T69973	F70
Earl C. Johnson	T69974	F/O
Frank D. Jones	T69974	F/O
James W. McKnight	0842883	2LT
Louis U. Murray	T69976	F/O
George J. Parker	T69977	F/O
Roscoe C. Perkins, Jr.	T69978	F/O
Willis E. Sanderlin	0842884	2LT
Mansfield L. Session	0842885	2LT
Thomas J. Tindall	T69979	F/O
George E. Eanamaker	T69980	F/O
Harry W. White	T69981	F/O
Kenneth O. Wofford	0842888	2LT

Benjamin Young, Jr.	0842887	2LT

CLASS TE-45-C Date of Graduation: May 23, 1945

Frederick D. Smith	0842877	2LT
William A. Tyler, Jr.	0842878	2LT

CLASS SE-45-D Date of Graduation: June 27, 1945

Walter G. Alexander,II	0842999	2LT
Reuben B. Bilbo	T70093	F/O
Joseph R. Blaylock	0843000	2LT
Grady E. Bryant	0843001	2LT
James O. Bryson	T70094	F/O
Clarence J. Carter	T70095	F/O
Wilson N. Cobbs	0843002	2LT
Victor L. Connell	0843003	2LT
Matthew J. Corbin	T70027	F/O
William V. Francis	T70098	F/O
Ivie V. Giles	T70099	F/O
Leonard C. Hall, Jr.	0843004	2LT
James E. Harrison	0843005	2LT
Clarence Johnson	0843006	2LT
William A. Johnston, Jr	T70100	F/O
Thomas A. Kelley	T70101	F/O
Calvin M. Knight	T70102	F/O
George L. Prather	T70103	F/O
Joseph A. Prince	T70104	F/O
Frank R. Raymond	T70112	F/O
Robert L. Robinson, Jr.	0843007	2LT
Albert B. Simeon, Jr.	T70105	F/O
Robert C. Smith	T70107	F/O
Walter H. Thomas, Jr.	T70108	F/O
Robert G. Trott	0843008	2LT
Emmett J. Wilhite	0843009	2LT
Raymond L. Williams	T70111	F/O
Phillip C. Yates	T70110	F/O
Leo W. Young	T70113	F/O

CLASS SE-45-E Date of Graduation: August 4, 1945

Henry T. Holland (SO)	02075546	2LT
Clinton E. McIntyre (SO)	02075549	2LT
Gordon G. Tuener (SOS)	02075566	2LT
William H. Bailey	0843102	2LT
Herman A. Barnett	T70221	F/O
Russell L. Collins	T70222	F/O
Roger B. Duncan	0843104	2LT
William A. Fuller, Jr.	T70223	F/O
Aaron C. Gaskins	0843105	2LT
Wesley D. Hurt	0843109	2LT
Clarence E. Reynolds, Jr.	T70224	F/O
Logan Roberts	T70225	F/O
Martin G. Saunders	0843106	2LT
Joseph P. Scott	0843107	2LT
Reginald V. Smith	T70226	F/O
Marvin C. White, Jr.	T70227	F/O
Leonard W. Wiggins	T70228	F/O
Eugene W. Williams	0843108	2LT
Isaac R. Woods	T70229	F/O

CLASS TE-45-E Date of Graduation: August 4, 1945

George B. Choisy (SO)	02075531	2LT
Harold B. Maples (SO)	T136668	F/O
Clifford E. Masley (SO)	T136674	F/O
Harry J. Satterwhite (SO)	02075559	2LT
William E. Broadwater	T70231	F/O
George A. Brown, Jr.	0843110	2LT
Joseph C. Bryant, Jr.	T70232	F/O
John C. Curry	0843111	2LT
Harry E. Ford, Jr.	T70233	F/O
Jerrold D. Griffin	0843112	2LT
John S. Harris	0843113	2LT
George R. Miller	T70235	F/O
Walter N. O'Neal	T70236	F/O
Mexion O. Prewitt	T70238	F/O

Oliver W. Proctor	T70239	F/O
John B. Roach	T70240	F/O
William H. Taylor, Jr.	T70241	F/O
Mitchel N. Toney	T70242	F/O
Albert Whiteside	T70243	F/O

CLASS SE-45-F Date of Graduation: September 8, 1945

Donald F. Davis (SO)	T140090	F/O
Sylvester S. Davis (SO)	02080883	2LT
Bennett G. Hardy (SO)	02080900	2LT
Thomas D. Harris, Jr.(SO)	0843233	2LT
Herbert A. McIntyre (SO)	02075551	2LT
Rueben H. Brown, Jr.	0843235	2LT
Walter P. Curry	T70420	F/O
Elliott H. Gray	0843236	2LT
Earl Kelly	0843237	2LT
August J. Martin	0843238	2LT
Ralph W. Manson	0843239	2LT
William B. Morgan	T70422	F/O
Augustus L. Palmer	0843240	2LT
Floyd R. Scott, Jr.	T70423	F/O
Edward W. Watkins, Jr.	T70424	F/O
Julius C. Westmoreland	0843241	2LT
James L. Williams	T70425	F/O
Thomas E. Williams	0843242	2LT
Sandy W. Wright, Jr.	T70426	F/O
William W. Young	0843243	2LT

CLASS TE-45-F Date of Graduation: September 8, 1945

George C. Bolden (SO)	02075526	2LT
Quinten V. Cheek (SO)	02075530	2LT
Edward M. Cooper (SO)	02080879	2LT
Roscoe J. Dabney, Jr.(SO)	0843244	2LT
Donald S. Jamison (SO)	T140106	F/O
Calvin V. Porter (SO)	02075556	2LT
James E. Talton (SO)	T136691	F/O
Clifford W. Davis	T70427	F/O
Otis B. Finley, Jr.	0843245	2LT

Victor L. Hancock	T70428	F/O
Jerry T. Hodges, Jr.	0843246	2LT
Robert L. Maxwell	0843247	2LT
David M. Mozee, Jr.	T70429	F/O
Pierce T. Ramsey	T70430	F/O
Charles J. Roach	T70431	F/O
Kenneth E. Terry	T70432	F/O
Vertner J. White, Jr.	0843248	2LT
Oscar L. Wilkerson, Jr.	0843249	2LT
LeRoy J. Wilson	0843250	2LT

CLASS SE-45-G Date of Graduation: October 16, 1945

Lorenzo W. Holloway, Jr.	02082800	2LT
William M. Jones (SO)	02082604	2LT
James A. Thompson (SO)	T141246	F/O
Page L. Dickerson	T70546	F/O
Alfred E. Garrett, Jr.	T70547	F/O
Alfonso L. Harris	T70548	F/O
Julien D. Jackson, Jr.	T70549	F/O
George Sherman	T70350	F/O

CLASS TE-45-G Date of Graduation: October 16, 1945

Granville C. Coggs (SO)	02082572	2LT
Arthur C. Harmon (SO)	0208259	2LT
William A. Leslie (SO)	02082651	2LT
Ferry W. Lindsey (SO)	02068905	2LT
Herbert C. Thorpe (SO)	02080935	2LT
James R. Williams (SO)	02068906	2LT
Daniel Keel (SO)	T131953	F/O
Marcellus L. Hunter	0843343	2LT
Julius P. Echols	T70553	F/O
Lonnie Harrison	T70543	F/O
Charles R. Price	T70556	F/O
James C. Russell	T70558	F/O
Richard Weatherford	T70557	F/O

CLASS SE-45-H Date of Graduation: November 20, 1945

Sylvester H. Hurd, Jr.	T70545	F/O

Herbert Lewis, Jr.	T70551	F/O
Godfrey C. Miller	0843344	2LT
Lincoln J. Ragsdale	0843349	2LT
Thurman E. Spriggs	0843350	2LT

CLASS TE-45-H Date of Graduation: November 20, 1945

Nathaniel W. Coins (SO)	0582758	1LT
Joshua J. Lankford (SO)	02069227	2LT
Robert Ashby	0843351	2LT
Henry Baldwin, Jr.	T70554	F/O
William V. Bibb	0843352	2LT
Lawrence W. Carroll	0843353	2LT
Jose R. Elfalan	0843354	2LT
Alvin E. Harrison, Jr.	T70447	F/O
Lyman L. Hubbard	T70485	F/O
Donald E. Jackson	T70489	F/O
Frederick D. Knight, Jr.	0843355	2LT
Lloyd B. McKeethen	0843356	2LT
John W. Nelson	T70559	F/O
Norman E. Proctor	T70561	F/O
Isaiah E. Robinson, Jr.	0843357	2LT
Theodore W. Robinson	0843358	2LT
Wayman E. Scott	T70561	F/O
Clifford C. Smith, Jr.	0843359	2LT
Cecil Spicer	0843360	2LT
William A. Streat, Jr.	T70562	F/O
Andrew B. Williams, Jr.	T70563	F/O

CLASS SE-45-I Date of Graduation: January 29, 1946

Joseph Bruce Bennett	02102013	2LT
Thomas Hamlin McGarrity	02102014	2LT
Merrill Ray Ross	02102015	2LT
Frank Griffin	T149962	F/O
Lee Archer Hayes	T144946	F/O
James M. Dillard, Jr.	02102016	2LT
Olivcr M. Dillon	02102017	2LT
Everett M. Ellis	02102018	2LT
Donehue Simmons	T149963	F/O

CLASS SE-46-A Date of Graduation: March 23, 1946

Jewel B. Butler (SO)	02078770	2LT
James H. Gallway (SO)	02078775	2LT
Jacob W. Greenwell (SO)	02090283	2LT
Harry E. Lanauze (SO)	02084156	2LT
Charles W. Chambers	02102097	2LT
Thomas W. Love, Jr.	02102098	2LT
James M. Barksdale	T149986	F/O
Eugene A. Briggs	T149987	F/O

CLASS TE-46-A Date of Graduation: March 23, 1946

Charles R. Matthews (SO)	02090286	2LT
Floyd J. Carter (SO)	T146021	F/O
George A. Bates	T149984	F/O
Abe Benjamin Moore	T149985	F/O

THE TUSKEGEE AIRMEN 1939--1949 43 Units:

Civil Pilot Training Program
Godman Field Station Hospital
Lockbourne AB Station Hospital
Tuskegee Army Flying School
Tuskegee AAF Station Hospital
66th AAF Flying Training Detach't
84rd Fighter Control Squadron
96th Air Service Group
99th Pursuit Squadron
99th Fighter Squadron
100th Fighter Squadron
118th AAF Base Unit (RTU)
126th AAF Base Unit (RTU)
301st Fighter Squadron
302nd Fighter Squadron
313th AAF Band
318th Base Hdqs & AB Sve Sq.
332nd Air Base Group
332nd Fighter Group
332nd Fighter Wing
366th Air Service Squadron
387th Hdqs Service Squadron
477th Bombardment Grou (M)
477th Composit Group
553rd Replacement Training Unit
590th Air Material Squadron
616th Bombardment Squadron
617th Bombardment Squadron
618th Bombardment Squadron
619 Bombardment Squadron
648th Ordnance Company
389th Signal Air Warning Squadron
717th Signal Air Material Squadron
889th Single Engine Fly'g Train'g Sq
890th Single Engine Fly'g Train'g Sq
941st Guard Squadron
964th Quartermaster Platoon
1062nd Air Material Squadron
1155th Single Eng. Fly'g Train'g Sq
1451st Quatermaster Company
4413th Women Air Force Squadron
Squadron "W (WAF)

AAF BLACK MILITARY PERSONNEL
SEPTEMBER 1942--MARCH 1946

Month/Year	Total	Officers	Enlisted
September, 1942	37223	142	37081
December, 1942	71824	129	71695
March, 1943	106409	255	1061542
June, 1943	114075	359	113716
September, 1943	130372	605	129767
December, 1943	145025	636	144389
March, 1944	140857	904	139953
June, 1944	145242	1107	144135
September, 1944	140728	1243	139485
December, 1944	137806	1303	136503
March, 1945	136827	1464	135363
June, 1945	140462	1559	138903
September, 1945	133447	1511	131936
December, 1945	69016	1050	67966
March, 1946	42565	778	41786

(Source: Army Air Forces Statistical Digest, 1946, p 23, Albert F. Simpson Historical Research Center 134. 11-6.)

AAF BLACK FLYING TRAINING GRADUATES.

Course	Total	Prior to October 1944	4th Qtr 1944	1945	1946
Advanced Pilot					
Training	926	520	105	263	38
Single Engine	673	429	61	161	22
Two Engine	253	91	44	102	16
Liaison Field Artillery	58	57	--	1	--
Navigators	136	54	25	53	--
Bombardier-Navigators	261	--	123	136	2

(Source: Army Air Forces Statistical Digest, 1946, p 75, Albert F. Simpson Historical Research Center 134.11-6.)

Top: LT James L. Warthall, Advanced Basic Flying Instructor; MAJ Gabe Hawkins, Director of Flight Training (TAAF). Bottom: COL Donald McPhearson, Director of Flight Training; LT Luther Davenport, Basic Flight Instructor (TAAF).

Top: Basic Flight Instructors: LT Richard Kraft, LT Owen Peterson. Bottom: Basic Flight Instructors: LT Philip H. Heard, LT Wayne E. Cook

(List of first 19 officers arrested)

HEADQUARTERS
FREEMAN FIELD
Seymour, Indiana

11 April 1945

SUBJECT: Disciplinary Action.
TO: All Concerned

1. Pursuant to authority conferred by the 69th Article of War, the following named commissioned and flight officers are ordered into arrest in quarters, effective 2245 hours, 11 April 1945.

2LT Robert S. Payton, Jr.
F/O Adolphus Lewis, Jr.
2LT Edward E. Tilman
2LT Leonard E. Williams
2LT Roy M. Chappell
F/O Charles E. Malone
F/O Charles R. Taylor
F/O Roland A. Webber
2LT Rudolph A. Berthoud
F/O Marcus E. Clarkson
2LT Theodore O. Mason
2LT Luther Oliver
F/O Frank V. Pivalo
F/O Norman A. Holmes
2LT LeRoy A. Battle
2LT Walter R. Ray
2LT Roger Pines
2LT Samuel Colbert, Sr.
2LT Clifford C. Jarrett

2. It is ordered that each commissioned and flight officer acknowledge receipt of this order, by placing his signature opposite his respective name.

ROBERT S. SELWAY JR.,
Colonel, Air Corps
Commanding

(List of 101 officers arrested)

HEADQUARTERS
FREEMAN FIELD
Seymour, Indiana

13 April 1945

SUBJECT: Disciplinary Action
TO: All concerned

1. Pursuant to authority conferred by the 69th Article of War, the following named commissioned and flight officers are ordered into arrest in transit from Freeman Field, Seymour, Indiana to Godman Field, Kentucky, and arrest in quarters upon arrival at Godman Field until further notice, effective 0800 hours 13 April 1945.

1LT Arthur L. Ward
1LT James B. Williams
2LT David A. Smith
2LT William C. Perkins
2LT James Shyte, Jr.
2LT Stephen Hotesse
2LT Wardell A. Polk
2LT Robert E. Lee
2LT George H. Kydd
F/O Eugene L. Woodson
2LT Charles E. Darnell
2LT James V. Kennedy
2LT Glen L. Head
F/O Harry R. Dickenson
2LT Quentin P. Smith
2LT Charles J. Dorkins
F/O Maurice J. Jackson, Jr.
2LT Herndon M. Cummings
2LT Mitchel L. Higginboyham
F/O Alfred U. McKenzie
2LT Herbert J. Schwing
F/O Wendell G. Freeland
F/O David J. Murphy Jr.
2LT Donald D. Harris
F/O Paul L. White
F/O Charles E. Wilson
F/O John E. Wilson
F/O Paul W. Scott
F/O McCray Jenkins
F/O Harris H. Robnett
F/O Donald A. Hawkins
F/O Glen W. Pullin
2LT Frank B. Sanders
F/O Walter M. Miller
F/O Denny C. Jefferson
F/O James H. Sheperd
F/O Edward R. Lunda
2LT James E. Jones
F/O Sidney H. Marzette
2LT Leonard A. Altemus
F/O Howard Storey
F/O James C. Warren
2LT Cleophus W. Valentine
F/O Ario Dixione
2LT Robert B. Johnson
F/O Calvin Smith

2LT Calvin T. Warrick
2LT Robert S. Payton, Jr.
2LT Theodore O. Mason
F/O Adolphus Lewis, Jr.
2LT Luther L. Oliver
2LT Edward E. Tillmon
F/O Frank V. Pivalo
2LT Leonard E. Williams
F/O Norman A. Holmes
2LT Roy M. Chappell
2LT LeRoy A. Battle
F/O Charles E. Malone
2LT Edward W. Woodward
F/O John R. Perkins, Jr.
F/O Alvin B. Steele
F/O Hiram E. Little
2LT George W. Priolieau, Jr.
F/O Marcel Clyne
2LT Arthur O. Fisher
F/O Charles E. Jones
F/O Charles S. Goldsby
F/O Wendell T. Stokes
2LT William W. Bowie, Jr.
F/O Bertram W. Pitts
2LT Silas M. Jenkins
F/O Harry S. Lum
F/O Robert T. McDaniel
F/O Haydel J. White
F/O Lewis C. Hubbard, Jr.
F/O William J. Curtis
2LT Cyril P. Dyer
2LT Victor L. Ranson
F/O Lloyd W. Godfrey
2LT Coleman A. Young
2LT LeRoy F. Gillead
F/O Connie Nappier, Jr.
2LT Argonne F. Harden
2LT Robert L. Hunter
2LT James W. Brown, Jr.
2LT Walter R. Ray
F/O Charles R. Taylor
2LT Roger Pines
F/O Roland A. Webber
2LT Samuel Colbert
2LT Rudolph A. Berthoud
2LT Clifford C. Jarrett
F/O Marcus E. Clarkson
2LT LeRoy H. Freeman
2LT George H. O. Martin
2LT Melvin N. Nelson
2LT Edward W. Watkins
F/O Edward R. Tabbanor
F/O Clarence C. Conway
F/O Frederick H. Samuels
2LT Edward V. Hipps, Jr.

2. It is ordered that each commissioned and flight officer acknowledge receipt of this order, by placing his signature opposite his respective name.

ROBERT R. SELWAY, JR.,
Colonel, Air Corps,
Commanding.

TUSKEGEE AIRMEN HISTORICAL CHRONOLOGY

--September 16, 1940
U.S. Congress passed Selective Service Act ending discrimination in selection of recruits for the Armed Forces.

--October 9, 1940
Col. B. O. Davis, Sr., became first Black American promoted to Brigadier General in U.S. History.

--January 16, 1941
U.S. War Department announced the formation of the 99th Pursuit Squadron.

--January 17, 1941
Mr. Yancey Williams filed suit in the U.S. Supreme Court of Washington, DC to compel the War Department to consider his application for Aviation Cadet Training.

--March 22, 1941
99th Pursuit Squadron activated at Chanute Army Field, IL with ground crew personnel training only.

--April 19, 1941
Eleanor Roosevelt flew with "Chief" Anderson at Moton Field, Tuskegee, AL, a grass airstrip located northeast of Tuskegee Institute's campus. The occasion was a visit by Mrs. Eleanor Roosevelt.

Some months earlier, Tuskegee Institute, along with Hampton Institute, Virginia State and Howard University, had been selected to offer Civilian Pilot Training Program (CPTP) to Black college students. With the advent of World War II, pressure was brought to bear on the War Department to utilize Blacks as officers and pilots in the then U.S. Army Air Corps. The choice as to where the Black pilots would be trained narrowed down to two locations: Tuskegee Institute and Hampton Institute.

Mrs. Roosevelt arrived at the airstrip along with an

entourage of Secret Servicemen, her purpose to evaluate the potential of Tuskegee's facilities and to meet the would-be director of the program, Charles "Chief" Anderson.

During the course of their conversations, Mrs. Roosevelt asked Chief Anderson, "Can Negroes really fly airplanes?" His reply was, "Certainly we can; as a matter of fact, would you like to take an airplane ride?"

Mrs. Roosevelt accepted! This threw the Secret Service men into a state of shock and panic! They forbade her to do so and ordered *Chief* not to fly her. Mrs. Roosevelt overruled their objections and proceeded to the aircraft with Chief. The Secret Service people rushed into the office and called President Roosevelt. After hearing the details of the situation, the President replied, "Well, if she wants to do it, there's nothing we can do to stop her."

With Mrs. Roosevelt in the back seat of his Piper J-3 Cub, Chief Anderson took off and gave her a 30-minute ride over the campus and the surrounding areas. Upon landing, Mrs. Roosevelt turned to the Chief and said, "I guess Negroes can fly."

An historical photo was taken at that point. Mrs. Roosevelt returned to Washington and it was announced a short time later that Tuskegee Institute would be the site at which the first Black Air Corps pilots would be trained. (Recollections by Charles "Chief" Anderson).

--July 19, 1941:

The first class (42C) of Black pilot trainees began Aviation Cadet Training at Tuskegee Army Flying School.

--July 23, 1941:

Tuskegee Army Airfield officially established.

--September 2, 1941:

CPT Benjamin O. Davis, Jr., became the first Black American to solo an aircraft as an officer in the U.S. Army Air Corps.

--March 6, 1942:

1st Class (42-C) graduated as Army Air Corps Pilots.

--May 15, 1942:

The 100th Fighter Squadron activated as a part of the 332nd Fighter Group.

--December 26, 1942:

Lt. Col. Noel F. Parrish assumed command of Tuskegee Army Air Field.

--March 27, 1943

332nd Fighter Group transferred from Tuskegee Army Air Field to Selfridge Field, MI.

--April 2, 1943:

99th Fighter Squadron left TAAF enroute to Port of Embarkation, Camp Shanks, N.Y.

--April 15, 1943:

99th Fighter Squadron boarded the S.S. Mariposa bound for combat overseas.

--April 24, 1943:

99th Fighter Squadron arrived at Casablanca, French Morocco.

--May 31, 1943:

99th Fighter Squadron arrived at Farjouna, Cape Bon, South Tunis to begin combat missions attached to the 33rd Fighter Group.

--June 2, 1943:

First combat mission for 99th pilots (LT Campbell, Hall, Jamison, and Wiley) as wingmen to pilots of the 33rd Fighter Group.

--June 9, 1943:

Six pilots of the 99th Fighter Squadron were the first Black U.S. Army Air Corps pilots to engage enemy pilots in aerial combat.

--June 11, 1943:

Pantelleria surrendered--first time in history that air power won surrender of a ground target. 99th was a key part of the air assault.

--July 2, 1943:

LT Charles *Buster* Hall downed a Focke-Wulf 190 and became the first Black American to score a victory in aerial combat as a U.S. Army Air Corps pilot.

--July 10, 1943:

LT Richard *Good Papa* Bolling ditched his P-40 in the Mediterranean and was the first 99th pilot to bail out in combat.

--October 7, 1943:

LTC B. O. Davis, Jr. assumed command of the 332nd Fighter Group.

--November 19, 1943:
99th Fighter Squadron moved to Modena, Italy with the 79th Fighter Group

--December 24, 1943:
332nd Fighter Group left Selfridge Field, MI enroute to overseas combat assignment.

--January 3, 1944:
332nd FG boarded troop transports at Camp Patrick Henry bound for Taranto, Italy.

--January 27, 1944:
99th downed 8 enemy aircraft over Anzio Beach.

--January 28, 1944:
99th downed 4 aircraft, including w confirmed by *Buster* Hall.

--February 5, 1944:
100th Fighter Squadron flew their first combat mission.

--February 15, 1944:
302nd Fighter Squadron pilots--LT Groves and Wilkins made initial contact with enemy aircraft.

--May 1, 1944:
99th Fighter Squadron assigned to the 332nd FG under the 12th Air Force.

--June 9, 1944:
39 pilots of the 332nd FG *Red Tails* engaged over 100 German fighters, destroying 5, damaging 1.

--June 25, 1944:
332nd FG pilots sank a German destroyer with machine gun fire in Trieste Harbor, Italy.

--July 6, 1944:
99th FS joined the 332nd FG at Ramitelli, Italy.

--July 12, 1944:
CPT Joe Elsberry of the 301st FS scored a triple victory on one mission.

--July 15, 1944:
332nd FG flew its first 4-Squadron mission with 99th, 100th, 301st, and 302nd pilots on a group mission.

--July 17, 1944:
332nd FG scored 3 victories over Avignon, France.

--July 18, 1944:

332nd pilots downed 11 aircraft, including a triple victory by LT Clarence *Lucky* Lester of the 100th Fighter Squadron.

--July 24, 1944:

332nd FG scored 4 victories over Southern Germany.

--July 26, 1944:

332nd destroyed 5 enemy aircraft and 2 probable over Markendorf, Austria.

--July 27, 1944:

332nd destroyed 8 enemy aircraft while escorting B-24 Bombers.

--March 24, 1945:

Target for today: Berlin, Germany. Three *Red Tail* pilots shot down 3 enemy ME-262 Jet aircraft.

--March 31, 1945:

332nd FG shot down 13 enemy aircraft on mission to Linz, Austria.

--April 1, 1945:

332nd FG destroyed 12 enemy aircraft on mission to Wels, Austria.

--April 5, 1945:

Pilots of the 477th Bombardment Group attempted to integrate the Officers Club at Freeman Field, Syemour, IN.

--April 13, 1945:

332nd FG destroyed the last four enemy aircraft in the Mediterranean area before WW II ended.

--May 8, 1945:

VE-Day -- End of WW II hostilities in Europe.

--June 21, 1945:

COL Benjamin O. Davis, Jr., assumed command of the 477th Composite Group at Godman Field, KY.

--August 6, 1945:

First atom bomb dropped on Hiroshima, Japan.

--August 9, 1945:

Second atom bomb dropped on Nagasaki, Japan.

--August 14, 1945:

VJ-Day. End of hostilities with Japan.

--September 30, 1945:

99th, 100th, and 301st Fighter Squadrons returned to the US from European Theatre.

--February 12, 1946:
LT Nancy C. Leftenant became the first Black American appointed in the Regular Army.

--March 13, 1946:
COL Benjamin O. Davis, Jr., assumed command of Lockbourne AFB, Columbus, OH.

--June 28, 1946:
The last class (46-C) graduated from Aviation Cadet training at TAAF after VE-Day.

--July 26, 1948:
President Harry S. Truman issues Executive Order #9981 desegregating the Armed Forces.

--October 27, 1954:
COL Davis, Jr., is promoted to BG, the first Black American to wear one star in the USAF.

--May 15, 1955:
First edition of *THE TUSKEGEE AIRMEN--The Story of the Negro in the U.S. Air Force* by Charles E. Francis is published, Boston, MA.

--May 22, 1959:
BG Davis promoted to MG, the first Black American to wear two stars.

--April 30, 1965:
MG Davis promoted to LTG, the first Black American to wear three stars.

--November 20, 1968:
Second printing of *THE TUSKEGEE AIRMEN--The Story of the Negro in the U.S. Air Force* by Charles E. Francis is published, Boston, MA.

--August, 1971:
Under the impulse of Charles Francis, the Airmen formed their first national organization, now widely known and accepted as the prestigious Tuskegee Airmen, Inc.

--September 1, 1975:
Daniel *Chappie* James promoted to General, the first Black american to wear four stars.

--February 28, 1978:

General James dies less than one month after retiring from active duty with the USAF.

--September 23, 1982:

Black Wings exhibit opened as part of the National Air & Space Museum, Smithsonian Institution, Washington, DC.

--August 8, 1985:

Tuskegee Airmen monument unveiled at the USAF Museum, Wright-Patterson AFB, OH.

--July 20, 1988:

Second edition of *THE TUSKEGEE AIRMEN--The Story of the Negro in the U.S. Air Force* by Charles E. Francis.

--September 15, 1993:

Third edition of *THE TUSKEGEE AIRMEN--The Men Who Changed a Nation* by Charles E. Francis.

--Summer 1997:

Fourth edition of *THE TUSKEGEE AIRMEN--The Men Who Changed a Nation* by the late Charles E. Francis, enlarged and edited by Adolfo Caso.

INDEX